Intercultural Sourcebook: Cross-Cultural Training Methods

VOL. 2

Sandra M. Fowler
Editor

Monica G. Mumford
Associate Editor

Intercultural Sourcebook: Cross-Cultural Training Methods

VOL. 2

Sandra M. Fowler

Editor

Monica G. Mumford

Associate Editor

INTERCULTURAL PRESS, INC.

For information, contact:
Intercultural Press, Inc.
P.O. Box 700
Yarmouth, Maine 04096 USA
207-846-5168

ISBN 1-877864-64-1 (v. 2)

Permissions Statement for Intercultural Sourcebook vol. 2

Book design and production by Patty J. Topel
Cover concept by Greg Frizzell
Cover design by Lois Leonard Stock

Printed in the United States of America

03   02   01   00   99   2   3   4   5   6

Library of Congress has Catalogued Volume 1 as Follows

Intercultural sourcebook : cross-cultural training methods / Sandra M.
   Fowler, editor; Monica G. Mumford, associate editor.
      p.   cm.
   Includes bibliographical references.
   ISBN 1-877864-29-3 (v. 1)
   1. Multicultural education.   2. Employees—training of.   3. Cross-
cultural orientation.   I. Fowler, Sandra M. (Sandra Mumford)   II. Mumford,
Monica G.

LC1099.I596   1995
370.19'6—dc20   94-48401
                                                                      CIP

Table of Contents

Acknowledgments

Our goal was always to expand the reference shelf for intercultural trainers by two books. The *Intercultural Sourcebook,* Volume 2, was begun at the same time as Volume 1, but despite our goal and our good intentions, it has taken three years longer to produce. Psychologist C. R. Snyder, in his 1994 book, *The Psychology of Hope,* has this to say about goals:

> We are inherently goal-oriented as we think about our futures. In the words of the noted psychotherapist Alfred Adler, "We cannot think, feel, will, or act without the perception of a goal." Indeed, goals capture our attention from the time we awaken in the morning until the time we go to sleep (where, should we dream, goals still appear in the theater of our minds). This conclusion holds whether you live in a Western or an Eastern culture, or any other for that matter. It is simply unthinkable not to think about goals. Can you do it? Careful, because if you try not to entertain a goal, you have one (4).*

Goals can be thought of as guideposts—hopefully our guides served us well. Achieving the complex web of goals represented by this volume required dedication and the support of many. We offer our gratitude to the authors for their fine work on their chapters and their devotion to intercultural training.

Special thanks are extended to David Hoopes for his trust, patience, and incisive editing, and to the professionals at Intercultural Press, most notably Toby Frank and Patty Topel. We also owe a debt of gratitude to Peggy Pusch.

And for the family and friends who sustained us with hope and belief in our shared goals, we thank you. Finally we would like to dedicate this book to Ray and Scott, who were the wind beneath our wings, and to Gene Zacher, who was there at the beginning.

—Sandra M. Fowler
Monica G. Mumford
Washington, DC
January 1999

---

* C. R. Snyder, *The Psychology of Hope: You Can Get There From Here* (New York: Free Press, 1994).

Preface

Ever since the publication of the first volume of the *Intercultural Sourcebook* we have been waiting for the second. Here it is and it was well worth the wait. As in Volume 1, Volume 2 carries on the effort to provide guidance for cross-cultural trainers and educators who want to use extant training methods and materials. It even provides guidance for those interested in developing methods to meet specific needs.

As Sandra Fowler notes in the Introduction, Volume 1 covered, for the most part, more traditional training methods. Volume 2 encompasses new or divergent methods: the use of inventories, videotapes, visual imagery, dialogues, cultural self-awareness practice, and culture heroes, among others. Particular attention is given in this volume to the link between research and training and to adapting training to meet alternative needs. Where it focuses in on one of the more traditional approaches, for instance, area studies, it exemplifies the method with a remarkably detailed and insightful description of a China training program, which pulls together an arsenal of techniques to accomplish its aims.

It seems to me that the completion of the *Sourcebook* is particularly opportune. While we may not be at a "crossroads" or a "watershed," as one's rhetorical inclinations might tempt one to suggest, we certainly have a broad, strong constituency—if not a critical mass of acceptance—for the basic premises of intercultural communication and cross-cultural training.

What the *Sourcebook* does, at this important time, is provide a rich resource through which trainers can expand their repertoire and increase the sophistication and effectiveness of their training. The *Sourcebook* contributes to raising the level of professionalism of the field as a whole, thus benefiting all who pursue careers in it.

Again, Sandra Fowler and Monica Mumford have done a remarkable job of corralling, working with, and channeling the creative energy of a large and disparate group of people. We thank and congratulate them.

—David S. Hoopes
Intercultural Press

Introduction

Sandra M. Fowler

Some people carry around an expectation that they have control over all aspects of their lives. As unrealistic as it seems, the allure of this unmeetable expectation is powerful. Intercultural encounters provide good lessons in reality. There is not an intercultural trainer alive today who would dispute that "people typically have difficulties when moving across cultures. Suddenly, and with little warning, behaviors and attitudes that proved necessary for obtaining goals in their own culture are no longer useful" (Brislin, Cushner, Cherrie, and Yong 1986, 13).

Cross-cultural trainers are in the business of helping people achieve a healthy management of reality. When the training is truly successful, our clients depart with a sense of both control and hope. They are actively open-minded about what they can expect and realistically control. Even a small sense of control helps blunt the effects of stress in intercultural experiences. At its very best, intercultural training plays a part in making the intercultural encounter a watershed experience, filled with excitement and even joy.

How does the intercultural trainer accomplish this? The making of a trainer takes time. The Intercultural Trainer Model (Figure 1) outlines the developmental areas in which trainers need knowledge and practice. **Culture** washes over everything we know and do. If the model were in color and the color of culture were green, everything would be green. Grounded in the basics of culture, intercultural trainers then need to focus on the central core—themselves. The **trainer** needs self-knowledge; in fact, to be a good intercultural trainer it is essential to know one's values and assumptions, personal style and traits, and skills and limitations. Knowledge of one's own cultural influences results from study and self-examination, which never stops. The expert intercultural trainer knows **content** inside and out, both culture-general and culture-specific concepts and theories. Trainers need to be cognizant of and comfortable with a wide variety of training **designs** and flexible enough to create on the spot when necessary. An example of an exciting design can be found in this volume in the chapter by George Renwick in which he describes a training program for people going to live and work in China. **Resources** are developed early, increase over a lifetime, and provide the guides needed to make intercultural training accurate, timely, grounded, and fresh. Resources are the cornerstones of area studies programs, and many excellent sources are listed in the chapter by Sandra Fowler, Monica Mumford, and V. Lynn Tyler.

Figure 1. The Intercultural Trainer Model

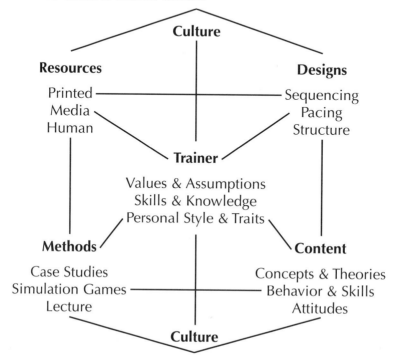

The **methods** you use when conducting training are also part of the skill package you offer clients. Our spotlight, continuing from *Intercultural Sourcebook, Volume 1,* is on the kinds of methods being used by intercultural trainers around the world. The methods in Volume 1 might be regarded as more traditional. Most of them have been with us for a long time and have been used in a wide variety of training situations beyond those involving intercultural issues. The methods in Volume 2, for the most part, have not been around so long—films, videos, and self-assessment instruments are good examples. On the other hand, area-specific training (described toward the end of this book) was where cross-cultural training started, though the culture-specific chapters here reflect the evolution of the method into a participative, experiential style that was missing in the didactic area studies programs of the first half of the twentieth century.

Some Things Not Included

As mentioned in Volume 1, there are some things you will not find in these volumes. For instance, there are no significant references to diversity training. Even though the content, context, and target groups are described in primarily cross-cultural terms in the *Sourcebook,* almost all the methods will work as effectively in training situations that are more specifically diversity oriented. For example, with appropriate content small group exercises, guided imagery, and workbooks can play important roles in a diversity program. Area studies may work well for intercultural trainers, but it is difficult to see how they might be used for diversity training.

The ability to perform needs assessments and training evaluations is a necessary skill for intercultural trainers. When you are designing a training program you should be responding to your needs assessment, and it is important to check on how well you are meeting those needs throughout a program. However, needs assessments cannot be regarded as a training method and therefore are not addressed in any depth in this book. If you would like to see what good ones look like, we suggest you check out the chapter by Renwick, since he included both a needs assessment and an evaluation for his China program. These can be found as appendices for his chapter, and they are offered as proven examples for creating your own.

Overview of the *Intercultural Sourcebook,* Volume 2

Thirty-four authors contributed the chapters in Volume 2. As before, they were invited to write chapters because they are associated in some way with the method they are writing about. Their combined perspectives, cultures, and backgrounds provide a richness that can add spice to your training as you dip into this collection to meet your own needs.

Structure of the *Intercultural Sourcebook,* Volume 2

Authors in Volume 2 received the same general guidelines as Volume 1 authors. The sections begin with a general description or overview of the method, followed by several specific examples. Authors of overview chapters were asked to describe the method in some detail, identify important considerations in using it, and describe specific intranational and international situations in which it might be used. They were also asked to list the benefits of using the method and mention some outcomes trainers could expect. They were asked to compare, when possible, their method with other methods and to list the most important resources for learning more about the method.

Authors of the specific exercises that serve as examples of the methods were asked to provide an introduction to their example, a history of the exercise, and a step-by-step procedure for using it. They were also asked to describe contexts in which the exercise has been used, discuss problems or pitfalls to watch for, and provide a resource list.

Content of the *Intercultural Sourcebook,* Volume 2

Volume 2 begins with Mitchell Hammer exploring the empirical roots of our profession in his chapter, **Cross-Cultural Training: The Research Connection**. Hammer points out that trainers owe a debt of gratitude to research for the scientific knowledge we have of training outcomes, how to measure effectiveness, and the nature of intercultural communication competencies.

Self-Awareness Inventories as a training tool are introduced by Chris Brown and Kasey Knight. They describe how these inventories can be used effectively in cross-cultural training and present a chart that helps you evaluate any instrument you are considering using.

Four examples are provided to demonstrate the range of applications this method offers. Pierre Casse describes a Four-Value Orientation Exercise that you can copy and use to help trainees understand their dominant value orientation. Michael Tucker gives us insight into the most empirically based, predictive instrument to date that was developed specifically for cross-cultural use: the Overseas Assignment Inventory (OAI). Colleen Kelley and Judith Meyers describe the Cross-Cultural Adaptability Inventory (CCAI), a well-constructed, easily obtainable instrument that assesses four skill areas to determine adaptability. Our sample of self-assessment instruments is completed by Hammer's detailed description of the Intercultural Development Inventory (IDI). This instrument measures intercultural sensitivity and can be analyzed at the individual or group level.

Videotapes as training tools are described by Robbins Hopkins. Her step-by-step guidelines for using videos show how they can enhance training by creating a window on the world.

Four videos illustrate the versatility of this method. Cay Hartley and Robbins Hopkins describe how video can be used for *Developing a Dual Perspective*. The video provides a vehicle for developing basic communication skills needed when working with people from other cultures. Nan Sussman tells us about one of the first business videos developed for culture-specific training of Americans, *Taking Your Product into the Japanese Market*. Nessa Loewenthal and Robert Hayles introduce Going International and Valuing Diversity, two film series useful for developing skills critical to success and productivity in an international, intercultural, and multiculturally diverse environment. Louis Meucci and Noriko Ogami describe how *Cold Water* evolved from Ogami's experiences as a foreign student. This film, designed for foreign students and scholars, is useful in many settings.

Small Group Exercises are defined for us by Sandra Fowler and Monica Mumford. They tell us how intercultural trainers use small group exercises to give trainees an opportunity to practice behaviors that will work well in other cultures and help them understand the underlying concepts.

In the first of the examples, Paul Pedersen describes Draw A House, a short, small group exercise that makes a good icebreaker. He also presents The Outside Expert, a useful intercultural communication exercise for small groups. Piglish, discussed by Cay Hartley and Terri Lapinsky, is an exercise for people who are preparing to learn a language—or who are dealing with someone who is. L. Robert Kohls describes three exercises that provide frameworks that trainers can fill out with their own content. Norma McCaig describes the Malonarian exercise, which gives participants the sense of a field trip—what it is like to explore mainstream U.S. cultural behaviors while in another culture—without leaving the training site.

The section on **Other Methods** used in training programs covers methods that do not easily fit into other categories. In her overview, Margaret Pusch describes the steps to consider when developing a new method.

Seven examples are included as types of other methods often used in intercultural training. Michael Gottlieb Berney explores Field Studies: Individual and

Group Trips, Expeditions, and Hunts and describes how to use them effectively. Visual imagery and its successful use as an intercultural training method are described by Fanchon Silberstein and Dorothy Sisk. Designing and Using Training Manuals effectively is outlined by Robert Cyr, with plenty of helpful hints on how to make this a dynamic part of your training program. Craig Storti describes his method of using Cross-Cultural Dialogues to improve skills in recognizing cultural differences and improving communication skills. Albert Wight gives us the steps to accomplishing Cross-Cultural Analysis and identifies a number of ways to use cultural informants. Alfred Kraemer describes his method for achieving Deep Cultural Self-Awareness. Finally, Edward Stewart and Jun Ohtake explore the values embedded in deep culture and revealed in their Culture Heroes exercise.

An overview of **Area-Specific Training**, presented by Sandra Fowler, Monica Mumford, and V. Lynn Tyler, offers a "map" that can be used to guide the development of a program for a specific culture or region of the world. Practical concerns and goals as well as other challenging issues are addressed. A valuable list of sources and resources for designing culture-specific training is included.

L. Robert Kohls provides a Conceptual Model for Country/Area Studies. It includes suggestions for a wide variety and an imaginative sequencing of training activities to convey the information required in a culture-specific program. George Renwick's description of his China Training Program concludes this section.

A section on **Adapting Training Methods** contains information any trainer will appreciate having at his or her fingertips. Sheila Ramsey discusses Adapting Intercultural Methods for Training across Cultures. She reminds us of our role as guides or counselors and explains how to be effective as we train people in cultures other than our own. Lance Descourouez offers his suggestions for Adapting Cross-Cultural Training Methods for Different Age Groups. Although we perhaps most often train adults, the whole family is involved when they are moved into another culture and we cannot take for granted that our training is appropriate for all ages—young or old.

This volume concludes with a peek by Sandra Fowler and Sheila Ramsey at where we might be going—Intercultural Training: The Future. They offer several observations and pose a number of questions to spark the imagination of intercultural trainers worldwide.

Final Thoughts

In the Volume 1 Acknowledgments we wrote, "There is no way to predict how a book will be received. We believe all books are created with the hope that each person who reads them finds something special to take away and use. We are no exception and harbor the hope that the *Intercultural Sourcebook* becomes a treasured resource and guide." One of the nicest responses we heard was from seasoned trainers who said how often they were surprised by what they learned in the first volume of the *Sourcebook*. Peggy Pusch remarked on how the significance of the *Sourcebook* goes beyond what is contained between the covers. It embodies the community formed by the authors of the chapters. It is telling that most of the authors know each other, have had at least a few interactions over the years, and together are considered to be among the builders of the intercultural profession. Peggy commented on how, for her, the *Sourcebook* rekindled relationships that have endured over the years.

We, of course, hold the same hope for Volume 2—that it will become a treasured resource and will rekindle or kindle relationships between you and the authors. I hope we are not being unrealistically optimistic, because, as I see it, the concept of hope is closely related to being a confident interculturalist. According to Snyder (1994, 12), "How we think about and interpret our external environment is the key to understanding hope." He refers to us as travelers through time, going from point to point, giving careful thought to where we want to go and what our goals are. Snyder believes that life is made up of thousands and thousands of instances in which we think about and navigate from Point A to Point B. When Point A is the home culture and Point B is a different culture, our clients are forced to change their mindset and learn new ways of interacting to be successful.

Aiming at our goals has been likened to constantly engaging in mental target practice. As interculturalists, we aim at the cultures represented by our clients and the cultures to which our trainees are headed. We need to instill the hope that you *can* get there from here. We hope you will find this book a helpful guide as you chart your course as an interculturalist.

References

Brislin, Richard W., Kenneth Cushner, Craig Cherrie, and Mahealani Yong. *Intercultural Interactions: A Practical Guide.* Beverly Hills, CA: Sage, 1986.

Snyder, C. R. *The Psychology of Hope: You Can Get There From Here.* New York: Free Press, 1994.

Cross-Cultural Training: The Research Connection

Mitchell R. Hammer

As I sit in my office ready to begin writing on the rather daunting topic of research and cross-cultural training, I am struck by the enormity of the task. I just finished reading the *Washington Post*. This morning there were articles on (1) the cultural adjustment difficulties of Vietnamese teenagers in the United States, (2) a murder/suicide by a troubled Hmong father who, evidently, was suffering great mental stress trying to cope with the cultural changes involved in living in the United States, (3) "ethnic cleansing" in Bosnia, (4) various misperceptions in Japanese/U.S. trade talks, (5) the problems health care agencies face when confronted with "folk" health practices which are at odds with mainstream medicine, and (6) a scathing editorial about diversity training being conducted in various organizations and institutions.

In each of these articles, the writer noted that cultural differences were at the core of the conflicts and/or difficulties being experienced. What a change! It was only twenty years ago that interculturalists met resistance by suggesting that greater intercultural understanding and skills were needed when living and working with people whose cultural backgrounds differ from one's own. Today, very few people need convincing of the value of increased cross-cultural capabilities. The task before us as we enter the twenty-first century is to effectively apply our insights and research findings in addressing the myriad "intercultural" issues arising in our multicultural world.

In this chapter, I look at a few of the conceptual models and a sampling of findings that demonstrate and support the connection between research and training. The research literature is a useful place to start when designing cross-cultural training efforts to meet our global needs in the next century.

There are two significant ways in which the research connection makes a difference for intercultural trainers: (1) real-world field and outcome validations and (2) cross-cultural training improvements. When intercultural trainers are asked by a client, "What do I get for my money?" they had better have answers. The answers come from research and evaluation measured against real-world criteria (such as productivity, employee satisfaction, promotion, profitability) of importance to the client. In the first half of this chapter, I turn my attention to outcome studies by examining the following factors that make a case for cross-cultural training:

- ❖ *Importance:* Trainers must often defend the importance of cross-cultural training in presentations to potential clients or at the beginning of training programs. Research findings support their case.

- ❖ *Costs:* Research studies suggest that the dynamics of the intercultural experience are the preeminent cause of early returns and difficulties in effectively living and working in a foreign culture. These studies bolster the case for cross-cultural training.

- ❖ *Effectiveness:* Research helps pinpoint the effectiveness of training, tying it to such positive outcome measures as increased information exchange; more rapid promotions; reduced anxiety; increased productivity, skills, commitment, and financial savings; and reduced culture stress.

Cross-cultural trainers owe a great deal to the research that developed some of their specific techniques, such as culture-specific assimilators (Fiedler, Mitchell, and Triandis 1971), the intercultural sensitizer (Cushner 1989; Cushner and Landis 1996), and the contrast-culture method (Stewart 1966; Stewart, Danielian, and Foster 1969). Trainers also need to remain current in the cross-cultural field by knowing the results of research focusing on training methods. In the second half of this chapter, I explore selected research findings regarding appropriate goals and outcomes for cross-cultural training. Finally, I examine the connection between intercultural communication competence and cross-cultural training.

The Importance of Cross-Cultural Training

We do not know when the first cross-cultural trainer emerged among human groups. Brislin, Landis, and Brandt (1983) suggest, however, that cross-cultural training owes its initial support to three kinds of international enterprises: war, religion, and commerce. As armies began the process of pacifying newly conquered peoples and missionaries began to spread the word of God and merchants began to trade for goods, the need for cross-cultural understanding and effective training increased.

There are, however, a number of more recent (twentieth century) factors that have influenced the growth and development of cross-cultural training efforts. First, the improvement of global transportation systems increased our ability to meet and interact with people from all areas of the world. Tourism, international educational exchange programs, and other forms of global travel allow people from different cultures the opportunity to interact with one another to a greater extent than at any other time in world history (Porter and Samovar 1994; Chen and Starosta 1996). This increased contact raises the demand for more in-depth cross-cultural preparation.

Second, the development of modern information and communications technology has increased our knowledge and awareness of peoples from other cultures. Television, radio, telephone, facsimile transmission, and computer networks are all made possible through the technological advances in ground and satellite communications. This has resulted in a dramatic increase in information exchanges across national borders. As a result of this communications revolution, we are experiencing exponential growth in information capabilities, both in the transmission and in the storage of data, which transcends national borders. Today, estimates of the "rate at which world knowledge doubles range from eighteen months to five years" (Frederick 1993, 8). This increased international communication effort is made all the more critical because of the substantial growth of nation-states since World War II (from 42 to more than 180 today). This communications revolution significantly raises the demand for accurate and timely cross-cultural training designed to manage the rapidly expanding global information flow.

Third, the increased economic interdependence in the world of business and trade raises the demand for effective, cross-cultural training aimed at improving global commercial transactions. Mary O'Hara-Devereaux and Robert Johansen, in their book *Globalwork* (1994), present the results of interviews with thousands of managers and team members from more than one hundred organizations in at least eighteen countries concerning the intersection of technologies, teamwork, and organizational change in today's world of international commerce. They conclude that

> a new landscape is emerging across the business world: the old boundaries of national economies and markets are bowing to globalization even as traditional office walls are giving way to new, borderless vistas (1).

This new landscape represents significantly different demands and requirements for long-term effectiveness in global business endeavors. The 1987 Canada-U.S. Free Trade Agreement; the recent NAFTA trade agreement with the United States, Canada, and Mexico; the economic integration of the European Union; and the increased economic cooperation evidenced among ASEAN (Association of South East Asian Nations) represent clear indications of increased trade within the global economic community.

Global assignments are similarly being viewed by multinational organizations as critical for long-term survival. General Electric, for instance, "estimates that 25 percent of its managers will need global assignments in order to gain the knowledge and experience necessary to understand the global market, customers, suppliers, and competitors the company will face in the 1990s and beyond" (Black, Gregersen, and Mendenhall 1992, 5). Cross-cultural training is essential in helping prepare employees to effectively assume international responsibilities within the new global landscape (Adler 1991).

Fourth, the demand is raised for effective transfer of technology and information training programs due to the growth of international cooperative efforts. This is reflected, for instance, in international development efforts such as the Peace Corps and the Agency for International Development as well as in the unprecedented global cooperation among American, Japanese, European, Canadian, and Russian space agencies on the International Space Station project.

Fifth, demands for cultural diversity training to improve interactions among ethnic groups within the United States are on the increase as the U.S. continues to move away from an assimilationist model of accommodation to a pluralist model of social integration (Kochman 1989). As the new workforce in the twenty-first century embodies increasing diversity in race, culture, age, and gender, greater citizen and institution capability is needed in intercultural communication, which can be achieved through targeted educational and diversity training experiences (Chen and Starosta 1996).

Finally, the nuclear, chemical, and biological weaponry currently dispersed throughout the world clearly raises challenges for effective intercultural communication and training for global institutions (like the United Nations) and government leaders from all nations in the areas of peacekeeping, peacemaking, and peacebuilding (Frederick 1993; Chen and Starosta 1996). Focused attention, for instance, is being given to increased capabilities for resolving conflicts that arise in crisis situations (Rogan, Hammer, and Van Zandt 1997; Hammer 1997; Hammer and Weaver 1994; Weaver 1997).

Professionals in the intercultural field have taken on these challenges, with both researchers and cross-cultural trainers engaging in systematic efforts to identify the primary concepts, goals, methods, and results from cross-cultural training activities. The results of these efforts are perhaps most clearly reflected in the excellent three-volume series on cross-cultural training edited by Landis and Brislin (1983a, 1983b, 1983c) along with the recent second edition edited by Landis and Bhagat (1996). This increased professionalism has led to more empirical research focusing on cross-cultural training activities, enabling the development of more effective cross-cultural training strategies, significant refinements in the methods and techniques for helping individuals adapt and function effectively in foreign cultures, and increased positive outcomes for international organizations and institutions.

The "Costs" of Cross-Cultural Training

Effective cross-cultural training is not easily designed or implemented because it is oftentimes fraught with a variety of "intercultural" interaction difficulties (Black, Gregersen, and Mendenhall 1992; Hammer 1984). Cross-cultural difficulties often lead not only to poor overseas job performance but ultimately to a premature return home for individuals on an overseas business assignment, technical advisers working within international development efforts, and others who work and live for an extended period of time in a foreign culture environment. In one graphic case, Feldman (1976) describes the experience of two U.S. multinational corporations then under contract to the government of Iran. These companies employed a total of 2,500 expatriates who lived in Iran with their families. Each company suffered, respectively, a 50 percent and 85 percent premature return rate among their U.S. hired employees and families, the cost of which was estimated at $55,000 per returned family.

Consider as well these research results relevant to cross-cultural training. Within the international development arena, Kealey (1990) estimates that as few as 20 percent of expatriate employees perform highly effectively while living overseas. Gertsen (1990) suggests that the technical competence of these workers is not typically problematic; it is the cross-cultural skills that are lacking. A number of researchers estimate that anywhere from 15 to 40 percent of U.S. multinational corporations' expatriate placements experience premature return because of cross-cultural adjustment problems (Dowling and Schuler 1990; Bird and Dunbar 1991; Henry 1965; Lanier 1979; Tung 1982; Tung 1987). These adjustment difficulties not only relate to the expatriate employee but also include adaptation problems experienced by the expatriate's spouse and children, which impact on the early return of the family unit (Kealey 1990; Kealey 1996; Solomon 1994).

The average cost of a failed overseas assignment ranges from $250,000 to $1,000,000 (Caudron 1991; Landis and Bhagat 1996; Harris and Moran 1987; Schaff 1981) and is estimated to cost U.S. companies over $2 billion each year in direct costs alone because of early expatriate returns (Bhagat and Prien 1996; Dowling and Schuler 1990; Lissy 1993; Nauman 1992; Kealey 1996). If proper assessment and training for international assignments result in prevention of just one family's premature return, the cost savings would pay for assessment and training of an additional thirty-five managers and their families (Tucker and Wight 1981).

Interestingly, work by Tung (1987) suggests that premature return rates for expatriates among Japanese international firms are substantially lower, averaging only 5-10 percent. This lower rate might suggest that the Japanese expatriates are more adept at living and working in a foreign environment than are American expatriates. This conclusion may not be warranted, however, given findings from a study I conducted with Dr. Bruce Stening (Stening and Hammer 1992). We examined aspects of intercultural effectiveness among Japanese managers in the United States, American managers in Japan, and Japanese and American managers in Thailand (a third-culture environment for both Japanese and American managers). We found that Japanese managers' satisfaction with living in a foreign culture; their perceived effectiveness in functioning well in a foreign culture; and their ability in managing stress, intercultural relationships, and communicating effectively were significantly lower compared with a similar sample of American managers.

Given these findings, why do Japanese firms have lower premature return rates for their managers than American firms? It is likely to be caused by differences between Japanese and American cultures (as reflected in greater corporate social pressure, for instance) rather than the superior intercultural adaptability and skills of Japanese managers. Quite simply, there is greater shame and there are more negative consequences for Japanese managers who return home early from an overseas assignment compared with American managers. When researchers use premature return rate as a measure of intercultural success achieved by Japanese firms in managing their expatriates, by the nature of the pressures imposed by Japanese society (and by extension, the corporation), Japanese firms will appear better than American firms. However, premature return rate may well mask difficulties and anxieties felt by individual expatriate Japanese managers.

Research suggests that the predominant reason for premature return rates and difficulties encountered in effectively managing and living in a foreign culture is not due to a low level of technical competence among the managers (which, in fact, is typically quite high) but to the dynamics of the intercultural experience—the fundamental concern of cross-cultural training activities (Brislin 1981; Tung 1982; Dinges 1983; Kealey and Ruben 1983; Bhagat and Prien 1996; Dinges and Baldwin 1996; Gudykunst, Guzley, and Hammer 1996; Kealey 1996). Neglecting to ensure the best possible training program is false economy when the costs of cross-cultural training are viewed within the context of the total business enterprise. The costs of cross-cultural incompetence are severe and the predominant reason for failure in this area is due to cultural differences in the communication and interaction patterns that take place between the expatriate manager and host nationals.

The Effectiveness of Cross-Cultural Training

Surprisingly, cross-cultural training is still not consistently undertaken by the majority of international companies. Goldstein (1989) found that 68 percent of U.S. companies did not engage in cross-cultural training as recently as 1984. Work by Black (1988), Tung (1981), and Dowling and Schuler (1990) reveals that only about 30 percent of American managers receive any kind of cross-cultural training before they leave for their international assignment. Surveys of multinational firms have found that over half of the cross-cultural training conducted is for one week or less (Arvey, Bhagat, and Salas 1991), and "over 80 percent of the firms surveyed focused on training the employee only, with no provision for training the spouse or family" (Bhagat and Prien 1996, 219).

The question arises: why has cross-cultural training not been used more extensively? While various reasons have been advanced, by far the most common is the assumption that cross-cultural training is not effective (Mendenhall and Oddou 1985; Tung 1981).

How effective, then, is cross-cultural training? In one recent case, a comprehensive training program lasting approximately one year was conducted for American and Japanese managers of an American-owned subsidiary in Japan. By the company's own estimates, the training was responsible for a savings of 16 million dollars and resulted in the start-up of a new plant in Japan one year earlier than projected. These positive outcomes occurred, according to the company, as a direct result of the improved transfer of technology and management competence of the American and Japanese managers, which, in turn, was due to the effectiveness of the cross-cultural training program conducted for the managers (Clarke and Hammer 1995).

I conducted two recent studies that also point to the effectiveness of cross-cultural training.

Effects of Short-Term Training

In the first study, the focus was on the effects of shorter-term training between Japanese and American managers working on a joint venture in the United States

(Hammer and Martin 1992). Managers participated in two types of training. In the first, American and Japanese managers met separately and learned about one another's culture and business practices. In the second program, participants were brought together in interactive training, where specific business problems were jointly addressed and intercultural communication techniques were demonstrated and applied to these business issues. The results indicate that both types of training were significantly more effective than no training at all in increasing knowledge about the other culture, reducing anxiety toward working with members of the other culture, and increasing information exchange between managers from the two cultures.

In related studies, O'Brien and Plooij (1977) found that programmed instruction had a greater effect on retention and generalization of cultural knowledge than cognitive (book) training or no training at all. McDaniel, McDaniel, and McDaniel (1988) concluded that training that emphasized intercultural attitudes transferred less effectively to application contexts for schoolteachers compared with training that focused on intercultural experiences.

A number of other studies found that no one training method is considered singularly effective in adequately preparing expatriate managers for an overseas assignment. Research by Gudykunst, Hammer, and Wiseman (1977), Harrison (1992), and Early (1987) clearly shows that an integrated (multimethod) approach to cross-cultural training is more effective than a monomethod approach (for example, factual briefing) in preparing sojourners for an international assignment. As Blake, Heslin, and Curtis (1996) conclude, "combinations of techniques may optimize the learning from each and thus give the participants opportunity to rehearse skills and apply information received from books, lectures, films, and programmed instruction" (170).

Effects of Long-Term Training

In the second study (Hammer, 1995), the focus was on the organization-wide effects of a long-term intercultural management development (IMD) program developed by the Clarke Consulting Group in Redwood City, California, for Japanese employees of an American corporation's subsidiary operation in Japan. The study tracked the eight-year progress of seventy-one employees of the Japan subsidiary who participated in the IMD program and a comparison group of employees who did not receive intercultural training.

The training program focused on both intercultural knowledge and skill development in such areas as meeting management, conflict resolution, and intercultural negotiation and was continued with intensive training in English language for business usage. The results indicated that intercultural training significantly increased employees' productivity, business skills, and commitment to their employer. Specifically, Japanese employees who participated in the IMD program were promoted twice as fast as their untrained counterparts, were selected for important overseas assignments three times as often, and had significantly higher levels of commitment to the organization compared with those who did not receive the training. Further, the IMD group participants were also rated by supervisors as possessing significantly higher levels of intercultural management skills in relation to the comparison group. This study clearly indicates that cross-cultural training can have a direct impact on an organization's bottom line.

Black and Mendenhall (1990) conducted an exhaustive review of cross-cultural training effectiveness studies prior to 1990. Their findings clearly indicate that cross-cultural training positively affects the overall success of international organizations. They examined the results of twenty-nine empirical studies of cross-cultural training effects. Ten of these studies (three of which used control groups in their design) examined the effectiveness of cross-cultural training in helping trainees better manage culture stress. All ten found a positive relationship between training and the reduction or effective management of culture stress.

Nine of the studies looked at the effects of cross-cultural training on long-term psychological adjustment. All nine found a positive relationship between training and increased psychological adaptation to the foreign living experience. Seven of the nine studies used control groups, while three used longitudinal designs.

Intercultural effectiveness, including a measure of job/task accomplishment, was investigated in fifteen of the studies. Eleven of the fifteen studies found positive relationships between cross-cultural training and various performance measures. The three studies that did not produce such findings were laboratory rather than field studies and thus were the most artificial in their design.

Overall, Black and Mendenhall (1990) suggest a clear, positive "relationship between cross-cultural training and the following dependent variables: cross-cultural skill development, cross-cultural adjustment, and performance in a cross-cultural setting" (119-20). In short, cross-cultural training has been shown to develop cross-cultural skills that affect subsequent success in an overseas assignment, improve expatriates' psychological comfort and satisfaction with living and working in a foreign culture, and improve task accomplishment in the cross-cultural environment.

Goals and Outcomes of Cross-Cultural Training

Cross-cultural training refers to those activities designed to help people work and live effectively in a foreign cultural environment. The content and focus of cross-cultural training are varied, ranging from diplomatic relations to development and technology transfer projects. Cross-cultural training is not defined so much by the specificity of its methods or content, however, as it is by its applied focus on the interpersonal dynamics that take place when individuals from one culture interact and communicate with people from another culture. It is this applied, interactional focus which constitutes the practice of cross-cultural training.

Cross-cultural training is also fundamentally concerned with cultural differences as they arise in interaction between individuals. Cultural differences between people can arise because of differences in what we do (actions), what we produce (artifacts), and what we mean by what we do and produce (interpretations). In one sense, culture is a blueprint or guide we use to make sense out of the world we live in. Cross-cultural training, then, is concerned with the ways in which cultural differences can influence how we communicate and interact with people who have a fundamentally different "blueprint" of the world.

There have been times when I have been particularly frustrated with cross-cultural trainers' apparent lack of clear intercultural training goals (for an excellent discussion of cross-cultural training goals and design, see Brislin and Yoshida 1994). Fortunately, cross-cultural research has nicely articulated the fundamental goals and outcomes one can expect as a result of an intercultural training effort. As mentioned earlier, cross-cultural training is designed to help individuals learn and adapt to new and unfamiliar cultural values, practices, and behaviors found in the foreign environment.

There are three fundamental outcomes that indicate the success or failure of expatriate adaptation and that guide the development of cross-cultural training efforts: personal/family adjustment and satisfaction, intercultural interaction, and professional effectiveness (Kealey 1996; Blake, Heslin, and Curtis 1996). These three dimensions are based on the early work of Ruben and Kealey (1979), Hawes and Kealey (1981), and Kealey (1990) and have been confirmed by more recent work by Black (1988) and Black, Gregersen, and Mendenhall (1992).

Personal/family adjustment and satisfaction is concerned both with the temporary effects of culture stress, which arise from one's initial adjustment to a foreign culture environment, and with long-term psychological satisfaction with living in the foreign culture. Culture stress or culture shock, according to Ruben and Kealey (1979) is concerned with "an individual's initial, transitory reactions during the first few months in a new culture" (21). These reactions oftentimes include a desire to return home, serious questioning of one's long-term commitment to remain in the host culture, a strong negative attitude toward host nationals, and a variety of stress-related symptoms (for example, inability to sleep, sleeping too much, digestive disorders, nervousness, lack of concentration). While culture stress/shock reactions can be quite severe, they are considered temporary, as they are most commonly associated with the unfamiliarity of the host culture during the initial period of living in it.

Most sojourners come to terms with their foreign assignment and develop more stable, long-term attitudes and strategies for coping with the foreign culture and its people. This aspect of personal/family adjustment and satisfaction is concerned with the sojourner's "general psychological well-being, self-satisfaction, contentment, comfort with, and accommodation to a new environment after the initial perturbations which characterize culture shock have passed" (Ruben and Kealey 1979, 21). This dimension reflects the individual's own judgments and feelings concerning his or her work and living activities in the host culture. Essentially this element is concerned with the mental health of the expatriate while living/working in a foreign culture environment.

A second outcome is termed *intercultural interaction* and is broadly concerned with the dynamics of social interaction that take place between the sojourner and host country and other foreign nationals (Kealey 1996; Ruben, Askling, and Kealey 1977). As Kealey (1996) states, "intercultural interaction refers to being socially involved with nationals and demonstrating interest in and knowledge of the host culture" (89). Central to this aspect of overseas success are the number and types of relationships the expatriate forms while living in the foreign culture (Hawes and Kealey 1981; Ruben and Kealey 1979).

The third outcome of overseas success is concerned with *professional effectiveness* of the expatriate. This refers to the ability of the sojourner to accomplish his or her professional goals in a culturally appropriate manner (Kealey 1996). Intercultural effectiveness is concerned with the degree of success the expatriate achieves in fulfilling the task/job responsibilities of the overseas assignment (Ruben, Askling, and Kealey 1977; Hawes and Kealey 1981) and when appropriate, achieving success in the transfer of knowledge, skills, and/or technology to host country nationals (Ruben and Kealey 1979).

Results from studies suggest that an intense experience of culture shock is related to positive (rather than negative) long-term psychological adjustment and intercultural effectiveness (Ruben and Kealey 1979). That is, expatriates who are open to learning about the host culture most directly confront the differences between their own cultural blueprints and the host's blueprints. This confrontation is often unsettling. However, these intense feelings of anxiety which are associated with culture shock are indicative of the shift in frame of reference the expatriate is undergoing. In short, a relatively intense experience of culture shock often stimulates a greater degree of learning about how to live and work in the host culture (that is, the expatriates' repertoire is increased). This can translate into a successful adaptation to the host culture, which will be reflected in positive long-term attitudes toward the host culture and effective job performance and social interaction.

Intercultural Communication Competency

Intercultural communication competencies have been found to be strong predictors of culture shock, psychological adjustment, overall intercultural effectiveness in living in the host culture, extent of social interaction with host nationals, job performance, and transfer of technology (Ruben and Kealey 1979; Hammer 1989; Hawes and Kealey 1981; Clarke and Hammer 1995). This finding suggests that intercultural communication competencies are an underlying and essential aspect of cross-cultural adaptation and therefore one of the most important topics for cross-cultural training efforts to address.

Kealey and Ruben (1983), after an extensive review of the literature, identified the following key intercultural skills or competencies: empathy, respect, interest in local culture, flexibility, tolerance, technical skill, initiative, open-mindedness, sociability, and positive self-image.

Six years later, I reviewed the literature on intercultural communication competence and identified five core intercultural communication skills relevant to cross-cultural interaction (Hammer 1989). The first communication skill is termed *interaction management* and refers to the degree to which participants easily engage one another and take turns in the conversation. The second skill is *immediacy* and involves the degree to which participants are approachable during an interaction. The third skill is *social relaxation* and refers to the degree to which those interacting manage the stress and anxiety felt during an interaction. The fourth skill is *expressiveness* and is concerned with the degree to which participants are able to express their opinions and ideas during an interaction. The fifth skill is *other orientation* and refers to the degree to which participants are attentive, interested in, and adaptable toward one another during an interaction.

These five skills seem to be culture-general in their underlying dimensions, but culture-specific in their behavioral manifestation. In other words, how one takes turns, signals approachability, manages internal stress and anxiety during interaction, expresses opinions and ideas, and communicates interest and adaptability to the other varies from culture to culture. Nevertheless, these five skill domains appear to capture the deeper evaluative process that people from different cultures engage in when determining how competent they and their other-culture counterpart are during an interaction. Therefore, these five skill dimensions possess at least some level of cultural generalizability. People from different cultures tend to view individuals who are interculturally skilled in interaction management, immediacy, social relaxation, expressiveness, and other orientation as highly competent communicators.

In a recent summary of research, Kealey (1996) proposes a model of an effective intercultural communicator: (1) *adaptation skills:* positive attitudes, flexibility, stress tolerance, patience, marital/family stability, emotional maturity, and inner security; (2) *cross-cultural skills:* realism (that is, realistic expectations), tolerance, involvement in culture, political astuteness, and cultural sensitivity; and (3) *partnership skills:* openness to others, professional commitment, perseverance, initiative, relationship building, self-confidence, and problem solving.

In another comprehensive review of studies, Chen and Starosta (1996) present a model of the effective interculturalist, which, consistent with the early work of Gudykunst, Wiseman, and Hammer (1977), focuses on affective (intercultural sensitivity), cognitive (intercultural awareness), and behavioral (intercultural adroitness) components. Specifically, Chen and Starosta (1996) view affective competence in terms of the ability to "project and receive positive emotional responses before, during, and after intercultural interactions" (362). Four personal attributes are posited: self-concept, open-mindedness, nonjudgmental attitudes, and social relaxation. The cognitive aspect of intercultural competence is concerned with reducing the ambiguity and uncertainty that are inherent in intercultural interactions. Cultural self-awareness and cultural awareness constitute this dimension. Finally, the behavioral aspect of intercultural competence focuses on how people act or behave in intercultural interactions. This element focuses on verbal and nonverbal behaviors and includes message skills, appropriate self-disclosure, behavioral flexibility, interaction management, and social skills.

From a research point of view, the identification of intercultural competencies reflects advancement in our understanding of the dynamics of the intercultural encounter. However, in terms of cross-cultural training, these intercultural skills remain at a level of abstraction that makes them difficult to teach to trainees. While we can discuss the concept of interaction management or behavioral flexibility, it is much more difficult to improve trainees' intercultural skills in these areas. One of the tasks facing intercultural researchers and trainers alike is to adequately address this important, applied concern.

As a profession, there is a need for greater specificity and application of identified intercultural communication competencies to specific cross-cultural training contexts (such as identifying concrete intercultural skills needed for effectively dealing with culture stress). In my own work, I have "translated" research findings on intercultural communication competence into an identified set of intercultural communication skills (defined as verbal and nonverbal behaviors or messages), which are essential in minimizing misunderstanding and building trust and affiliation with a person from a different culture. I have specifically applied these intercultural skills in training programs I conduct around issues of conflict and negotiation.

Briefly, I have identified four clusters or sets of intercultural communication skills that are central to effective negotiation across cultures. These clusters represent two fundamentally different foci when interacting in a conflict situation. The first focus is on reflecting understanding of the other, which I term "reflecting skills." Because reflecting skills focus on the other, they are considered receiver-centered skills. Reflecting skills involve two central skill sets: active listening (such as paraphrasing, pauses/silences) and questioning (such as open-ended questions). The second focus is aimed at eliciting information from the other person by moving the conversation toward topics the speaker wishes to address. These skills are termed "piloting skills" and are considered speaker-centered. Piloting involves two core skill clusters: directing (for example, explanations) and disclosure (for instance, background). I have found that these behaviorally based communication skills are highly welcomed by trainees who urgently desire to learn additional coping strategies and skills when interacting with others across the cultural divide.

Conclusion

A researcher-practitioner is not defined by job title or role, but rather by an integrated approach to both research and training—my academic and professional life has been devoted to advancing this concept. Some cross-cultural trainers (for example, Sandra Fowler) began their careers as researchers and shifted to training, while others (such as William Gudykunst) began as cross-cultural trainers and became researchers.

Although a young field and profession, cross-cultural training is already supported and shaped by a substantial body of research. The practice of intercultural training is becoming more sophisticated and relevant. Integrating research and practice was one of the original goals of the founders of the Society for Intercultural Education, Training and Research (SIETAR) International. The intention was to produce practitioners who integrated research findings in their training and researchers who incorporated practical concerns in their research. This integrative approach to research and practice—wherein each continually informs the other—is a fundamental and important link that must be protected as we move into the twenty-first century.

References

Adler, Nancy J. *International Dimensions of Organizational Behavior*. Belmont, CA: Wadsworth, 1991.

Arvey, R. D., Rabi S. Bhagat, and E. Salas. "Cross-cultural and Cross-national Issues in Personnel and Human Resources Management: Where Do We Go from Here? *Personnel and Human Resources Management* 9 (1991): 367–407.

Bhagat, Rabi S., and Kristin O. Prien. "Cross-cultural Training in Organizational Contexts." In *Handbook of Intercultural Training*, 2d ed., edited by Dan Landis and Rabi S. Bhagat, 216–30. Thousand Oaks, CA: Sage, 1996.

Bird, A., and R. Dunbar. "Getting the Job Done over There: Improving Expatriate Productivity." *National Productivity Review* 10, no. 2 (1991): 145–56.

Black, J. S. "Workrole Transitions: A Study of American Expatriate Managers in Japan." *Journal of International Business Studies* 19 (1988): 277–94.

Black, J. S., H. B. Gregersen, and M. E. Mendenhall. *Global Assignments*. San Francisco: Jossey-Bass, 1992.

Black, J. S., and M. E. Mendenhall. "Cross-cultural Training Effectiveness: A Review and a Theoretical Framework for Future Research." *Academy of Management Review* 15, no. 1 (1990): 113–36.

Blake, B. F., R. Heslin, and S. C. Curtis. "Measuring the Impacts of Cross-Cultural Training." In *Handbook of Intercultural Training*, 2d ed., edited by Dan Landis and Rabi S. Bhagat, 164–84. Thousand Oaks, CA: Sage, 1996.

Brislin, Richard W. *Cross-Cultural Encounters: Face-to-Face Interaction*. New York: Pergamon, 1981.

Brislin, Richard W., Dan Landis, and M. Brandt. "Conceptualization of Intercultural Behavior and Training." In *Handbook of Intercultural Training, vol. 1: Issues in Theory and Design*, edited by Dan Landis and Richard W. Brislin, 1–35. Elmsford, NY: Pergamon, 1983.

Brislin, Richard, and T. Yoshida. *Intercultural Communication Training*. Thousand Oaks, CA: Sage, 1994.

Caudron, S. "Training Ensures Success Overseas." *Personnel Journal* 70, no. 12 (1991): 27–30.

Chen, G. M., and William J. Starosta. "Intercultural Communication Competence: A Synthesis." *Communication Yearbook* 19 (1996): 353–83.

Clarke, Clifford, and Mitchell R. Hammer. "Predictors of Japanese and American Managers' Job Success, Personal Adjustment, and Intercultural Interaction Effectiveness." *International Management Review* 35, no. 2 (1995): 153–70.

Cushner, Kenneth. "Assessing the Impact of the Culture-General Assimilator." *International Journal of Intercultural Relations* 13 (1989): 125–46.

Cushner, Kenneth, and Dan Landis. "The Intercultural Sensitizer." In *Handbook of Intercultural Training,* 2d ed., edited by Dan Landis and Rabi S. Bhagat, 185–202. Thousand Oaks, CA: Sage, 1996.

Dinges, Norman G. "Intercultural Competence." In *Handbook of Intercultural Training, vol. 1: Issues in Theory and Design,* edited by Dan Landis and Richard W. Brislin, 176–202. New York: Pergamon, 1983.

Dinges, Norman G., and K. D. Baldwin. "Intercultural Competence: A Research Perspective." In *Handbook of Intercultural Training,* 2d ed., edited by Dan Landis and Rabi S. Bhagat, 106–23. Thousand Oaks, CA: Sage, 1996.

Dowling, P. J., and R. S. Schuler. *International Dimensions of Human Resource Management.* Boston: PWS-Kent, 1990.

Early, P. C. "Intercultural Training for Managers: A Comparison of Documentary and Interpersonal Methods." *Academy of Management Journal* 30, no. 4 (1987): 685–98.

Feldman, M. J. "Training for Cross-Cultural International Interaction in the Federal Government." *Training and Development Journal* 30, no. 11 (1976): 19–23.

Fiedler, Fred E., R. Mitchell, and Harry C. Triandis. "The Culture Assimilator: An Approach to Cross-Cultural Training." *Journal of Applied Psychology* 55 (1971): 95–102.

Frederick, H. H. *Global Communication and International Relations.* Belmont, CA: Wadsworth, 1993.

Gertsen, M. "Intercultural Competence and Expatriates." *Journal of Human Resource Management* 4 (1990): 341–61.

Goldstein, I. L. "Critical Training Issues: Past, Present, and Future." In *Training and Development in Organizations,* edited by I. L. Goldstein and Associates, 1–22. San Francisco: Jossey-Bass, 1989.

Gudykunst, William B., R. M. Guzley, and Mitchell R. Hammer. "Designing Intercultural Training." In *Handbook of Intercultural Training,* 2d ed., edited by Dan Landis and Rabi S. Bhagat, 61–80. Thousand Oaks, CA: Sage, 1996.

Gudykunst, William B., Mitchell R. Hammer, and R. L. Wiseman. "An Analysis of an Integrated Approach to Cross-Cultural Training." *International Journal of Intercultural Relations* 1, no. 2 (1977): 99–109.

Gudykunst, William B., R. L. Wiseman, and Mitchell R. Hammer. "Determinants of a Sojourner's Attitudinal Satisfaction: A Path Model." In *Communication Yearbook* 1, edited by Brent D. Ruben, 415–25. New Brunswick, NJ: Transaction Press, 1977.

Hammer, Mitchell R. "Negotiating across the Cultural Divide: Intercultural Dynamics in Crisis Incidents." In *Dynamic Processes of Crisis Negotiation,* edited by R. G. Rogan, Mitchell R. Hammer, and C. R. Van Zandt, 105–14. Westport, CT: Praeger, 1997.

———. "Making the Case with the Corporation: Tracking the Effects of an International Management Development Program." Presentation given at the 21st annual Congress of the Society for Intercultural Education, Training and Research, Phoenix, AZ, May 14–17, 1995.

———. "Intercultural Communication Competence." In *The Handbook of International and Intercultural Communication,* edited by Molefi K. Asante and William B. Gudykunst, 247–60. Newbury Park, CA: Sage, 1989.

———. "The Effects of an Intercultural Communication Workshop on Participants' Intercultural Communication Competence." *Communication Quarterly* 32 (1984): 252–62 (refereed academic journal article).

Hammer, Mitchell R., and Judith N. Martin. "The Effects of Cross-Cultural Training on American Managers in a Japanese-American Joint Venture." *Journal of Applied Communication Research* 20, no. 2 (1992): 161–82.

Hammer, Mitchell R., and Gary R. Weaver. "Cultural Considerations in Hostage Negotiations." In *Culture, Communication and Conflict: Readings in Intercultural Relations,* edited by Gary R. Weaver, 499–510. Needham Heights, MA: Ginn Press, 1994.

Harris, Philip, and Robert T. Moran. *Managing Cultural Differences.* Houston: Gulf, 1987.

Harrison, J. K. "Individual and Combined Effects of Behavior Modeling and the Culture Assimilator in Cross-Cultural Management Training." *Journal of Applied Psychology* 77 (1992): 952–62.

Hawes, Frank, and Daniel J. Kealey. "An Empirical Study of Canadian Technical Assistance." *International Journal of Intercultural Relations* 5, no. 3 (1981): 239–58.

Henry, E. R. "What Business Can Learn from Peace Corps Selection and Training." *Personnel Journal* 42 (1965): 17–25.

Kealey, Daniel J. "The Challenge of International Personnel Selection." In *Handbook of Intercultural Training,* 2d ed., edited by Dan Landis and Rabi S. Bhagat, 81–105. Thousand Oaks, CA: Sage, 1996.

———. *Cross-Cultural Effectiveness.* Hull, Canada: CIDA, 1990.

Kealey, Daniel J., and Brent D. Ruben. "Cross-Cultural Personnel Selection Criteria, Issues, and Methods." In *Handbook of Intercultural Training, vol. 1: Issues in Theory and Design,* edited by Dan Landis and Richard W. Brislin, 155–75. New York: Pergamon, 1983.

Kochman, Thomas. "Black and White Cultural Styles in Pluralistic Perspective." In *Test Policy and Performance: Education, Language and Culture,* edited by B. R. Gifford, 259–96. Boston: Kluwer Academic Publishers, 1989.

Landis, Dan, and Rabi S. Bhagat, eds. *Handbook of Intercultural Training.* 2d ed. Thousand Oaks, CA: Sage, 1996.

Landis, Dan, and Richard W. Brislin, eds. *Handbook of Intercultural Training, vol. 1: Issues in Theory and Design.* New York: Pergamon, 1983a.

————. *Handbook of Intercultural Training, vol. 2: Issues in Training Methodology.* New York: Pergamon, 1983b.

————. *Handbook of Intercultural Training, vol. 3: Area Studies in Intercultural Training.* New York: Pergamon, 1983c.

Lanier, Alison R. "Selecting and Preparing Personnel for Overseas Transfers." *Personnel Journal* 58, no. 3 (1979): 160–63.

Lissy, W. E. "International Issues." *Compensation and Benefits Review* 17 (1993).

McDaniel, C. O. Jr., N. C. McDaniel, and A. K. McDaniel. "Transferability of Multicultural Evaluation from Training to Practice." *International Journal of Intercultural Relations* 12 (1988): 19–33.

Mendenhall, M. E., and G. Oddou. "The Dimensions of Expatriate Acculturation: A Review." *Academy of Management Review* 10 (1985): 39–48.

Nauman, E. "A Conceptual Model of Expatriate Turnover." *Journal of International Business Studies* 23, no. 3 (1992): 499–532.

O'Brien, G. E., and D. Plooij. "Comparison of Programmed and Prose Culture Training upon Attitudes and Knowledge." *Journal of Applied Psychology* 62 (1977): 499–505.

O'Hara-Devereaux, Mary, and Robert Johansen. *Globalwork.* San Francisco: Jossey-Bass, 1994.

Porter, Richard E., and Larry A. Samovar. "An Introduction to Intercultural Communication." In *Intercultural Communication: A Reader*, 7th ed., edited by Larry A. Samovar and Richard E. Porter, 4–25. Belmont, CA: Wadsworth, 1994.

Rogan, R. G., Mitchell R. Hammer, and C. R. Van Zandt, eds. *Dynamic Processes of Crisis Negotiation.* Wesport, CT: Praeger, 1997.

Ruben, Brent D., and Daniel J. Kealey. "Behavioral Assessment of Communication Competency and the Prediction of Cross-Cultural Adaptation." *International Journal of Intercultural Relations* 3 (1979): 15–48.

Ruben, Brent D., L. R. Askling, and Daniel J. Kealey. "Cross-Cultural Effectiveness." In *Overview of Intercultural Education, Training, and Research, vol. 1: Theory*, edited by David S. Hoopes, Paul B. Pedersen, and George W. Renwick, 92–105. Washington, DC: Society for Intercultural Education, Training and Research, 1977.

Schaff, D. "The Growing Need for Cross Cultural and Bilingual Training." *Training/HRD* (January 1981): 85–86.

Solomon, C. M. "Success Abroad Depends on More than Job Skills." *Personnel Journal* (1994): 51–60.

Stening, Bruce W., and Mitchell R. Hammer. "Cultural Baggage and the Adaptation of Expatriate American and Japanese Managers." *Management International Review* 32, no. 1 (1992): 77–89.

Stewart, Edward C. "The Simulation of Cultural Differences." *Journal of Communication* 16, no. 4 (1966).

Stewart, Edward C., Jack Danielian, and Robert J. Foster. "Simulating Intercultural Communication through Role Playing." Technical report 69–7. Alexandria, VA: HumRRO, 1969.

Tucker, Michael F., and Albert R. Wight. "A 'Culture Gap' in International Personnel Programs." *The Bridge* (Winter 1981): 11–13.

Tung, R. L. *The New Expatriates: Managing Human Resources Abroad.* Cambridge, MA: Ballinger, 1988.

———. "Expatriate Assignments: Enhancing Success and Minimizing Failure." *Academy of Management Executive* 1, no. 2 (1987): 117–26.

———. "Selection and Training Procedures of U. S., European and Japanese Multinationals." *California Management Review* 25, no. 1 (1982): 57–71.

———. "Selection and Training Procedures of Personnel for Overseas Assignments." *Columbia Journal of World Business* 16, no. 1 (1981): 68–78.

Weaver, Gary R. "Psychological and Cultural Dimensions of Hostage Negotiation." In *Dynamic Processes of Crisis Negotiation*, edited by R. G. Rogan, Mitchell R. Hammer, and C. R. Van Zandt, 115–28. Westport, CT: Praeger, 1997.

Introduction to Self-Awareness Inventories

Chris Brown and Kasey Knight

Paolo Freire (1970) uses the term *praxis* to describe the process of learning as an interplay of action and reflection. Self-awareness inventories are used in training, at the beginning and at other points, to stimulate reflection on where past experiences are leading the learner and what future actions are contemplated as a result. When you use self-assessment inventories in training, the interplay of past action and current reflection leads to praxis.

Introduction

To distinguish self-awareness or self-assessment inventories from the array of other inventories, we propose the following definition:

> A *self-awareness inventory is a systematic self-reporting of perceptions, using a scored questionnaire, that allows reflection on a particular issue.*

Scoring involves analyzing responses to groups of items that indicate patterns of preference. Since there are *no right answers*, an inventory is not a test—merely a snapshot in time. Individual responses may or may not change with time or context. These inventories are not meant for psychodiagnostic or therapeutic purposes.

Self-awareness inventories serve as a springboard for exploring thinking patterns and behavioral styles and for considering the possibility of modifying these patterns and styles. They are most effective when combined with other training activities and not used as an end in themselves. They assist trainers in helping trainees see where they are now, in identifying areas for development, and in moving in the direction they choose. Self-awareness inventories introduce concepts and vocabulary that give trainees a nonjudgmental framework within which to examine their attitudes and behaviors. Trainers can identify group trends, then tailor program design to place more or less emphasis on certain topics or skills.

Uses of Self-Awareness Inventories

Self-assessment inventories have numerous uses in training. Here are some of them:

❖ Provide instrumented feedback to group members

❖ Introduce training concepts

❖ Supply a nonthreatening vocabulary

❖ Serve as a frame of reference

❖ Orchestrate group composition

❖ Analyze individual and group functioning

Trainees—especially in the corporate sector—seem to appreciate instruments (inventories are frequently referred to as "instruments") that supply them with quantitative feedback about themselves. While feedback from the trainer or other members of the group may be welcomed, it is regarded as subjective, based on the fact that it is someone else's perception. However, the feedback provided by an inventory is considered more objective and easier for the receiver to accept. For many low-context culture members, this is an advantage, because identity and meaning are embedded in words and numbers, not in personal relationships.

Self-awareness inventories can be used to introduce concepts, supply a common vocabulary, and provide a frame of reference. The four value orientations (action, process, people, and ideas) in the exercise described by Pierre Casse are an example of a frame of reference. The dimensions in the inventories described in the chapters by Michael Tucker and by Colleen Kelley and Judith Meyers introduce new concepts and a new vocabulary to the trainees, for example, *open-mindedness, personal autonomy,* and *perceptual acuity*. For most trainers or trainees, these phrases are not likely to be ones they use regularly. They therefore become a specialized vocabulary that encourages the individuals in the group to talk about themselves and others in a way that others in the group understand—even though they may come from diverse cultural backgrounds. This process can further group or team cohesion.

Inventory results can also aid in grouping trainees. Many times during a training program we want to break the large group into small groups to work on a specific task or complete an exercise. The groupings suggested by the inventory accomplish this division. At the same time, group members get a clearer picture of the dimensions they share with other group members and learn more about working with people like themselves. The effects of mixing the groups may produce valuable insights. Trainees can learn to appreciate the strengths and understand the limitations of people different from themselves. This is especially helpful in training that focuses on team building. The potential for conflict exists in both homogeneous and mixed groups, but the capacity for growth is vast and the effects are powerful. These groupings help you and the trainees analyze the level of functioning for both the individual and the group. It can help individuals explore ways to improve their effectiveness as group members.

It is important to be aware of both the advantages and disadvantages of using self-awareness instruments.

Advantages	Disadvantages
Enhance training relevance	Produce fear of exposure
Motivate the learner	Cause undue focus on individual inventory items
Enable early theoretical learning	
Develop understanding of terminology	Provide an overload of feedback
Increase personal commitment	Foster dependency on the trainer
Supply individual feedback	Induce fear of being stereotyped
Bring latent issues to the surface	Give the impression of superficiality
Provide comparison with group norms	
Assess longitudinal change	

Three of the disadvantages deserve additional comment. The first is the fear of personal exposure. Members of many cultures are uncomfortable in learning situations that require them to share their personal values, attitudes, or thoughts. Their fear can manifest itself in introverted or hostile reactions. Hostility can also be an indication that the participant thinks the instrument is unreliable, irrelevant, a waste of time, or stereotypical of a "touchy-feely" culture.

Secondly, inventories can generate a great deal of argument over specific items or questions on the inventory itself. Focusing on specific items can be a form of resistance. This resistance is often caused by the participants receiving information they are unable to accept. They may feel the feedback is inaccurate or too accurate, and they fear they will be judged negatively by others.

Finally, inventories can supply more feedback than the participant is able to accept at one time. This could be due to the actual amount of information or the speed with which it is given. Your training program may not allow sufficient time for assimilation. One way to deal with this situation is to arrange a time outside the workshop to meet with individual participants who have these kinds of questions or concerns. Some participants will feel more comfortable talking one-on-one with you.

Overcoming Pitfalls

Self-assessment inventories are not foolproof, but many of their pitfalls can be avoided with careful facilitation on your part. First of all, it is important to remove the mystery connected with self-assessment inventories. They are not error-free; they only suggest behavioral or attitudinal preferences. There are no right or wrong answers, no best or worst types. You as the trainer should explain that the individual scores are the results of how each trainee chose to answer a series of questions at that point in time. The participants' interpretation of the questions could vary at different times in their lives if their self-concept or skills have changed. Responses can also vary according to the setting in which they are asked to answer the questions; for example, attitudes or behaviors at work may differ significantly from those at home.

Another way to avoid some of the pitfalls is to ensure that individuals have sufficient training time to process the new data. There are two techniques that we have found helpful. The first one is to ask trainees to predict their own inventory results based on the conceptual framework that you present, and then ask them to compare their prediction with their actual scores. Be sure to allow them ample time for questions regarding similarities and differences they find. If there is sufficient trust within the group and if it is appropriate to the training goals, you can encourage your participants to discuss and compare their scores with the scores of other participants. Many participants find it comforting and enlightening to share their inventory results with others. This often increases the cohesiveness of the group.

If you sense your participants fear personal exposure or are especially resistant, it is time to back off, relax, and reevaluate your expectations. It is never helpful to push the participants into doing something they resist intensely; they will not benefit from the training if they are too defensive. Sometimes it works to review the purpose of the instrument and to help trainees frame the training session as a chance to receive feedback in a nonthreatening manner. You should emphasize that all individuals have strengths as well as areas for improvement. Rather than be ashamed about their areas for improvement, they should be encouraged to view these as opportunities for personal growth.

How to Use Self-Awareness Inventories

A self-awareness inventory is not an isolated training tool. It should be used as part of a larger training program. In other words, do not use an inventory by itself or just because you want to try it. The self-awareness component of the inventory needs to be integrated into the main purpose or objective of the training program. For example, the primary training objective may be multicultural team building or development of leadership skills or preparation for an overseas assignment.

To obtain the most benefit from an inventory, we suggest including the following six phases in your session design:

Before

1. *Briefly describe the purpose and benefits* of the particular instrument. Trainees are more likely to cooperate in completing the inventory if they understand what they will gain from the experience. Possible benefits may include awareness of the personal strengths they bring to a multicultural team, knowledge of their behavioral tendencies under pressure, or identification of areas where skill building is needed.

2. *Create a nonthreatening environment* by emphasizing that the inventory is not a test. There are no right or wrong answers, and (if appropriate) trainees will have control over how much of the results they share with others. Tell trainees to answer each item so that it reflects how they see themselves now, not how they would like to be seen. Pass out the inventory and read through the directions and example(s) together. Ask the trainees to answer the items in the context appropriate for the training session, that is, work group, family, or other group. Address questions and give appropriate time to complete the items. Emphasize spontaneity. Ask trainees to remain quiet until all are finished.

After

3. *Describe the theory* on which the inventory is based. Include the dimensions and characteristics that the instrument delineates. Give specific examples, address questions, and check for understanding.

4. *Ask trainees to predict their own results* based on their understanding of the theory. This gives value to their self-perceptions, reduces overreliance on the inventory scores, and emphasizes the importance of future verification and development.

5. *Score the inventory* according to the specific directions. Give individuals time to reflect and to compare the results for similarities and differences with what they predicted. Follow this with pairs discussing their results with each other. Address questions and concerns as they arise during the scoring and interpretation.

Debriefing

6. *Conduct a large or small group discussion* on the specific applications of the inventory results. Encourage trainees to discuss their insights as appropriate to the goals of the training program. For example, if you are training a team on their way to a business venture in another culture, you can ask the team members to discuss how their identified strengths and weaknesses will work for or against them based on their knowledge of the target culture. If you are working with families, you might ask them to develop plans for supporting each other during an overseas assignment based on their inventory results.

A powerful benefit of self-assessment inventories is that they supply the participants with a common framework within which to describe behaviors and attitudes, their own and those of others, and to make comparisons in nonjudgmental ways. Tie results into subsequent activities where possible. This phase is the foundation from which other training activities flow, whether their purpose is self-awareness or skill building.

Contexts and Applications

Contexts

Self-assessment inventories are used in a wide variety of multicultural contexts, which is a testimony to their versatility. Some of the contexts or situations are

Foreign service, military, and government agencies. The training in which these people find themselves is often just prior to an overseas assignment. The U.S. Navy and the Foreign Service Institute, for instance, have included inventories in their cross-cultural training.

Educational settings. Exchange programs for students and faculty often include self-assessment inventories in predeparture training.

Business and industry. Companies sending employees overseas for short or extended work assignments provide cross-cultural training prior to departure. Some, such as AT&T, have modified part of their management curriculum to reflect their multicultural workforce. Self-awareness inventories have strengthened these training programs.

Community groups. A multicultural grassroots group banding together to improve the safety and quality of life in their neighborhood may use self-awareness inventories to provide a needed frame of reference through which to communicate.

Families. Two possible scenarios are (1) training for family members who are accompanying employees being sent on an overseas assignment or (2) training for host families about to receive a foreign exchange student.

Nonprofit and religious organizations. Self-awareness inventories can be integrated into cross-cultural training to prepare volunteers and members of religious organizations to live and work overseas. Another use may be for church leaders attending a cross-cultural training session to increase their sensitivity to people from other cultures who belong to their congregation.

Applications

The possible applications for inventories underscore their usefulness. Specific applications include but are not limited to the following:

Orientation	Problem solving or decision making
Reentry	Conflict resolution
Management or staff development	Leadership training
Executive education	Negotiation
Career development	Teacher training
Outplacement	Counseling
Team building	Research

Potential for Misuse

While there are many highly effective uses for self-awareness inventories, there is also potential for misuse. As long as the participants are interpreting the results for themselves, you are safe. However, the danger—and temptation—is for the trainer or some other "authority" to try to interpret the results for the trainee. However accurate those interpretations may be, it can be seen as a form of manipulation. The inventories can take on an appearance of greater psychological validity than they were ever intended to possess. Therefore, avoid giving "your" interpretation; this is a time to listen, observe, and clarify when needed.

Breaching confidentiality is another way in which self-assessment inventories can be misused. This happens when either the trainer or trainees share information they learn about another trainee to individuals outside the group without prior consent or knowledge of the trainee. An example would be your divulging specific inventory results with a supervisor of one of the trainees, which should not be dictated by the training goals.

Self-assessment inventories can be misused if they are presented as sources of fact or "hidden truths" about the trainees. Explain the instrument's validity and reliability accurately. We have also found it helpful to position (that is, describe) both *self-perception* and *perceptions of others* realistically for what they are—perceptions, not facts.

Very rarely a participant will become agitated by the results of the inventory. You might hear something like "Well this just proves that I am hopeless. I will never be able to make it." The self-awareness inventory does not cause this reaction; the person already has a sense of hopelessness or low self-esteem. But the self-awareness inventory can precipitate the response—one this person probably uses often. Make sure the participant understands the limitations of the instrument, as described earlier, and reemphasize the fact that there are no right or wrong answers or best styles or types. Usually the person will be able to continue the training program but occasionally may need to be removed for counseling before proceeding. This action can benefit both that individual and the other participants.

Selected Self-Awareness Inventories

There are four inventories described in this section of the *Sourcebook*. The first, *The Four-Value Orientation*, designed by Pierre Casse, assesses the learner's orientation toward action, process, ideas, and people. Individuals discuss their own preferences regarding these orientations in relation to their own communication style and to that of others.

The Overseas Assignment Inventory (OAI) measures fourteen attitudes and attributes found to be important for successful cross-cultural adaptation. It is a useful tool for identifying individual motivation and personal development.

The purpose of the *Cross-Cultural Adaptability Inventory (CCAI)* is to increase individual awareness of how people function cross-culturally. This self-scoring instrument aids in the identification of personal strengths and areas for improvement.

The Intercultural Development Inventory (IDI) is based on Milton Bennett's developmental model of intercultural sensitivity. This instrument can be used to assess the intercultural sensitivity of an individual or group in terms of primary stages and secondary strategies.

All of these are excellent inventories for cross-cultural training. In addition it is important to become familiar with other inventories that are available to cross-cultural trainers, thus increasing your likelihood of selecting the best instrument for your unique situation.

Other Inventories

There are a large number of instruments available that can be adapted for cross-cultural use with a little effort and creativity. A primary consideration is always the comfort level of the trainees. As Joyce L. Francis (1989) stated in her article, "The Cultural Relativity of Training Techniques" (based on Geert Hofstede's work), each culture has its unique learning styles. It is important to develop trust with your trainees, and one way to do so is to initially use the training methods that most closely match their learning styles and then introduce new methods gradually as the trainees become comfortable.

Three self-awareness inventories that have been used successfully in cross-cultural contexts are the Myers-Briggs Type Indicator (MBTI), the Thomas-Kilmann Conflict Mode Instrument, and ACUMEN.

The Myers-Briggs Type Indicator

The MBTI is based on psychological types identified by the Swiss psychologist Carl G. Jung. It was developed by Katherine Briggs and Isabel Briggs Myers over a thirty-year period. In one recent year, over two million MBTI answer sheets were sold in North America alone.

This instrument consists of four dimensions that assess an individual's preferences:

❖ Basic orientation toward inner or outer world (Extroversion-Introversion)

❖ Modes of perception; taking in information (Sensing-Intuition)

❖ Ways of processing information and making decisions (Thinking-Feeling)

❖ Ways of responding to the outer world (Judging-Perceiving)

Each dimension contains two poles, for example, introversion/extroversion. The two polar aspects of each dimension come into play at different times, not both at once and not with equal confidence. Just as we have inborn preferences for writing with our right or left hand, the authors of the MBTI have found that we favor one of the two poles in each dimension. The total number of possible combinations results in sixteen personality types. As interesting as they are, there is not room here, nor is it appropriate in this overview chapter, to provide the details of these personality types. Your best resource for an in-depth description of the MBTI personality type is Myers and Myers (1980). (Please note that in order to administer the MBTI, certification is required).

In our training sessions we have found that focusing on the four functional types (subsets of the sixteen personality types) provides a straightforward framework for understanding differences. People with a strong technical background who have had little or no exposure to psychology find this model easy to understand, since only four styles are delineated. Based on the information they receive regarding the tendencies of their functional type, trainees understand more fully why they react the way they do in particular situations, especially in those that include interaction with others. Demonstrating a nonjudgmental approach (no one type is best) is essential. A source for more information on the four functional types is Keirsey and Bates (1984).

One effective way to show the value of diverse personality preferences is to lead a small group, decision-making activity such as a desert or arctic survival exercise, a project-planning exercise, or any decision-making task where the outcomes are tangible or quantifiable. The power of the lesson comes from grouping people with the same functional preferences together—with one exception: one group is composed of representatives from *all* preferences, in other words, as heterogeneous a group as possible. When the *best performing* group is discovered to be the *most diverse*, the value of diversity is dramatically demonstrated.

The MBTI has been used extensively in cross-cultural training worldwide and has been translated into other languages. Substantial research has been done on

Japanese culture, where findings have revealed that people holding certain professional jobs in Japan scored the same on the MBTI inventory as Americans holding similar jobs. This does not mean that it is true for all cultures or for all members of a specific culture, but it does attest to the usefulness of the MBTI in cross-cultural training.

The Thomas-Kilmann Conflict Mode Instrument

Cross-cultural encounters can be very stressful. Rational responses are often short-circuited under stress, making behavior difficult to predict. It is helpful to learn more about our own styles of dealing with conflict, since the more we know about how we *might* react in a situation, the greater the chance we have of selecting an appropriate course of action. Self-assessment inventories such as the Thomas-Kilmann Conflict Mode Instrument are one way of increasing this knowledge about ourselves.

The Thomas-Kilmann Conflict Mode Instrument is designed to assess an individual's typical behavior in conflict situations. Conflict between and among individuals or groups starts when one or both parties feels he or she is not in agreement. A person's behavior can be described along two dimensions:

1. **assertiveness**—the extent to which the person attempts to satisfy his or her own needs.

2. **cooperativeness**—the extent to which the person attempts to satisfy the needs of the other party.

The Thomas-Kilmann inventory is built on identifying people along these two basic dimensions and five specific methods of dealing with conflict: competing, avoiding, accommodating, compromising, and collaborating. All five modes of behavior are valuable and can be used in response to requirements of the situation. However, most people have a strong preference for one of the modes, and, consequently, they tend to use it to the exclusion of the others.

Since the Thomas-Kilmann Conflict Mode Instrument assists trainees in identifying their preferences for dealing with conflict, it can be useful for training programs in which the goal is team building. Personality differences—whether individuals are from the same or a variety of different cultures—produce conflict. This inherent conflict needs to be addressed and managed in order to build a smoothly functioning team. When team members learn to recognize and understand their own preferred method for dealing with conflict and the preferred methods of the others, they can develop ways of working together to manage conflict and stress more effectively.

This instrument can be the central feature of a training session. When it is used as a "stand alone," the goal of the training is likely to focus on conflict resolution. The Thomas-Kilmann inventory can also be used in sequence with other instruments and activities. For example, you might want to start with the MBTI to provide a conceptual framework for general personality differences and differences in processing information. Then you can move from general personality differences to a specific context by introducing trainees to the Thomas-Kilmann instrument so they can learn their preferred mode for dealing with conflict. Finally, you can conduct a consensus-building activity such as a project-planning or a desert survival exercise or a cross-cultural simulation game like *Barnga* (Steinwachs 1990) to help trainees assess their new skills in managing conflict and functioning at a higher level.

ACUMEN

This inventory is designed for those who manage relationships with other people—executives, managers, supervisors, salespeople, teachers, and other professionals. Over a twenty-year period, specialists found that certain thinking styles are associated more frequently with successful managers.

The theoretical basis for ACUMEN assumes that our interactions with others are a reflection of the view we hold of ourselves and the world around us. ACUMEN helps individuals identify their worldview, major patterns of thinking styles and attitudes, motivation styles, ways they attempt to lead others, preferences in interpersonal communication, and conflict resolution styles. It enables participants to examine how each of these factors impacts their interpersonal world and management performance.

ACUMEN is a 124-question inventory. Standardized scores are generated for twelve scales. Each scale represents a particular character trait or thinking style that has been associated with managerial and interpersonal effectiveness. The twelve scales are

Humanistic-Helpful	Affiliation	Approval
Conventional	Dependence	Apprehension
Oppositional	Power	Competition
Perfectionism	Achievement	Self-Actualization

ACUMEN is a powerful tool that can be used when preparing managers or executives for negotiations across cultures. Each profile gives a wealth of information that offers insight into the individual's interpersonal communication and management styles. It has been used extensively overseas, both in English and in a number of other languages.

ACUMEN can be completed on a computer or on a paper-pencil form. If paper-pencil forms are used, you have to enter the data into the ACUMEN Report Writer program on a computer or send it to Human Factors in San Rafael, California, to have it entered commercially. The beauty of this inventory is that team members, colleagues, superiors, and subordinates can all give anonymous feedback regarding an individual that is then compiled as a group report. The personalized report includes both a self-assessment profile and a group profile. Because of the sensitive nature of the personalized reports, specialized training is recommended before one administers ACUMEN. Training is offered by Human Factors and by Human Synergistics in Ypsilanti, Michigan.

Selection Considerations

How do you decide which self-awareness inventory is best for you? Major considerations include certification training, scoring, reporting, research, and additional resources. The information regarding these considerations for each inventory highlighted in this section is presented in the table below.

Consideration	ACUMEN	CCAI	MBTI	OAI	IDI	Thomas-Kilmann	Four-Value Orientation
Need training to administer	X		X	X			
Self-scorable	X	X	X		X	X	X
Trainer scored	X	X	X		X***		X
Commercially scored	X		X	X			
Personalized report	X		X	X			
Extensive research data	X	X*	X	X	X**	X	X**
Used 10+ years			X	X			
Supplementary references	X		X	X	X	X	

* Ongoing research in progress
** Based on researched concepts
*** Group profile score needs to be compiled by IDI expert

Conclusion

Self-assessment inventories are helpful tools in cross-cultural training. Selection can be from one of the instruments especially designed for use in cross-cultural situations or an inventory that you adapt. These inventories encourage self-discovery and open communication and serve as a strong foundation on which to build a training program. They assess *what is* so the trainee can decide *what could be.*

References

Francis, Joyce L. "The Cultural Relativity of Training Techniques." *Bay Area OD Network Journal* (1989).

Freire, Paolo. "Cultural Action for Freedom." *Harvard Educational Review.* Monograph series no. 1 (1970): 13.

Keirsey, David, and Marilyn Bates. *Please Understand Me.* Del Mar, CA: Prometheus Nemesis, 1984.

Myers, Isabel Briggs, and Peter Myers. *Gifts Differing.* Palo Alto, CA: Consulting Psychologists, 1980.

Thiagarajan, Sivasailam, and Barbara Steinwachs. *Barnga: A Simulation Game on Cultural Clashes.* Yarmouth, ME: Intercultural Press, 1990.

Instruments

ACUMEN. Human Factors, San Rafael, CA. Phone: 415-499-8181.

Myers-Briggs Type Indicator. Consulting Psychologists Press, 3803 East Bayshore Road, Palo Alto, CA 94303.

Thomas-Kilmann Conflict Mode Instrument. Xicom, 60 Woods Rd., Tuxedo, NY 10987. Phone: 800-759-4266.

Resources

Conte, H. R., and R. Plutchik. "A Circumplex Model for Interpersonal Personality Traits. *Journal of Personality and Social Psychology* 40 (1981): 701–11.

Cooke, Robert A., and James C. Lafferty. *Level 1: Life Styles Inventory—An instrument for Assessing and Changing the Self-Concept of Organizational Members.* Plymouth, MI: Human Synergistics, 1981.

Freire, Paolo. *Pedagogy of the Oppressed.* New York: Herder and Herder, 1972.

Gordon, Lawrence D. *People Types and Tiger Stripes: A Practical Guide to Learning Styles.* 2d ed. Gainesville, FL: Center for Applications of Psychological Type, 1982.

Hirsh, Sandra, and Jean Kummerow. *Life Types.* New York: Warner Books, 1989.

Hofstede, Geert. *Culture's Consequences: International Differences in Work-Related Values.* Beverly Hills: Sage, 1980.

Kilmann, Ralph H. *Managing Beyond the Quick Fix.* San Francisco: Jossey-Bass, 1989.

Kroeger, Otto, and Janet M. Thuesen. *Type Talk.* New York: Delacorte Press, 1988.

The Four-Value Orientation Exercise Using a Self-Awareness Inventory

Pierre Casse

Intercultural training is growing. There is no question that more and more organizations are getting interested in promoting intercultural awareness among their managers and staff. They have no choice. The world is indeed becoming increasingly global, and its complexity and ambiguity require a better understanding and control of cultural diversity. Corporations like Alcatel, Shell, Phillips, and AT&T are looking for practical, effective ways to enhance their leaders' cultural sensitivity. They are searching for trainers who can help them perform better in today's world. One useful training tool is the Four-Value Orientation Exercise, which helps trainees understand their dominant value orientation. This is an important part of their "cultural software."

Introduction

A challenge that intercultural specialists must repond to is fine-tuning their training technologies to meet the expectations of their customers. Among the many expectations and learning needs clients or customers have, some of the strongest are:

❖ to understand, in a nonstereotyping way, what cultural differences are all about;

❖ to work with instruments which are neither so sophisticated that they cannot be understood nor so simple that they are ineffective; and

❖ to learn how to learn so that they will be able to cope with whatever situation they find themselves in tomorrow.

Self-awareness inventories are powerful training tools to meet these expectations, but to understand why this is so, we need to know more about them.

Definition and Characteristics

A self-awareness inventory (or self-assessment instrument) is *not* a test. It is not supposed to reveal the inner truth about somebody. It is a subjective measure which has been constructed in such a way that people who complete it get a chance to reflect on aspects of their own personality. They are the only judges regarding the relevance (and validity) of the information they have at the end of the exercise. They decide if it makes sense or not. A good definition to use is this:

> A self-assessment inventory is a subjective training tool which uses a questionnaire to give people an opportunity to reflect on aspects of their own personality in relation to a selected theme or topic.

You will recognize a good (effective) self-assessment inventory because it has certain characteristics:

❖ Trainees are excited about using it. They are *motivated* by it to learn about themselves.

❖ It is easy to understand and constructed in such a way that people have no problem going through it. The *instructions* are clear.

❖ The outcome is clearly meaningful and enriching even if the learners still have doubts about the accuracy with which it reflects their personality. (Debriefing the exercise is critical because it provides an opportunity for *reflection*.)

Successfully using a self-assessment inventory in a training program means carefully designing the session or exercise in which it is embedded. The design process consists of setting the goals for the session, introducing the self-assessment instrument, completing and scoring the instrument, debriefing it in a way that helps participants understand its meaning for them individually, and group work that ties the self-assessment scores to the goals of the session and to the real world of the participants. Success criteria for a self-assessment inventory exercise are:

❖ The questionnaire must be well constructed and the wording clear.

❖ The introduction explaining what the questionnaire is about and how to fill it out must be motivating, stimulating, and anxiety-reducing.

❖ The debriefing must meet the learning goals and encourage participants to find ways of using the outcome of the questionnaire.

Types of Self-Awareness Inventories

Self-awareness inventory exercises can be classified into three categories: the one-question self-assessment exercise, the multiple-choice self-assessment exercise, and the in-depth self-assessment exercise.

The one-question self-assessment exercise. One open-ended question is asked of the learners, who must answer for themselves. For example, what are your strengths as a communicator? Or, identify three ways to improve your own negotiating effectiveness. Then trainees meet in small groups to share reactions and learn from each other.

The one-question self-assessment exercise is extremely effective when used to supplement a theory or a model which has just been presented; to enable trainees to relate what has just been covered to their own experience; to change the pace of the learning process; and/or to foster motivation, participation, and the sharing of personal views.

The multiple-choice self-assessment exercise. This approach is characterized by the use of a forced-choice questionnaire. This type of questionnaire is usually filled out by the learners during the session. Different models can be used, for example,

❖ the selection model. Choose the item in each pair presented to you that is most typical of you.

❖ the rating model. For each item presented in the questionnaire, rate yourself on the following scale: 1=never; 2=sometimes; 3=all the time.

The in-depth self-assessment exercise. These instruments are more sophisticated and have generally been developed and tested by professionals in various fields. The Myers-Briggs Type Indicator, the Minnesota Multiphasic Personality Inventory (MMPI), and Fundamental Interpersonal Relations Orientation-Behavior (FIRO-B) are examples of in-depth self-assessment instruments. An exercise based on an in-depth self-assessment questionnaire requires enough time to fill out the questionnaire (the MMPI has 362 questions), well-prepared interpretation or feedback (often in writing) for the trainees, and professional processing of the outcome of the exercise, sometimes with private counseling sessions with the learners.

Advantages and Disadvantages

The key advantages and disadvantages of self-awareness inventories are summarized in the following chart.

Advantages	Disadvantages
1. Motivates learners to get involved	1. Can be perceived as superficial
2. Makes the learning experience more relevant	2. Can be taken too seriously by some people, who then feel hurt
3. Promotes sharing among the learners	3. Can be used by the learners outside the training framework without appropriate precautions

The Four-Value Orientation Exercise

The Four-Value Orientation Exercise is a good example of the multiple-choice self-assessment exercise. It is an opportunity for learners to explore four value orientations (action, process, people, ideas) to find out about their dominant orientation, what impact it has on their communication styles, and how this relates to their culture-based patterns of thinking and behaving, or "cultural programming."

History

I developed this exercise during my tenure at the World Bank. It was originally intended to be used in advanced cross-cultural training programs for managers at the bank. I have since used it in a variety of situations.

The conceptual scheme and items in the inventory are based on the work of Carl G. Jung (1964). A version of the exercise was first published in my book, *Training for the Cross-Cultural Mind* (1979).*

Procedure

Introduction. Begin by telling the group that the purpose of the exercise (which is not a test) is to enable the learners to identify and analyze four different value orientations, or "software." These value orientations can be seen as four ways to define and control things, internally and externally. They are subject to cultural influences and are manifested in culturally appropriate ways that differ from culture to culture. I refer to them as "software" because they operate within the individual much as a software program controls a computer.

Instructions. Hand out the questionnaire and tell the learners to select, in each pair of attributes, the one which is most typical of their own personality. Each pair is an either-or proposal; either one item or the other is more like them. They should make their choices as spontaneously as possible and not skip any pairs. There are no wrong answers. There are 80 items (40 pairs), and when all the participants are finished, they will receive scoring instructions. Refer to Appendix A for the questionnaire.

Scoring. When everyone has completed the self-assessment inventory, hand out the scoring instructions (Appendix B). Read the instructions aloud and make sure everyone is clear about how to proceed.

Debriefing. Although debriefing is important for any learning exercise, it is especially important for self-assessment inventories. You are dealing with the self-images of the learners. They are eager to know what their scores mean to them as individuals and are curious about the scores of others in their group. You need to be sure they understand the scores in the context of the learning situation and, since this is cross-cultural training, the cultural significance of knowing the value orientations for themselves and others. Conduct the debriefing in five phases.

Phase 1. First the learners should check to make sure they have a score for each value orientation. It is all right to have a zero score in one or two orientations, but the total score must be 40. They should pay attention to

❖ the highest score(s) they got (likely to be their dominant value orientation or the most important part of their cultural software).

❖ the various levels of scores (1–7 = underdeveloped value orientation; 8–15 = well-developed value orientation; 16–20 = overdeveloped value orientation).

---

* The World Bank holds copyright under Protocol 2 of the Universal Copyright Convention. However, this material may be copied for research, educational, or scholarly purposes in member countries of the World Bank. If the exercise is reproduced or translated, the Economic Development Institute of the World Bank would appreciate a copy.

Phase 2. Present the model to the learners step by step, using the following model and moving from Value Orientation 1 (VO 1) to Value Orientation 4 (VO 4):

VO 1	VO 2
ACTION	PROCESS
VO 4	VO 3
IDEA	PEOPLE

Tell the learners that four value orientations have been used to construct this self-assessment inventory, with two assumptions underlying the model: (1) the four orientations can be found in any individual or culture and (2) the four orientations have an impact on the way an individual communicates. Next, describe the four value orientations.

Value Orientation 1: ACTION (*what*). Individuals with a high score on this orientation like action, doing, achieving, improving, solving problems, and so forth.

Value Orientation 2: PROCESS (*how*). Individuals with high scores in this orientation like facts, organizing, structuring, developing strategies, tactics, and the like.

Value Orientation 3: PEOPLE (*who*). Individuals who are people-oriented like to focus on social processes, human relations, interactions, communications, teamwork, and motivation.

Value Orientation 4: IDEA (*why*). Individuals who are idea-oriented like concepts, theories, innovation, creativity, novelty, and the exchange of ideas.

All individuals possess the four orientations, but most generally have a dominant value orientation or style with which they feel most comfortable. The dominant value orientation may change and is determined by the particular situation in which the person is involved. People, therefore, have the capability of switching from one orientation to another. However, when a crisis occurs, most individuals switch back to the orientation with which they are most familiar.

Cultures tend to value certain orientations over others. This can be called "cultural programming." Most people would agree that action is the dominant value orientation in the United States. Many factual, logical, process-oriented people can be found in Germany. A dominant people-orientation can be found in the traditional cultures of the Middle East and Asia. Many French people are proud of their idea-orientation. This does not deny the rich complexity of value orientations in every culture. It does indicate that cultures have observably dominant value orientations, just as individuals do.

Phase 3. Have learners with the same dominant value orientations meet as a group to clarify the impact of the value orientation on their behavior and to brainstorm how to communicate with people who have different dominant value orientations. To guide the discussion, give them the handouts—Value Orientations: Main Characteristics (Appendix C) and Communicating with Other Value Orientations (Appendix D). Participants looking at Appendix D may ask, "How do I know the value orientation of the person I'm talking to?" You can suggest they use the lists in Appendix C. Watch for those characteristics. They may want to practice with a different group.

Phase 4. Have the learners return to the value orientation model and mark the quadrants in which their two highest scores fall. Show them the following version of the model and explain how to find out what their two highest scores indicate about them. For example, if the two highest scores are in the Action and Process quadrants, the learners tend to be Implementors. If the highest scores are Process and People, then they are likely to be Organizers. They can also find out about themselves if their two highest scores are on the diagonals. High Process plus Idea orientations combine in people who are Planners, and Action plus People orientations are often found in Leaders.

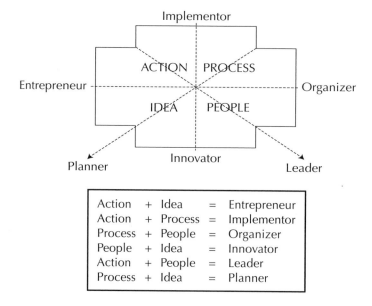

Phase 5. You can use this model to divide into six small groups: all the "implementors" in one group, the "organizers" in another, and so on. Have discussion questions prepared. I suggest you begin by asking them to examine the relevance of the model from a personal viewpoint. Then ask them to discuss experiences from their own lives that illustrate how their value orientation is supported (or not supported) in their culture. Can they become aware of their cultural programming? Can they expand on it? How? Where can they start?

Constructing a Self-Awareness Inventory

You can design and write your own self-awareness inventory by carefully following these steps.

Step 1: The Objectives

Identify the main theme of the exercise and clarify its objectives. In the illustration in this chapter, the main idea was to examine four different ways people orient themselves to the world. The objective was to give learners a chance to discover the nature and structure of their own cultural programming in terms of these value orientations.

Step 2: The Model

Start at the end and develop the model which you will use to achieve the objectives. I selected the four-value orientation model based on Jung's (1964) theory on psychic functions and orientations to illustrate some key cultural differences.

Step 3: The Questions (Items)

Develop questions or items to illustrate the various points or elements of the model. Here are examples from the four-value questionnaire:

Action Orientation
1. I like action.
8. Deadlines are important for me.
9. I cannot stand procrastination.

Process Orientation
2. I deal with problems in a systematic way.
7. I like to attend well-organized meetings.
10. I believe that new ideas have to be tested before being used.

People Orientation
3. I believe that teams are more effective than individuals.
6. I enjoy working with people.
11. I enjoy the stimulation of interaction with others.

Idea Orientation
4. I enjoy innovation very much.
5. I am more interested in the future than in the past.
12. I am always looking for new possibilities.

Step 4: The Questionnaire (Instrument)

Mix up the items (note the differing numbers in above examples) or provide ratings for each item (such as: never—sometimes—always).

Step 5: Instructions

Develop the proper instructions and check them many times for clarity.

Step 6: Field Trials

Test your questionnaire with a sample of people. Fine-tune it and test it again. Check the wording and validate the outcome through feedback from several groups of people. Confirm the relevance of the model. Since you are asking people what they think, you are getting their subjective opinion. This subjective validation is a necessary step. With a subjective validation you can construct a useful questionnaire for training purposes. If you have the expertise, however, to conduct an *objective* validation using random samples and statistical tests, you can produce a more psychometrically robust instrument that can be used for research as well as training. But subjective validation is sufficient for practical training purposes.

Step 7: Polishing

Finalize the questionnaire and be ready to improve it after using it with various groups of learners. A final piece of advice: do not look for perfection. A questionnaire can be useful before it is perfect—if there is such a thing as a perfect questionnaire. But make sure the exercise does indeed stimulate meaningful self-awareness.

Conclusion

In the first edition of *Training for the Cross-Cultural Mind* I said,

> To understand the world is easy since we are part of the world. The problem is that we sometimes have a tendency to forget it on the one hand and deny it on the other. Why such a reaction? It looks like a characteristic of human nature to be able to separate itself from the parts which make up what we are as well as from the whole which, in a way, possesses us. This continuous process can be attributed to the human drive toward identity, and the fulfillment of what one actually is…. To understand oneself is maybe the most challenging endeavour that we face (ix and x).

Self-assessment inventories such as the Four-Value Orientation Self-Awareness Inventory are one of the best tools any trainer can use to help learners discover personal, interpersonal, and intercultural realities.

References

Casse, Pierre. *Training for the Cross-Cultural Mind: A Handbook for Cross-Cultural Trainers and Consultants.* Washington, DC: SIETAR International, 1979.

Jung, Carl G. *Man and His Symbols.* New York: Doubleday, 1964.

Self-Assessment Inventories

Fundamental Interpersonal Relations Orientation–Behavior. Consulting Psychologists Press, 3803 East Bayshore Road, Palo Alto, CA 94303.

The Minnesota Multiphasic Personality Inventory. NCS Assessments, 5605 Green Circle Drive, Minnetonka, Minnesota 55343 (800-627-7271).

The Myers-Briggs Type Indicator. Consulting Psychologists Press, 3803 East Bayshore Road, Palo Alto, CA 94303.

Appendix A

Self-Assessment Exercise

1. I like action.
2. I deal with problems in a systematic way.
3. I believe that teams are more effective than individuals.   *9*
4. I enjoy innovation very much.
5. I am more interested in the future than in the past.
6. I enjoy working with people.
7. I like to attend well-organized group meetings.
8. Deadlines are important for me.
9. I cannot stand procrastination.
10. I believe that new ideas have to be tested before being used.
11. I enjoy the stimulation of interaction with others.
12. I am always looking for new possibilities.
13. I want to set up my own objectives.
14. When I start something I go through until the end.
15. I basically try to understand other people's emotions.
16. I do challenge people around me.
17. I look forward to receiving feedback on my performance.
18. I find the step-by-step approach very effective.
19. I think I am good at reading people.
20. I like creative problem solving.
21. I extrapolate and project all the time.
22. I am sensitive to others' needs.
23. Planning is the key to success.
24. I become impatient with long deliberations.
25. I am cool under pressure.
26. I value experience very much.
27. I listen to people.
28. People say that I am a fast thinker.
29. Cooperation is a key word for me.
30. I use logical methods to test alternatives.

31. I like to handle several projects at the same time.
32. I always question myself.

33. I learn by doing.
34. I believe that my head rules my heart.

35. I can predict how others may react to a certain action.
36. I do not like details.

37. Analysis should always precede action.
38. I am able to assess the climate of a group.

39. I have a tendency to start things and not finish them.
40. I perceive myself as decisive.

41. I search for challenging tasks.
42. I rely on observation and data.

43. I can express my feelings openly.
44. I like to design new projects.

45. I enjoy reading very much.
46. I perceive myself as a facilitator.

47. I like to focus on one issue at a time.
48. I like to achieve.

49. I enjoy learning about others.
50. I like variety.

51. Facts speak for themselves.
52. I use my imagination as much as possible.

53. I am impatient with long, slow assignments.
54. My mind never stops working.

55. Key decisions have to be made in a cautious way.
56. I strongly believe that people need each other to get work done.

57. I usually make decisions without thinking too much.
58. Emotions create problems.

59. I like to be liked by others.
60. I can put two and two together very quickly.

61. I try out my new ideas on people.
62. I believe in the scientific approach.

63. I like to get things done.
64. Good relationships are essential.

65. I am impulsive.
66. I accept differences in people.

67. Communicating with people is an end in itself.
68. I like to be intellectually stimulated.

69. I like to organize.
70. I usually jump from one task to another.

71. Talking and working with people is a creative act.
72. Self-actualization is a key word for me.

73. I enjoy playing with ideas.
74. I dislike wasting my time.

75. I enjoy doing what I am good at.
76. I learn by interacting with others.

77. I find abstractions interesting and enjoyable.
78. I am patient with details.

79. I like brief, to-the-point statements.
80. I feel confident in myself.

Appendix B

Scoring Instructions

When everyone has completed the self-assessment inventory, use these scoring instructions to obtain your value profile. Note the item numbers included in the first value orientation and circle the ones you selected. Next add the number of items you circled for a total score for that orientation. The maximum is 20 per value orientation and your total for the four styles should be 40. You must repeat the process for each value orientation.

Value Orientation 1

1 - 8 - 9 - 13 - 17 - 24 - 26 - 31 - 33 - 40 -41 - 48 - 50 - 53 - 57 - 63 - 65 - 70 - 74 - 79

<u>   </u>
20

Description of Value Orientation 1 (Action) =

Value Orientation 2

2 - 7 - 10 - 14 - 18 - 23 - 25 - 30 - 34 - 37 - 42 - 47 - 51 - 55 - 58 - 62 - 66 - 69 - 75 - 78

<u>   </u>
20

Description of Value Orientation 2 (Process) =

Value Orientation 3

3 - 6 - 11 - 15 - 19 - 22 - 27 - 29 - 35 - 38 - 43 - 46 - 49 - 56 - 59 - 64 - 67 - 71 - 76 - 80

<u>   </u>
20

Description of Value Orientation 3 (People) =

Value Orientation 4

4 - 5 - 12 - 16 - 20 - 21 - 28 - 32 - 36 - 39 - 44 - 45 - 52 - 54 - 60 - 61 - 68 - 72 - 73 - 77

<u>   </u>
20

Description of Value Orientation 4 (Idea) =

Appendix C

Value Orientations: Main Characteristics

1. Action	They talk about	They are
	Results/Responsibility	Pragmatic
	Objectives/Feedback	Direct (to the point)
	Performance/Experience	Impatient
	Productivity/Challenge	Decisive
	Efficiency/Achievements	Quick
	Decisions/Change	Energetic

2. Process	They talk about	They are
	Facts/Trying out	Systematic
	Procedures/Analysis	Logical (cause and effect)
	Planning/Observations	Factual
	Organizing/Proof	Verbose
	Controlling/Details	Unemotional
	Testing	Cautious/Patient

3. People	They talk about	They are
	People/Self-development	Spontaneous
	Needs/Sensitivity	Empathic
	Motivation/Awareness	Warm
	Teamwork/Cooperation	Subjective
	Beliefs/Communication	Emotional
	Feelings/Values	Perceptive
	Team spirit/Expectations	Sensitive
	Relationships/Understanding	

4. Idea	They talk about	They are
	Concepts/Interdependence	Imaginative
	Innovation/New ways	Charismatic
	Creativity/New methods	Difficult to understand
	Improving/Opportunities	Ego-centered
	Possibilities/Problems	Unrealistic
	Potential/Grand designs	Creative
	Issues/Alternatives	Full of ideas/Provocative

Appendix D

Communicating with Other Value Orientations

Communicating with an action-oriented person.

Focus on the results first (state the conclusion right at the outset).
State your best recommendation (do not offer many alternatives).
Be as brief as possible.
Emphasize the practicality of your ideas.
Use visual aids.

Communicating with a process-oriented person.

Be precise (state the facts).
Organize your presentation in logical order: background, present, outcome.
Break down your recommendations.
Include options (consider alternatives) with pros and cons.
Do not rush a process-oriented person.

Communicating with a people-oriented person.

Allow for small talk (do not start the discussion right away).
Stress the relationship between your proposal and the people concerned.
Show how the idea worked well in the past.
Indicate support from well-respected people.
Use an informal writing style.

Communicating with an idea-oriented person.

Allow enough time for discussion.
Do not get impatient when he or she goes off on tangents.
In your opening, try to relate the topic to a broader concept (be conceptual).
Stress the uniqueness of the idea or topic at hand.
Emphasize future value or relate the impact of the idea on the future.

Self-Awareness and Development Using the Overseas Assignment Inventory

Michael F. Tucker

One of the most thoroughly researched cross-cultural self-assessment instruments, the Overseas Assignment Inventory (OAI), is available to cross-cultural trainers and consultants for selection, development, and training. An excellent selection instrument, it contributes significant information to the overall data that managers use for making overseas assignment decisions. In addition, the OAI is a powerful training tool.

History

The development of the OAI has been a longitudinal effort under my direction since the early 1970s. The OAI is continuously refined and revised as new research data become available. The OAI in its current form has drawn upon a number of empirical studies based on a variety of populations.

Corporate Sector (1985 to present)

Substantial long-term research is focused on the corporate sector (Moran, Stahl and Boyer International 1990). To date, the OAI has been completed by 4,450 corporate employees and spouses being considered for assignments to sixty different countries. OAI scores are regularly entered into a master database for ongoing analysis of the reliability and validity of the instrument. In order to continuously enhance the validity of the OAI, respondents are contacted one year after their arrival in the country of assignment and asked to complete an adjustment criterion instrument. The OAI dimensions are correlated with the adjustment dimensions to obtain estimates of the predictive power of the OAI.

Peace Corps

Research was conducted using 1,045 volunteers. The earliest work, begun in 1972 (Center for Research and Education 1973), identified adjustment issues among Peace Corps volunteers. Later work (Tucker, Baier, and Golesorkhi 1984) produced normative data for Peace Corps volunteers.

Youth For Understanding

This work involved 960 foreign exchange students from the United States, Brazil, Spain, Finland, and Sweden. The validity of the OAI in predicting cross-cultural adaptability was the focus of this research (Tucker, Baier, and Montgomery 1983).

Canadian International Development Agency

This study (Hawes and Kealey 1979) examined cross-cultural effectiveness using the OAI. The sample included 250 Canadian technical advisers and their spouses in Afghanistan, Haiti, Kenya, Pakistan, Peru, and Senegal.

U.S. Navy

The Navy Overseas Assignment Inventory (NOAI) was completed by 4,000 Navy personnel from 1973 to 1975. The final validation study was conducted on 1,627 individuals around the world on whom the NOAI data and both self-rating and supervisory criterion forms were available (Tucker, Benson, and Blanchard 1978).

Description of the OAI

Qualifying to Use the OAI

A decision was made to restrict the OAI to persons trained in its development and use. Information regarding the regularly scheduled OAI certification course can be obtained from Tucker International, Boulder, CO (phone: 303-786-7753; fax: 303-786-7801). The two-day training consists of a review of the state of the art in selecting and screening international personnel; a review of the research-based definition of intercultural adjustment; a complete understanding of the OAI dimensions—what they measure, what they are and are not; an introduction to behavioral-event interviewing and how to use that technique in conjunction with the OAI profiles; practice cases—doing behavioral-event interviews with sample OAIs and analyzing the videotaped interviews; and practice in giving feedback and conducting discussions based on the OAI results.

The OAI is a paper-and-pencil instrument that measures fourteen attitudes and attributes found to be important for successful cross-cultural adaptation. The OAI also provides a measure of the respondent's motivation for an international assignment. There are fourteen dimensions to the OAI, briefly defined as follows:

1. *Expectations*: Anticipations, positive and negative, about living in a new country

2. *Open-mindedness*: Receptivity to the ideas, values, and ways of other cultures

3. *Respect for Other Beliefs*: Ability to be accepting and nonjudgmental of other religious and political beliefs

4. *Trust in People*: Ability to have trust and faith in other people

5. *Tolerance*: Willingness and ability to adapt to unfamiliar and sometimes uncomfortable surroundings and circumstances

6. *Personal Control (Locus of Control)*: Internal versus external locus of control over the direction and outcome of one's life events

7. *Flexibility*: Willingness to consider new ideas and approaches in dealing with problems and tasks

8. *Patience*: Ability to remain patient in dealing with frustrating situations and unanticipated delays

9. *Social Adaptability*: Ability to adjust to new, unfamiliar social situations

10. *Initiative*: Willingness to be the first to take charge of new or challenging situations

11. *Risk Taking*: Willingness to take risks, meet challenges, and cope with change

12. *Sense of Humor*: Ability to use humor in difficult or confusing situations

13. *Interpersonal Interest*: Interest and enjoyment in being with other people

14. *Spouse Communication*: Level and quality of communication between spouses

Individual scores on these dimensions are plotted in relationship to a normative base and form a profile of cross-cultural adaptability. See the example in Figure 1. The shaded area represents scores for people predicted to adapt well (the normative base). The points connected by a single line represent sample scores for one individual.

Figure 1. Sample Overseas Assignment Inventory Profile

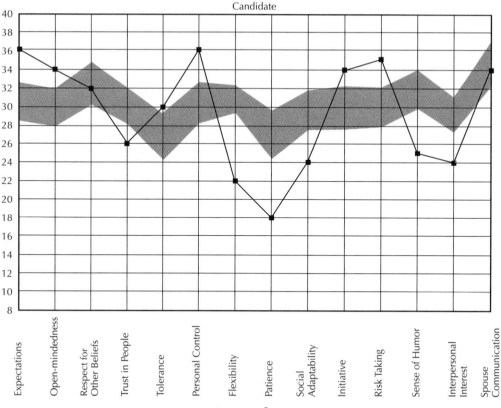

Procedure

Trainees are usually quite eager to see their OAI profile, so you might be tempted to reduce preparation time and jump directly into processing them. Do not give in to this temptation, which can lead to confusion and disappointment. We recommend the following procedure.

Before the Training Program Begins

To prepare for the OAI training session, you should do the following:

1. Have all trainees complete the OAI.

2. Send answer sheets to Tucker International for scoring. They will prepare an individualized OAI *Assessment and Development Guide* for each trainee. This report explains to the trainees what their individual OAI scores mean, discusses the importance of each dimension to successful intercultural adjustment, and offers suggestions and readings where improvement is needed.

3. Review the definitions of the OAI dimensions.

4. Study the OAI profile of each trainee.

5. Decide where the OAI training session would best fit into the overall program design.

6. Allocate at least one hour to the OAI training session.

During the Training Program

To achieve the best results, you should do the following:

7. Review origins and purpose of the OAI and discuss the results with the trainees. Then explain how the results will be used in the training program.

8. Give each trainee his/her own OAI Assessment and Development Guide.

9. Define the OAI dimensions and discuss why each is important to cross-cultural adjustment.

10. Ask the trainees to discuss their feelings about how accurately they feel their OAI profiles represent their attitudes and attributes.

11. Have them discuss their motivation for living and working in their destination country, and convey to them the importance of having positive, specific, well-balanced, and sustaining motivation and wanting to go for the sake of the experience abroad rather than to get away from a bad situation at home or at work. Ensure that couples are aware of each other's motivations for wanting the international assignment.

12. Identify the key dimensions that are most crucial for successful adjustment to life and work in the destination country, for example, Flexibility (in Japan), Respect for Other Beliefs (in Saudi Arabia), or Patience (in Spain). If the trainees scored high on these key dimensions, ask for behavioral examples illustrating their strengths and encourage them to help other family members who may not be as strong in those areas. If they scored low on those dimensions, help them understand how their weaknesses may result in culturally offensive behavior jeopardizing their relationships in the destination culture. It is helpful to include in the discussion a national of the destination culture as a resource person who can offer special insight into how the attitudes and attributes of the trainees will affect their living in his or her country.

13. Help the trainees arrive at personal development strategies specifically designed to reinforce their strengths and develop more effective attitudes and attributes in their weaker areas.

14. Encourage the trainees to study carefully their personalized Assessment and Development Guide and use it as a resource for personal development.

Successful Contexts

The OAI has been successfully incorporated as a self-awareness training tool in many different types of cross-cultural training programs. It is especially effective with the following.

Large Groups

The OAI is a strong team-building tool for large groups of employees and their spouses or partners bound for the same destination. The OAI scores are used to calculate norms for the trainee group as a whole, then are broken out separately for the employees and spouses or partners. This allows you to identify the strengths and weaknesses of the whole group as well as the employees and spouses as subgroups. The norms permit each individual trainee to compare his or her own attitudes and attributes with those of the group and recognize how he or she can best contribute to the group. During training, individuals who scored high on certain OAI dimensions can help those who scored lower. For example, individuals with high scores on Sense of Humor share with others how humor helps them deal with stressful or difficult situations, or those with high Patience scores discuss how they handle frustrating situations or unanticipated delays. Trainees are encouraged to describe behaviors that illustrate their strengths. The result is that the trainees come to understand and appreciate each others' strengths and commit themselves to helping one another assure a successful expatriate community.

Couples

The OAI is a useful tool for helping couples understand each other's motivations, expectations, attitudes, and attributes. The OAI is especially valuable for couples who received either low or discrepant scores on the Spouse Communication scale. Couples who are initially surprised about information they discover about their partner often benefit the most from talking about the reasons they answered the way they did. It is important to point out to couples that spouses are the most immediate source of support, so good communication between them often means the difference between success or failure on assignment. Therefore, couples are encouraged to discuss their Spouse Communication scores as well as the rest of their profiles to find out if there are any surprises and to talk through what the profiles mean to them.

People with No Previous International Experience

The OAI is particularly helpful for people who have little or no previous international living or travel experience. These people may have never been exposed to the idea that their basic attitudes and behaviors may not all be appropriate for living in another country or understand how their culture and background have shaped their worldview—all of which may be reflected in the way they respond to the OAI questions. For example, it is possible that a low score on Open-mindedness is due to lack of exposure to other cultures rather than ethnocentrism or bigotry. The OAI helps them sort out which of their attitudes and attributes are most important for successful cross-cultural adjustment.

Expatriate Development

The OAI is valuable for companies interested in developing a pool of qualified expatriates for unspecified future international assignments. In such cases, the focus is on understanding the implications of the OAI profile for successful cross-cultural adaptation and arriving at a personal development strategy for strengthening weaker OAI scores. For example, if individuals have low scores on Social Adaptability and Interpersonal Interest, it might be suggested that they participate in activities that will help them develop their interpersonal skills in cross-cultural situations. Such activities might include hosting international visitors, conducting meetings with members of other cultures, taking short business trips to another country, participating in social activities with people of other countries, or enrolling in foreign language conversation courses.

Business Travelers

The OAI helps business travelers understand how their own attitudes and behavioral tendencies can affect the outcome of their trip. For example, travelers going to Asia to conduct negotiations have benefited from knowing what their particular level of patience and flexibility is. Similarly, someone visiting Latin America would find it useful to know his or her scores on interpersonal styles and social expectations.

Pitfalls to Avoid

To avoid the effectiveness of the OAI being undermined by mistaken attitudes among the trainees, watch for the following pitfalls.

Faking

Like any other paper-and-pencil instrument, the OAI is subject to distortion by respondents. Sometimes individuals answer the questions according to how they would like themselves to be or how they think others expect them to be. This tendency to respond to the OAI questions in a socially desirable way is measured by a scale comprising questions randomly distributed throughout the instrument. Tucker International will alert you to evidence of faking or of unacceptably high Social Desirability scores. Such profiles should be treated with caution and care taken to explain to the trainee that it is a natural tendency to respond that way and while not bad per se, it reduces the usefulness of the profile.

The All or None Problem

Unsatisfactory results may be expected when the OAI is administered to some of the trainees but not all. In such situations, those who have not taken the OAI feel cheated, and those who have taken it feel uncertain as to why they were singled out to do so. If it is not possible to administer the OAI to all participants, it is best not to administer it to anyone.

Taking a Test

Do not assume that the trainees will automatically understand that the OAI is an information resource rather than a test. If trainees view the OAI as a pass-fail test, they are more likely to try to guess the "right" answer than the one that is accurately self-descriptive. Assure the trainees that there are no right or wrong answers and no cutoff scores.

Overreliance on Numbers

Understanding a trainee's general OAI profile is more important than relying on the specific numerical score. A specific score is not an absolute measure of an individual's attitude. Therefore, it is best to focus more on whether a score falls above or below the average than to rely on its exact value. You can verify the OAI scores by asking the participants to give examples of their behaviors that verify the scores they have on the OAI dimensions.

Conclusion

Cross-cultural trainers use many training tools because they seem right. In this world of subjective decisions, there is one tool we can use because it has been empirically validated and its data evaluated for almost three decades. This inspires a confidence we can pass on to the people who need a great deal of self-knowledge to succeed in meeting the demands of an overseas assignment.

Availability

For certification requirements contact Tucker International, LLC, 900 28th Street, Suite 200, Boulder, CO 80301.

References

Hawes, Frank, and Daniel J. Kealey. "Canadians in Development: An Empirical Study of Adaptation and Effectiveness on Overseas Assignment." Communications Branch Briefing Centre. September 1979.

Moran, Stahl & Boyer International. "OAI Technical Status Report." An unpublished paper. September 1990.

Tucker, Michael F. "Improving Cross-cultural Training and Measurement of Cross-cultural Learning." Volume I of the Report of Supplemental Activities Conducted by the Center for Research and Education under Peace Corps Brazil Training Contract PC-72-42043. Submitted to ACTION, Washington, DC, March 28, 1973.

Tucker, Michael F., V. Baier, and Banu Golesorkhi. Peace Corps Normative Study: Technical Report. April 1984.

Tucker, Michael F., V. Baier, and J. Montgomery. "The Measurement and Prediction of Intercultural Adjustment of YFU Students." A Report Prepared for Youth For Understanding's Research Project in Intercultural Exchange. December 1983.

Tucker, Michael F., P. G. Benson, and F. Blanchard. "The Measurement and Prediction of Overseas Adjustment in the Navy." Final Report on the Development and Longitudinal Validation of the Navy Overseas Assignment Inventory. August 1978.

The Cross-Cultural Adaptability Inventory

Colleen Kelley and Judith Meyers

Introduction

Suppose you are training people who are preparing to live abroad and you want to help them assess their ability to adapt to another culture. Or perhaps you want to train employees to get along with those of other cultures within a local multinational company. Or you are teaching a class on international relations and you want to introduce students to the research on cross-cultural adjustment. The Cross-Cultural Adaptability Inventory (CCAI) was designed to assist you in these and related situations.

Background

The CCAI is a direct response to the needs expressed by cross-cultural trainers and teachers for a well-constructed, easily obtainable self-assessment training instrument on cross-cultural adaptability. After a thorough search failed to turn up such an inventory, the decision was made to develop the CCAI.

Developing the Instrument

The first step was to study the literature on cross-cultural adaptability with the help of an extensive electronic search. A composite list was made of all traits and skills associated with the ability to adapt to other cultures.

Next, in light of their own experience, a group of cross-cultural training experts rated each trait or skill on the list, indicating the ones that they believed to be most important for adapting to other cultures. Four skill sets were consistently rated most highly by the experts. All four were among those most often cited in the research literature.

Another skill set that stood out in the literature and had been rated well by the experts was added to complete the CCAI's original five dimensions.

Finally, a pool of cross-cultural trainers administered the CCAI to 653 people in order to refine the scoring. The results were entered into the computer and statistically analyzed. On the basis of this analysis, the fifth dimension (Positive Regard for Others) was eliminated because it was a subset of one of the other dimensions. Based on statistical analysis, certain items were shifted from one dimension (skill set) to another.

In its final version the CCAI is a self-assessment inventory. An inventory is a list of questions or statements relating to specific topics or issues. Usually people are asked to write their responses to these questions or statements and to score them in some organized way. Self-awareness inventories help people focus on specific aspects of their personality, behavior, skills, and/or knowledge and to become more conscious of their strengths and weaknesses in these areas.

Uses of the CCAI

The CCAI organizes responses to its fifty items into four dimensions which have been named Emotional Resilience, Flexibility/Openness, Perceptual Acuity, and Personal Autonomy. A profiling section is provided so that each person can graph his or her scores. This makes it easier to see how the scores compare with each other and how other people have scored on the same dimensions. In addition a worksheet offers suggestions for improvement and gives guidelines for developing an action plan.

A multiple-rater version of the CCAI was designed to provide feedback on a person's cross-cultural adaptability. The Multi-Rater Set includes an individual survey plus three observer surveys. The profile sheet in this set accommodates all four profiles. This allows "360-degree feedback" from a supervisor, a peer, and a subordinate. Through research it was discovered that more than three raters provide too much data, and fewer than three, not enough. This version is useful both in corporations and with families.

Purposes of the Instrument

The CCAI Manual (1987, 9) lists five reasons why you might decide that this is the right instrument for your training program. Your trainees may need to
1. *understand* the factors or qualities that facilitate cross-cultural effectiveness.
    The CCAI helps people to focus attention on four skill areas that research has shown to be critical in adapting to other cultures.
2. *become self-aware* regarding those factors or qualities in which they are strong and those that need improvement.
    The CCAI provides feedback on relative strengths and weaknesses vis-à-vis the four CCAI dimensions. This feedback increases self-knowledge and raises awareness regarding potential difficulties and concerns.

3. *improve* skills in interacting with people from other cultures, when they are in a multicultural or new-culture setting.

   The same information can be used both to continuously improve in the four CCAI skills areas and to intermittently take time for a "checkup" and "on-the-job" skill practice.

4. *decide* whether to work in a culturally diverse company or multinational company, whether to live abroad, and so on.

   Information obtained from the CCAI can help individuals to make decisions about their participation in activities with people from other cultures encountered in the workplace or during their sojourn abroad.

5. *prepare* to enter another culture, such as a multinational environment or a new country, through preparatory training customized to the individual.

   Armed with the knowledge obtained from the CCAI, a person can develop an action plan to maximize strengths and improve weak areas.

The CCAI Dimensions

The CCAI Manual provides explanations of the four CCAI dimensions and a brief description of each dimension.

The first dimension is *Emotional Resilience*. People can experience feelings of frustration, confusion, or loneliness when interacting with those of other cultures. The emotionally resilient person has the ability to deal with stressful feelings in a constructive way and to "bounce back" from them. Emotionally resilient people like new experiences and have confidence in their ability to cope with ambiguity. They tend to have a sense of humor and positive self-regard.

The second dimension is *Flexibility/Openness*. When people live or work with those from other cultures, they usually encounter ways of thinking and behaving that are different from their own. Open, flexible people enjoy interacting with those who are different and think differently from themselves. They like and feel comfortable with all kinds of people. They tend to be nonjudgmental and to think creatively.

The third CCAI dimension is *Perceptual Acuity*. People sometimes find communication with those from other cultures difficult because of unfamiliar or confusing values, assumptions, customs, body language, and words. People who are perceptually acute are attentive to verbal and nonverbal behaviors, to the context of communication, and to interpersonal relations. These people are sensitive to the feelings of others and to their own impact on others. They tend to be empathic and accurate communicators.

The fourth dimension is *Personal Autonomy*. People who interact with those of other cultures may not receive the types of reactions and reinforcement they are accustomed to. Personally autonomous people are not overly dependent on cues from the environment for their identity, whether that identity is with an individual- or group-oriented culture. They have a strong sense of who they are, clear personal values, and respect for self and others. They feel empowered, know how to make their own decisions, and can eventually feel at home in any environment.

Using the CCAI—A Basic Sequence

The CCAI can be administered in a short training session to raise awareness and increase knowledge about cross-cultural adaptability (about one and one-half hours), in a longer training program to develop skills in cross-cultural adaptability (a half day or more), and in an intermittent program to practice these skills on the job between training sessions (over several weeks or months).

The Manual describes basic steps for administering the CCAI (or any other self-assessment training instrument). An abbreviated version of these steps is listed here.

First, describe benefits participants can gain from the instrument. For example, completing the CCAI produces an individualized baseline for measuring one's growth, and it provides a framework or model for analyzing cross-cultural behavior. The CCAI can also stimulate participants to think in general about the potential impact of new environments and new ways of interacting.

Second, distribute the CCAI, which includes the inventory and scoring and profile sections, to each participant.

Third, read the instructions, give a time limit, and tell participants the results will only be as accurate as the information they provide. Emphasize that this is not a test but a self-scoring learning tool. Ask participants to respond to each item as it applies to them *at this time.* Ask them to select one setting (for example, the work setting) and to answer all items from that perspective.

Fourth, after everyone has completed the inventory, show participants how to obtain a score for each of the four dimensions.

Fifth, briefly discuss the concept of cross-cultural adaptability and describe the CCAI dimensions, using examples relevant to the group.

Sixth, show how to develop a personal profile from the CCAI scores—usually best demonstrated on a large poster or overhead projector—and how to interpret CCAI score patterns. Ask participants to complete their own profiles.

Seventh, answer questions and conduct a general discussion about learnings, implications of those learnings for cross-cultural adaptability, and plans for future change or action steps.

Using the CCAI—Enhancements to the Basic Sequence

If more time is available, one or more of the following variations can be added to the basic sequence outlined above.

Before the scoring instructions at step four, ask participants to predict their scores. After they have torn off the top section of the CCAI, and after you describe each dimension, ask participants to predict their scores by writing an H (High), M (Medium), or L (Low) above the appropriate letter on the scoring section worksheet. These are predictions of each person's scores relative to one another, and not relative to others' scores or to the maximum possible scores.

At step five, request examples illustrating the behaviors characterizing the four dimensions.

After step six, ask each participant to choose a partner and discuss his or her scores with the partner. For example, they might examine discrepancies between predictions and actual scores and share perceptions about the accuracy of the scores. The pairs can review the items associated with the scores.

The above variations help participants understand and interact with the CCAI data, which in turn help them to commit to further growth in cross-cultural adaptability. Preparatory and follow-on CCAI-related activities can be added to foster behavior change and skill improvement. These activities usually take the form of structured experiences, role plays, and skill practice sessions. For example, in the area of perceptual acuity, the trainer might ask participants to role-play their usual behavior when communicating with a person from the target culture; provide a structured experience which helps them understand how a person from the target culture would perceive their communication style; and provide skill practice in various aspects of perceptual acuity, such as attention to verbal and nonverbal behaviors. The ancillary CCAI training tools can be helpful in this growth process.

The CCAI has also been used intermittently over several months with training groups to help them examine their progress and refocus their learning.

Contexts for Use of the CCAI

The CCAI can be used effectively with those planning to travel, live, or work abroad. Examples include the following groups and their families: business executives in international companies, people doing business abroad, missionaries and other international volunteers, students, and diplomats. The CCAI has been used effectively with those returning from life abroad and readjusting to their "home" culture. Examples include expatriates, their families, and students. The CCAI has been used effectively with those who do not plan to travel but who work in a multicultural environment or who interface with those of other cultures. Examples are employees of foreign subsidiaries, their coworkers, and educators. The CCAI can be used with immigrants, both those who voluntarily emigrate and those who are forced to relocate. The CCAI is also appropriate for professionals who work with the foregoing groups.

In addition to its applications in cross-cultural training, the CCAI can be used for team building in culturally diverse work groups, as a self-selection instrument for people making decisions about their cross-cultural future, and as a counseling tool for people in the process of cross-cultural adjustment.

Benefits and Limitations

Some of the benefits of the CCAI as a training instrument include the fact that it is research-based, easy to understand and administer, self-scoring, inexpensive, and easily available. Norms exist for the inventory, and it has been tested in a variety of settings.

Selection and Self-Selection

The CCAI is a self-selection instrument, as contrasted with a selection instrument. Because selection instruments are often used for evaluation and prediction, items must be worded in such a way that respondents cannot guess the "right" answer. Since they generally are not designed to be used in training, these instruments can contain a greater number of items and require a longer administration time. Scoring is done by someone other than the respondent—often by a computer—and the results may or may not be communicated to the respondent. Selection instruments should have a high degree of predictive validity. No instrument, however, can be 100 percent accurate in its predictions, and no one instrument can address such a many-faceted area as that of cross-cultural adaptability.

The CCAI is not designed to predict success or failure in cross-cultural adaptation. In other words, we do not recommend that the CCAI be used to make decisions about another person's future, such as who to send abroad or who to put in charge of a multicultural team. Self-selection means that the people taking the instrument make decisions about their own future, after learning about cross-cultural adaptability and examining their own assets and liabilities in this area.

Transparency

The CCAI is a self-assessment training tool, so the more "cross-culturally adaptable" response to an item is often obvious. Some negatively worded statements have been included to make sure that all the items are actually read. However, a self-scoring training instrument is meant to remain in the hands of the participant and to be used as a learning tool. As such it must be somewhat straightforward and easy to understand. Two points should be made clear to those taking the inventory:

1. The CCAI is not a test where the goal is to get the "right" answers. It is an inventory where the only right answer is based on accurate self-perception and honesty. "Cheating" on the inventory means cheating oneself out of useful information and potential learning and growth.

2. There is a difference between answering as one would *like* to be and as one actually *is*. Participants should honestly respond to items according to how they perceive themselves now. Although scores can be elevated because of item transparency, the relative positions of scores should remain constant. In addition, norms are provided as a point of comparison.

Relative Position of Scores

Participants should understand that it is more important for each person to look at how his or her own scores relate to one another (which scores are higher and which lower) than to compare personal scores with maximum possible scores or with those of fellow participants. The goal is to learn about one's relative strengths and weaknesses and to take steps to become a more cross-culturally adaptable person, no matter at what level one begins. In addition other factors distort scores. For example, some people tend to use the ends of a scale ("Definitely True," "Definitely Not True") more than others.

Culture-General versus Culture-Specific

The CCAI is a culture-general instrument. It explores a person's abilities to adapt to any culture. A culture-specific instrument measures a person's compatibility with a particular culture. Even though an individual may be highly adaptable, he or she may currently have traits or skills which are more compatible with a specific culture. Examples of these are knowledge of the culture, ability to speak the language, and previous residence in the culture.

Summary

The CCAI is a practical, cross-cultural, self-assessment training tool. It is the result of careful development, is easy to use and understand, and can be incorporated into a variety of training formats. It can be used to help people develop the knowledge and skills to (1) adapt to another culture, (2) interact effectively with people from other cultures, and (3) promote harmony between cultures. The Cross-Cultural Adaptability Inventory is published by NCS Assessments, 5605 Green Circle Drive, Minnetonka, MN 55343 (800-627-7271). NCS makes the CCAI available throughout such areas as Canada and Europe. The Intercultural Press is the only other distributor of the CCAI in the United States.

Technical Note: The CCAI is considered to have face, content, and construct validity and has an overall reliability of .89. Although it probably also has predictive validity, this has not yet been established.

Resources

Cross-Cultural Theory

Benson, Philip G. "Measuring Cross-Cultural Adjustment: The Problem of Criteria." *International Journal of Intercultural Relations* 2 (1978): 21–37.

Casse, Pierre. "The Psychological Dimension of Intercultural Communication." *Training for the Cross-Cultural Mind.* 2d ed. Washington DC: Society for Intercultural Education, Training and Research, 1981.

Dinges, Norman G. "Intercultural Competence." *Handbook of Intercultural Training* 1 (1983): 176–202.

Hammer, Mitchell R., William B. Gudykunst, and R. Wiseman. "Dimensions of Intercultural Effectiveness." *International Journal of Intercultural Relations* 2 (1978): 99–110.

Kealey, Daniel J., and Brent D. Ruben. "Cross-Cultural Personnel Selection Criteria, Issues and Methods." *Handbook of Intercultural Training* 1 (1983): 155–75.

Paige, R. Michael. "Trainer Competencies: The Missing Link in Orientation." *International Journal of Intercultural Relations* 10 (1986): 135–58.

Ruben, Brent D. "The Study of Cross-Cultural Competence: Traditions and Contemporary Issues." *International Journal of Intercultural Relations* 13 (1989): 229–40.

Instrumentation and Other Instruments

Harris, Philip R. *Intercultural Relations Inventory.* Jacksonville Beach, FL: Talico, 1984.

Pfeiffer, J. William, et al. *Instrumentation in Human Relations Training.* 2d ed. San Diego, CA: University Associates, 1976.

Reddin, W. J., and Ken Rowell. *Culture Shock Inventory.* Fredericton, NB, Canada: Organizational Tests, 1976.

A Measure of Intercultural Sensitivity: The Intercultural Development Inventory

Mitchell R. Hammer

Where do you turn when you need a measure of sensitivity to cultural differences and need to know how certain people deal with these differences? The Intercultural Development Inventory (IDI) may be one of the most important cross-cultural instruments you can use to help in a wide variety of situations. You might consider using the IDI in the following situations:

❖ You are preparing to conduct cross-cultural training for a family about to leave for an overseas assignment and you would like to help them assess their intercultural sensitivity toward other cultures.

❖ Your organization wants to develop a diversity program and you need to have some data upon which to begin program development.

❖ You have recently completed a major organizational change effort in which effective global management of cultural differences is a key ingredient for success. Now you want to assess the impact of this change program on the management team.

❖ Your university has recently inaugurated a cultural diversity component in its freshman course requirements. Your committee now has to determine how to assess the impact of this new educational component among its students.

❖ A manager and spouse have been selected for a 3–5 year assignment overseas. As part of a cross-cultural training effort, you would like to help them assess their sensitivity toward other cultures.

❖ You and your staff work as human services providers within a multicultural community. In order to build better relations between your staff and the community, you want to develop intercultural training for your staff members that will improve their sensitivity and competence.

❖ As an administrator in charge of preparing government officials and diplomats for international postings, you want to provide feedback to participants in your training program on their intercultural sensitivity.

Introduction

The Intercultural Development Inventory is a sixty-item paper-and-pencil instrument that measures intercultural sensitivity based on the Developmental Model of Intercultural Sensitivity (DMIS) first proposed by Milton Bennett in 1986 (1993). The IDI takes about 15–20 minutes to complete and is a theoretically based, valid, and reliable assessment instrument that can be used for individual- or group/organizational-level analysis.

Conceptual Foundations

The IDI is an empirical measure of intercultural sensitivity. The term *intercultural sensitivity* generally refers to "a sensitivity to the importance of cultural differences and to the points of view of people in other cultures" (Bhawuk and Brislin 1992, 414). As Bennett (1993) cogently points out, however, "intercultural sensitivity is not natural.… Cross-cultural contact usually has been accompanied by bloodshed, oppression, or genocide" (21). Intercultural sensitivity has been identified in a number of studies focusing on overseas effectiveness of international sojourners (Cleveland, Mangone, and Adams 1960; Brislin 1981; Landis and Bhagat, 1996; Landis and Brislin 1983a, 1983b, 1983c; Kealey and Rubin 1983), international business adaptation and job performance (Adler 1991; Black 1990; Black, Gregersen and Mendenhall 1992), foreign student adjustment (Klineberg and Hull 1979), international transfer of technology and information (Hawes and Kealey 1981, 1979; Kealey 1996, 1989), and as a key capability for working and living effectively with people from different cultures (Bhawuk and Brislin 1992). Indeed, intercultural sensitivity is viewed by many as the defining characteristic for transcending ethnocentrism and establishing positive relations across national and cultural boundaries (Bennett 1993). As Bhawuk and Brislin (1992) conclude:

> To be effective in another culture, people must be interested in other cultures, be sensitive enough to notice cultural differences, and then also be willing to modify their behavior as an indication of respect for the people of other cultures. A reasonable term that summarizes these qualities of people is intercultural sensitivity, and we suggest that it may be a predictor of effectiveness (416).

The IDI is an assessment of intercultural sensitivity which captures major elements of the DMIS and, consistent with Bhawuk and Brislin's (1992) conclusions, offers a powerful explanation of effective interaction across cultural boundaries.

Purpose of the IDI

The IDI provides useful and valid information regarding respondents' orientation toward cultural differences. The inventory can be used to help achieve a number of goals. First, you can use the IDI to help increase respondents' understanding of the developmental stages of intercultural sensitivity which enhance intercultural effectiveness. The IDI focuses attention on the stages of intercultural sensitivity which prior research suggests are central to effective interaction with people from different cultures. Since the IDI can provide both individual-level feedback and an organization-wide profile, both individuals and identified groups within an organization or institution can examine their predominant orientations toward cultural differences.

Second, you can use the IDI to evaluate the effectiveness of various training, counseling, and education interventions. The instrument can be used to develop a baseline profile of individuals and/or groups prior to an intervention (for example, training). Then, administer the IDI following completion of the designated intervention to determine the degree to which the intercultural sensitivity of the targeted respondent(s) improved.

Third, because it is a feedback instrument, you can use the IDI to improve people's intercultural skills and to assist them in making a decision to work or live in a culturally diverse setting.

Fourth, you can use the IDI to identify cross-cultural training needs of targeted individuals and groups within the context of a foreign country or within a domestic, culturally diverse setting. The IDI is a powerful needs assessment tool when it is important to know the developmental levels of intercultural sensitivity for trainees or students.

Populations Appropriate for the IDI

The IDI can be effectively administered to a wide variety of people. The instrument is appropriate for people from all world cultures because it was developed within the intercultural context—not any specific cultural context. At this time, the primary requirement is that the individual's command of spoken and written English is sufficient to appropriately respond to the questionnaire, since the IDI has not yet been translated into other languages. The IDI, because of its uniqueness and sensitivity, should not be translated into other languages without express written permission and guidance from Mitchell Hammer and Milton Bennett.

People preparing for short- and long-term international travel and living are appropriate populations for the IDI. Also, people who work and/or live in culturally diverse communities and organizations can learn much from the IDI. In general, the IDI is appropriate for anyone who interacts regularly with people whose cultural backgrounds are different, such as business managers; hospital and clinic physicians, nurses, and other medical care personnel; public relations managers; social workers; judges and lawyers; counselors; military and law enforcement personnel; teachers; and cross-cultural trainers and consultants.

The Six Scales of the IDI

The IDI consists of six scales that measure six core orientations toward cultural differences based on the DMIS outlined by Bennett (1993). It should be noted that some of the terminology and descriptions of these scales that measure specific orientations (stages) of intercultural sensitivity have been slightly revised to establish a more descriptively accurate portrayal of the meaning of some of the orientations.

Bennett (1993) proposes two broad categories for construing cultural differences that he terms "ethnocentric" and "ethnorelative." An ethnocentric orientation is based on the assumption that "the worldview of one's own culture is central to all reality" (Bennett 1986, 33) and involves the interpretation of events and behavior from one's own cultural viewpoint. In contrast, an ethnorelative orientation is based on "the assumption that cultures can only be understood relative to one another and that particular behavior can only be understood within a cultural context" (Bennett 1993, 46). Three scales in the IDI measure ethnocentric orientations (Denial, Defense, and Minimization), and three scales assess ethnorelative orientations toward cultural differences (Acceptance, Cognitive Adaptation, and Behavioral Adaptation).

The Denial Scale

The *Denial scale* is a reliable (coefficient alpha = .87) ten-item scale which reflects an orientation toward construing cultural differences that incorporates aspects of the "isolation" and "separation" forms of denial identified in the DMIS. This scale measures the most basic form of ethnocentrism and reflects an orientation that assumes no real differences between people from different cultures. Respondents who reflect a denial orientation typically do not possess the basic cultural categories in which to make differences meaningful. In a small number of cases, circumstances of physical or social *isolation* from people who are culturally different can reinforce selective perception, whereby a person sees what he or she wants to see and does not see what he or she is unaccustomed to perceiving. An isolation pattern can lead a person to assume, for instance, that his or her interaction with people from other cultures is culturally appropriate when in fact, it may be quite inappropriate. More common, however, is the *separation* pattern of denial: "the intentional erection of physical or social barriers to create distance from cultural difference" (Bennett 1986, 35). Maintaining living arrangements distinct from people who are culturally different perpetuates a cultural distance. While separation does acknowledge some differences between groups, these differences are generally viewed with suspicion.

The Defense Scale

The *Defense scale* is a reliable (coefficient alpha = .91) ten-item scale which reflects an orientation toward construing cultural differences that incorporates aspects of the "denigration" and "superiority" forms of defense identified in the DMIS. This scale measures a form of ethnocentrism that refers to a more explicit recognition of differences coupled with more overt attempts at erecting defenses against them. In this state, differences are not only viewed with suspicion; they are considered threatening to one's self-esteem and identity. One strategy for defending against differences perceived as a threat is to negatively judge the identified differences—denigration. A person may also emphasize "the positive evaluation of one's own cultural status" (Bennett 1986, 38), thus exhibiting a sense of "superiority." For example, a Japanese executive who views the inherent technological superiority of Japanese products over similar products made in the United States, Canada, Korea, or Taiwan may be operating from a defense perspective.[1]

The Minimization Scale

The *Minimization scale* is a reliable (coefficient alpha = .87) ten-item scale which reflects an orientation toward construing cultural differences that incorporates aspects of the "physical universalism" and "transcendent universalism" forms of minimization identified in the DMIS. This scale measures a form of ethnocentrism that concerns efforts by a person to overgeneralize similarities between self and other. When this is done, cultural differences are trivialized and therefore rendered "harmless." Bennett (1986; 1993) identifies two minimization strategies: (1) physical universalism, which views all cultures as "merely elaborations of fundamental biology" (1993, 42), and (2) transcendent universalism, which suggests all human beings are the product of a single, transcendent, and universal imperative or entity. This pattern of thought minimizes the truly important differences that exist between people who have different blueprints of their social world.

The Acceptance Scale

The *Acceptance scale* is a reliable (coefficient alpha = .80) ten-item scale which reflects an orientation toward construing cultural differences that incorporates aspects of the "respect for behavioral differences" and "respect for value differences" forms of acceptance identified in the DMIS. This scale measures a form of ethnorelativism that involves a fundamental acknowledgment that differences are important, they do exist, and they should be respected. The Acceptance scale measures both (1) respect for behavioral differences, which is an acceptance of verbal and nonverbal behavior differences which exist at deeper cultural levels, and (2) respect for value differences, which is an acceptance and affirmation of different worldviews that underlie cultural variation in behavior. At a deeper level than exists in the ethnocentric stages, acceptance of differences involves a fundamental shift in mindset: one now sees that to understand another culture can only be done from that particular cultural perspective.

The Cognitive Adaptation Scale

The *Cognitive Adaptation scale* is a reliable (coefficient alpha = .85) ten-item scale which reflects an orientation toward construing cultural differences that incorporates aspects of the "empathy" form of the adaptation stage and the "contextual evaluation" form of the integration stage posited in the DMIS. This scale measures an individual's deeper understanding of other cultural values and practices from the perspective of the other culture (empathy) as well as an ability to evaluate situations from different cultural viewpoints. The Cognitive Adaptation scale measures a form of ethnorelativism that involves a more proactive effort on the part of an individual to use cultural differences and intercultural skills in ways which maximize his or her understanding of and relationships with people from other cultures.

The Behavioral Adaptation Scale

The *Behavioral Adaptation scale* is a reliable (coefficient alpha = .80), ten-item scale which reflects an orientation toward construing cultural differences that incorporates aspects of the "pluralism" form of the adaptation stage identified in the DMIS. This scale does not mean a person "assimilates" to a dominant pattern by giving up his or her own cultural values, beliefs, or practices. Rather, it represents an expansion of one's perspective and skills to incorporate other ways of communicating and interacting. Behavioral adaptation refers to a more complete internalization of two or more cultural interpretive frameworks, which translates into an ability to adapt behavior to different cultural contexts. Behavioral adaptation, because it is a more complete integration of different perspectives with behavior, tends to be experienced by individuals "as a part of their normal selves" (Bennett 1993, 55).

Compared to acceptance, cognitive adaptation and behavioral adaptation represent a capacity for interpreting and responding to the world from another frame of reference, while acceptance involves a temporary shift in perspective that permits an individual to experience aspects of the foreign culture in a way which is different from that provided by his or her cultural background.[2]

General Assumptions Underlying the DMIS and the IDI

The Developmental Model of Intercultural Sensitivity and the IDI instrument are related to, but at the same time different from, other intercultural models and self-assessment instruments. Certain aspects of the model and the instrument are important to keep in mind as we proceed. Six general assumptions will be reviewed before guidelines for administering the IDI are discussed.

First, the DMIS and the IDI capture the individual's *experience of cultural difference*, not objective behavior. This is in contrast with, for instance, the Bhawuk and Brislin (1992) measure of intercultural sensitivity, which focuses on behaviors associated with individualism and collectivism and the self-reported intention of the respondent to modify his or her behavior when moving from one culture to another. In this sense, the DMIS model is phenomenological in nature.

Second, intercultural sensitivity is viewed in *developmental* terms rather than static terms. Intercultural sensitivity is conceptualized as a *continuum* ranging from a more ethnocentric to a more ethnorelative perspective.

Third, the DMIS model implies a certain degree of *progression*, in the sense of increasing awareness and understanding, although Bennett (1993) makes a point of stating that "it is not assumed that progression through the stages is one-way or permanent" (27). Nevertheless, "each stage is meant to characterize a treatment of cultural difference that is fairly consistent for a particular individual at a particular point of development" (27).

Fourth, the DMIS is based on *clinical observations* from more than twenty years of work with people who are making transitions across cultural boundaries, whereas the IDI is *empirically derived*. Psychometric development of the IDI is presented at the end of this chapter, and a full discussion of the psychometric properties of the IDI can be found in Hammer and Bennett (1998).

Fifth, the DMIS model offers a social-psychological explanation of how individuals' orientations toward cultural differences exist in terms of their *social identifications*. More specifically, the model describes an individual's generalized perspective toward peoples and cultures seen as different from his or her own group. Ingroup/outgroup perspectives are a key to understanding the dynamics of the model.

Sixth, for each developmental stage, individuals tend to maintain a *consistent perspective* in their orientation toward differences in terms of their own culture group identification compared with other culture groups. According to Bennett (1986, 1993), individuals tend to be *consistent* in the manner in which they interpret social reality in relation to ingroup- and outgroup-based differences within each developmental stage. Conceptually, the fundamental ingroup-outgroup social categories are one's own cultural group versus another culture group. The IDI examines respondents' orientations toward cultural differences in terms of the respondents' own culture group identification compared to other cultures.

Bennett (1993) states that individuals tend to maintain consistency in the manner in which they construe social reality vis-à-vis group-based differences. As Bennett (1993) suggests, "New cultural differences, *once they are defined as cultural*, will be treated in more or less the same way as familiar differences" (27). Therefore, people in one developmental stage in their orientation toward cultural differences will tend to view differences encountered from another new social category from a similar orientation. Further, moving from one developmental stage to another vis-à-vis one social group (for example, Asian Americans) will tend to lead to a reevaluation of other group categories (for example, a reassessment of one's orientations toward Hispanic Americans, Koreans, and people from other cultures more generally). Theoretically, the Intercultural Development Inventory is designed to reflect the broadest social categories ("my culture group relative to other cultures in general").

Administering the IDI

There are three basic approaches for administering the IDI. In the first, individual participants in a training program, for instance, complete the IDI either before or during the program. This *individual-focused approach* is designed to provide immediate, individual-level profiles of IDI results to each participant in the training program. This approach typically involves training procedures following the self-scoring of the instrument so that meaningful interpretation and action planning is incorporated into the training process. This approach is designed to increase individuals' awareness about their orientations toward cultural differences and can be successfully completed in one to two days of a training program, which also includes a review of the developmental model of intercultural sensitivity.

The second approach is to administer the IDI for the purpose of obtaining a *group* profile. For instance, the IDI can be administered prior to a training program and a group profile developed. When used this way, the IDI becomes a needs assessment for that particular training group. The resulting profile is not completed on data from any one individual but rather on the total aggregate group. Individual-level feedback is not presented and the self-scoring aspect of the IDI is not used. Therefore, individual respondents complete the IDI and then return their completed questionnaires to a designated central location where someone else (probably a researcher familiar with the IDI) develops group-level profiles. A variation of this group approach is to use the IDI to obtain a profile of an entire organization, perhaps as a baseline assessment. Again, the purpose is to obtain a group profile (or subgroup comparisons), not individual-level profiles.

The third approach is to use the IDI as a measurement of *program effectiveness* or impact. When used in this way, the IDI is administered prior to a designated intervention and, then, following it. When used for program evaluation, it is recommended that a comparison or control group also be used in the study. For example, an organization such as a corporation or a university may want to evaluate whether a particular program impacts on the intercultural capabilities of its members. In this case, the IDI can be used to assess the development of intercultural sensitivity both before the program is implemented and following it.

Psychometric Development of the IDI

The Intercultural Development Inventory was developed in response to numerous requests from cross-cultural educators, counselors, trainers, international student advisers, and domestic diversity trainers for a valid, accessible, self-assessment instrument that provides participants with feedback, based on Bennett's Developmental Model of Intercultural Sensitivity. Hammer and Bennett began developing the IDI in 1993, and instrument development and validation efforts were completed in 1997. A brief review of the reliability and validity testing conducted on the IDI follows. For more in-depth presentation of the psychometric properties of the IDI, see Hammer and Bennett (1998).

Initial Scale Construction

Guidelines for scale construction provided by DeVellis (1991) formed the basis for developing the IDI.

Interviews. We conducted forty interviews with people from a wide variety of cultures. Written transcriptions of the forty interviews were then completed. Following this procedure, four members of the research team independently reviewed twenty-five of the forty transcripts and rated the overall stage and form that the individual interviewee most consistently expressed during the interview. Inter-rater reliabilities were then calculated across these twenty-five interviews for ratings given by the research team. For both the stage ratings and the form ratings, quite high inter-rater reliabilities were obtained among the four raters (.87 and above). These results suggest that the Developmental Model of Intercultural Sensitivity can be reliably assessed based on in-depth interviews of a culturally diverse group of individuals.

Items. We systematically generated the items for the inventory. However, one consideration in generating items is the degree to which the items are researcher-imposed and therefore may reflect conscious or even unconscious cultural bias. Obviously, this is an important concern when developing an instrument that is designed to have cross-cultural generalizability.

We addressed this concern by individually reviewing each of the forty interview transcripts. Because these transcripts were verbatim, we were able to read the actual statements people from a wide range of cultures use when talking about cultural differences. We knew from our previous analysis that these statements clustered within specific stage and form orientations. We listed every statement made by the respondents that we identified as indicative of the specific stage and form they were rated to most consistently reflect. This produced quite a large list of statements across the six stages and thirteen forms. Therefore, the initial group of items were not statements "imposed" by the researchers, but were in fact actual statements made by people from a wide variety of cultures which reflected the stages and forms of intercultural sensitivity.

Pilot Tests. Two pilot test administrations of the IDI with culturally diverse groups of people were completed in order to identify difficulties respondents may have with such issues as clarity of instructions, item clarity, response option applicability, and overall amount of time taken to complete the instrument. Based upon feedback from respondents, the IDI was further revised.

Reliability and Validity Testing

Expert Panel. We assembled a panel of seven cross-cultural experts to review the item pool. This helped ensure the relevancy of the items to the construct of intercultural sensitivity as well as providing initial reliability and validity estimates. The intercultural communication experts, intimately familiar with the DMIS, were sent the complete list of items to review. The coded stage and form for each item were not identified. Then the experts independently categorized each item into the thirteen forms. If they felt an item could not appropriately be categorized into one of the thirteen forms, they were to indicate this on the rating form.

Inter-rater reliability among the expert ratings was determined for each item. Criteria for selecting items from this analysis included the following: (1) a minimum of five of the seven experts were able to categorize the item (that is, if more than two of the seven experts felt the item was too difficult to categorize, the item was eliminated from further consideration) and (2) inter-rater agreement for placing the item in the same form category among the experts had to be .60 or above. Those items that could not be reliably categorized were eliminated. Finally, each expert provided comments concerning the clarity and conciseness of each item. This produced a further refinement of the IDI, resulting in a measure of 145 items.

Construct Validity. In order to examine the construct validity of the IDI, two measures were included in the final questionnaire (a modified version of the World-mindedness scale and an Intercultural Anxiety scale). The first measure used was a six-item version employed by Wiseman, Hammer, and Nishida (1989) of the World-mindedness scale (Sampson and Smith 1957). The second measure employed was a modified version of the Social Anxiety scale developed by Stephan and Stephan (1985). Respondents indicated how they felt overall when interacting with people from other cultures (on a 1–7 scale): less or more anxious, comfortable, accepted, irritated, awkward, impatient, defensive, suspicious, self-conscious, careful, and nervous.

Gathering and Analyzing Data. This revised version of the IDI was administered (including the six-item version of the World-mindedness scale, the Intercultural Anxiety measure, and selected demographic items), and a total of 312 respondents completed the IDI questionnaire. This sample consisted of respondents who came from all walks of life, not primarily drawn from the university class-room environment.

Extensive statistical analyses (factor analysis, reliability analysis, correlation analysis, for example) were conducted to identify a smaller set of items and unidimensional scales. The result was a sixty-item inventory which includes six, ten-item scales: Denial, Defense, Minimization, Acceptance, Cognitive Adaptation, and Behavioral Adaptation.

Overall results from these analyses demonstrate that the IDI is a highly reliable, valid, cross-cultural measure of intercultural sensitivity applicable to a variety of groups of people from different cultural backgrounds. It provides a theoretically derived profile in terms of the stages of intercultural sensitivity identified in the DMIS. The results of testing the validity of the IDI clearly show that higher scores in Denial, Defense, and Minimization orientations are related to *lower* levels of World-mindedness and *higher* levels of Intercultural Anxiety. In contrast, higher scores in Acceptance, Cognitive Adaptation, and Behavioral Adaptation are related to *lower* World-mindedness scores and *higher* Intercultural Anxiety scores. Further, analysis of IDI scores by gender and social status (educational level) reveals no significant differences. Overall, these findings provide powerful evidence that the IDI is a robust measure of intercultural sensitivity which is generalizable not only across culture groups but also across gender and social status differences.

Conclusion

Self-assessment instruments are designed to focus on specific patterns of human behavior in order to assist people in better understanding the dynamics of their interaction with others. The IDI is a self-assessment inventory that focuses on how individuals construe their social world in terms of dealing with cultural differences between themselves and people from other social/cultural groups. The IDI is a self-scoring instrument that provides feedback to respondents concerning their general orientations or viewpoints toward cultural differences, that is, their intercultural sensitivity. As such, the IDI can be profitably employed whenever intercultural sensitivity is important to assess.

Endnotes

1. Not as common but equally polarizing in orientation is what is termed in the DMIS as "reversal," which involves the "denigration of one's own culture and an attendant assumption of superiority of a different culture" (Bennett 1986, 41). Analysis was undertaken to develop a scale to measure this orientation; however, unsatisfactory reliabilities were obtained. Therefore, "reversal" is not assessed in the IDI.

2. For a full discussion of the stages of intercultural sensitivity identified in the DMIS and the specific IDI scales, see Hammer and Bennett (1998). Essentially, the forms of isolation and separation within the denial stage are incorporated within the Denial scale of the IDI. The forms of denigration and superiority within the defense scale are incorporated within the Defense scale of the IDI. As mentioned earlier, the reversal form of defense is not incorporated within the IDI measure due to unsatisfactory reliabilities. The forms of physical universalism and transcendent universalism within

the minimization stage are incorporated in the Minimization scale of the IDI. The forms of respect for behavioral differences and respect for value differences within the adaptation stage are incorporated in the Acceptance scale of the IDI. The empathy form of the adaptation stage and the contextual evaluation form of the integration stage are incorporated in the Cognitive Adaptation scale of the IDI. The pluralism form of the adaptation stage is incorporated in the Behavioral Adaptation scale of the IDI. It should be noted that Bennett (1993) identifies a sixth stage, termed *integration,* in his developmental model. This stage focuses on the ways individuals incorporate different aspects of cultural identity into their sense of self. One aspect of the integration stage identified by Bennett (1993) is *contextual evaluation*, while a second form is *constructive marginality.* As stated earlier, contextual evaluation has been incorporated in the cognitive adaptation measure (see Hammer and Bennett 1998, for a fuller explanation of this theoretical shift). An effort was undertaken to develop a measure of the constructive marginality form of integration discussed in the DMIS. However, reliability for this scale was not sufficient and therefore not included in the IDI. The authors are working on finalizing a constructive marginality measure consistent with the DMIS.

References

Adler, Nancy. *International Dimensions of Organizational Behavior.* 2d ed. Belmont, CA: Wadsworth, 1991.

Bennett, Milton J. "Towards Ethnorelativism: A Developmental Model of Intercultural Sensitivity." In *Education for the Intercultural Experience*, edited by R. Michael Paige, 21–71. Yarmouth, ME: Intercultural Press, 1993.

———. "Towards Ethnorelativism: A Developmental Model of Intercultural Sensitivity." In *Cross-Cultural Orientation: New Conceptualizations and Applications,* edited by R. Michael Paige. New York: University Press of America, 1986.

Bhawuk, D. P. S., and Richard W. Brislin. "The Measurement of Intercultural Sensitivity Using the Concepts of Individualism and Collectivism." *International Journal of Intercultural Relations* 16 (1992): 413–36.

Black, J. S. "The Relationship of Personal Characteristics with the Adjustment of Japanese Expatriate Managers." *Management International Review* 30 (1990): 119–34.

Black, J. S., H. B. Gregersen, and M. E. Mendenhall. *Global Assignments.* San Francisco: Jossey-Bass, 1992.

Brislin, Richard W. *Cross-Cultural Encounters: Face-to-Face Interaction.* Elmsford, NY: Pergamon, 1981.

Brislin, Richard W., Kenneth Cushner, Craig Cherrie, and Mahealani Yong. *Intercultural Interactions: A Practical Guide.* Beverly Hills, CA: Sage, 1986.

Cleveland, H., G. Mangone, and J. Adams. *The Overseas Americans.* New York: McGraw-Hill, 1960.

DeVellis, R. F. *Scale Development.* Thousand Oaks, CA: Sage, 1991.

Hammer, Mitchell R., and Milton J. Bennett. *The Intercultural Development Inventory Manual.* Portland OR: Intercultural Communication Institute, 1998.

Hawes, Frank, and Daniel Kealey. "An Empirical Study of Canadian Technical Assistance." *International Journal of Intercultural Relations* 5, no. 3 (1981): 239–58.

———. "Canadians in Development: An Empirical Study of Adaptation and Effectiveness on Overseas Assignment." Communication Branch Briefing Center, Canadian International Development Agency, September 1979.

Kealey, Daniel. "The Challenge of International Personnel Selection." In *Handbook of Intercultural Training,* 2d ed., edited by Dan Landis and Rabi S. Bhagat, 81–105. Thousand Oaks, CA: Sage,1996.

———. "A Study of Cross-Cultural Effectiveness: Theoretical Issues, Practical Applications." *International Journal of Intercultural Relations* 13 (1989): 387–428.

Kealey, Daniel, and Brent D. Ruben. "Cross-Cultural Personnel Selection Criteria, Issues, and Methods." In *Handbook of Intercultural Training, vol. 1: Issues in Theory and Design,* edited by Dan Landis and Richard W. Brislin, 155–75. New York: Pergamon, 1983.

Klineberg, Otto, and Frank Hull. *At a Foreign University.* New York: Praeger, 1979.

Landis Dan, and Rabi S. Bhagat, eds. *Handbook of Intercultural Training.* 2d ed. Thousand Oaks, CA: Sage, 1996.

Landis, Dan, and Richard W. Brislin, eds. *Handbook of Intercultural Training, vol. 1: Issues in Theory and Design.* New York: Pergamon, 1983a.

———. *Handbook of Intercultural Training, vol. 2: Issues in Training Methodology.* New York: Pergamon, 1983b.

———. *Handbook of Intercultural Training, vol. 3: Area Studies in Intercultural Training.* New York: Pergamon, 1983c.

Sampson, D. L., and H. P. Smith. "A Scale to Measure World-Minded Attitudes." *Journal of Social Psychology* 45 (1957): 99–106.

Stephan, W. G., and C. W. Stephan. "Intergroup Anxiety." *Journal of Social Issues* 41 (1985): 157–76.

Wiseman, R. L., Mitchell R. Hammer, and H. Nishida. "Predictors of Intercultural Communication Competence." *International Journal of Intercultural Relations* 13 (1989): 349–70.

Using Videos as Training Tools

Robbins S. Hopkins

Videos have the capacity to bring experiences, ideas, emotions, and people from different countries into a training program and are often the closest alternative to the real thing. With both audio and visual components, the video settings can evoke powerful feelings in participants; therefore they need to be carefully managed in training.

Description of the Method

"Video" refers to any audiovisual materials which have been recorded on video-tape cassettes to be played on a videocassette recorder and seen on a television monitor. The materials may have originally been films, slide shows, plays, television shows, live discussions, and so forth. Confusion often arises for trainers when the generic term *film* is used to refer to videos; however, both films and videos have similar guidelines for use in training. Bear in mind when reading this section that films can be easily substituted for videos and should be if they are more readily available for a given audience.

Specific Uses for Video

Standardizing Information

There are several situations in which video contributes effectively to training. When many people are being trained in geographically dispersed areas, video provides a shared and therefore standardized experience for these people despite the distances between them. For example, when instructions or complicated procedures are being given to employees in several countries, video is probably the most effective medium. Both the accuracy of the information exchange and the standardization of this information across countries can be ensured through video.

Standardizing Delivery

Video is also a good choice when trainers are not experienced professionals. Video materials can provide a minimum standard in the instruction quality because the video acts as a constant. Videos used in training can ensure a consistent level of quality in the training not always available from volunteer trainers.

Emotional Content

Certain types of content can be presented most effectively on videos. Highly emotional content, group interactions, or the experiencing of specific cultural differences are hard to present in person. For example, video can capture an argument between people from different countries that would be hard to re-create in person. Emotionally charged topics such as abortion, divorce, child abuse, and human rights can often be more effectively explored through the use of a videotape than through live presentations. Video gives the trainer some control over the session because the catalyst for the session is known in advance.

Modeling Behavior

Video is a good training tool when there is a need to provide models in specific skill areas to produce behavior change in participants. For example, video can model desired behavior for interacting with an employee from another country or for training people to be more effective in recruiting committee members from different ethnic groups in the United States. Video is an excellent medium for training people in discrete skill areas because the skills can be demonstrated so effectively on video.

Providing Feedback

Video can also be used effectively in training as a feedback mechanism. For example, it can be used to tape participants practicing skills and then played back for critiquing. This is a microteaching approach to cross-cultural training. It allows the participants to use video to improve their individual abilities in specific areas.

Change in people often occurs when they are faced with an image of themselves that is in clear contrast with what they perceive themselves to be or what they wish to become. Therefore, if viewers are presented with a video that shows them being ineffective in interviewing, counseling, managing, supervising, or training, the contrast with their desired behavior alone will do more to motivate toward change than anything else one might do. When used to help individuals change their behavior, video is a powerful medium and one that should be considered when such is the goal.

Important Considerations for Using Videos

Designing the Session

First you must design your session, since many of the videotapes available to trainers are usually developed with the emphasis on the content of the video (such as the story to be taped) rather than on the training outcomes the video might produce (such as the ability to counsel, negotiate conflict, or interview others). In most cases the video will have to be adapted for use with a particular audience. Since you cannot change the video, you will have to carefully construct the session goals and discussion questions. There are some exceptions. Video training programs do exist where the entire program is on tape. However, this is rare in cross-cultural training because production is expensive and has to be narrowly focused for a limited audience, thereby becoming poor investments for producers. For the vast majority of videos used in cross-cultural training, the integration of the video with the training objectives is the key to successful video-based training.

Training for Awareness or for Skills

Is the emphasis of the cross-cultural training session going to be on raising awareness (knowledge, attitudes, perceptions) or on teaching skills (behaviors)? All support materials, exercises, and discussions used in conjunction with the videotape should be designed with the appropriate training objectives in mind. Actually, the most comprehensive cross-cultural training programs have a combination of sessions designed to do both. Each session, however, must be designed to reach its specific objectives.

For example, a video-based awareness training session for U.S. families hosting students from Argentina might highlight some of the general differences between teenagers' lives in these two countries. The video supporting this training could show interviews with exchange students from Argentina about their lives at home and how they differ from the lives of their friends in the United States. The training session could then have participants discuss the differences and the implications of these differences.

A video-based skills training session for the same participants could enable participants to negotiate a resolution to a conflict between a U.S. host family and a student from Argentina. The video for this session would show the specific conflict, and the accompanying training session would have the participants practice negotiation skills relating to the situation. The first session, designed to raise awareness, and the second session, designed to develop skills, could be combined to offer a multidimensional training program for the U.S. host parents.

It is also possible to use the same video for both awareness and skill development. The film *Gung Ho* is about a Japanese auto plant coming to a small town in the United States. The plot revolves around the cultural differences between Japanese and American workers and would be a rich source of material for either a general or culture-specific discussion of cultural differences. This would be the awareness dimension. To develop skills, selected clips from this video could be the basis for asking trainers to describe an example of intercultural interaction nonjudgmentally, which for most would be a new skill.

The specific video examples covered in this section of the *Sourcebook* provide information about videos that can be used both as skills training tools and as tools to raise awareness of cultural issues.

General Steps for Using Videos in Training

The general steps for using videos in training are these: (1) state goals for the training session and introduce the video, (2) present tasks for viewers, (3) view the video, and (4) process the video. The content of each of these steps could vary widely from session to session depending on the intended use of the video, but all of the steps should be covered in any event.

State Goals and Introduce the Video

Take care to note the major goals for the session and the specific objectives for use of the video.

Tell the viewers what to expect, giving special attention to elements that are emotionally powerful or visually graphic or shocking. If the video is not properly introduced, valuable time (and impact) can be lost while the audience adjusts to it, or valuable time can be lost in the processing of it if viewers are angry about not being appropriately prepared for what they were shown.

Give Viewers Special Tasks

Give viewers instructions on what especially to attend to. For example, some viewers might be asked to pay attention to the dialogue between two actors while others watch their actions. Or give groups of viewers one or two questions to think about as they watch the video. Specific tasks produce more focused observations and richer follow-up discussion.

View the Video

Make sure the video is ready to go!

Process the Video

Start by asking for general reactions in order to give the viewers a chance to get out their strongest responses and feelings before moving into the planned debriefing. In the discussion, ensure that the tasks assigned to the viewers are highlighted and given special attention, even though a broad focus is sought. Participants can be needlessly annoyed if an assignment they have been given and have taken seriously is not followed up on.

Benefits for the Trainees from Using Video

One benefit of using videotapes in training is that this medium comes the closest to reflecting real-life situations familiar to the trainees. Seeing real people giving real reactions to real problems can be highly motivational if the trainees are experiencing similar problems in their own lives. They are often encouraged to see that *their* issues are important enough to be captured on videotape, stirring them to a renewed effort to learn new behaviors to deal with the problems. In cross-cultural training, the videotape often gives legitimacy to the issues the trainees are dealing with by affirming the difficult and unique nature of intercultural and/or interpersonal interactions.

Video can also demonstrate both negative and positive consequences of certain behaviors in intercultural situations. For example, hotel personnel need to remain calm and use courteous language even when working with a hostile traveler. Picture a video showing an individual from the United States who is angry, loud, and accusatory toward a hotel clerk in the Caribbean. The video then shows the hotel clerk responding in three different ways, accompanied by the American's reaction to each of these responses.

Consequences of one's behavior motivate trainees to change. If you show the consequences of certain actions on video, the trainees can see in an especially powerful way (audiovisually) what they are moving toward. The training takes on new meaning and direction with the use of video.

General Rules for Producing Videotapes for Training

Some training situations may call for the development of your own videos. There are several rules that, if followed, will result in an effective video production, particularly those designed to change behavior.

1. The highly technical nature of a video production should not overshadow the hard work of designing an effective training program.

    Videotape is a popular and flashy communications medium. There is a tendency to think that the simple act of putting something on videotape will improve the training. Videotaping an ineffective training session, however, only means the ineffective training can now be shown to more people. Design a sound training program, then determine whether video can enhance the impact of the training.

2. Use video to show situations similar to those the trainees experience in their own lives.

    Video is an action medium with the potential of bringing to training programs the events, emotions, images, and experiences the trainees face daily. Do not use precious dollars to present lectures or other "talking heads" on the video. Telling never engages the audience as showing does. Even though talking heads can be used successfully (commercially, at least) to provide information, they do not change behavior. When you are working to change behavior, the most effective material reflects real life. Consider the ultimate application of this thinking as the video projection flight simulators used to train fighter pilots. This should be your model, not the evening news.

3. Low-quality production communicates "low-quality training" to the trainees.

    Hire a professional video production staff. Audiences already have established standards in mind for acceptable video quality because of television. If you expect the content of the training to be taken seriously, the production must be professionally managed, even if you are an amateur. So, cut back on the length of the video rather than on the production quality.

4. Integrate the video development with the training objectives from the beginning.

    Your training design team should include both training specialists and video specialists. The planning process should be completely determined before any footage is shot unless there is ample money for reshooting. The goals and objectives of the project will greatly affect the video that is developed.

5. The trainees have to see themselves in the video.

The more easily the trainees can identify with the people and situations in the video, the easier it will be for them to focus their attention on the learning objectives. When language, settings, story lines, or actors' dress or mannerisms are not familiar to the viewers, they tend to focus on the irrelevance of the video rather than on the potential learning opportunities.

How This Method Compares to Other Training Methods

Videos can be used in training exercises to change behavior by modeling desirable and undesirable behavior and as experiences to enable trainees to develop analytical skills. They are excellent alternatives to written case studies, critical incidents, and certain types of role plays. Videos cannot substitute for role plays where skill practice is the goal, but they can substitute for role plays used to set up a situation in order to explore different attitudes and perspectives. In fact, skill practice role plays are often a good companion activity to videos because trainees can role-play responses to visually presented situations.

Videos are excellent at raising issues, perspectives, and attitudes about other countries and cultures. They can bring experiences into the training setting that cannot be accessed in any other fashion. Through videos you can invite people from around the world into the classroom or training session who could not otherwise be there. Conflict and consensus, history and news, group perceptions and individual comments, facts and interpretations can all be presented to audiences through this medium, which is perhaps the most versatile of any training method. The challenge, as with any training program, is to determine what the group wants or needs as an outcome of the training experience and then to design a program around the video to produce the desired outcome. Only then will a video realize its full potential.

Conclusion

Video training programs designed for cross-cultural communication are rare and often very specific to the audience for which they were developed. Therefore trainers will most frequently need to locate good videos and design the learning sessions around them. No matter how video is used in cross-cultural training, it offers both the trainers and the viewers an expansive window on the world, one that would not otherwise be accessible.

Resources

Begin by reading *Crossing Cultures through Film* by Ellen Summerfield (Yarmouth, ME: Intercultural Press, 1993); PO Box 700, Yarmouth, ME 04096; Phone: 207-846-5168 or 800-370-2665; Website: www.interculturalpress.com

There are numerous organizations offering excellent business training videos such as Films Incorporated of Chicago, Illinois. I have yet to see a video addressing cross-cultural communication or any related topics offered through these types of organizations. There are, however, some individual efforts in this field, several of which are reviewed in this section of the *Sourcebook*. Individual productions are often hard to track down precisely because no publication or organization exists specifically to promote them.

A good source for general films that can be used in intercultural training remains the university film catalogues. All the state universities have film catalogues—you can call your local state university and ask for its film catalogue. Typically they offer the films on their list for rent or purchase. One of the most extensive holdings of these is Syracuse University. Most of the university holdings can be obtained both as films and videos. Most local libraries also have copies. Another good source of interesting cross-cultural films is the National Film Board of Canada, Constitution Square, 360 Albert Street, Suite 1560, Ottawa, Ontario K1A 0M9 Canada; Phone: 613-992-3615; Website: www.nfb.ca

Several on-line databases are also available to aid in the location of appropriate audiovisual materials. One is KIDSNET in Takoma Park, Maryland, specializing in video materials for preschool through high school, with entries of 25,000 titles. They have extensive holdings in multicultural and international areas. Search services are available domestically and internationally on a subscription basis.

Developing a Dual Perspective

Cay Hartley and Robbins S. Hopkins

This chapter deals with the development of training materials, print and video, which are designed to teach basic skills to anyone who works with persons from other cultures. Some background is needed to understand the context for the development of this material.

History

In 1980 the training department at Youth For Understanding International Exchange (YFU) was faced with the task of developing effective communication skills in more than 2,000 volunteers who serve as local contacts for international students and host families. At that time, the practice was to develop training materials in response to requests from YFU regional offices around the United States and design them to meet local needs. There was little concern given to their replicability for use in other regions or their comprehensiveness in meeting larger organizational objectives. As a problem arose, a session would be designed to address that particular area of concern. The trainers were sometimes experienced but were often chosen because of other achievements such as their ability to recruit host families and place international students. Training modules tended to be short (one or two hours) and aimed at challenging participants to consider their attitudes about a topic relevant to educational exchange.

YFU made the decision to undertake a revision of its training system on a national basis and to organize training units around volunteer functions. Results from a needs assessment indicated three major areas of volunteer activity and need: (a) intercultural communication, (b) interpersonal communication, and (c) promotion and marketing. Skills in each of these areas were identified, and over the next five years, with partial support from the W. K. Kellogg Foundation, sixteen units were developed, all but one with a central videotape component. The units average six hours in length (a range of four to nine hours) and place primary emphasis on skill development, which is reinforced by practice sessions. In this manner, skills were demonstrated in a variety of situations commonly encountered by volunteers. The effectiveness of this strategy became increasingly evident as volunteers reported their ability to transfer the use of these skills to other professional and personal settings.

Developing a Dual Perspective, one of the core training units from this set of materials, will be the specific focus in the rest of this chapter. Being able to view any situation from a dual cultural perspective—one's own and that of someone from a different culture—is a major skill, essential for everyone working cross-culturally; in YFU's case, with international students and their American host families.

In developing the materials, we assessed the behavior of persons who were judged to be exceptional in their ability to work cross-culturally. We found the following skill areas to be present:

- ❖ the ability to describe a situation nonjudgmentally
- ❖ the ability to determine what information is missing
- ❖ the ability to seek out that missing information
- ❖ the ability to describe any given situation from the perspective of more than one person

YFU volunteers are frequently in the position of being a "third party helper," assisting the student and family to understand one another. This task is complicated by the fact that most often the helper's own cultural perspective matches that of the host family and, therefore, an extra effort is needed to see the student's perspective.

Video and Training Design

A five-step model designed to enable the participant to understand more than one cultural perspective is presented during the dual-perspective training. The steps in the dual-perspective model are as follows:

1. describing the situation while recognizing the impact of one's own cultural point of view,
2. reviewing the description to assure that it is nonjudgmental,
3. determining areas of missing information,
4. seeking the missing information, and
5. describing the situation from two cultural perspectives.

The dual-perspective materials represent a major departure from culture-specific training programs, which focus on the delivery of information about any given culture. While that information is useful in certain cases, it depends on the correctness of the source and in some cases can lead to the promotion of stereotypes. By contrast, these materials are aimed at helping a person working in cross-cultural situations to develop a set of generic skills useful in understanding any culture.

The premise that understanding one's own culture is essential to the process of trying to figure out and understand another culture underpins this material, as it does many others in the intercultural field (Stewart and Bennett, 1991).

The dual-perspective unit begins with small group discussions of one's own cultural and personal perspectives on a number of familiar topics such as education of children, use of time, family activities, and use of space in homes. After a discussion of the similarities and differences, the participants are invited to imagine how their ideas would be viewed by someone from a different culture. For example, American groups often report that the kitchen/breakfast room is a favorite gathering place for family members as well as guests. It is not hard to imagine that in other cultures, the very idea of entertaining guests in the kitchen would produce great embarrassment.

At this point, the video is introduced. In this 45-minute video, we meet Kimiko, an exchange student from Japan, her American family (mother, father, little brother, and sister), and the YFU volunteer. The video is divided into five scenes, each adding more information to the story and the situation as it unfolds. The situation (exchange student and host family) was chosen because it is familiar for all YFU volunteers, and the problem presented is also familiar (adjustment between student and family) but not of a critical nature. It has the added benefit of building up a body of culture-specific information about life in Japan through introducing this particular Japanese student and her host family.

The video medium was specifically chosen over a less expensive audio case study for two reasons; the video captures the nonverbal behavioral component, and the visual scenes heighten the emotional aspects of the story. Participants usually become quite taken with this young Japanese girl's tale and listen carefully to her observations about Americans and her recollections of her life and family in Japan.

The reactions of participants to the situation need to be carefully monitored. We have found that after each scene, trainers need to ask for reactions from the group prior to asking the participants to carry out a task.

The first scene on the video shows Kimiko with her host mother and the YFU volunteer. After viewing scene 1, participants are asked to generate all possible options for action that might be considered as a result of the conversation they have just observed. Scene 2 shows Kimiko's perception of the same events described in scene 1. It is immediately clear to the participants that many of the options they proposed, had they been carried out, would not have been appropriate. This exercise draws viewers in as they begin to realize that what at first seems appropriate may not be without further investigation and understanding of the situation.

You can now complete step 1 of the model. Show the first scene again and ask participants to carry out the first step of the model: describing the scene from one's own point of view.

Step 2 of the model requires participants to review their descriptions for judgmental elements. Judgmental attitudes are easily observed in the verbal content of what one says as well as the accompanying nonverbal aspects of communication. Experience has shown that though spotting the judgmental language of others may be relatively easy, identifying it in oneself and changing the description of an action, situation, or person to nonjudgmental terms is much more difficult. This realization often sparks a personal reassessment of assumptions that have led to the judgmental language, and this experience inevitably motivates participants for continued involvement in the training.

Video scenes 3 and 4 provide material to practice steps one and two of the dual perspective model. They also give enough information to carry out step 3— determining what information is still needed for adequate understanding of the situation. There are moments of hilarity, such as a harried dinner scene with the host family, and ones of poignancy as the concerned host mother tells Kimiko to look her directly in the eyes when she talks with her. With each new video scene, more of Kimiko's story of her life with her host family is revealed (step 4). Participants steadily build the skills to achieve the goal of step 5, which is to develop a dual perspective.

Part of the ability to develop a dual perspective is being able to understand each party's point of view. With that in mind, the training design involves all workshop participants simultaneously in a role play in which a "volunteer" talks with Kimiko and one person observes each interaction. Briefing information is provided and a third of the participants attempt to take on the Japanese student's perspective.

The training objectives are several: to increase information about Japanese youth and their ideas, to increase empathy for a student from this culture, and to increase the ability of the volunteer helper to talk with students from a different culture. The video ends with a scene where Kimiko talks with the YFU volunteer, who models good listening skills and (more successfully than in earlier scenes) guides Kimiko into talking about life in America and Japan. At this point, participants complete the fifth step of the model by describing the situation from both the American and Japanese points of view.

Successful Uses and Variation

Since its development in 1983, *Developing a Dual Perspective* has been used frequently with YFU volunteers in the United States. All volunteers received this training unit as part of their basic grounding in cross-cultural skills. The unit, introduced into the YFU system in Europe in 1985, has been widely used there as well. It was first used in Australia in 1986 and in Latin America in 1989. In each case, volunteers report that the skills they acquire and polish during this training are vital and essential to their work in the cross-cultural field.

The first portion of the unit (being able to describe a situation nonjudgmentally) has been used as a basic approach and first step for conflict management and negotiation programs. This same portion has also been adapted for use at the Foreign Service Institute of the U.S. Department of State. Further, portions of the unit have been used with receiving host families in a number of countries to raise their awareness about different cultural perspectives and how they affect behavior in exchange students. Another manner of using the training material is to prepare sojourners for their reactions to a new culture.

Whereas the existing video has most often been used with this training material, it is also possible to accomplish at least steps one, two, and three (describing the situation, reviewing the description to make sure it is nonjudgmental, and determining areas of missing information) using commercially available video footage. There are many commercial films presenting cross-cultural encounters which provide opportunities to describe scenes nonjudgmentally. Some examples are *Gung Ho, El Norte, Passage to India,* and *The Gods Must Be Crazy.*

One advantage to using a video that portrays scenes very familiar to the participants is that it increases receptivity to the training. However, scenes from films such as those mentioned above may be more neutral in content, thus allowing a broader range of participants to focus on skill development.

Important Considerations in Using This Content

There are several problems that experience has taught us are fairly predictable. As mentioned earlier, the emotional impact of the tape produces a high level of participant involvement with the material. Participants need help resisting the temptation to delve into the *content* of the video story instead of attending to the skills/steps being taught. YFU volunteers frequently want to problem-solve to help out this appealing Japanese student, moving directly to the solution and usually blaming the insensitive American host family. The trainer needs to strike a balance between allowing ventilation and reactions to the video scenes and reminding participants that the story is presented to allow a focus on skill development.

It is also essential to help participants recognize that the process is more difficult than is immediately apparent. This usually occurs when participants compare their initial descriptions about the scene with deliberate attempts to be nonjudgmental. The difficulties encountered usually serve to increase the participants' commitment to the material.

As always, a skilled trainer is crucial. Though the material looks simple on paper, if it is presented in a simplistic fashion, participants will feel talked down to and assume the concepts are self-evident. The trainer needs to be able to integrate the training concepts with the experience level of the group and to be able to use experienced participants by verbally soliciting their stories or accessing experiences from their journals (customarily part of longer training programs) and tying these experiences to the principles being discussed. The key is getting the participants to make the connections between principles and experience and leading them into discovering the complexities of high-level cross-cultural communication skills.

Summary

The videotape with the written training material had a number of advantages. The video provided a shared standard viewed by all, which created a consistency of training throughout our training system. It added an affective element to the training and increased the interest and involvement of the participants. It enabled us to present culture-specific information and, at the same time, provided a vehicle for developing the basic communication skills needed by anyone working with people from a culture other than one's own.

Distribution

Youth For Understanding International Exchange
Attn: Training Unit
3501 Newark Street, NW
Washington, DC 20016 USA
202-966-6808

Reference

Stewart, Edward C., and Milton J. Bennett. *American Cultural Patterns: A Cross-Cultural Perspective.* Rev. ed. Yarmouth, ME: Intercultural Press, 1991.

Training with Video: *Taking Your Product into the Japanese Market*

Nan M. Sussman

Over the years there has been a continuous stream of Western business personnel attempting to conduct negotiations, sell products, or establish joint ventures in Japan. More often than not these Westerners have left Japan frustrated, disappointed, and angry with their Japanese counterparts and with their failure to accomplish their goals. Something needed to be done.

History and Development

In 1984 two business colleagues, Frank O'Brien, an Irish national representing a U.S. firm in Japan, and Takuro Tsukatani, a Japanese consultant educated in the United States and working for the European Economic Community and a Japanese automobile company, compared their observations of the seemingly insurmountable cultural barriers to the Japanese and Americans doing business together, and decided to try to come up with a remedy. The result was a training package which would teach Westerners about the Japanese style of business and how to do business with the Japanese. Of the training modes available, only videotape, they reasoned, could convey both the dynamism of business encounters and the visual images so effective in preparing newcomers for the Japanese business setting.

Their first step was to immerse themselves in the cross-cultural literature, theoretical and practical (including videotapes), and in the literature on Japanese business. From their perspective, based on their own experience, all the current material was too academic to be useful to businesspeople. The few available videotapes that focused on Japan touched on only a portion of the relevant business customs and were often not practical enough. Books about Japanese business practices were dry and static and did not convey the dynamic nature of doing business across cultures. Yet, while they did not want to ignore the accumulated knowledge about cross-cultural communication, their goal was to produce a series of training videotapes that had a solid grounding in cross-cultural theory and learning models, yet at the same time were practical for the business expatriate.

The second step was to create a story line. It featured a hypothetical American businessman, Lloyd Maxwell, who resembled the dozens of Westerners O'Brien and Tsukatani had watched depart from Japan disgruntled and confused. The story traced Maxwell over an eighteen-month period in which he attempted to sell his company's product to a midsized Japanese engineering company.

Scripting parameters grew out of the desire to highlight three underlying cross-cultural differences between Japanese and Western business styles: differences in interpersonal communication, in negotiation processes, and in decision-making styles.

The producers also wanted to correct deficiencies of other training products: lack of sufficient explanation of cultural differences; lack of insight into the thinking of the Japanese and Western businesspeople during frustrating encounters; lack of visual images of Tokyo, Japanese offices, street scenes; and lack of visual and content information regarding the role of "informal" but mandatory business relationship building through after-hours entertaining.

A final concern about content of the videotape was their desire to ensure a balanced and nonjudgmental view of both American and Japanese business customs and processes.

Production

Video. Production began early in 1985, and the entire project took over twenty-four months to complete. It was filmed exclusively in Tokyo, using actual corporate offices, restaurants, hostess bars, and neighborhood drinking places. Despite their best estimates of the cost of production, O'Brien and Tsukatani far exceeded initial budgets. Final production figures for the two and one-half hour video package, including comprehensive editing, was over $550,000.

Several challenges to production emerged, in part due to the cross-cultural nature of the video. The first important decision was to determine which language would be used in the dramatized conversations. If all the actors, American and Japanese, in the tape spoke English, this would represent an unrealistic picture to the trainee. Clearly one of the problems of working in Japan is the language difference. The producers wanted trainees to become accustomed to hearing Japanese being spoken in business meetings, simulating the experience they would have in Japan. However, would trainees tire of reading subtitles for all the Japanese conversations? A compromise was reached: the language problem would be handled in three ways.

In those situations which involved direct U.S.-Japanese conversation, the story line would create interpreters for the participants. This was also a way of demonstrating the preparation needed when working with an interpreter, a frequent problem for Westerners who are not accustomed to simultaneous interpretation.

In those situations where the Japanese were speaking to each other but in the presence of the Americans, either subtitles would be used or voice-overs. In situations of lengthy discussions carried on in Japanese with no foreigners present, voice-overs would be used. Even with the voice-overs, the Japanese language could be heard softly in the background.

Finding appropriate-sounding voices proved to be surprisingly difficult. Initially, the voice-overs were done by Japanese who spoke English. However, even the least accented speaker was distracting to a pilot group of trainees. Instead of focusing on the content of the tape, trainees struggled to understand the translated, accented English. Thus, all the voice-overs had to be redone using thirty-five different native English speakers who did not already appear in the tape, as their voices would be familiar to viewers.

A second production challenge was the selection of actors. Choosing Japanese actors was relatively simple despite the fact that over one hundred were needed. There was a large supply of trained actors in Tokyo. Even so, the producers considered using Japanese-American or Japanese-Canadian actors because of their English language fluency, but they could not master appropriate postures, gestures, and other native Japanese nonverbal behaviors. In an effort to ensure authenticity, Japanese actors were chosen. But ten experienced American actors were needed, and finding them in Tokyo was a more difficult task. In the end the producers had to resort to amateur actors and to "creative casting."

A third production difficulty was on-location shooting. A few scenes ostensibly took place in U.S. offices, restaurants, and golf courses and had to be simulated in Tokyo and neighboring areas. Tokyo scenes proved a challenge, too, since to convey realism, they were actually shot, as noted above, in real Japanese corporate offices, hostess bars, *yakitori,* and *nomiya* (casual restaurants and bars). Even the ever-present uniforms of "office ladies" (the term they use) and technical employees needed to be supplied for the actors.

Training Manuals. As the video production ended and pilot testing of the tape started, work began on the training manuals. The producers knew that trainers would need guidance to maximize the potential training value of the tape and would appreciate supplemental material for lectures. Trainees, too, would benefit from a manual that supplemented the tape.

Production of these two comprehensive manuals became an unexpectedly complex task but vital to the success of the project.

The Training Package. The final product was six half-hour tapes which followed Lloyd Maxwell from his arrival at Narita Airport through consultations with Americans in Tokyo, initial meetings with the Japanese client, follow-up meetings, in-house discussions among the Japanese, long negotiation sessions, and final agreement to a sale.

The unique features of the training package are as follows:

1. An engaging simulation of a cross-cultural business process in which trainees are active participants.

2. A practical training product which covers Japan-U.S. cross-cultural negotiation and relationship-building steps in great detail, from the correct method for exchanging business cards to the after-hours protocol for socializing.

3. A behind-the-scenes perspective on Japanese organizational behavior, that is, what they do and say to each other away from the bargaining table.

4. A close-up of the small, interpersonal details that are necessary for one to model or, at the very least, understand when working with the Japanese.

5. A visual introduction to all the settings in which Japanese business takes place.
6. A five-minute review at the end of each tape to highlight the important cross-cultural themes.
7. A detailed trainer's manual and a trainee's manual with material explaining the various scenes and supplementing the tapes.

The tapes debuted in Japan in February 1986, to great acclaim. *Nihon Keizai,* the Japanese equivalent of the *Wall Street Journal,* featured the video training series in a major article, as did the *Japan Times* and several other Japanese periodicals. The foreign community in Japan, struggling on a daily basis to understand and succeed in the Japanese business environment, were most interested in the tapes.

The U.S. debut followed soon thereafter. The tapes were reviewed and showcased in *USA Today* and the *Washington Times.*

Using the Training Package

The videotapes and manual are designed to be used together. The tapes come in six individual cases, convenient for playback. They are available in several video formats including 3/4 inch u-matic, 1/2 inch VHS, 1/2 inch beta, and VHS/PAL. Both the trainer's and trainee's manuals are bound together in one book. Supplemental readings, general information, and an extensive bibliography are provided.

Training Mode

With access to both manuals, it is possible for a trainee to use the program as a self-instructional training package. This is often desirable, as many expatriates are given no time or opportunity for training in their hectic predeparture schedule. Also, since many training programs, when they are available, do not include the spouse, this training package could be taken home for the benefit of the whole family.

A more likely and, from my experience, preferable training mode is in a group setting with a trainer or leader. The trainer can direct attention and discussion to the more crucial cultural points. She or he can gauge trainee comprehension and supplement the tape with additional materials and clarification of the tape. A group setting provides trainees with a richer learning environment, and questions and comments from other participants can add knowledge and stimulate thinking. Trainees can more easily participate in group exercises and simulations that complement the tapes and text.

Timing

Timing of training is a decision which needs to be determined in the early stages of planning. *Taking Your Product into the Japanese Market* is appropriate for predeparture training or on-arrival training, and equally useful during the course of a Japan assignment as the difficulties of conducting business in Japan become more salient and pressing. In fact, using the tape both in predeparture and midassignment training would be ideal, because trainees become more sophisticated during their time in Japan and can better appreciate the complexities involved.

Target Groups

The comprehensiveness of the tape allows it to be used with a wide range of trainees. U.S. business personnel who regularly work with the Japanese, either on a periodic basis in Japan or in the United States, or American expatriates in Japan are obvious training targets. These would include company representatives in Japan, sales and marketing staff, and some technical personnel.

However, there are many others who would benefit from this program. For example, top management needs to understand the Japanese market in order to formulate policy decisions. Managers of corporate planning need to understand the value system and organizational structure that form the basis for the conduct of Japanese management. International managers who supervise staff working in Japan will benefit from understanding the culture/business climate impinging on their employees and what the employees must do to be successful in that environment. Human resources managers who select and train employees for overseas assignments will find additional knowledge about the Japanese business style helpful.

Western European business personnel could also find the training package beneficial. They would learn something about American business customs and concerns as well as about those of the Japanese.

A special training market is the Japanese themselves. The tape serves as a cultural mirror which can help Japanese become more aware of the cultural underpinnings of their own business practices. It is then a comparison point for understanding business behavior in other countries.

Procedure for Using the Training Package

Three Training Designs

Design 1. With a competent trainer, the tapes and manuals can be a stand-alone training package. Armed with good training skills and a thorough understanding of the tape and the manuals, a non-Japanese expert can guide trainees through the tape. Because of the detail imbedded in the tape, I suggest that sessions be spread out over several days. This will enable trainees to better digest the material, read some of the supplemental articles, and practice the behavioral activities (exchanging *meishi* [business cards], elementary greetings in Japanese, and the like). Each tape is approximately thirty minutes long, which allows a half-hour for discussion in a one-hour session.

Design 2. A second design assumes additional knowledge of Japan on the part of the trainer. This design uses the tape as the backbone or skeleton of a three- to five-day training program. Extensive supplemental sessions precede each tape segment. Such sessions might include Japanese history; current politics and economic environment; an overview of Japanese customs and social and nonverbal behavior; the educational system; eating rituals and a visit to a local Japanese restaurant; and detailed discussions of Japanese corporate structure, decision making, and negotiating. More culture-general information can be included, such as an introduction to the concept of culture, cultural differences, and cultural adaptation.

This expanded training can also include lengthy sessions practicing greeting behaviors, studying the language, and participating in negotiation simulations. Additional special speakers could join the training: managers repatriated from Japan, culturally aware Japanese businessmen in the United States, and in-house corporate planning managers, who can discuss a company's long-range plans vis-à-vis Japan.

Design 3. A third design uses portions of the tape rather than the entire two and one-half hour package. In the manual, the producers have conveniently divided the tape's twenty-seven scenes into three components: scenes in which there are cross-cultural encounters between the Japanese and Americans, scenes in which the Americans are interacting, and scenes in which the Japanese are interacting. Thus, if your training design includes a unit on business/cultural self-awareness for Americans (for use in culture-general training or the culture-general segment of culture-specific training), the indicated scenes would be an excellent source of visual information and subsequent discussion for the trainees.

Conversely, a unit focusing on Japanese behavior apart from cross-cultural interactions might use only the seven scenes which feature Japanese businessmen.

Important Considerations for Use

While *Taking Your Product into the Japanese Market* is an excellent training tape, it is not without its flaws. Despite the producers' best efforts, there are several technical problems which mar what is substantially a professional production. These slipups are most salient to a corporate audience that is accustomed to flawless, Hollywood-type training productions. The most glaring problem is the amateurishness of the American actors. Their stilted performances detract from the story line and inappropriately focus the attention of the trainees on actor skills. There are also one or two instances where the story line lacks continuity in the script.

As mentioned above, finding enough "voices" for the voice-overs was a problem and several of the choices were inappropriate because of accent or voice tone or quality. Additionally, the attempts to interpret the Japanese language in colloquial English were occasionally comical, especially when the translators were the Japanese and Irish producers. Subtitles were generally well worded and legible but in a few instances contained typographical errors.

The manual contains very useful information for comprehending the story line. Organizational and seating charts, scene-by-scene cast of characters, and summaries of each tape are welcome additions. However, the trainer-and-trainee-combined manual is cumbersome and expensive. In order to provide each trainee with a copy of his or her own user's manual, it is necessary to buy copies of the entire manual and remove all the trainer manuals. It is time-consuming and you are left with dozens of useless trainer copies. This would be easily remedied with the reprinting of the manuals separately for separate purchase.

One final and somewhat unusual complaint: the tape is intricate and detailed and contains so much information that inexperienced trainers or those completely unfamiliar with Japanese culture will surely miss the finer points of the cultural differences in the story. While the manuals assist in comprehension, subtleties are often lost on both trainers and trainees, certainly on trainees using the package as self-instructional material.

Distribution

The tapes can be purchased in the United States through

> PacificVision Inc.
> Attn: Susan Place
> 1441 Broadway Street
> Boulder, Colorado 80302
> 303-938-1883

Cost, as of the writing of this chapter, for the six-set package including the two manuals is $850.00.

Equipment needs are minimal: an appropriate VCR and monitor and a room suitable for viewing, discussion, and note taking. A blackboard or whiteboard is also highly recommended as well as easel paper, which can be removed and retained for later reference.

While the appendices of the manual give references for general books on Japan, most of the references are business-specific. They are most helpful to the corporate trainees. I have listed, for trainers' use, some additional selected resources.

Resources

Brannen, Christalyn, and Tracey Wilen. *Doing Business with Japanese Men: A Woman's Handbook.* Berkeley: Stone Bridge Press, 1993.

Christopher, Robert C. *The Japanese Mind: The Goliath Explained.* New York: Simon and Schuster, 1983.

Condon, John C., and Mitsuko Saito. *Intercultural Encounters with Japan: Communication-Contact and Conflict.* Tokyo: Simul Press, 1974.

Discover Japan: Words, Customs and Concepts, vols. 1 and 2. Tokyo: Kodansha International, 1982.

Hall, Edward T., and Mildred R. Hall. *Hidden Differences: Doing Business with the Japanese.* New York: Anchor/Doubleday, 1987.

Lebra, Takie S., and William Lebra. *Japanese Culture and Behavior: Selected Readings.* Honolulu: University of Hawaii Press, 1974.

March, Robert M. *Working for a Japanese Company.* Tokyo: Kodansha International, 1992.

Reischauer, Edwin O. *The Japanese.* Cambridge, MA: Harvard University Press, 1977.

Going International +
Valuing Diversity = Tools for Training

Nessa Loewenthal and Robert Hayles

Produced by Lennie Copeland and Lewis Griggs, the Going International and Valuing Diversity series were developed to create an awareness of cultural differences and the ways in which these differences affect communication and understanding between people. The films are useful in facilitating the development of those skills critical to success and productivity in an international, intercultural, and/or multiculturally diverse environment.

Going International

History

In 1983 Copeland Griggs Productions with its first film/video series, Going International, provided those working with international relocation and exchange a new tool. In the process of marketing the series, Copeland Griggs made a significant contribution to the field of intercultural communication by increasing the visibility of the concept of "culture shock" to the U.S. public and to the media. The influence of culture on communication styles, on perception, and most importantly on the ways people of different cultures work, manage, and interact became more generally recognized because of the media coverage received by the films.

Overview

Going International, a seven-part series available in film or video format, covers all aspects of the international cross-cultural life cycle. These films are designed to be used in predeparture and on-site training programs that prepare people to live and work effectively in cultures other than their own. Because of the nature of the material and the style of presentation, they are beneficial for managers and for students preparing to study or work abroad. Executives, salespeople, negotiators, frequent travelers, and others who have contact with people from different cultures, whether at home or abroad, will also benefit from these films. Each of the films, with the exception of the shorter Part IV, *Welcome Home, Stranger,* is approximately thirty minutes long. Because of the breadth of the subject matter and limited film lengths, the material introduces the concepts and ideas, rather than exploring them in depth.

The series is divided into three segments, each designed for a particular audience or specific purpose:

Segment 1—International Effectiveness. The original films in the Going International series are designed for use with Americans who are or will be in prolonged contact with other cultures while working in or visiting other countries.

Part I, *Bridging the Culture Gap,* introduces the concepts of cultural values and variables. It shows the need to develop skills and strategies for recognizing and dealing with differences as it lays the groundwork for cultural adjustment and cross-cultural effectiveness.

Part II, *Managing the Overseas Assignment,* consists of a series of vignettes showing the difficulties and misunderstandings which arise when Americans try to do business overseas as they do at home. Cultural taboos, business practices, and differences in expectations and perceptions are discussed by host country nationals who also present examples of effective business behavior in their cultures. Although each scenario is set in a specific country—Japan, Saudi Arabia, England, India, and Mexico—the situations and concepts are applicable worldwide.

Parts III and IV, *Beyond Culture Shock* and *Welcome Home, Stranger,* are designed to assist the employee and family in developing strategies and skills for living in another culture and for their reentry into their home culture. Culture shock, coping skills, and adaptation strategies are presented by experts as well as by families who have experienced several successful international tours of duty. A candid presentation of the pleasures and pitfalls of living in another culture, *Beyond Culture Shock* focuses primarily on the spouse's needs and concerns, recognizing that the spouse's ability to adapt is critical to the employee's success and productivity. *Welcome Home, Stranger* presents, again through the eyes of experienced families, the unexpected problems encountered by employees and their families on reentry into their own cultures: national, family, and workplace. Families and experts share strategies for dealing with the new assignment and cultures found when one returns home.

Copeland and Griggs have written an excellent resource and ready reference, *Going International: How to Make Friends in the Global Marketplace* as a companion to the film series. This book provides general as well as culture-specific information for anyone planning on spending time in other cultures. It complements the material presented in the films without being repetitive or pedantic and offers support when needed.

Segment 2—Inward Bound. Parts V, *Living in the USA* and VI, *Working in the USA,* are directed toward employees from other countries and cultures relocating to the United States with their families. *Living in the USA* concentrates on the family, while *Working in the United States* is appropriate for use with all employees—male and female—whether they have a long- or short-term assignment. The information presented is also useful for the headquarters personnel receiving and working with the newcomers.

Segment 3—Security and Safety. Part VII, *Going International Safely,* examines realities with which anyone living, working, or traveling abroad should be familiar. Security measures are presented and strategies developed for dealing with personal, family, and organizational safety. As the saying goes, "Forewarned is forearmed!"

Contexts for Use

Tapes in the Going International series are appropriate for use in a wide variety of training programs with differing goals, including

❖ predeparture training for the international employee and his/her family (I–IV and VII);

❖ reentry preparation and debriefing (IV);

❖ orientation for the foreign employee and family in the United States (I, IV, VI);

❖ cultural awareness and cross-cultural management for the managers and co-workers of these employees (I,II,V);

❖ management and intercultural communication skills for the manager working internationally (I, II, V);

❖ management of the multicultural workforce (I, II, VI); and

❖ cultural awareness and/or intercultural communication skills (I, II).

These films are excellent vehicles through which to introduce ideas and initiate discussions as a part of a facilitated training session. They are designed to be used in a discussion session and as a part of a larger program. A second viewing of a film, after its initial presentation and discussion, is helpful, because the breadth of information presented makes it difficult to absorb everything in one viewing. Many organizations find it useful to show the films again as part of on-site support and orientation programs, even when people have seen the series as part of predeparture preparation.

Tapes I and II are useful in training personnel who will be working with the international employee and family. Part II has been used extensively in international business classes, and it presents the concepts of culture and communication in a way that is understandable even at the high school level.

Procedures for Effective Use

Introducing Concepts. To gain the maximum benefit from these films, preface their showing with some activity designed to introduce the concepts to be developed. Because of the variety of applications of these films, the introductory activities will vary to meet program objectives.

One of the best ways to involve participants or trainees is to determine their prior experiences, their level of knowledge, their concerns, and their perceptions. This can be done through the use of questions or statements such as these: When I think of_____culture, three thoughts come to mind; The

_____ think that Americans are_____; Three things that I am excited about or look forward to during this assignment are_____; Three things that concern or frighten me are_____.

Another effective method is to use culture-general or culture-specific critical incidents or role-play situations based on specific values or potential difficulties. Exercises such as *BaFá BaFá*, described in *Sourcebook,* Vol. 1 (see pages 93–100), or *RaFá RaFá* if one is working with children below junior high school age, work well in programs with cultural differences and serve as an effective introduction to training in intercultural communication. *Barnga* is another activity that serves the same purpose.

When using any of the above methods, it is necessary to facilitate group discussion to draw out the desired responses and to summarize and clarify the ideas. Following any of the above methods for introducing the concepts, tie participants' responses or experiences to the content of the film/tape. Direct the viewers to watch for additional information and ideas that can be found in the film. Show the film and process the trainees' thoughts and responses to it.

The concepts to be developed are determined by the goals and objectives of the program in which the films are used. For example, in a Family Predeparture Program, the focus is on

❖ an understanding of the International Life Cycle: Selection, Preparation, International Experience, Reentry; an examination of the potential difficulties and benefits of each phase; and the development of strategies and coping skills for functioning effectively during each phase;

❖ an examination of culture shock and strategies for managing transition (that is, survival skills and strategies); strategies can be developed from participants' previous experiences with transition (moves, leaving home, marrying, and so forth);

❖ an awareness of culture and values and how these affect the ability to communicate effectively;

❖ an introduction to the potential difficulties of "coming home" after a successful international experience, combined with a program for developing reentry strategies that can be worked on and developed the entire time away (from departure until actual reentry).

In a Cultural Awareness Program the concepts to be developed include the following:

❖ Differences exist in implicit/hidden values as well as in those that are readily apparent. (We are not all the same under the surface.)

❖ Deep-seated differences in attitudes, behaviors, and perceptions are the cause of miscommunication and unintentional misconduct.

❖ We are unaware of these differences until we come in contact/conflict with someone from a culture with different perspectives.

❖ We develop a knowledge and understanding of cultural values and their manifestations as held by the macroculture and by each individual participant.

A program in Intercultural Communication combines the content of the Cultural Awareness Program with the development of skills and procedures leading to the ability to communicate effectively with those whose culturally based attitudes, behaviors, and perceptions are different from one's own. The primary objectives are to

❖ understand how perceptions, behaviors, and beliefs based on cultural values can inhibit or enhance communication;

❖ recognize the "red flags" which signal missed communication; and

❖ develop strategies for correcting misunderstandings and minimizing the "damage."

The ultimate goal of these programs, individually or combined, is to help trainees avoid potential difficulties in understanding and being understood by those from other cultures.

Strengths and Benefits

One of the greatest strengths of these films is the realistic picture they present. In films III and IV, the use of expatriate families sharing their experiences, combined with experts providing information and ideas, provides situations in which the trainees can imagine themselves and creates an atmosphere in which they can begin to develop their own strategies for coping. *Bridging the Culture Gap*, film I, probably has the widest range of uses, from the American preparing to go overseas to those from other cultures who need to understand how the American sees himself or herself. *Managing the Overseas Assignment* is the only film in the first series using professional actors. One of the greatest benefits of this segment is that it helps Americans recognize that some behaviors and attitudes may have a negative effect on the success of intercultural business encounters. For Americans, this is truly a case of "see yourself as others see you." Analysis by experts and expatriates builds validity for the concepts presented, and, combined with the presentation of alternative behaviors, these concepts are clarified and discussion stimulated.

Living in the USA and *Working in the USA* are accompanied by transcripts for those viewers whose aural English may not be sufficient to understand the films adequately. Providing the transcripts prior to viewing the films gives viewers a chance to become familiar with the content and concepts. Transcripts read or reread after seeing the films lead to understanding at a deeper level.

An extremely productive use of these two films is in programs designed to help American managers see and change their perceptions and expectations of employees and colleagues from other cultures. This objective can be achieved most effectively if representatives of other cultures participate openly and honestly in the discussion following the films. Since there are some cultures where one does not participate openly and honestly in this kind of discussion, it is important to talk with cultural informants to make sure your expectations are realistic before using this activity.

Valuing Diversity

History

Valuing Diversity is a seven-part film/video series produced by Copeland Griggs Productions. Developed in two stages, the first three films were produced in association with Price M. Cobbs and deal with issues of race, gender, and cultural differences in the increasingly multicultural American workplace. These earlier films, developed to help managers and employees perform and communicate more effectively with people different from themselves, address such issues as stereotypes and assumptions, cultural differences, unwritten rules and double standards, the "glass ceiling," the "white male club," mentoring and networking, communication styles and accents, and the stresses of being bicultural.

Overview

Part I, *Managing Differences*, presents through drama and interviews, examples of good and not-so-good ways of evaluating, developing, and motivating diverse employees. Part II, *Diversity at Work*, illustrates how stereotypes and differences affect employees' ability to succeed. Strategies for self-development, teamwork, and relationship building are portrayed. Part III, *Communicating across Cultures*, uses drama to show how misunderstandings result from different styles of communication. It also explores the discomfort people feel when dealing with issues of race and gender, suggesting alternative approaches to the communication process. Each part is approximately thirty minutes in length and is more broad than deep regarding specific diversity issues.

In the second stage, four additional films, released in early 1990, update and expand the Valuing Diversity series. These additional films, which can stand alone or be used in conjunction with the earlier ones, are directed more specifically at the members of the diverse workforce, the first-line supervisor, and those institutions implementing programs of change.

Part IV, *You Make the Difference*, designed for entry-level employees, shows the necessity for people to work well with those different from themselves. Issues, including stereotypes, teamwork, and cultural differences are presented in brief vignettes and interviews.

Part V, *Supervising Differences*, directed at the first-line supervisor, presents strategies for dealing with the issues of diversity and for creating an environment based on recognizing the values of a diverse workforce.

Parts VI and VII, *Champions of Diversity* and *Profiles in Change*, look at organizations that are instituting—or have instituted—programs of change to maximize their diverse human resources. In *Champions of Diversity*, senior executives discuss the benefits of diversity realized by their organizations and examine changes that have occurred both in the organizations and within themselves. *Profiles in Change* provides insight into the areas of effective recruitment, training, mentoring, and motivating in the culturally diverse workplace.

The seven-film Valuing Diversity series can be used as the core of a series of programs on diversity in the workplace. However, for learning to take place, the trainer or facilitator should be prepared to facilitate discussions, elicit ideas, and present additional materials. Useful information and ideas can be found in the leader's guide, which includes transcripts of the films, analysis of the issues, and suggestions for presentations and resources.

Procedures for Effective Use

Introducing the Topic of Diversity. When introducing the concept of diversity, a short discussion of demographic changes in the United States over the past several years and the relationship of these facts and figures to the projected changes in the workforce is an attention grabber. Pointing out the connection between the sensitive issues of complaints because of affirmative action and equal employment opportunity compliance personalizes the subject and assures attention. The best introductions also note the positive business reasons for addressing diversity. Documentation is provided in the Trainer's Guides for the increased productivity, profitability, and competitive edge resulting from working with diversity. The Epilogue in Volume 1 of the *Intercultural Sourcebook* provides empirical and anecdotal evidence supporting the positive relationship between valuing diversity and excellent individual, group, and organizational performance. Finally, balanced introductions present the work as good business practice and the right, correct, proper, and ethical thing to do.

Facilitating Discussions. The introduction and use of these videos require professional facilitation skills. Because the presentation of change (demographic) and negative consequential information (costs of discrimination) often evoke strong emotional reactions (anger, feelings of exclusion and fear, resistance to change, and latent prejudice), skilled leadership is necessary to help participants work through their feelings. Examples of reactions to introductory issues requiring facilitation include the following: Why are we spending money on this stuff? Why can't minorities just be American—like everyone else—and play by the rules we already have? Why do *we* have to change? Why are we diluting efforts to deal with racism and sexism by adding other differences to the list?

When the videos are used, one can either show an entire part and then discuss it or stop the film after one of the many excellent vignettes which demonstrate effective and ineffective behavior. Either of the above options, combined with either large or small group processing, is equally viable. Sample issues requiring facilitation frequently raised by participants during and after viewing the films include these:

- ❖ All_____(fill in with women, Asians, Hispanics, etc.) are not like that.
- ❖ Is there more than one effective way to handle that situation?
- ❖ What if I do the "wrong" thing?
- ❖ How do I figure out what is best for a specific person?
- ❖ How realistic was that?
- ❖ What if I really don't like people like that or just can't understand them?
- ❖ Do we have to lower our standards to have a diverse workforce?
- ❖ Isn't talking about differences just reinforcing stereotypes?

❖ Which differences are cultural and which are more related to personality?

Caution and multicultural competence are vital, because these issues carry high potential for misunderstanding and counterproductive responses. When processing these and other issues, activities like the following are suggested:

❖ Have participants develop alternative effective ways of handling situations portrayed in the films.

❖ Role-play events depicted in the videos.

❖ Ask participants to describe demographic changes (if any) that have taken place in their office, department, organization, community, and the like.

❖ Have participants project what their community, church, school, office, and so on, will look like one, five, and ten years from now.

❖ Describe several members of one particular cultural group with an emphasis on both similarities and differences within the group.

Context for Successful Use

The Valuing Diversity films are appropriate as training and development tools for use in management education/development, multicultural team building, equal opportunity/affirmative action programs, and training for communication skill building. They are extremely useful as staff meeting discussion material and can be used to set a context for human resources planning. These films can play an important role in all activities designed to create and sustain effective organizations with diverse populations.

Going International and Valuing Diversity

The technical quality of the films is excellent. In the Going International series, the use of experienced expatriate managers and their families supports the concepts and strategies provided by the experts. Together they lend credence to the information and ideas presented in the films.

In Part II—*Managing the Overseas Assignment*—and in the Valuing Diversity series, the acting is professional and situations portrayed are realistic. Women and people of color are shown in all except the most senior roles. People with different physical and mental ability levels and from different countries are also included.

A valuable feature of these films is the use of replays of poorly handled situations in order to present more appropriate and effective behaviors.

Important Considerations for Use

Relevance in Specific Geographic Areas

Because all the films are produced primarily for U.S.-based businesses and their employees, whether U.S.-born or foreign, they strongly reflect American culture. The Valuing Diversity films are relevant for businesses operating in the United States; in Canada the appropriateness is fair, and in Australia it is limited.

In Japan and in most of Europe the applicability and use are quite limited and probably not worth considering. Parts I, III, IV, and VII of Going International are designed specifically for use with the outward-bound U.S. employee and family but can be used with those from other cultures as an introduction to the values, behaviors, and attitudes of the United States.

Limitations and Pitfalls

The two Going International films for non-U.S. citizens (Parts V and VI), geared toward preparing international employees and families for living and working in the United States, are based on the point of view of American managers. The selection of situations which may be potentially difficult for a newcomer and the managers' perceptions of "what we wish they knew" misses the mark of what the foreigner really needs to know in order to adapt and function effectively.

In Valuing Diversity, the situations used in the videos are typical of American business. The language (vocabulary, style, and idioms) is also representative of U.S. business settings and may need some clarification when viewed by others such as educators and public servants.

In both series, the producers chose to cover a broad range of issues rather than go into depth on fewer issues. As a result, the presenter must provide the substance for in-depth explorations of most issues, and—as noted earlier—professional facilitation is necessary.

Commentary

In organizations dealing with both globalization and local diversity issues, a combination of these films is worth exploring. This is particularly true in North America and somewhat applicable in other places where the English language is frequently used. In countries where equality and social justice for women are not receiving much attention, the Valuing Diversity series might be viewed as unrealistic. On the other hand, contrasting it with the Going International series can help educate viewers about the variation in social justice for women worldwide. By introducing both series as focusing on diversity, local and global, learnings from each can be integrated by skillful facilitators.

Future Needs

The intercultural field needs generic films in the areas of global, national, cultural, racial, and ethnic diversity dealing with

- ❖ the increasingly global environment (in the educational, public, and private sectors);
- ❖ the issues of adaptation, adjustment, and effectiveness as experienced by those living and/or working with people who are different from themselves;
- ❖ the issues of and constraints on functioning effectively within major geographic or organizational boundaries; and
- ❖ cultural influence on communication and management styles and practices, on language patterns and thought processes, and on expectations for and perceptions of health care.

While some culture-specific and area-specific visual materials are available, most have been developed for the mass media and present only a visual impression of an area and its people or analysis of the obvious in cultural differences. Very few products developed for public consumption delve below the surface or touch on the hows and whys of intercultural interaction.

Distribution

Griggs Productions
5616 Geary Boulevard
San Francisco, CA 94121 USA
Phone: 415-668-4200
Fax: 415-668-6004
Provides user guides and seminars to enhance the competence of people using their products (cross-cultural films and videos).

As of this writing, the films are available on a two-tiered pricing system (non-profit and for-profit). Call or fax for details.

Resources

Copeland, Lennie, and Lewis Griggs. *Going International: How to Make Friends in the Global Marketplace.* New York: Random House, 1983.

Fowler, Sandra M., and Monica G. Mumford, eds. *Intercultural Sourcebook: Cross-Cultural Training Methods,* vol. I. Yarmouth, ME: Intercultural Press, 1995.

Summerfield, Ellen. *Crossing Cultures through Film.* Yarmouth, ME: Intercultural Press, 1993.

Thiagarajan, Sivasailam, and Barbara Steinwachs. *Barnga: A Simulation Game on Cultural Clashes.* Yarmouth, ME: Intercultural Press, 1990.

Sources of Diversity Videos

ABCNEWS
PO Box 51790
Livonia, MI 48151

Advantage Media
21601 Marilla Street
Chatsworth, CA 91311

AIDS Action Committee
131 Clarendon Street
Boston, MA 02116

AM Videos
One Hallidie Plaza, Suite 701
San Francisco, CA 94102

The American Management Association
135 West 50th Street
New York, NY 10020

AMI (American Media, Inc.)
4900 University
West Des Moines, IA 50266-6769

American Society for
  Training and Development
1640 King Street
Box 1443
Alexandria, VA 22313

Audio Graphics Training Systems
500 Gabbettville Road
LaGrange, GA 30240

Barr Films
1201 Schabarum Avenue
Box 7878
Irwindale, CA 91706-7878

Big World, Inc.
1350 Pine Street, Suite 5
Boulder, CO 80302

BNA Communications, Inc.
9439 Key West Avenue
Rockville, MD 20850

California Newsreel
630 Natona Street
San Francisco, CA 94103

Cambridge Documentary Films, Inc.
PO Box 385
Cambridge, MA 02139

The Carle Foundation
Carle Medical Communications
611 West Park
Urbana, IL 61801

Coronet/MTI Film and Video
108 Wilmot Road
Deerfield, IL 60015-9925

Crisp, Inc.
95 First Street
Los Altos, Ca 94022-9803

CRM Films
2233 Faraday Avenue
Carlsbad, CA 92008

Dartnell Corporation
4660 Ravenswood Avenue
Chicago, IL 60640

Films for the Humanities
PO Box 2053
Princeton, NJ 08543

Kay Poyner Brown Associates
5938 North Drake
Chicago, IL 60659

Kochman Communication
  Consultants, Ltd.
649 West Deming Place
Chicago, IL 60614

Menninger Management Institute
Menninger Foundation
5800 Southwest Sixth
Box 829
Topeka, KS 66606

MGD
3780 Kilroy Airport Way, Suite 200
Long Beach, CA 90806

Microtraining Associates
PO Box 641
North Amherst, MA 01059

MTI Film and Video
420 Academy Drive
Northbrook, IL 60062

PBS VIDEO
Public Broadcasting Service
1320 Braddock Place
Alexandria, VA 22314-1698

Professional EEO Consultants, Inc.
416 East Hennepin, Suite 3219
Minneapolis, MN 55414

Resolution, Inc./California Newsreel
149 Ninth Street
San Francisco, Ca 94103

RMI Media Productions
2807 West 47th Street
Shawnee Mission, KS 66205

Soup to Nuts Video Productions
41 Union Square, Suite 1023
New York, NY 10003

Stir-Fry Productions
1222 Preservation Park Way
Oakland, CA 94612

Sum Fun Productions, Inc.
1442 Camino del Mar, Suite 204
Del Mar, CA 92014

UNAPIX Entertainment
PO Box 4055
Santa Monica, CA 90411

United Training Media
6633 W. Howard Street
PO Box 48718
Niles, IL 60714-0718

Wellspring Media, Inc.
PO Box 2284
South Burlington, VT 05407-2284

Witcom
A Video Communications Company
55 Wheeler Street
Cambridge, MA 02138

The Working Group
1611 Telegraph Avenue, Suite 1550
Oakland, CA 94612

Cold Water: Intercultural Adjustment and Values Conflict of Foreign Students and Scholars

Louis M. Meucci and Noriko Ogami

History of *Cold Water*

Cold Water is a videocassette produced by Noriko Ogami, accompanied by the Facilitator's Guide by Louis M. Meucci. Ninety-two hours of on-camera interviews and background scenes with students were edited—cutting through to the essence and weaving a fast-moving, fascinating forty-eight-minute tapestry.

Ms. Ogami describes how she came to produce *Cold Water.*

> Like most foreign students who come to the United States, I experienced feelings of tension, frustration, and disorientation. It wasn't until I had been here over a year, however, when I realized that these feelings were part of culture shock.
>
> When I was studying television production at Boston University, especially during my first six months, I was too busy to stop and think about my adjustment process. Keeping up with all the readings and getting good grades were my top priorities. After all my hard work to come to the United States to study, I really wanted the experience to be successful. I had a lot to deal with, including language, schoolwork, culture, and personal issues. I tried very hard to fit in, but I felt somewhat overwhelmed. Remarkably, after a year went by, I came to feel quite happy about my adjustment. It was like a fog had slowly cleared up.
>
> Then I began working with the International Orientation Program. I met many other foreign students who were experiencing the same feelings that I had once felt. It was almost like looking into a mirror.

One of our orientation training techniques for helping students make cultural adjustments to life in the United States was to show and discuss videotapes. Unfortunately, most of these videos seemed artificial, and focused on negative issues. Some students became upset while watching them.

Right about that time, I was looking for a suitable topic for my thesis project. It was a degree requirement and had to be a significant piece of work. I decided, with the encouragement of Mr. Meucci, my orientation supervisor, to make a videotape exploring the intercultural adjustment process in a manner which educated in a positive way. I wanted new foreign students to realize their adjustment was a normal process. And I wanted foreign student advisers, American professors, American students, and American host families to understand the process that foreign students go through.

The title came to me much later, during a student interview, when Tina Lang, from Germany, told me that coming to the United States was, for her, like jumping into cold water.

How *Cold Water* Is Unique

The aim of *Cold Water* is to generate lively discussion, not to provide answers or solutions. It avoids the preachy mode of "don't do this, don't do that" that Ms. Ogami found in other intercultural videos she viewed. She used real people telling their real, personal experiences. There were no scripts and no rehearsals. This approach adds an authentic sincerity and freshness. Ms. Ogami did all the research, producing, directing, interviewing, and editing herself.

Goals of the Video

The main goals *of Cold Water* are to describe the intercultural adjustment process and to explain how a number of core American values conflict with foreign values and cause misunderstandings. It examines the key areas of stress during intercultural adjustment. Facilitators using the video should elicit from their particular groups whatever solutions to the problems identified are appropriate in their context.

Another goal is to let people, frustrated by the adjustment to a new culture, know that they are not alone; that they are experiencing a normal, somewhat predictable, and universal process of change. Finally, *Cold Water* is intended to inform and sensitize various people (foreign student advisers; American host families; university administrators; Americans in education, business, and community contexts) to what foreign visitors experience and why they react to life in the United States in certain ways.

The Research and Production Process

Cold Water took about eighteen months to produce: conducting the research, planning for the production, enlisting and videotaping interviewees, making transcripts of each taped interview, and finally editing. For almost a year before she actually interviewed the subjects, Ms. Ogami did extensive reading, reviewed other relevant videocassettes, and conducted interviews with professionals to familiarize herself with the fields of international education and intercultural training. She gained valuable experience working as an international orientation leader for Mr. Meucci at Boston University's International Students and Scholars Office. In that capacity, she played a key role in designing, implementing, and evaluating an extensive orientation program (60 events over a six-week time span) for about 1,000 students from almost 100 countries.

After the research was complete, interviews began. Interviews were between 30 and 120 minutes long. First Ms. Ogami interviewed 100 people without a camera. Then she did a second interview with 50 of the original 100, again without camera. Next she interviewed on-camera 30 people from those 50. After that, she did second on-camera interviews with the final 13 students and 3 professionals. In addition, she filmed extensive background scenes of orientation activities and landscapes, accumulating a total of 92 hours of videotaped material.

Suggestions for Using *Cold Water*

The Facilitator's Guide

Accompanying each copy of *Cold Water* is a Facilitator's Guide, which offers clear, concise recommendations. It provides suggestions for optimizing use, expanding potential applications and audiences, and a summary of the contents and timing of the videocassette.

Timing Presentations

The total viewing time of *Cold Water* is 48 minutes. It contains so many emotional and thought-provoking personal observations that it is better to view and discuss the video in sections, rather than in one continuous viewing.

With a sixty-minute session, rather than showing the entire video, it might be more productive to select and view only the segments most relevant to achieving your goals for that session, then discuss the issues involved at greater length.

If you are using the video with an English as a foreign language group with minimal or medium levels of English, we recommend that you present it in 10–15 minute segments, stopping to clarify and discuss each one before moving on.

A number of *Cold Water* facilitators have suggested using the following segments in a session of fewer than sixty minutes:

1. Start from the beginning and continue through the intercultural adjustment segment (which ends at 13:30 minutes).

2. Advance to the closing segment (beginning with the scene of sailboats on the Charles River, at 41:25 minutes) and view to the end. This makes a total viewing time of about 20 minutes, leaving the remaining time for discussion.

A Chronology of the Contents

Cold Water divides easily into four sections.

The first section is two minutes of introduction, including a logo (designed by Ms. Ogami), titles, and opening quotes from students.

The second section is eleven minutes specifically about the intercultural adjustment process, interweaving quotes from students and professionals.

The third and longest section, about values conflict, is twenty-eight minutes. The areas of conflict and confusion most commonly mentioned by the interviewees are

❖ openness and directness

❖ privacy

❖ time management

❖ Americans' lack of knowledge about world geography

❖ language versus communication (in the context of a Burger King story)

❖ finding an apartment

❖ how Americans greet each other

❖ Americans' superficiality in friendships

❖ appropriate classroom behavior, competitiveness, and respect for authority

The last section is three minutes of closure, covering advice to new students: how to ask for help and how the students feel once they have adjusted.

Facilitating the Discussion

The students and professors interviewed on film speak frankly about their own impressions of America and Americans. Be prepared to deal with some Americans who personalize the comments and become defensive. This defensiveness can turn into an excuse to deny the meaningfulness of the video's content. Those interviewed in the video are drawing conclusions based on their own experiences. Their views are not presented as "facts" applicable to all Americans. They are presented to record these experiences and thereby generate discussion which can make the intercultural adjustment process more understandable to others.

It is preferable to show *Cold Water* when there is ample time to process it. The video is designed to generate discussion, not necessarily to provide answers. It has a high concentration of data, challenges basic assumptions and expectations, and deals honestly with emotion-charged issues and values. You need to allow time for the audience to express their reactions, seek clarification, challenge, ask for additional information on special points of interest, and leave with a feeling of closure. Use the Facilitator's Guide to select an appropriate time frame and format that allow ample discussion.

Keep in mind that the people speaking in the video are honestly sharing their experiences in realistic terms. When Ms. Ogami interviewed the students, she asked open-ended questions, yet they uniformly focused their responses on the more difficult aspects of adjustment.

In your discussions of conflicting values, the goal is for people to understand, articulate, and accept differences without being judgmental.

The discussion is just as important a part of your presentation as the video itself. That is when you will have the opportunity to customize the video content to your particular context. One of the best ways to stimulate discussion is to mix the audience; for example, a mix of new and continuing students, a mix of Americans and internationals, or a mix of students and staff. Another approach that works well is a panel presentation. Have an international student panel and an American student panel react to the video and to specific questions from you. After the panel presentation, open the discussion to the entire audience.

Overview of the Students and Professionals in *Cold Water*

Students

The thirteen students finally selected to be in the video were chosen because they were able to articulate their experiences, because they represented a wide range of countries, continents, and cultures, and because their experiences were representative of all the students interviewed. One of the students is American.

Professionals

Dr. L. Robert Kohls (see "About the Authors," page 361).

Dr. Oliva Espin, during the filming of *Cold Water*, was assistant professor in the Counseling Psychology Program of the Boston Univeristy School of Education. Dr. Espin was born in Cuba and has lived in the United States for almost thirty years. Espin is currently associate professor in the Counseling Psychology Program at Tufts University.

Noriko Ogami (see "About the Authors," page 361).

Louis M. Meucci (see "About the Authors," page 361).

Contexts in Which *Cold Water* Has Been Used Successfully

Most frequently *Cold Water* is used in educational (campus- and community-based) contexts. Yet many users realize it is as applicable to the business world as it is to the educational world. In both situations people experience basically the same process as they adjust to another country, culture, and language. Many of the professor/student experiences in the video are analogous to manager/employee relationships. Classroom anecdotes have many similarities in business.

Possible Uses

❖ all university students (American and international)
❖ professional associations, such as those for student unions, housing, support staff, and so on
❖ resident adviser training
❖ workshops for residents in dorms with international students
❖ predeparture orientation for those preparing to study or work in another country
❖ training/orientation for faculty, teachers, and academic advisers

❖ training of American and international teaching assistants

❖ English as a foreign language programs: workshops for teachers, administrators, support staff, and students

❖ refugee orientation (if language capacity is adequate)

❖ workshops for administrators who deal with international students: residence life, comptroller, registrar, and the like

❖ orientation leader training

❖ training for foreign student advisers, their supervisors (dean of students, director of counseling, and so forth), and their support staff

❖ training international host and/or homestay families

❖ classes in psychology, sociology, education, international relations, counseling, communications, history, and American culture

❖ community or church groups which have outreach/support networks for international students

Cold Water is obtainable from Intercultural Press, PO Box 700, Yarmouth, ME 04096; phone 800-370-2665.

Small Group Exercises as Intercultural Training Tools

Sandra M. Fowler and Monica G. Mumford

Without small group exercises, intercultural trainers oriented toward participative, experiential training would find their training tool kits rather empty. People who do a lot of training fill these kits with a variety of small group exercises they have designed, because they are effective training tools. These exercises are especially useful for cross-cultural training, since they give people a chance to practice behaviors that will work well in other cultures and help them understand conceptual frameworks for these new ways of behaving.

Description of the Method

Trying to imagine the earliest small group exercises can lead to some interesting conjecture. Perhaps the history of small group training dates back to the cohort groups of adolescent African boys, who—following their circumcision ceremony—were taught to hunt and dance by their tribal elders in the Great Rift Valley or Olduvai Gorge at the dawn of human history. Fortunately for training program participants today, surgery is not a necessary precursor; however, you can generate a trace of the bonding experience and mutual support by skillfully using small group exercises.

Definition

With such a wide variety of small group exercises being used in the training world today, it is difficult to construct a definition that encompasses them all. It helps to recognize that both parts of the term (*small group* and *exercise*) are important. A small group exercise engages the group in an interactive and structured way. The exercise acts as a focus for the group to be able to make decisions, solve problems, analyze situations, generate ideas, clarify issues, build commitment, reach consensus, or prioritize their immediate concerns. That is by no means an exhaustive list, but it describes the kinds of activities that can take place in a small group exercise.

It is far easier to say what such exercises are not, rather than what they are. Whatever we say is common to them all, someone, somewhere will know of an exception. Taking that risk, we would identify three basic characteristics of successful small group exercises:

❖ A focused activity takes place in a group.

❖ Both content and process are considered acceptable matters for discussion.

❖ Synergistic results are intended; that is, the group outcome is greater than the participants could have achieved individually.

One of the best ways of deciding whether you are running a small group exercise or something else is to look at the core of the activity. For example, when you put participants into small groups to go out in the community to observe nonverbal interaction patterns between people of different cultures, are you doing a small group exercise? The answer, of course, is no, you are doing a field trip. If participants are reading a case study or a critical incident or participating in a role play, then the method you are using is a case study or a critical incident or a role play, even when you have divided them into small groups for the activity or for debriefing. Dividing people into small groups for educational and training purposes is a *technique* (any systematic procedure by which a complex task is accomplished) usable in a vast range of training methods. It does not itself constitute a small group exercise. Another way of defining a small group exercise is by a process of elimination: when there is no identifiable core training method, the activity is likely a small group exercise.

One of the most common confusions arises out of mistakenly equating small group exercises with simulation games. Legitimately, to be a simulation game, the training activity must have both simulation and game elements. It is easier to make a case for a small group exercise being a simulation than for it being a game. Both relate to or attempt to "simulate" an aspect of the real world—the simulation game simply does it for larger, more complex processes or systems. After all, almost anything that happens in a classroom or workshop is somehow analogous to something in the outside world.

The comparison falls down, however, where "game" is concerned. Barbara Steinwachs, drawing on ideas from Pierre Corbeil, Stewart Brand, Allan Feldt, and others suggests that to be a game, an exercise must have some of the following: a scenario, ritual, suspense, constraints and/or rules, personal risk taking, accounting or scoring, challenge, visible—and possibly striking—feedback, keen competition, artifacts, roles, wit, activities (steps of play), an underlying model, choices of strategy, the thrill of victory, and the agony of defeat.

Small group exercises do not have to have any of the above, although they are likely to have at least a few. Blohm (1990) says that "there are many other teaching/training activities that are neither simulations nor games. Rather they are structured learning experiences with specific purposes which involve participants actively without simulating or having essential game elements" (1). She refers to them as "exercises, activities, and structured experiences."

At this point you may be asking, what is an example of a learning activity that has only a few of the simulation game elements but not enough to be called a simulation game, so it must be a small group exercise? Let us return to our three defining characteristics and use as an example one that most trainers are familiar with: the survival exercise, where participants have landed on the moon, in a desert, in a jungle, or in the Arctic and have a list of survival items they must prioritize. This *focused activity* is often done in *small groups*, sometimes after people have prioritized the list individually, so that you can ask them to contrast their outcome with that of a like-minded group. Both *content* (the prioritized lists) and *process* (how they worked together and their performance contrasted with other groups) are points of discussion. The *group outcomes* when compared with recommendations by survival experts are almost always better than what the individuals produced by themselves.

Another exercise of the same genre is the lifeboat exercise in which people of different backgrounds and capabilities are in a lifeboat that will sink if everyone remains in the boat. This can be done with people taking the designated roles, which makes it a role play-like small group exercise, but not a role play per se. The key element in this exercise is not the way people function in the roles (the essence of a role play), but the group decision-making process that results in someone being pushed overboard.

Conceptual Foundations

It is important to keep several concepts in mind when you are designing and facilitating small group work. The ideas discussed below are adapted from Low and Bridger (in Smith and Farrell 1979, 85–88). They are important because they deal with some of the special aspects of life in small groups.

❖ While groups consist of individuals, the group itself is an entity with its own identifiable culture; in other words, a group is more than the sum of its parts. Individuals bring many things to a group, among them, the need to learn, adapt, and resist. The group develops its own life and its own tensions, trying to balance growing and changing with resisting change and avoiding work. Groups will strive for both stability and movement. It is important for you to keep this in mind, since a group's culture affects its output.

❖ Group culture is not always predictable just by knowing the individuals who compose it. However, you can predict that the group culture will form rapidly—the less time the group has to work together, the quicker its culture becomes apparent, since it cannot take the time to evolve slowly. It can appear full-blown, and one of the first indications is when the group questions your instructions, limits, or constraints. One of the most effective ways to deal with group culture is to trust the group and, to the extent possible, remain open and accessible to the group's ideas.

❖ Participants find a trainer helpful for drawing lessons from the shared experience in the small group. For example, you can help participants relate these lessons to a conceptual framework and apply the lessons to the real world. Even though a small group may seem to be an artificial, temporary system, learning can take place without the constraints and pressures normally present in the everyday world. Learning from both the content and process in a safe environment can encourage trainees to transfer new ways of viewing and solving problems from the small group to the real world.

❖ Individuals and the group can simultaneously deal with matters of content and process. Tasks (content) are valuable vehicles for learning about internal dynamics (process). Small group work offers an opportunity to develop awareness of the group process and its relationship to the content. Your role is to facilitate the dual learning.

❖ It is possible for individuals to modify behavior through lessons learned during group experiences; however, the learning is particular to each individual, as is any modification of behavior. Your responsibility is to find the right way to assist this learning.

❖ It is important to understand the influence of any hidden agendas or of what is not being expressed. It can be a key to understanding what *is* happening in a group. With your help, a group can create an environment of trust and a capacity to explore hidden agendas that impede learning.

❖ There is an opportunity for feedback skills to be improved in small group work. In particular, you can help trainees see that nonjudgmental observations are more effective and useful than judgments or evaluations.

These dynamics are implicit in any small group work. It is better to recognize and deal with them than to ignore them and pay the price of dissatisfied trainees and lost learning.

Types of Small Group Exercises

Small group exercises can be categorized by where they appear in the training program.

Opening exercises (icebreakers) are often small group exercises. University Associates' *The Encyclopedia of Icebreakers* (Forbess-Greene 1983) describes six types according to the primary function of the activity: energizers and tension reducers, feedback and disclosure, games and brainteasers, getting acquainted, openers and warm-ups, and professional development (1).

Instructional or training activities. Small group exercises can provide information, teach skills, and influence attitudes to meet the goals and purposes of a training program. They are a good way to present core course material. Participants' understanding is maximized when they have to work with the material they are expected to learn. These exercises provide the opportunity to work with the models, concepts, and behaviors and to practice using them. Exercises in this category focus on specific themes commonly encountered in organizational life, for example, problem solving, leadership, or stress management.

Closing exercises. A small group exercise can help make your training unforgettable. Mel Silberman (1995) says that "one of the surest ways to make training 'stick' is to allow time for participants to review material that has been learned. In fact, material that has been reviewed by participants is five times as likely to be retained as material that has not. Reviewing allows participants to 'save' the information in their brains" (241). He describes an array of strategies, including a number that make reviewing fun. If you believe in participative training, Silberman's book *101 Ways to Make Training Active* (1995) needs to be on your bookshelf.

Benefits and Outcomes

An intriguing question confronts intercultural trainers: does the value of small group exercises lie in creating an experience that can result in participants looking at themselves, their culture, and their relationships and interactions from a new perspective, or does the value lie in providing a way for participants to learn new skills and procedures useful for interacting with people from other cultures? Of course, these two outcomes could, and probably in most cases do, overlap. An answer is proposed by B. Babington Smith (Smith and Farrell 1979):

> It is not clear that the two approaches are divergent, representing two distinct routes for making progress, or whether each is incomplete in the sense that concentration on either would in the long run reveal how necessary the other was becoming. For, if a changed outlook be regarded as an end product, the question remains open as to what are the practical effects of such a change. When, however, emphasis is on learning new techniques for interaction with other people, behavioural changes can turn out to be no more than rituals, with no basis of understanding or, in the worst case, to be ploys deliberately adopted by someone who has concealed aims of his [or her] own. The implication is that change of outlook and change of behaviour must develop together (127).

From our years of training experience, we feel that the beauty of a well-designed small group exercise is that it encourages both types of learning.

Involvement. Probably the most frequently cited reason for using small groups is that this is the only way some participants will ever say anything during the entire training program. The smaller the group, the more likely the shy person will say something. That brings up the issue of whether a pair is a small group. You may want to create pairs in some training sessions. And yes, a pair is a small group, just as a triad is a small group. They are special small groups and offer interesting alternatives in training designs. It is easy to combine pairs to increase the size of the small group when you want to take the discussion to the next level. Pairing has another advantage. Participants who are angry or upset about some aspect of the training and who may not bring it up in the large group or with you will often use their partner as a sounding board for their discomfort. Pairing up might be the only way you can give those persons an outlet for their feelings.

Customizing. Small group exercises can be customized easily to fit your situation and the needs of your client precisely. Most of these exercises are designed specifically for a particular client, a program, or a group rather than coming off the shelf.

Energizing. A small group exercise is an excellent energizer after a break or a series of presentations, or during a lull. There is nothing more satisfying to a trainer than the heady feeling when you have set up a small group exercise well and the room bursts into myriad conversations. The energy bounces off the walls.

Considerations and Helpful Hints for Using Small Group Exercises

With a lot of experience, you develop almost a sixth sense about small group exercises—how to design, run, and recover when things go awry. Here are several tips for maximizing your success. Our list is not exhaustive, but we think these are among the most important things to know.

Consider the culture. Taking into consideration that training is not done the same way around the world, you need to select carefully the small group exercise that fits not only your content but also the cultural assumptions of your audience. The level of impact and degree of intensity varies significantly among different exercises. Cultures with expectations that teaching is done by lecture will be less inclined to respond positively to active, participative learning strategies. In these situations, you need to develop trust and begin by selecting the least threatening exercises in your repertoire.

Watch the time. Small group exercises, like any participative method, take time. In fact, since much small group work is learning by discovery, an exercise can be quite time-consuming, because no one can tell how long it will take to make the discovery.

It is especially important to start on time. This sends a message that you are serious about the schedule. One strategy to get people into their seats at the beginning of the day or after a break is to use a minilecture or story to reward the punctual. Tim Dalmau, an Australian trainer, uses unusual stories that he says are for the "third eye" (the inner eye that sees elusive messages). The stories are so intriguing, participants find they do not want to miss them. You can also start with short warm-ups like a massage circle (where everyone rubs the back of the person on the right) that participants soon learn they do not want to miss.

Plan your instructions. Another thing that can waste time is not giving clear instructions before starting an exercise. Complicated instructions should always be in writing; simple ones are best mapped on newsprint or an overhead projection. Do not start an activity if you sense any confusion among participants about what they are being asked to do. Trying to introduce something new without adequate preparation is inefficient. Even with excellent preparation, implementing the instructions may prove too hard or complicated for the trainees. When you sense this, you can have them go through the procedure as a dry run, then go through a planning process of their own and repeat the activity. Planning and repetition can develop the expertise needed to apply a skill in a fresh situation.

Expedite reporting out. Very often at the end of an activity you want the small groups to report the essence of their discussion to the large group. Keep in mind ways for facilitating this report. Having insights, conclusions, recommendations, and the like presented visually helps. You can also ask for one idea at a time so that the next group will not repeat a point already made. Norma McCaig, in her chapter in this section of the *Sourcebook*, describes a technique taught to her by

L. Robert Kohls called "traveling newsprint" (see page 165). This technique can also save time during the report-out session, since participants will have been reading each other's ideas throughout the exercise. That way they are already familiar with the contributions of each group. In any case, do not let reports go on too long. Remind people how much time is left and how many people will have an opportunity to speak if contributions are kept short.

Create interesting ways to form groups. Counting off by the number is a popular American technique for creating small groups, but if you try it with other cultures, you may find unexpected resistance. Marvina Shilling, who does a lot of training for French companies, cautions that the French do not learn to count off at an early age. You can either take the additional time to teach them or you can form the groups yourself by suggesting that "these people in front can be one group, those over there are a second group, and the ones back there form a third group." This casual, directive style works well in cultures where trainers are seen more as teachers than as facilitators.

Even trainers training in the United States find counting off gets boring after awhile. Silberman (1995) has many creative suggestions for forming groups (23–24). For instance, he suggests using six-piece children's jigsaw puzzles (or make your own), and when you are ready to form groups, give each participant a puzzle piece and tell each person to locate other group members by completing their puzzle. He says you can also create "families" by using famous people or fictional characters. For example, Peter Pan, Tinkerbell, Captain Hook, Wendy, and the Crocodile form a family. Put one of these names on an index card in the participant's packet and when you need to form groups, ask participants to find the other members of their family. Colored dots will do, if you do not want to use families.

Hone your facilitator skills. Possessing developed facilitator skills is important no matter what method you are using, but it is essential with small group exercises. Remember that your goal is to smooth the way for ideas to flow easily. One thing to avoid is the appearance that you are looking for the *right* answers. However, when you are pressed for time, you may find that you have to lead and direct the discussion more than you would normally.

It is best not to tell participants what they should have learned. In any case, they will only learn what they were ready to learn, not what you think they should. Remember the basic interventions of a good facilitator: paraphrase, elaborate, clarify, give examples, energize, affirm, and summarize. You can do those things yourself or ask the group to "summarize where we are now," "elaborate on that last point," or "give an example."

Situations in Which Small Group Exercises Can Be Used

To explore situations where small group exercises might be used, let us look at the sample exercises included in this section of the *Intercultural Sourcebook*.

Paul Pedersen's Draw A House makes a good icebreaker. It is short, zippy, and piques participants' interest in what will happen next. The partners will get to know each other, and getting acquainted is often one purpose of an icebreaker. It is also a good exercise to use after lunch when people are apt to be sleepy. They will not fall asleep in the middle of this exercise! It can be used with all ages; it works as well with corporate executives as with family members. Pedersen's other exercise, The Outside Expert, can be used at the beginning of a training program, but it is not an icebreaker as such. It has more content and is more complicated than Draw A House. It would be useful in any situation where communication is an issue.

Piglish, described by Cay Hartley and Terri Lapinsky, was designed to help teachers, host families, and foreign students analyze what happens when people begin to learn and actually communicate in a new language. This exercise allows participants to explore the dependency relationship between the learner and helper and to examine other emotional and psychological aspects of language learning. People who are in the process of learning a language are already experiencing these firsthand and do not need Piglish to create the feelings, so this exercise works best with people who are preparing to learn a language or who are dealing with someone who is. The exercise is always done in small groups, which makes the point that language learning in a supportive group is one of the best ways of going about it.

The small group exercises described by L. Robert Kohls are "frame" exercises. The frames, or frameworks, they provide can accommodate a variety of content, making them useful in many different kinds of cross-cultural training programs. For example, the Consensus exercise focuses on confronting stereotypes and prejudices, but the content can be altered to focus instead on ethnocentrism, culture shock, cultural baggage, or a variety of other topics. Every trainer needs some frame exercises and Kohls' frames are favorites. Since the content is so customized, frame exercises can fit almost any training program. In the beginning of his chapter, Kohls provides more details about where small group exercises can be used.

The Malonarian exercise described by McCaig gives participants some of the experience of a field trip without leaving the room. This small group exercise incorporates both role play and simulation elements within its structure. The exercise can be conducted with colorful trappings that add to its interest or in a more streamlined version which requires fewer props and is somewhat easier to set up.

Conclusion

We know that the experience of merely being part of a small group is not enough. Our trainees must be clear that the small group experience is only the start of the learning process. It is up to them to make good use of what has begun in the small group. As with anything new, they need to practice, practice, practice.

There is reasonable evidence that all trainers need a wide variety of small group exercises in their tool kits. Sivasailam Thiagarajan, a trainer highly skilled in the use of small group exercises, uses his Web page to remark on the strong, silent revolution taking place in corporate training. The revolution he is referring to is the use of experiential methods, and if he is correct, small group exercises are in the vanguard of the movement.

References

Blohm, Judith. *Some Thoughts on Using Activities and Games in Cross-Cultural Training.* Unpublished presentation to SIETAR Washington Metro Group, December, 1995; material from 1990.

Forbess-Greene, Sue. *The Encyclopedia of Icebreakers.* San Diego: Applied Skills Press, 1983.

Silberman, Mel. *101 Ways to Make Training Active.* San Diego: Pfeiffer & Company, 1995.

Smith, B. Babington, and B. A. Farrell. *Training in Small Groups: A Study of Five Methods.* Oxford: Pergamon Press, 1979.

Thiagarajan, Sivasailam. www.Thiagi.com

Identifying Culturally Learned Patterns: Two Exercises that Help

Paul B. Pedersen

Culture influences the patterns of behavior we use to react to each different situation. Before we can understand and predict a person's (or our own) behavior in a cultural context we need to recognize the relevant patterns. Most exercises and structured experiences are attempts to help people learn behavior patterns in one way or another. The two exercises being described here demonstrate several such patterns as examples so that participants can better identify other patterns in themselves and those around them.

Exercise 1

Draw A House

I learned this exercise from a trainer at the German Foundation for International Development at Bad Honnef, Germany. She introduced it as a simple and frequently used warm-up exercise among German and European trainers—although I have not seen it widely used either in Europe or in the United States. I have also found it to be more useful than just a warm-up exercise, even though it does function well in that capacity. I have found the exercise valuable in marriage or relationship counseling and in a variety of settings where persons who might otherwise disagree can be persuaded to cooperate.

Objectives

- ❖ Demonstrate situational leader and follower patterns
- ❖ Demonstrate situational relationship and task orientation patterns
- ❖ Report patterns of the participant's own personal cultural orientation

The learning objective for the exercise is to learn how cultural differences are displayed in situational patterns of behavior.

Procedure

Participants are asked to select a partner as culturally different from themselves as possible. A single sheet of paper and one pen or pencil is distributed to each two-person team. The team is warned that the only difficult aspect of this exercise will be that they will not be allowed to talk out loud to one another during it. They are then told again that the "no talking rule" will be difficult to observe but is very important to the successful outcome of the exercise.

Next, the two persons are asked to hold on to the same pen or pencil at the same time and, *without talking*, cooperatively draw a house on the paper. Others have adapted this exercise by asking participants to draw a Chinese house or an object from whatever culture is appropriate for the workshop or training program. By keeping it simple the results will be easier to interpret and the focus will be clear.

After about two or three minutes ask the participants to stop and show their drawing of the house to those around them. You may want to collect the papers, but sometimes participants become quite possessive about their house. There is usually a lot of talk with one another about their house, so you may have to wait a minute or two before going on.

When you have the group's attention again, you might want to suggest that the houses offer several examples of culturally learned patterns. You may also want to emphasize that this is not a sophisticated measure of their inner thoughts. Such extraneous variables as who owned the pencil or pen being used or whose hand was at the bottom of the pen or pencil will influence what was drawn and how.

Context for Use and Interpretation

Usually three kinds of houses are drawn. The first kind of house looks like a house any primary-school child would draw. I point out that the influence of our primary-school teachers is often more profound than we realize. This might suggest that either both persons saw the house in the same way from the same perspective or that one person drew the house and the other person was a hitchhiker.

The second kind of house looks like two houses that do not quite fit together. When you see this, it is very likely that somewhere in the middle of the exercise the person drawing the house began to feel guilty for taking control. Then most often he or she will let the other person finish drawing the house as the other person chooses.

The third kind of house does not look like a house at all but rather like an aimless wandering of the pen or pencil without any obvious image. In that case, it may be that either both persons were trying so hard to help one another that neither one would take control or else that both were competing so hard that neither would give up control. There was an incident where a British civil servant and a Pacific Island chief did the exercise and became so angry in their competition that they tore the paper in half, left the room, and did not return.

The way two people work together to accomplish the goal of drawing a house demonstrates two behavioral patterns: a relationship-oriented pattern, where the person seeks to facilitate the partner's agenda (whatever that might be), and a task-oriented pattern, where the primary objective is to draw a very nice house. If a participant has not already mentioned it, I point out that the dominant culture in the United States is so typically task oriented that even a task with no consequences, such as drawing a house, is likely to become more important than facilitating a relationship with one's partner, though the relationship may have much more profound consequences than accomplishing the goal.

I ask participants to ask themselves whether they were more relationship oriented or task oriented in the exercise and—more important—whether that is a cultural pattern evident in their interactions with others outside the training setting. The goal is not to change the participants' pattern, whatever it might be, but to help them become more aware of the patterns that control their lives.

The cultural patterns in real-life responses are of course situationally specific for each cultural group. The discussion should focus on examples of how two cultures might not share the same culturally conditioned expectations in the same situation. In some cases cultural differences may facilitate interaction, as in a work team, where one member favors the leader role and the other favors a follower role. In other cases cultural differences will present problems, as in a work team where one member favors relationships and the other favors task accomplishment.

Problems or Pitfalls to Be Aware of in Using This Exercise

A problem might arise because of the intensity of the exercise, such as could be seen in the occasion when the civil servant and the Pacific Islander ripped up the paper and left the room. In marriage counseling the exercise can stimulate a discussion on relationship issues. The partners usually want some time to talk about the experience and their implicit agenda in working together.

Another indication of the intensity of the exercise is that immediately after drawing the house, the noise level usually increases to the point where the leader cannot be heard for a couple of minutes. This provides a useful opportunity for partners to discuss their interaction and any implicit agendas they had. I often ask each pair to hold up their picture for others to see. If they are sitting around a table where that is easily done, then the group members might want to talk about one another's drawings.

Occasionally you may find that a number of persons choose not to be matched with partners and elect not to participate in the drawing. I do not embarrass them by pressuring them to join in. I do try to make sure that everyone who does want to participate has an opportunity. Sometimes this means that I become one of the partners.

Questions may arise among participants with management training, comparing this exercise with the Blake and Mouton (1964) Managerial Grid, where the optimum profile is to be *both* high-relationship and high-task oriented. I usually suggest that this exercise is much more simplistic than the Managerial Grid, with a much more limited application which neither confirms nor contradicts the Blake and Mouton hypotheses.

Exercise 2

The Outside Expert

The second exercise I have found helpful allows participants to apply their knowledge of cultural patterns to an actual task situation. Having learned the importance of cultural patterns, they will now find an example helpful.

History

This exercise was generated at a workshop in Seattle where we needed something to accomplish some of the same purposes as *BaFá BaFá* but did not have the time to run the longer simulation. I had been working with trainees in my National Institutes of Mental Health-sponsored training project in Hawaii, "Developing Interculturally Skilled Counselors," and needed special behavioral norms or rules to develop synthetic cultures. In this workshop one of the leaders was from the Pacific region and suggested that three of the actual norms enforced by his culture might provide convenient examples of cultural rules. We proceeded to develop the exercise along the lines of these three rules.

Objectives

❖ Identify communication cues in an unfamiliar culture

❖ Gather information systematically from an unfamiliar culture

❖ Report ambiguities and stress factors from the interaction

The learning objective is to recognize how misunderstandings occur between the expert and the host culture.

It is sometimes difficult for outside experts to understand the information being provided by a host culture. Patterns of response that are obvious and consistent from the host culture's point of view can seem frustrating, inconsistent, uncooperative, and even hostile by the outside expert who does not know the host culture's rules.

Procedure

I request a male and female volunteer—who will be called "outside experts"—from the group. More volunteers are needed if the group is large. The best ratio is about two volunteers for every ten participants. I tell the group that I will ask the volunteers to step outside the room for about three minutes to prepare for their visit to the culture (which we set up with the group while they are gone). The volunteers then return and work individually in the group to collect as much information about the culture as possible, but they can only ask yes-and-no questions. After about five or ten minutes of collecting data, the volunteers are asked to report back individually to the other participants on what they have learned from their contact.

I suggest that these outside experts are well paid in thousands of dollars a day, so they should be conscientious in their investigation. After very little coaxing I usually get as many volunteers as I need to leave the room. When possible, I have a cotrainer go with the "experts" to answer questions about what they are to do. The cotrainer's answers are purposefully vague, telling them essentially that it is up to them to decide how they would like to gather their data.

While the volunteer outside experts are preparing for their visit, I instruct the remaining participants in the three rules of their new culture. These rules are as follows:

1. Participants may only respond "yes" or "no" to the outside experts' questions (which I have already told the outside experts before they left the room).

2. Men may only respond to men and women may only respond to women. Each person must ignore any question from an outside expert of the opposite gender.

3. If the expert is smiling when asking the question, the host culture person of the same gender will say "yes," but if the expert is not smiling when asking the question, then the same-gender host culture person will say "no," irrespective of the question's actual content.

When the experts return to the culture, I usually remind them to ask their questions in a yes/no format. The experts are free to roam the room individually and question as many host culture participants as possible. The experts are also encouraged to speak loudly enough so that most host culture participants can hear what is going on among all the question-and-answer exchanges. I discourage the experts from consulting with one another, since each person's perspective is likely to be slightly different.

After about ten minutes, ask the experts to come to the front of the room and report back on what they have learned regarding the host culture's problems and provide suggestions for solving them.

Typically the experts have generated elegant interpretations of their data based on the yes and no answers they have received. To encourage the experts as they individually report back on what they have learned, I often ask them: Were the host culture people friendly? Reasonable? Rational? Consistent? Good persons? Would the expert spend summer vacations in this culture given the opportunity?

When the experts have shared their observations, I thank them and lead a round of applause for their contribution. Then I disclose to the outside experts the second and third rules of the host culture and lead a discussion of what can be learned from the exercise.

Discussion

Be sure to ask both the outside experts and the culture members some questions. I like to start by asking the experts to reflect on their experience and tell us what they learned about entering another culture to gather data. The points I am looking for in the discussion are the importance of understanding a culture's rules before trying to collect information from it, emphasizing that inconsistencies may be in the outside expert (that is, whether he or she is smiling or not) rather than in the host culture, and the fact that messages sent may be quite different from messages received.

Also ask the experts about their feelings as they participated in this exercise. Often they experience the culture as inconsistent and hostile, even though members of it were attempting to be as helpful as possible within the limits of their rules. People who find the culture hostile tend not to smile much. People who smile a lot generally perceive the culture to be more friendly.

It is useful to ask members of the host culture if they think there was anything they could have done differently within the limits of the rules. How they were feeling is also worth discussing, since some are likely to feel stressed by their cultural constraints and others rather enjoyed being obtuse. You can help participants make connections between their feelings in this exercise and real-world situations and how they might deal with the feelings to be more effective.

LaRay Barna, an experienced intercultural trainer, has asked, "Why is it that contact with persons from other cultures so often is frustrating and fraught with misunderstanding?" She concludes that there are major stumbling blocks that are not easily circumvented present in most intercultural encounters. I have found Barna's (1985) five stumbling blocks or barriers useful in debriefing this exercise. I ask participants to consider each barrier and what impact it had on the outcomes of this exercise. The barriers are

❖ assuming similarity instead of difference,

❖ language,

❖ nonverbal misinterpretations,

❖ preconceptions and stereotypes, and

❖ tendency to evaluate.

Dr. Barna also describes the high anxiety that accompanies cross-cultural interactions and its effect as a barrier to communication. Anne Pedersen has developed the concept of organizational constraints that act as barriers, and this is also useful in debriefing the exercise.

Contexts in Which This Exercise Can Be Used

I have used this exercise at conferences, workshops, and as a small group warm-up exercise. I have also used it to develop a shared point of reference for cross-cultural training programs and in classes on multicultural counseling or communication. The exercise helps participants become aware of important assumptions in multicultural contact as well as gaps in their own cultural sensitivity. Typically it would be used following a series of other awareness exercises so that the participants have the opportunity to put insights they have gained into practice. I have never used this exercise by itself but always in a larger training context, so that the learning can be integrated with what has come before and what will come after.

The exercise can be used in a lecture presentation, but I have usually reserved it for groups of from ten to a hundred participants in a workshop or training setting. Banquet seating facilitates the success of the exercise and the ease of movement as experts circulate among the other participants.

Problems and Pitfalls to Be Avoided

The exercise needs to be approached seriously; otherwise, it may be treated as a parlor game that is fun but results in little learning.

The groups need to be prepared ahead of time to observe the success or failure of the experts in collecting data and, of course, to be thoroughly debriefed after the exercise.

The experts should not be made to feel set up more than necessary. One round of applause before they sit down and an opportunity to ventilate what they were feeling during and after the exercise are usually enough to prevent a negative reaction. Occasionally you have to continue to work with them at a later time—perhaps during a break—in order to allay lingering emotions.

Sometimes it is difficult to establish a lively discussion with the whole group. You can divide the large group into smaller groups of eight or ten to come up with a question, insight, or observation that can then be shared with the group as a whole. This turns the design of the discussion over to participants and works well to engage their interest and energy.

Be very clear about the three rules. Even then, there will always be some deviants who forget or defy them. In debriefing, I point out that this is also true in real life. Again, it is important to make your point and move on without overinterpreting the exercise.

Conclusion

By examining in the workshop setting what culturally learned patterns are and why they are important, it might be possible for participants to identify other culturally learned patterns in their life outside the workshop. To be able to be successful in intercultural encounters, you cannot take refuge in intellectual detachment, you must engage with behavioral patterns different from your own, become intimately familiar with them, and learn to work with and within them.

References

Barna, LaRay M. "Stumbling Blocks in Intercultural Communication." In *Intercultural Communication: A Reader*, 5th ed., edited by Larry Samovar and Richard Porter. Belmont, CA: Wadsworth Publishing, 1985.

Blake, Robert, and Jane Mouton. *The Managerial Grid.* Houston: Gulf, 1964.

Resources

The Draw A House exercise and the Outside Expert exercise are both described along with other similar exercises in Paul Pedersen, *A Handbook for Developing Multicultural Awareness.* Alexandria, VA: American Counseling Association, 1988.

Piglish: A Language Learning Simulation

Cay Hartley and Terri Lapinsky

"Language learning depends on the deeper reaches of the personalities of all those who are involved in the process" (Stevick 1976, 3). This statement accurately reflects our experience with some of the important components of language learning. From both sides of the equation, as language learners and as cross-cultural educators and trainers in the field of international education, we knew, for example, that the experience of foreign language learning is a catalyst for mutual (if fluctuating) dependency between the learner and those in the role of helper or teacher. The dilemma was how to help both teachers and learners achieve a perspective on the process that would enable the strong, positive aspects of their personalities to meet the challenges inherent in language learning. The answer was to develop Piglish, an exercise that simulates the process of learning a language.

Theoretical Background

While working for Youth For Understanding International Exchange (YFU), we found we needed not only to be able to distinguish between the intellectual and linguistic abilities of exchange students as learners but also to understand the emotional and personal characteristics of both the learner and the host family members, peers, and other teachers with whom the student interacts. The relationship of a nonnative speaker to peers and to those in authority became crucial to our assessment of that student's total academic, social, and linguistic adjustment.

According to Stevick (1976), one's readiness for interaction with another depends on expected consequences of the interaction. We saw evidence of this phenomenon in our students and often heard our host families lament the inconsistent communication produced by varying expectations. For example, the threat to a student's ego that language learning can produce may result in verbal aggression or withdrawal. Rudy and Lapinsky (1988) explored these behaviors in composite case studies of exchange students.

Since both language learners and helpers react defensively according to varying circumstances, it is particularly important for teachers and trainers to understand these ego defenses and why people use them. Stevick cites several psychodynamic principles of language learning, among which is the tendency for learning to slow down if the learner is busy "defending himself" from someone else.

In addition, Stevick describes studies implying that empathy and acceptance in language learning are likely to be related to one's sensitivity to others and to the existence of a positive relationship with foreigners early in one's life.

Charles Curran (1976) also contributed to our theoretical framework for developing materials on language learning. In his community language learning approach, Curran attempts to instill empathy and acceptance in both helpers and learners. His methods seek to cultivate an ability to provide greater security and independence for the learners. He does this by fostering the self-esteem and positive attitudes of all parties in the language learning process.

Background

This theoretical background and our practical experience combined to develop the training unit, Learning about Language, in which Piglish is the opening exercise. The overall unit goals are to increase understanding, self-awareness, and skills related to language learning and cross-cultural adjustment. One of the specific goals is to help our volunteers to "understand some of the relationships between language learning and adjustment in a new culture." This includes being able to identify feelings and problems that can occur during the process of learning a language.

Most of our U.S. volunteers were people without expertise in foreign language learning. Many had never traveled in non-English-speaking countries. New volunteers may not even have worked previously with foreign students. The numbers of U.S. students going abroad and the expanding exchanges between non-English-speaking countries created a pressing organization-wide need for a language learning unit. The developers of the unit decided that a climate-setting, language learning simulation would be the most effective and efficient training method to initiate the process.

We wanted something interactive and fun as well as instructive to begin a training workshop. We wanted the participants to begin to learn and actually communicate in a new language. Then we wanted them to analyze what happened to them, how they felt, and what they saw as challenges of the language learning process. Dan Edwards of Training Resources Group (TRG) conceived the idea of using a fairy tale context for the language simulation and wrote the first draft of the Piglish story. The vocabulary, grammar, and training methodology were tested with groups of volunteers and revised numerous times by YFU staff before the present version was finalized. The process questions have also been tested repeatedly and can be adapted to be relevant to a variety of training situations.

Procedure

Although language learners derive many benefits from participating in Piglish, the audience for this procedural description is language trainers.* Introduce the unit by telling participants that the exercise is designed to enable the participants to experience some of the feelings associated with learning a new language, and that understanding this process is an important step in being able to work with students as they try to cope with a new environment in a new language.

Then review "The Story of the Three Little Pigs" (Appendix A) and set participants to the task of learning the Piglish language. They are to learn enough of the language contained in the dictionary sheets (Appendix B) to be able to tell the story in Piglish. Examples of vocabulary in Piglish include the following: bricks = *baaba*; wolf = *groof*; chin = *chuga*. The past tense is formed by squatting down and the future by standing on your toes. Some frequently used sentences would be "Once upon a time" = *Uber squa snip-snip* (squatting down) and "Open the door" = *Uudle-uuh der puhbbb-ah*. Participants are encouraged to try out all methods of learning and to pay attention to their feelings as they work through the story with the dictionary sheets.

In small groups, the participants learn and tell a portion of "The Story of the Three Little Pigs" in Piglish. After the storytelling, the following questions may be used for discussion.

Small Group Process Questions

1. *What was the most difficult thing about learning to communicate in a new language?*

   This question builds empathy for the challenge of language learning.

2. *Describe the feelings you had while trying to speak and understand others.*

   This question elicits empathy for both parties in the language learning equation: speaking (in this case associated with learning) and understanding (in this case associated with helping).

3. *How were these feelings affecting your behavior?*

   This question promotes a deeper understanding of the roots of one's attitudes and actions toward nonnative speakers.

After the small groups have had time to discuss how the exercise went, the participants gather in a large group.

---

* A more extensive description of procedures is contained in "Piglish: A Language Learning Exercise," Judith Blohm, Cay Hartley, and Terri Lapinsky, *International Journal of Intercultural Relations* 19, no. 2 (Spring 1995).

Large Group Process Questions

These questions were designed specifically to counteract stereotypes and negative experiences we had heard from volunteers with respect to students who were struggling to learn the new language. Another objective was to demonstrate that, as Stevick says, "People tend to use over and over again the kinds of solutions that proved satisfactory in the past" (51).

1. *How did you learn the language?*

> Answering this question helps participants begin to analyze their learning styles and appreciate the legitimacy of different ones. It also allows them to see the impact and influence of prior learning experiences on new experiences.

2. *Were you more comfortable learning alone or in a group?*

> This is asked to provoke some discussion on how interpersonal styles and relationships as well as learning styles can affect one's comfort level and effectiveness in a group.

3. *How many of you used some English or other foreign language words or pronunciations while trying to tell the story?*

> This question reminds people that it is common to fall back on prior knowledge and familiar strategies when learning something new. In fact, such methods can facilitate foreign language learning even though they are sometimes viewed negatively or misunderstood by the native speaker.

4. *What were some examples of the feelings derived from this exercise that were identified in your small group?*

> This question should help bring out the commonality of the language learning experience. It helps prevent blaming a student (or oneself) for insufficient language skills.

5. *How did these feelings affect your individual and group behavior?*

> This question points out how attitudes affect the helper's behavior toward the student as well as the student's own behavior.

6. *How did it feel to be called on or to have to perform?*

> This should help elicit empathy for the highs and lows, the exhilaration and humiliation of language learning.

After the group discusses these points, you can share the observations you noted during the language learning period. Relate your observations to the discussion and reinforce the learning.

Finally, elicit a process-oriented conclusion from participants by using the questions below.

7. *How does it feel to communicate with a student who has limited English proficiency?*

8. *What might happen if that young adult can only communicate at a five-year-old level?*

9. *What is the impact of dealing with a student each day who appears extremely dependent on you as an interpreter?*

> These questions show the direct relevance of the simulation to the participants' work with exchange students. The three questions try to get participants to understand their own reactions to students with limited target language proficiency and to empathize with the students' frustration and with the challenge these students present to their host families and school personnel.

Alternative Procedures

When time is limited, the procedures may be shortened to decrease the total amount of time needed for this simulation or to emphasize certain points. For example, the story might be told in pairs or in the large group or studied in pairs or small groups—each participant or small group may be given only a few lines to recite in Piglish. The process questions can also be modified to emphasize certain points or to fit the particular needs of the participant/client group. On occasion, we have changed the process questions to reflect an emphasis on the interaction between participants and how they worked together (or did not!) to learn Piglish.

For participant groups when there were distinct subgroups—such as families that could easily be compared with one another—we have focused attention on the differences in how the groups worked. In this kind of instance, the final questions related to the roles taken in the groups, to feelings of accomplishing a task in a group instead of alone, and to factors for successful learning.

Context for Successful Use

With appropriate modifications, this simulation could be used successfully with university faculty, administrators, businesspeople, new field-workers in an agency, or people in any setting where host country nationals work with nonnative speakers of their language. The process questions would need to be modified to conform with agency goals and behavioral objectives for those being trained.

Considerations for Use

Our experience has been that the more specific the initial instructions are, the more anxiety the participants may have during the simulation. Participants have said this is because they were trying to perform so many tasks exactly as described in a short time frame. Specific instructions also tend to lessen spontaneous reactions and methods of language study (translating, memorizing, using dictionary sheets, working together and so forth).

Some participants will insist on more instructions. Those requests can be granted individually and processed during the large group discussion as an example of one way in which people react to the task of language learning.

Sometimes, performance anxiety attacks people, and you must be ready to reassure them and lower the tension. You may also need to deal with other reactions such as participant resentment, passive or active resistance to the activity, vocal frustration, and withdrawal. It is possible that these responses are unconscious barriers to their language learning process and might be approached as such. Some variables to consider when trying to predict the reactions are

1. the relationship of group size to participants' willingness to perform;
2. how well the group members know each other and the potential for ego involvement; and
3. the amount of positive experience participants have had with foreign languages, peoples, and cultures, and its effect on participants' ability and motivation to perform the tasks.

During the large group discussion, participants sometimes comment on the lack of reality in having to learn a language so quickly. Whether or not participants make such a comment, you need to explain that pressure plays a major part in the achievement and trauma of total immersion in a new language. Exchange students, for example, must perform immediately upon arrival in the host country despite disorientation, travel fatigue, homesickness, or culture shock.

We have found that to conduct this simulation well you need to feel comfortable with both its conceptual principles and specific procedures. This means knowing "The Story of the Three Little Pigs" and Piglish history, practicing speaking Piglish, keenly observing interactions and making conscious decisions about encouraging participants, and knowing which process questions to use and how much time to allow for each part of the exercise.

To obtain a better perspective on these variables, especially if you are not a language specialist, it may be useful to participate in or run a related exercise such as the ones described in this section of *Intercultural Sourcebook*. The references mentioned in this chapter can assist you in developing more background and insight into the language learning process and should increase your confidence in conducting such an exercise. Experience with simulations such as *BaFá BaFá* (Shirts 1983) would be useful as well.

Conclusion

We have had consistent success for over ten years using this simulation in a variety of contexts. Even experienced foreign language teachers from different countries have enjoyed and positively evaluated this activity. The challenge to the trainer lies mostly in an enthusiastic presentation and in the facilitation and processing of the discussions. Otherwise, you just "Ugh-puhbbb" and stand on your toes!

References

Blohm, Judith, Cay Hartley, and Terri Lapinsky. "Piglish: A Language Learning Exercise." *International Journal of Intercultural Relations* 19, no. 2 (Spring 1995).

Curran, Charles A. *Counseling Learning in Second Languages.* Apple River, IL: Apple River Press, 1976.

"Learning about Language," from the Intercultural Communication Skills series, *Volunteers in Intercultural Programs.* Washington, DC: Youth For Understanding International Exchange, 1985, 1989.

Rudy, Sharon, and Terri Lapinsky. "Differentiating Language and Adjustment Issues to Improve Counseling Support." In *Building the Professional Dimension of Educational Exchange,* edited by Joy M. Reid. Yarmouth, ME: Intercultural Press, 1988.

Shirts, R. Garry. *BaFá BaFá.* Del Mar, CA: Simulation Training Systems, 1983.

Stevick, Earl. *Memory, Meaning and Method: Some Psychological Perspectives on Language Learning.* Rowley, MA: Newbury House Publishers, 1976.

Appendix A

The Story of the Three Little Pigs

Once upon a time, there were three little pigs who lived by a forest. They were very happy. One day they decided to build houses. One of the pigs built his house of straw. The second little pig built his house of sticks. The third pig built his house of bricks.

After the houses were finished, the pigs went to sleep, each in his own house. A big bad wolf came out of the forest and went to the house of straw.

"Little pig, little pig—let me in!" said the wolf.

The first pig said, "Not by the hair of my chinny-chin-chin."

The wolf said, "I'll huff and I'll puff and I'll blow your house down!"

So he huffed and puffed and blew the house of straw down. The pig ran to the house of his brother, the house made of sticks.

The wolf went to the house of sticks next and shouted, "Little pigs, little pigs, let me in, or I'll blow this house down too!"

The two pigs were afraid, but they said, "Not by the hair of our chinny-chin-chins!"

So the wolf huffed and puffed, and huffed and puffed, and down went the house of sticks. The two little pigs ran to the brick house their brother pig had built. The wolf followed close behind.

"I know you're in there, little pigs. Let me in, or I'll blow your house down."

While the two little pigs hid under the bed, the third pig stood in front of his door and said, "NOT BY THE HAIR OF MY CHINNY-CHIN-CHIN, WOLF!!"

With that, the wolf began to huff and puff, and he tried to blow down the brick house but nothing happened. The wolf huffed and puffed until he had to lie down and rest. Then he decided to get up onto the roof and try to go down the chimney. The third pig put a large pot of water in the fireplace and waited for the wolf.

The third pig heard the wolf on the roof as he tried to get down the chimney. Suddenly, with a big splash, the wolf fell down the chimney into the pot. Quickly, the third pig tied up the wet wolf and left him in the water.

The three little pigs were so happy, they danced around the room singing, "Who's afraid of the big bad wolf, the big bad wolf, the big bad wolf. Who's afraid of the big bad wolf, the big bad wolf—NOT I!"

Appendix B

Piglish: A Modern Language
Instructions and Vocabulary List

Introduction

Piglish is a modern language and is derived from an island culture that was established when European settlers were shipwrecked with a load of swine destined for the New World in the sixteenth century. The survivors were mainly a group of children and 1,400 swine. The language was developed on the basis of the interactions between the swine and a two-year-old human's command of English. Such notions as time and space also reflect a two-year-old's perceptions. You will be happy to know that both the children and the swine flourished together in the new society. The language and the culture have evolved over the years to a point where fluent native speakers can meet all needs for survival. You must realize, of course, that fluent speakers use a great number of gestures and nonverbal cues to make up for the lack of extensive vocabulary and complexity of language structure.

Grammar

The vocabulary included here is enough to get you started in the language. It is approximately what a two-year-old, modern pigler would know. The basic grammar of the language (word order to form sentences) follows English closely. For example, an ordinary sentence starts with a noun or pronoun (pig, I), followed by a verb (am, is, are), followed by an adjective (hungry). You will also notice that Piglish does not have separate pronouns for *I* or *we*, *you*, or *they*. The island culture is very group oriented, and pronoun distinctions are meaningless to a pigler!

Verbs in Piglish have only a single tense, and gestures are used to indicate past, present, and future. Verbs are not conjugated to agree with pronouns. For example, *I am happy* sounds the same as *We are happy;* so does *You are happy, She is happy,* and *He is happy.* They are all said exactly alike. However, it will be perfectly clear in communication that by pointing in different ways (indicating *I, you, we,* or *they*) and squatting (or rising on the toes) at the right time, you are expressing a past, present, or future tense.

Pronunciation

The language is quite phonetic and sounds like a guttural or grunted English. It follows the same consonant sounds of English, and the vowel sounds are only as follows:

a = ah, as in *father*	o = oh, as in *bone*
e = ay, as in *hay*	u = oo, as in *fool*
i = ee, as in *me*	

Special combination sounds are varieties of grunting sounds. Here are some examples:

mmmm = said with lips closed and in the throat, as in *mmmm good.*

uug = said with the lips pursed in a round O, followed by a partial stop, as in *oo-ga.*

nhhh = said with the mouth closed and through the nose with a grunting sound in a low tone.

pldddd = made by moving the tongue in the mouth in a soft flutter.

puhbbb = made by buzzing the lips the way a horse does.

Gestures with Meaning

Finger points at the indicated person (*you, me, I, they, we*), accompanied by the generic pronoun for all persons, *uug,* pronounced *oo-ga.*

Squatting (used with verbs): indicates past tense; deep squat is long time ago; slight knee bend indicates yesterday or single past action.

Tiptoes (used with verbs): indicates the future tense.

Eyes wide open or eyes closed: indicates degree or emphasis, such as when an English speaker would use "er" on the end of a word (bigg*er*).

The negative can be formed by crossing the forearms over the chest as the verb is spoken.

Verbs

to go =	mnnph	to dance =	sqo
to be (is, are, am) =	uugh	to get (up/down) =	blugh*
to laugh =	snuff-snuff	to bind/tie =	sbynog
to look/see =	ibah	to wait =	tiple-pldddd
to let/allow =	huuba	to huff/puff =	ugh-puhbbb
to blow =	whiff	to say =	ilk-eh
tō live =	nnh-bah	to run =	mo-mo
to open =	uudle-uuh	to leave =	bibi
to sit =	chachu	to sing =	ugh-lala
to put =	di-shy	to finish =	nnb-fi
to build =	batuu		

Nouns

pigs =	uugi	thing =	daa
food =	mmmm	minutes =	snips
bricks =	baaba	hair =	mope
sticks =	waawa	roof =	topah

---

* Gesture up or down as appropriate!

pot =	daa-ruh	road/trail =	longa
water =	mot-ve	door =	puhbbb-ah
chimney =	waa-buh	time =	snip-snip
home/house =	sty	chin =	chuga
wolf =	groof	fireplace =	waa-daa
straw =	hesi	splash =	mot-whiff

Adjectives, Adverbs, Prepositions, and Conjunctions

big =	enorpub	bad =	yuk
good =	slurp	happy =	squil
scared =	trull	stupid =	owe
not/no =	nabba	and =	muucha
or =	da	down =	flak
of =	di	once =	uber
the =	der	in =	tut
little =	squiz	hungry =	supcha
upon =	squa	wet =	move

Numbers (same for first, second, etc.)

1 =	pee	4 =	pee sno
2 =	pee pee	5 =	sno
3 =	pee pee pee	6 =	sno pee

Commonly Used Expressions

Open the door =	Uudle-uuh der puhbbb-ah
I'm hungry =	Uug supcha (pointing to stomach)
Once upon a time =	Uber squa snip-snip (squatting down)
There were =	cog (squatting down)
Let me in =	Huba uug tut
Who's afraid =	Uug trull

A Selection of Small Group Exercises

L. Robert Kohls

Julius E. Eitington, in his book *The Winning Trainer* (1996, 13), calls the small group the *basic unit* for participative training. Certainly some of the simplest and most effective training techniques I have encountered can be classified as small group exercises.

Introduction

Small group exercises seem to fall naturally into place in training designs. Every trainer I know finds them useful.

Reasons for Using Small Group Exercises

I use small group exercises a disproportionately large percentage of the time for the following reasons:

- ❖ They add variety.
- ❖ They heighten the sense of individual involvement.
- ❖ They increase the chance of *all* of the trainees participating actively in the exercise.
- ❖ They are generally at an extremely low risk/threat level (as compared, for example, to role play).
- ❖ They provide an optimal chance for participants to learn from their peers rather than from the trainer.
- ❖ They provide a nonthreatening format for participants to test out new ideas (or lifestyles).
- ❖ They give a sense of support and solidarity, which is much more difficult to achieve in larger, less intimate groups.
- ❖ They are often the only practical, experiential exercise available when training time is extremely limited.
- ❖ They accomplish the most with the fewest resources.

Control of the Training Situation

In addition they provide the trainer with optimal control, for it is the trainer who decides the composition of the group each time. The small group may be made up of members with similarities of experience, interests, ethnic makeup, occupation, or whatever category the trainer decides on. Or they may be built around the greatest diversity. The same groups can be maintained throughout the entire training period, or they can be reconstituted at will if "new blood" and variety are felt to be needed.

Size of the Groups

Whenever I want to be certain that *all* members of the group will participate actively and each person will contribute orally, I limit the size of the group to four. I have found that it is virtually impossible for a person—even the shyest member—to remain silent in a group of four. The other members simply will not allow it. When the size of the total training group is too large (I consider anything over twenty as too large), it is absolutely necessary to spend a portion of the session broken out into smaller groups. This makes unmounted, movable chairs a must in the training room. Lecturing may be possible in an auditorium with bolted seats, but training is not!

Types of Small Group Exercises

Simply mentioning a few types of training activities which fall under the definition of small group exercises will demonstrate how vital they are to the trainer:

Icebreakers	Brainstorming
Question-and-Answer Sessions	Force-Field Analysis
Group Discussions	Decision by Consensus
Buzz Groups	Fishbowl
Task Forces	

All of these are, clearly, small group activities. We can begin to see, as we scan this list, just how ubiquitous small group exercises are. We could not get along without them even if we wanted to.

Small Group Tasks

You form small groups to have them do something. In other words, you give them a task to accomplish. Some people might consider a case study as a specific form of a small group exercise. I do not, even though in the typical case study format small groups could be asked, for example, to discuss and determine the most likely reason why the situation detailed in the case occurred. Or you might task them with developing several viable solutions for the case study problem. Since so much work goes into developing the case itself, I prefer to consider it a case study exercise instead of a small group exercise, even though the training process and group dynamics are similar.

In its simplest form, the small group is the perfect vehicle to receive the assignment of such basic yet important tasks as these:

❖ Reaching agreement on the three most important reasons for a particular phenomenon

❖ Creating a list of questions around a certain topic

❖ Sharing examples from the trainees' experience in relation to a particular situation or topic

❖ Determining objectives for a project

❖ Reaching agreement (or consensus) on a problem, debate, or dispute

❖ Writing a short case study to illustrate a certain point

❖ Developing a "worst case scenario"

❖ Making forecasts or predictions

❖ Preparing points for both sides of a debate on a certain issue

❖ Developing a "laundry list" of items relevant to a subject under consideration (for example, list all the factors that facilitate communication between groups that are different from each other)

❖ Developing checklists

❖ Agreeing on priorities

The list is virtually endless. Even though the above list is by no means exhaustive, it illustrates how simple the assignment can be for breaking out into small groups and how small groups so often seem to be just the right medium to use in a typical training session. It gives new meaning to Eitington's comment, referred to at the beginning of this chapter.

Small Group Processing

It may or may not be desirable—it definitely is not necessary every time—to have each small group report back their findings to the group as a whole. Obviously, each group may be working on the same task, or they may each be assigned separate and unique tasks. In this latter case, their findings will probably need to be shared with the entire body.

Three Examples of Small Group Exercises

The following are three examples of small group exercises out of literally hundreds of possibilities. I chose these three because they are nonthreatening, so that trainees are not at all reluctant to join in, yet they are stimulating enough to encourage each person to contribute his or her own ideas; they can be adapted easily to fit different training needs or groups; and they illustrate the breadth of what small group exercises can be expected to accomplish. Just reading through a description of them, before having had a chance to try them out, a trainer is likely to sense their potential.

Exercise 1: Consensus

Purpose

The purpose of this exercise is to have the participants confront their own and their neighbors' stereotypes and prejudices, all of which are so commonly encountered that they have become a part of our everyday language and way of thinking. The exercise also provides practice in tactfully correcting these prejudices when we encounter them in others.

Reproduce and distribute the following statements.

1. The fact that America was able to place a man on the moon proves America's technological superiority. _____

2. Foreigners going to live in a new country should give up their foreign ways and adapt to the new country as quickly as possible. _____

3. Orientals* do many things backwards. _____

4. Much of the world's population does not take enough initiative to develop themselves; therefore, they remain "underdeveloped." _____

5. English should be accepted as the universal language of the world. _____

6. The Vietnamese do not place any value on human life. To them life is cheap. _____

7. Americans have been very generous in teaching other people how to do things the right way. _____

8. Primitive people have not yet reached the higher stages of civilization. _____

9. The sooner the whole world learns to do things the way we do, the sooner all the people of the world will be able to understand each other better. _____

Time

This exercise takes about seventy minutes for the groups to make their corrections in an unhurried manner and to share their rewritten statements with the larger group.†

---

* If the participants have not caught it themselves, the trainer should make the point that *Orientals* is regarded as offensive; *Asians* is a better choice.

† If I do not have enough training time, I sometimes shorten the original rewriting time from 40 to 25 minutes, counting on having already assigned half of the small groups to start at the bottom of the list to make sure all of the statements will be covered. (I am reluctant to condense in this way, however, since I feel it is valuable to have all participants struggle with every concept inherent in each statement.)

Instructions

Ask each member, first of all, to read each statement and to write in the blank on the right-hand side an *A* or a *D*, depending on whether he or she personally Agrees or Disagrees with each statement. Then, if one or more of the members disagrees with a statement, the group is to rewrite that statement so that all of its members now agree with it. Proceed through the statements, changing each so that everybody agrees with them in their rewritten forms. The group members may not simply agree to disagree. They need to be warned ahead of time against doing this. Otherwise, someone inevitably thinks of this nonsolution to cop out of the assignment.

Do not tell the group (until after the completion of the exercise) that all of the statements are questionable in some way or another and should be rewritten.

In giving the initial instructions, assign half the groups to start at the bottom of the list and work their way toward the top so that in case the groups need more time than allowed (forty minutes) to get through the statements, at least all statements will be covered.

Processing

When the groups report back their rewritten solutions, you can freely add your comments to further clarify any points. But the beauty of this exercise is that not you, but the participants themselves correct the stereotypes, not only in the statements but in the minds of their fellow participants as well.

Exercise 2: Role Assignments

Purpose

The purpose of this exercise is to explore and actually experience how various roles we play in everyday life add to and/or detract from communicating with others.

Time

This exercise takes approximately one hour to run, in addition to the time it takes to watch the film. This hour is divided equally between the discussion in the assigned roles and the processing of the experience.

Instructions

Before watching a film on any relevant topic, divide the participants into six subgroups by counting off. Then assign the members of each of the six subgroups one of the roles and the hidden agenda listed below. Now show the film. While watching the film, all number ones will play the role of Objective Observers (with the indicated hidden agenda); all number twos will become Questioners, and so forth.

Role	**Hidden Agenda**
1. Objective Observers	Report, as objectively as possible, what happened in the film. Stay completely away from interpretations, feelings, and emotions.
2. Questioners	Question everything—what actually happened, what the intention was, what was being "said," why that was the message rather than something else, and so forth.
3. Clarifiers	Clarify and define points at every opportunity.
4. Agreers	Agree with everybody and everything that is said. Be supportive.
5. Disagreers	Disagree with everybody and everything. Play the "devil's advocate."
6. Implementors	Suggest how the concepts dealt with in the film might be applied to the workaday world.

Discuss the reactions of the participants to the film, with each participant playing the role assigned. This discussion session will have a mix of all six roles, either in a single group or, if the number of participants exceeds twelve or fifteen, in two or more discussion groups.

Processing

After the discussion, process the experience, inquiring whether some roles were helpful and others not, whether the discussion was livelier than it probably would have been if the role assignments had not been made, how natural each person's arbitrarily assigned role seemed, and other appropriate questions.

Exercise 3: Value Options

Purpose

The main purpose of this exercise is to provide the experience of negotiating through our differences to reach a compromise. A secondary purpose might be to use it as a variation on values exercises, making the point of difference in our value preferences. Before you run this exercise you might want to review the discussion of values (chapter 7) in *Survival Kit for Overseas Living* (Kohls 1996) and the "Cross-Cultural Value Cards Exercise" in *Developing Intercultural Awareness* (Kohls and Knight 1994).

Time

This exercise takes approximately 1 hour and 40 minutes. This allows 5 minutes to distribute the cards and explain the rules of the exercise, 15 to 20 minutes for round one, 10 for round two, 10 for round three, 25 for round four, and half an hour for processing.

Preparation

This exercise requires you to prepare a deck of cards, created by typing the fifty-two values statements in Appendix A (one per card) on a pack of plain 3x5-inch index cards. For every twelve people in your group, create a separate set of cards, but shuffle all the cards into one large deck.

Distribute the cards evenly. No one should have fewer than four cards. It is better, if possible, to have at least eight cards per person.

Instructions

After the cards have been dealt out, sight unseen, to all the players, the participants may look at their cards. The object of the exercise is to trade your cards with the other participants so that you end up with the cards that most nearly express your own values.

Round One: You may trade as many cards as you need in order to collect the card(s) you want most. There is no certain number of cards you must end up with at the end of the first round.

This initial trading round requires players to circulate freely and show their cards to the other players to try to find someone who is willing to trade.

Round Two: Circulate and team up with someone whose value cards are most like your own (without being exactly the same as yours).

Round Three: Now circulate together and find another pair whose value cards are most *unlike* yours.

Round Four: Sit down together with that pair and try to agree on a compromise statement of values which will be acceptable to all four of you. (Do not expect all groups to be able to reach resolution, but the experience will be valuable, since compromise and reconciling values are key cross-cultural skills.)

Processing

Debrief the experience, stressing the process more than the content of what has happened. Obviously, those groups that have been able to resolve their differences should be praised, but also point out that the process itself has been valuable if people listened actively, with open minds, even if agreement was not reached in the short time available.

Conclusion

Small group exercises are not without their risks. You must be sensitive to the intercultural sophistication of your group. Your purpose and instructions must be clear, clear, clear. Processing requires good facilitative skills. However, over three decades of training experience have led me to believe that small group exercises are the staff of this trainer's life.

References

Eitington, Julius E. *The Winning Trainer.* 3d ed. Houston: Gulf, 1996.

Kohls, L. Robert. *Survival Kit for Overseas Living.* 3d. ed. Yarmouth, ME: Intercultural Press, 1996.

Kohls, L. Robert, and John M. Knight. *Developing Intercultural Awareness.* 2d. ed. Yarmouth, ME: Intercultural Press, 1994.

Resources

Badger, B., and I. Chaston. *Fifty Activities for Effective Problem Solving.* Amherst, MA: Human Resource Development Press, 1992.

Casse, Pierre. *Training for the Cross-Cultural Mind: A Handbook for Cross-Cultural Trainers and Consultants.* Washington, DC: SIETAR International, 1979.

Cox, G., C. Dufault, and W. Hopkins. *Fifty Activities for Creativity and Problem Solving.* Amherst, MA: Human Resource Development Press, 1991.

Forbess-Greene, Sue. *The Encyclopedia of Icebreakers.* San Diego: Applied Skills Press, 1983.

Gochenour, Theodore, ed. *Beyond Experience: An Experiential Approach to Cross-Cultural Education.* 2d ed. Yarmouth, ME: Intercultural Press, 1993.

Kirby, A. *Icebreakers, Energizers, and Introductions.* Amherst, MA: Human Resource Development Press, 1992.

Pfeiffer, John W. *The Encyclopedia of Group Activities.* San Diego: Pfeiffer, 1989.

Pfeiffer, John W., and J. E. Jones. *A Handbook of Structured Experiences,* vol. 1-10 (plus Index volume). San Diego: Pfeiffer, 1974–1985.

Pfeiffer, John W., et al. *The Human Resources Development Annual Set* (separate volume for each year from 1972 to present). San Diego: Pfeiffer, 1972ff, to present year.

Smith, B. J., and B. L. Delahaye. *How to Be an Effective Trainer.* New York: Wiley, 1983.

Appendix A

The Values Statements

In large part I am the one who is responsible for what I make out of life and what I become in life.

I believe that fate or destiny—some force outside myself—ultimately determines what life will bring to me.

Change is the only constant in life, and, ultimately, change is a good thing, for it makes life rich and full of infinite variety.

We should hold fast to our traditions, for they give our lives stability and continuity. Change is disruptive because it kills tradition (in any society).

It is very important that we be on time for an appointment. It is rude to keep the other person waiting, and it says we don't think the other person is important if we keep him or her waiting.

Interpersonal relationships and human friendships are the most important things in life. We must nurture them at all costs.

All people, no matter what their status in life, should wait their turn in line. Line-bucking upsets me! Do they think they're better than I am not to wait their turn?

It's very important to know what level in society people have been born into so I can know whether to accept them or not.

Some people, by reason of their rank and status in life, deserve more "rights" than others.

As long as they don't hurt others, people should be allowed to do what they *choose* to do.

The group must be given preference over the desires of any individual member of the group.

All people must gain control of time, for if they don't, time will take control of their lives.

It is more important to take time to enjoy life with a friend—or simply to stop and smell the flowers—than it is to be exactly on time for every appointment.

Some people deserve more benefits than others because their station in life is higher.

I should be the one who decides what is best for me and what I want to do with my life.

What is best for the group is ultimately best for me, therefore I am willing to accept the decision of the group whenever it is different from my own individual wish.

All people should take the initiative to help themselves in this life. If people don't look out for their own interests, no one else will.

The position in society into which a person is born is very important.

Competition spurs us on to accomplish great things, therefore competition is good for any society.

It is better to cooperate with others than to fight or compete with them.

By working together we will accomplish far more than any of us could accomplish alone.

A person who starts out with very little and yet, in spite of all the difficulties, goes farther in life deserves all of our respect.

By competing with others and winning, we prove our true superiority and worth.

It is important to have a plan for your life so that it can get better and better.

All of my life so far, I have been planning and working for what I will become in the future.

We should look to the past for our models, our examples, and our inspiration. The past is the best teacher we could possibly have.

An active life is a productive life.

Hard work enables us to accomplish great things in life.

The heroes and important people of our history deserve our admiration and imitation.

I don't worry whether I break any records in life. To me just being a good person every day of my life is the most important thing I can achieve.

I have worked all my life, and I'm not ashamed of the material objects I have to show for that hard work. After all, I've earned them!

People should not be driven to acquire too many material possessions. A person's spiritual advancement is far more important than the amassing of material objects.

It is best not to tell everything I know, especially if revealing it might hurt another person (or myself).

The thing Americans should be most admired for is their practicality. Americans can always find a solution to any problem and always invent a gadget to do any task.

We should be more concerned with preserving our "golden" ideals than with what is actually happening to us at any given moment.

I don't like to dress up to go anywhere. I much prefer clothing which is more informal and comfortable. After all, I'm not trying to impress anyone.

We should not call older people by their "first" names (their "given" names). Such treatment would be too disrespectful.

I believe in "calling a spade a spade." I don't "beat around the bush." I say what I mean—even when it hurts a little.

It is more important to just be a good person than it is to achieve great success in life.

I don't like formal situations. They seem so unnatural. For me, the informal approach is preferable.

Certain situations in life seem to demand formality, ceremony, and ritual.

People should be direct and open in all their dealings. They should clearly say what they mean, and precisely where they stand, so there will be no confusion.

Sometimes it is best to tell a "little white lie" if it will save another person embarrassment or loss of face.

If something does not have a practical and useful application, then it is a waste of my time, effort, and money.

Sometimes theoretical and abstract thoughts can be more satisfying than the everyday, practical way to apply those thoughts.

It is natural for people to want to acquire a number of material possessions in this life. Such possessions can bring great happiness.

The greatest happiness is spiritual. It is through detachment from life and from material possessions that we gain the greatest happiness.

I must make the most out of whatever has been given to me in life. After all, most of my eventual lot in life will be a direct result of what I do with what I have. I shouldn't just sit around and cry about what I don't have. Instead, I should get up and go after what I want.

If one has been dealt a bad hand in the card game of life, it is best to just accept one's lowly position and learn to live with it than to fight one's natural condition.

People who act like they're better than I am irritate me! After all, no one is better than anyone else. We're all the same.

Changes in life can be somewhat disruptive at the moment, but they are ultimately best for our own good. They give us new and exciting opportunities that we wouldn't have had otherwise.

Changes are frightening and disruptive. I prefer a life which allows me to continue the experiences, people, and events with which I am already familiar.

These statements have been carefully prepared to be in balance for the exercise to work properly. Therefore, you should not shorten the list arbitrarily.

The Malonarian Cultural Expedition Team: Exploring Behavioral Reflections of Mainstream U.S. Values

Norma M. McCaig

"Malonarians" is a values exercise calculated to develop awareness of concrete ways in which U.S. values are manifested in daily life. Asking participants to assume the role of citizens from the fictional Republic of Malonaria, a traditional society, helps them view U.S. values from a very different cultural stance. The Malonarian exercise can either be used in its original long form or modified short form as a stand-alone workshop or as a component in a larger training design. Although in the past, interculturalists and other culturally aware participants have approached the tasks of the exercise with enthusiasm and, on occasion, great wit, those who are new to intercultural interaction or new to the notion that behavior may be culturally determined are the intended audience.

History

While on staff at the Washington International Center (W.I.C.) of Meridian House International, now the Training and Visitors Services Division of Meridian International Center, I was fortunate to work under the tutelage of former W.I.C. executive director and one of the founders of the intercultural field, L. Robert Kohls. Mentor and friend, he has generously shared his cross-cultural insights and creative models throughout the years and has granted liberal license for their inclusion in various works of my own since those early days. This exercise is no exception. Values included in the Malonarian exercise are found in "Values Americans Live By" (Kohls 1984), part of the U.S.A. in Brief series funded by the U.S. Agency for International Development.

The Republic of Malonaria (pronounced may-low-naria) was founded one day early in 1988 as I searched for a novel way to approach the cross-cultural segment of an upcoming host volunteer orientation. Participants needed to engage in a relatively short activity that would

1. make the abstract notion of cultural values concrete,

2. raise their awareness of the cultural transition stress experienced by their newly arrived international dinner guests, and

3. stimulate a discussion on stereotyping and cultural assumptions.

I wanted them to find ways to relate insights gained in the exercise to their hosting experience.

By evening's end, the core version of the Malonarian Cultural Expedition Team exercise had been developed to meet the learning goals. Embellishments were added in the days immediately following, and the first trial run was held with new host volunteers that weekend. Feedback was encouraging, some of the best observations coming from two recently repatriated teenagers who had decided at the last minute to join their parents for the orientation. The exercise was successfully tested at the University of Virginia in 1989, when student interns chose to use it in their Student Host Program orientation session. Their supervisor, Lorna Sundberg of the International House in Charlottesville, cofacilitated that workshop, as she did many times subsequently when we presented the exercise at national and regional conferences of the National Association for Foreign Student Affairs: Association of International Educators (NAFSA). The Malonarian exercise and modified versions of it have been used in a variety of training workshops over the past eight years. Feedback on the exercise is still welcomed, particularly with respect to training context, variations, and facilitation tips that can be added to the trainer's guidelines.

Description

This exercise is somewhat like a field trip—without the field trip itself. I happen to use this exercise in the United States, so I designed the Malonarian exercise to take advantage of the participants' experience of the United States, but I believe it could be adapted for use in other cultures.

People who use simulation games speak of a "frame game." The Malonarian exercise might be seen as a frame for increasing the participants' understanding of their home culture values and behavior, but it is not a game. It is an experiential, small group exercise, so it might not be the first choice in a didactic training design, but I think it has potential for even the most traditional training programs.

Scenario

Participants make up the Malonarian Cultural Expedition Team. They are gathered in a meeting room at the Ramardan Hilton (or Plaza Malonaria, if you prefer) in the capital of the Republic of Malonaria. They are all distinguished anthropologists who have recently returned from a year's sojourn in the United States, where they were tasked to observe how that country's cultural values influenced the living environment and behavior of its citizens. The Cultural Expedition Team's findings are to form the basis of a cross-cultural orientation manual for Malonarian exchange students bound for the United States.

Overview

The exercise begins when participants, as repatriating Malonarians, work in small groups to record the results of their study, which will then be presented to the entire Cultural Expedition Team. Several lists support their work. A list of Malonarian values grounds them in the traditional culture of Malonaria. These values serve as their reference point. Next, participants are given a list of U.S. values. Each small group is asked to take two of these values and list behavioral examples of them as observed in the United States. Another list suggests themes that might be helpful in accomplishing their task. When each group has completed work on both of their assigned values, they prepare their report for the entire team. The activity ends when the small groups give their reports and post them on the walls of the training room. The entire exercise is debriefed after participants are de-roled.

Procedure

Preworkshop Participant Preparation

It is important to prepare participants for the Malonarian experience, particularly if those attending know one another or if the Malonarian session is part of a conference. The goal is not only to open participants to an enjoyable exploration of values but also to avoid a sense of manipulation that they may feel without advance notice. Well prior to the session, I usually announce that participants will have the opportunity to set aside their current national identity and become Malonarians for a few hours.

Step 1—Room Setup and Materials Preparation—90 minutes

Two rooms are ideal. It is best to begin in one room arranged theater style for participant registration and preparation for the exercise. The training takes place in a room large enough to accommodate four groups of three to seven participants seated at round tables or in small group circles without tables. Each group needs an easel with newsprint and a magic marker. Use enough different colors so that each group is assigned its own magic marker color. An extra easel with newsprint is required for both the group reports and exercise debriefing. Walls in the training room should be suitable for posting newsprint with masking tape.

You need to prepare the following:

1. A sign for the training room door saying "Welcome Back to the Republic of Malonaria!" I usually create a mock national coat of arms or flag for this.

2. Two name tags for each participant: one (blank) for the real name, the other prepared in advance with a Malonarian name. With the exception of the president of the republic, I generally follow the alphabet and prepare two-

syllable names, such as Dr. Adan, Dr. Benat, Dr. Casat, Dr. Desan, and so on, which are easy to read and remember.

3. Brainstorming sheets (large newsprint: two per group), each with a different value written on the top. Note: Choose values from the list of thirteen provided in step 4, taking care to select those likely to generate numerous examples.

4. Task guidelines for small group work on large newsprint for posting in the training room (see step 4).

5. Two values lists—one U.S., the other Malonarian—on separate sheets of newsprint to post side by side (see step 4 for list and order of values).

6. A list of themes (also provided in step 4) to address while the group is brainstorming values.

Suggested mood enhancers. Robes (Asian, Latin American, or African robes work well) for "Malonarian" trainers Drs. Radan and Enat (see below). Caps are another option. This costuming gives participants strong visual reinforcement of the assumed identity. A podium with a sign reading The Ramardan Hilton or Plaza Malonaria helps participants sense they are in a different place. A cassette or CD playing culturally ambiguous music, ostensibly Malonarian, is one of the best mood enhancers.

Step 2—Introduction—30 minutes

Have people write their names on the blank name tag. Then conduct participant and presenter introductions and describe the purpose of the workshop and the agenda. Give a brief overview of the participants' roles and functions as the Malonarian Cultural Expedition Team. Ask them to assume their new names on the Malonarian name tags provided before they go into the main training room (which represents their reentry into Malonaria). At this point the lead trainer slips into the main training room and closes the door to assume the role of Dr. Radan. The cotrainer (or training assistant) waits a brief time and escorts the group into the room, donning a robe and Malonarian identity (through a name tag) as Dr. Enat, while group members seat themselves. Dr. Enat ensures that participants are evenly distributed in groups.

Step 3—Welcome to Malonaria—5 minutes

Dr. Enat introduces the group to Dr. Radan (lead trainer), who is a representative of the Malonarian president, Dr. Manat Ramardan, and who sets the stage for the debriefing with a message from the president welcoming them back to Malonaria and a brief recapping of the purpose of their study.

Step 4—Tasking the Groups—10 minutes

Participants' attention is drawn to two sheets of newsprint posted side by side in the training room: one listing traditional Malonarian values, the other listing U.S. values. The lists provide the starting point for tying cultural values to behavior. Dr. Radan reminds the team of their decision to use a values approach in their field study. They had decided that a critical first step was to understand their own behavior in its Malonarian cultural context. To do so they selected thirteen Malonarian values operative in their culture as their point of reference.

Malonarian Values

Fate/Destiny

Stability/Tradition/Continuity

Human Interaction

Hierarchy/Rank/Status

Group Welfare/Dependence

Birthright Inheritance

Cooperation

Past Orientation

Being Orientation (rather than "doing" or goal orientation)

Formality

Indirectness/Ritual/Face

Idealism/Theory

Spiritualism/Detachment

Radan then reviews the cultural values the team learned were operative in the United States. The group is reminded that their task while abroad was to study the relationship between these values and life in the United States.

United States Values

Personal Control over the Environment/ Responsibility

Change Seen as Natural and Positive

Time and Its Control

Equality/Fairness

Individualism/Independence

Self-Help/Initiative

Competition

Future Orientation

Action/Work Orientation

Informality

Directness/Openness/Honesty

Practicality/Efficiency

Materialism/Acquisitiveness

Dr. Radan notes that (1) no positive or negative worth is assigned to any values shown on either list, (2) lists show mainstream values that are not necessarily shared personally by all members of that society, and (3) in either society, the importance attached to values on each list are in flux rather than being rigid because, as with most societies today, both Malonarian and U.S. cultures are changing. Dr. Radan asks if the meaning of each value is clear and answers any questions about the values.

Next Dr. Radan asks each small group to conduct self-introductions (based on their Malonarian names) and to appoint a scribe to record all suggested behavioral examples for the two different U.S. values assigned to their group. Dr. Radan reviews the Task Guidelines listed on newsprint.

Task Guidelines

1. All examples are to be recorded: group consensus is not required on any.
2. Remember your Malonarian roots while brainstorming.
3. Behavioral examples should be concrete.
4. Spend approximately 7 minutes brainstorming each value.
5. Prepare a brief (5–minute) report for the entire team.

When the third task guideline item is read (behavioral examples), Dr. Radan or Dr. Enat should mention an example, such as the fact that many U.S. citizens put clocks—prominently displayed—in at least three rooms. This is an observation of the high value Americans hold for *time and its control*. Provide additional examples to prepare participants for accomplishing their task.

Dr. Radan then points out another newsprint sheet listing suggested cultural themes to use when trying to think of concrete examples of behaviors that reflect specific values.

Cultural Themes

Education	Professional Life
Family Life	Friendship
Male/Female Interaction	Hospitality
Politics and Government	Verbal and Nonverbal Communication

Note: If possible, this sheet should be posted near the values lists for easy reference.

Step 5—Small Group Work—15 minutes

Drs. Radan and Enat circulate around the room observing group interaction, intervening only when asked to keep groups on task or to offer concrete examples if a group seems bogged down. Note: The person who holds the magic marker controls the group. Scribes listing only comments agreeable to them or those who seek consensus on each observation may need to be reminded of the legitimacy of all comments.

After 7 minutes, groups are notified to begin work on the second value.

Step 6—Group Reports (in Role)—up to 25 minutes (approximately 5–7 minutes per group)

Scribes post their newsprint reports in turn on an easel at the front of the room. Time permitting, Dr. Radan encourages brief comments following each report. Scribes transfer their reports to the training room walls as the next scribe moves to the front to report. By the end of the report segment the room is a blaze of color.

The reporting process is often full of humor, particularly when participants do remain solidly in role. In one group a scribe, unable to read her own writing, explained, "Sorry! I've been away so long I've forgotten how to read Malonarian script." Spinning off that comment, another participant, stumbling verbally, apologized, saying she was "still thinking in English." Yet another scribe talked expressively of people who, at both the beginning and end of the workday, "put funny-looking long cards into machines that snapped at them."

Step 7—Adjourning the Malonarian Cultural Expedition Team—5 minutes

Dr. Radan closes the training activity portion of the exercise by asking if expedition team members have any final comments to make before their cultural debriefing ends. Appreciation is expressed for their time and research, which will be of great benefit to the university's study abroad program. Team members are asked to stand, shake hands, and bid farewell to one another, and all are encouraged to applaud their good work.

Step 8—Assuming Real Identities—5 minutes

Trainers shed their assumed identities by removing their Malonarian "national dress" and the sign on the podium. They then ask participants to turn around a time or two to return to the real world and put on their original name tags. Trainers reintroduce themselves and encourage participants to exchange greetings with those close by.

Step 9—Processing the Exercise—25 minutes

One trainer leads the processing while the other charts responses on newsprint. When processing the exercise, I ask how being Malonarian affected or did not affect their observations, what their reactions to the process and content of reports were, what insights they have gained, how these relate to the intercultural interactions that bring them to this training, and how these insights will affect their attitudes and behavior beyond the training room. Several themes generally emerge that are useful in guiding participants toward the goals of the training session:

❖ Their own tendency to stereotype. This is reflected in their remarks, beginning with "Americans always" or "Malonarians never...." This tendency can be pointed out by bringing their attention to these stereotyping statements.

❖ The perception by many participants that most of the comments listed are critical of the United States. This can lead to a discussion of attitudes typically associated with those present either when entering a culture for the first time or reentering a familiar or home culture.

❖ Surprise at how culturally determined individual behavior is and a sense of how much they themselves "are" their culture.

❖ Greater awareness of the potential for cross-cultural misunderstanding based on blind assumptions and rigid absolutes (one said the exercise gave new meaning to the term "value judgment").

❖ Heightened sensitivity to the complex task of cultural adaptation and adjustment facing someone entering a new culture or reentering a home culture. This occurs when attention is drawn to the newsprint, where voluminous comment on only a few values has been recorded. I often point out that in the cross-cultural setting people are adapting to many, if not all, the listed behaviors almost simultaneously while perhaps operating in a new or different language.

Considerations for Use

Duration of Training

Plan on two hours plus a half-hour segment for participant registration and a workshop overview. The exercise itself lasts an hour and a half; one hour to complete the Malonarian segment and 30 minutes to debrief the experience.

Minimum and Maximum Number of Participants

Twelve to twenty-eight participants (to be divided into four groups) produce the best results. The exercise works with more (fifty people turned up for the session at one NAFSA conference), but a higher number of Malonarians requires setting up more groups and carefully monitoring the length of each group's verbal report, to avoid tedium. Adding more participants per group, while another option, presents its own challenges, as side conversations are more likely to develop, distracting team members from the central task.

Number of Facilitators

Two trainers or one trainer and an assistant are recommended for welcoming and seating participants, for monitoring the small group work, and for processing the exercise.

Supplies and Material Development

The exercise fairly begs for colorful signs and exotic trappings to reinforce the difference between the United States and Malonaria. Have a good time with this. Let your imagination reign if time and courage permit. There are several essential supplies:
1. Two name tags per person, including trainers.
2. One easel and newsprint pad per group and one to be used for both group reporting and processing following the Malonarian segment.
3. Masking tape for posting on the walls: the two values lists, task guidelines, brainstormed behavioral examples, cultural themes, and reports.
4. Magic markers for trainers and group scribes. Assigning each group a different color marker lends visual energy to the reporting process. (Avoid orange and, of course, yellow, which are difficult to read).

Contexts for Use

What I call the "Complete Malonarian," resplendent with all the trappings, has been particularly effective with college students and with volunteers in host programs and other community-based services for international students or visitors. In all such cases, the learning environment has been informal and relaxed, and participants seem more prone to risk adopting a temporary Malonarian identity. The same has been true of international educators at NAFSA conferences, where sessions have been particularly interactive and well received.

Modified, albeit more restrained, versions of the exercise have been used with equal effectiveness when time constraints, training needs, or trainer's intuition deem the full-blown fantasy too risky to use. Ways to modify the design are described in Trainer Tips, below.

The shorter design has been used successfully in a prefield orientation preparing U.S. citizens who will be teachers or houseparents at boarding schools overseas (most for the first time), in cross-cultural awareness seminars for faculty and staff working with international students, in cross-cultural training of trainers work-shops, and in reentry workshops for global nomads (also called third-culture kids, or TCKs).

Either in full or modified form, the exercise works well as part of a larger program. A design I often use begins with a simulation game such as *Barnga* that effectively stimulates learning by encouraging behavioral and emotional responses of participants to an intercultural encounter, followed by either the long or short version of the Malonarian exercise. Then I present interactive lecturettes (content-oriented but seeking spontaneous input from participants) to expand on cross-cultural concepts and strategies specific to participant needs.

Trainer Tips

Climate Setting

Take time to get the group invested in the role-play aspect of the Malonarian exercise. Generally, the group needs to be certain that being put into a role serves a purpose beyond being fun, that insights into cross-cultural adaptation will be expanded by role-playing, and that they will not be called upon to act ridiculous. Encourage trainees to participate in a way that enhances group interaction during the exercise while enabling them to remain comfortable with their own behavior.

Small Group Work

Positioning an easel at each table or group, rather than asking participants to put the newsprint on the table or floor, more efficiently focuses the entire group's attention on the task. This is particularly important if you must have groups with over seven participants. Keeping all members of a group connected to the task is difficult when they must strain to read written comments.

Processing

Certain values are more likely to lead to controversy. For example, the values of *equality and materialism/acquisitiveness* have been known to generate intense discussion, which may provoke argument or may go beyond what can be dealt with in the debriefing. This can disrupt group reports, so it is important to keep participants on track by making sure their comments are recorded on the news-print and letting them know that the issue can be discussed again later. Subse-quently, when discussion of these values ensues during the processing of the ex-ercise following the reports, I have found it useful to guide participants into dis-cussions regarding stereotyping (the degree of disagreement within their groups about specific behaviors reflects the diversity of responses within any culture, based on such elements as subcultural contexts and individual experiences) and cultural relativity (values such as equality and materialism are perceived accord-ing to one's own cultural context).

The different colors used for each group become a metaphor for cultural iden-tity (the green group, the blue group, the red group, and so on), underscoring the diversity in our culture. They also graphically convey how much work the participants have done. Ask participants what the use of color represents for them. Their responses may underline regional and ethnic subcultural differences inherent in any society regarding values and behavior. Since there are differences within any culture, participants need to recognize they should not approach a culture as monolithic.

Another important point that can be raised during a discussion of the meaning of the colors is the difference between stereotyping and generalizing. Clarify the difference between rigid stereotyping and making flexible and more or less objective generalizations about culture-based behavioral tendencies as a starting point for understanding individual behavior. Reinforce the idea that locking yourself into stereotypes can prevent you from using the generalizations for fruitful analysis.

To include an affective or emotional element in the processing, encourage participants to relate the exercise to times when they felt like outsiders, felt judged by another standard or assumptions made by others, or any other emotional reaction to stereotyping, cultural miscommunication, or the stress of cultural transition. I generally point out that newcomers or those experiencing reentry are adjusting on five levels simultaneously—emotionally, socially, culturally, professionally, and practically. It is important not to stop there. Ask what effective coping strategies participants developed and how the actions and reactions of others facilitated adaptation.

Meeting Workshop Goals

Be clear about the learning outcomes you seek, which will depend on the purpose of your workshop. In all cases one insight that can emerge is a greater understanding of how values are reflected in behavior, as is an increased awareness of the degree to which participants reflect or operate by their home culture values.

When your goal is to enhance cultural awareness of volunteers interacting with international visitors or students, processing can encourage attitudes of greater sensitivity and flexibility.

When training those going abroad from the United States for work or study, your goal may be to promote recognition that in very concrete ways participants take their culture's values and assumptions with them. The Malonarian exercise can be a useful tool for examining whether or not their responses (or judgments) are based on culture or personality, for validating their assumptions, for helping them remain flexible in response to cultural nuances and individuality rather than settling into rigid judgments, and for avoiding stereotyping and gross or subjective generalizations.

When working with groups reentering the United States (or any home culture), draw attention to the fact that they are having a Malonarian experience in real life. They have changed through their adaptation to life abroad and life has continued to change in the United States while they were gone, so they are observing their own culture as if it were new to them. Doing it consciously can ease their transition. Here, especially, is the time to use the cross-cultural skills and attitudes they have developed rather than assuming they can pack them away because they are home.

Design Modifications and Suggestions

To suit a more formal training environment, drop the Malonarian framework and set the exercise up as a means of exploring ways in which U.S. culture is reflected in daily life.

Post a list of "traditional" values (formerly Malonarian) and suggest that participants imagine they are observing U.S. society from this non-U.S. cultural perspective (such as the fictional Republic of Malonaria) to encourage detachment from their own culture. Change other aspects of the original design to support this revised structure.

To increase participant input and small group interaction, I often use a method suggested to me by Kohls: "traveling newsprint." It is an ideal way to get everyone's input on each topic while somewhat lessening the amount of time needed for the small group report process. Instead of asking each group to brainstorm concrete, behavioral examples of two values and to present a report to the total group, ask each group to brainstorm examples for their assigned values for 10 minutes. Then, they pass their two newsprint sheets to the next group, take newsprint from the group behind them, and start the brainstorming process again, adding their comments to those already on the sheets. Continue this process (decreasing in each round the time allowed) until each group receives its original newsprint back and reads the examples and comments added after theirs. At the end of the brainstorming, all members have read most of the comments on each sheet and are heavily involved in interaction around them. Post all sheets for viewing and additional comments, then begin processing the exercise.

This can be done in either version. I prefer not to use it with the Malonarian version, because reporting—eliminated in the non-Malonarian version—is rich in humor, which adds a special element to the group dynamics.

To save time, brainstorm only one value per group and, during processing, point out the vast quantity of information and ideas that would be generated by doing all the values on the list. Choose only up to eight values—or ten at the most—to process in a workshop. Participants quickly become bored with the group reports if there are too many groups, the reporting time is too long, or an attempt is made to cover too many values. When using the traveling newsprint technique, brainstorming eight to ten values works well.

Conclusion

Creating a balance between an enjoyable experience in an informal environment and the commitment to increasing cross-cultural awareness is critical. Getting caught up in the Malonarian fantasy is fun, but staying on top of the process is vital to avoid sacrificing learning for a good time. Fortunately, with the Malonarian Cultural Expedition Team exercise, participants can have both.

References

Kohls, L. Robert. "Values Americans Live By." U.S.A. in Brief series. Washington, DC: Meridian House International, 1984. Article available in English and Spanish from the Meridian Training and Visitors Services Division.

Resources

For further information or materials on the Malonarian Cultural Expedition Team, write or call:

MCET
2507 Penny Royal Lane
Reston, VA 22091
703-758-7766

Other Methods
Used in Training Programs

Margaret D. Pusch

Introducing the section on "other methods" is a rather difficult task, since the possibilities of what to include are endless, but the reality of what exists, very limited. It appears that very few innovations occur in cross-cultural training that cannot be subsumed under familiar categories, because the tendency is to develop another version of what we already know rather than to try something that is completely different. It is difficult even to imagine something that dramatically alters how we approach training and create new training methods or strategies. Other methods, then, are not especially new but are methods that do not easily fit into the categories already provided in either volume of the *Sourcebook*.

Descriptions of the Methods

There are seven methods described here: field studies, visual imagery, training manuals, cross-cultural dialogues, cross-cultural analysis, a process for developing deep cultural self-awareness, and culture heroes. Even those brief names suggest methods that are familiar, but here the focus is on using them interculturally—and therein lies much of their value.

Field Studies

Michael Gottlieb Berney explores in depth one field study program and reviews others that are similar but not identical to it. The Drop Off exercise, developed at the Experiment in International Living (now World Learning), is one of the earliest structured approaches to this kind of experience. Field studies of many sorts are valuable for all the reasons that Berney suggests, but they also allow participants to learn from experience in a controlled situation. That is, the participants can be debriefed, during which process they can ask questions, gain clarification, and categorize their experience. They can also be helped to draw generalizations and discover how this experience might apply during their stay in a new culture.

When conducting orientation programs at Syracuse University for international students, I used a "do-it-yourself" orientation format developed by Gary Althen of the University of Iowa. With instructions to explore (in groups of four or fewer) those areas of the community and university that the students would regularly encounter, they became familiar with local stores, the health center, banks, and other places they would frequent during their stay.

In follow-up discussion groups it was possible to compare their experiences and ask questions as well as develop a conceptual set within which they could categorize their experience (patterns of rendering service, skills that are useful in more than one situation, ways to ask for assistance, categories of relationships, and the like). Together we created appropriate expectations to draw on in future interactions. Returning students led the small group discussions and, over several days, guided the new students through the entire do-it-yourself program. Many of the debriefing methods described by Berney were used, and large group meetings and events were designed to bring the entire group of two to three hundred together in ways that allowed them to meet others and acquire basic information about university procedures. In addition, the small group became the support group for the students' early days in a new place, and great care was taken to watch the dynamics in the group to be sure members or subsets of members were successfully relating to each other.

Visual Imagery

Visual imagery is used in a variety of settings to expand consciousness and identify the inner strengths of the individual by drawing on the unconscious as a resource for conscious activity. In cross-cultural training, visual imagery allows people to imagine what they might encounter and plan how they can meet the challenges of adapting to a new environment or even return to a familiar one. For example, the Canadian International Development Agency (CIDA) included a visual imagery exercise in its reentry booklet some years ago. In their chapter in this volume, Fanchon Silberstein and Dorothy Sisk describe various ways this method can be used successfully. Visual imagery is indeed powerful and should be used with considerable care and after a great deal of practice. This chapter provides suggestions for developing the skill and using it well.

Training Manuals

Developing workbooks or manuals to be used in training programs is not an easy task, so the explanation of how this can be done is quite useful. While it might be assumed that workbooks can be used independently, not requiring the presence of a trainer, someone must help integrate what is learned from the workbook exercise with other training events. Robert Cyr's materials are clearly designed with that in mind.

There really have been no materials devised that allow people, on their own, to prepare fully for an intercultural experience. Indeed, it would be sheer folly to assume that one could learn how to interact with people from other cultures by engaging in exercises that totally exclude another person! Information about a culture or country can be transferred in many ways. Self-discovery does not always require the presence of other people, but the goal of becoming more effective at interacting with people from other cultures is unlikely to be achieved without engaging in that experience.

Cross-Cultural Dialogues

Craig Storti comes closest to the goal of improving effectiveness in intercultural relations without actually interacting with the target group. His book *Cross-Cultural Dialogues* (1994), is devoted entirely to this method. Reading the dialogues he describes in this *Sourcebook* is very helpful, but to get the full flavor of the communication difficulties, cultural misunderstandings, and other interactive nuances, it is best, as he suggests, to role-play the dialogues with other people.

Cross-Cultural Analysis

Al Wight combines interaction with self-instruction to explore culture in his cross-cultural analysis activity. He accomplishes a great deal in this compact method: participants use various learning styles, develop skills in culture learning, and obtain solid, helpful information. In addition, several conceptual frameworks are used to encompass and organize the learning that occurs. Using informants from a target culture is not new, but this activity establishes a process for their participation that is often missing but is critically important.

Deep Cultural Self-Awareness

Al Kraemer reviews a method he developed twenty-five years ago to prepare government personnel for international assignments. Its goal is to provide participants with the opportunity to recognize the subtle influence of their own cultural conditioning on the interpretations of conversations and perceptions of others in intercultural situations. Kraemer uses videotapes of segments of conversations to help participants elicit and analyze the cultural aspects of each interaction and, eventually, synthesize what has been learned from a series of these conversations.

The content of the video segments is fairly mundane, because it is in rather routine, trivial conversations that most misunderstandings occur—largely because they make up so much of daily life. Those viewing the videotapes must ask themselves if this is what they might say, and they learn how to look for clues that would alert them to use a different approach. First, however, they must explore their own values and assumptions and how these influence their first, instinctive response. The process allows trainees to gradually become more aware of and more sophisticated in recognizing how cultural conditioning, latent content, and implicit assumptions subtly influence their behavior and cause them to project meaning that is inappropriate in an intercultural situation. The beauty of this method lies in the simplicity of the process and the complexity of the concepts that lie behind it, allowing deeper exploration than may, initially, be expected and learning that has immediate practical application in any cultural environment.

Culture Heroes

Cultural informants are essential to the culture heroes method devised by Ed Stewart and Jun Ohtake, who explore the values that heroes in different cultures exemplify and their continuing impact on individuals and culture groups. This method goes beyond just an identification and exploration of a particular hero's behavior. It requires looking deeper into the culture to discover what is generally believed to constitute heroic behavior, how people within the culture identify with the values that are demonstrated, and how they use the hero as a reference for appropriate behavior in their lives. The authors explore the significance of heroes on two levels: personal (a hero who had a strong influence on an individual's behavior and values) and cultural (a hero who is accepted as a reference point by most people in the culture). They also examine theories that help interpret the heroes selected by people in two specific cultures. Much of the cross-cultural learning occurs as the hero choices and interpretations are compared across cultures—in this case, Japanese and North American.

Developing Other Methods

Most trainers, faced with a new training assignment, immediately think of the methods that have served them well in other situations or search through books such as this to come up with innovative ideas. Few have the funding (a major constraint) or time (equally constraining) to devise a new approach. Reading the chapters in this section will suggest why this is not an easy task. However, there are trainers who do continue to explore new methods, and the field is grateful to them for finding the resources to make this possible. What entices a trainer to develop a new method rather than rely on the tried and true (but possibly tired) training tools?

There are several motivations for creating something new: boredom with what one has been doing for so long, even though it is being done very well, or an inability to find any method that appropriately fits a particular training situation. Intercultural trainers are also encountering the increasing sophistication of clients and participants who are veterans of intercultural experience or are familiar with training methods in other arenas. These clients challenge the trainer to engage their attention. The growing body of knowledge in the field of intercultural communication is another motive for developing methods that take advantage of new ideas, concepts, or research findings.

This does not always require the creation of a new method. Expanding or modifying an old one may be the most appropriate response. Far fewer steps are required to develop a new case study or create a different context for a new role play than to develop an entirely new method. Developing a new method, no matter how much we draw on past experience and familiar processes, requires considerable work and an environment in which the method can be tested. Embarking on this adventure requires, at the least, serious consideration of the issues and steps listed below.

Decide to Create a New Method

This may seem obvious, but it is important to think through why you want to initiate this process and how you will go about it. Consider all the constraints involved, using the suggestions below to reach a conscious and informed decision to go forward.

❖ Explore methods you have used before to determine if they can be adapted to meet the needs of the training.

❖ Do a force-field analysis: what are the positive reasons for designing a new approach and the constraints that will make it difficult or convince you to give up the idea? On the positive side, write down everything the new method will offer that you cannot obtain elsewhere. Be exhaustive and be honest; the only person you are fooling with arguments that are too optimistic is you. On the negative side, list all the reasons why this is not a good idea, with respect to the time and other resources it will require (over- rather than underestimate) and to the perceived quality of and need for the product.

❖ Finally, develop a work plan and fit it into your schedule.

Design the New Method

❖ Identify the target group for whom the method is being created. (This will most likely be factored into the decision process outlined above.) Usually you cannot afford to create a method for a limited engagement or a very specialized group unless you are the lucky recipient of a grant or have a visionary client. It is useful, however, to identify a particular group to whom the method will be applied immediately but also to imagine a much broader audience for its eventual use.

❖ Be clear about the skills and concepts that are being demonstrated. Outline the concepts you want to teach and the skills that must be developed. Determine what action (and interaction) must be taken by participants to learn the skills and concepts. Eliminate any activity that does not directly contribute to the transfer of skills and knowledge.

❖ Keep the method as concise as possible. Few training programs have the luxury of abundant time to accomplish the training. Most methods must have an impact in a relatively brief period. Define how much time the method will take to process, and test to be sure it fits within that time frame, making adjustments as needed.

Implement and Evaluate the Method

❖ Be aware of any collateral skills and concepts that may emerge. It is the rare idea or skill-building activity that does not produce collateral learning; nearly everything has a ripple effect. While these effects may not be the primary purpose of the method, be prepared to capitalize on their presence to the degree that time permits.

❖ If you are not working with another trainer or are not yet prepared to share the method (see final suggestion), it is helpful for you to prepare for yourself an outline or a script as carefully as if another person would use it without your presence.

❖ Assuming you want or expect other trainers to use it, provide clear guidance. Include, in your rendering of the method, information about the concepts that drive the activity and the skills it is expected to produce as well as thorough instructions on how to use and debrief the activity and materials that could be presented in its support. Even if a minilecture or other presentation is not used during the activity, the trainer should still be aware of the theoretical foundation on which the method was built. Ideas and reactions often emerge during discussion that the trainer should be prepared to address; an understanding of the theory is essential.

❖ Test the method. Find a willing group to try it out on or arrange to test it with clients who will allow you to experiment. Ask colleagues if they can test the method for you to get additional feedback on how it works in another setting and with another trainer.

❖ Testing can be done very systematically with a questionnaire that you develop or less formally with verbal feedback on how the method worked. The more formal, the better, to be sure the desired outcomes are achieved, the feedback is comparable, and the results can be replicated. The level of testing depends, of course, on the complexity of the method.

❖ Avoid using an untested new method in a situation that could be defined as high risk: where more self-disclosure is required than you are certain the audience can handle, when there is a great deal of psychological stress already present, where rapport in the group is minimal, where the client is distrustful of experiential methods, and when you are working in a totally new environment.

Revise the Method

❖ Few methods are completely designed the first time they are tested. It is almost always necessary to test for a while, revise with the benefit of feedback, test again, then revise again. This can go on for quite some time. You may have noticed even with an exercise you have used for years, which you obtained from a good source, that small adjustments seem necessary. This is even more important when creating something new.

❖ Know when to let go. It is tempting to tinker until the method is perfect. Perfection is almost never achieved; do not feel you have to be the first to do so.

Share the Method

Trainers are always looking for new methods, and people who develop them should be credited for their work. As you develop the new method, think in terms of eventually publishing your work. Be sure to note all the references you have used (including page numbers and full citations), prepare explanations of the theories you use, write every version of the action steps you consider (even if you end up discarding most of them), and number and date each version of the method—do this to avoid the miserable process of trying to track down information or remember a small but critical idea at a later date.

Devising new methods requires creativity and dedication, but it keeps training fresh and interesting, not only for the participants but also for the trainer. Unless the method is very simple, it is best to assume the development will occur over a long period of time, possibly years, as it is explored, perfected, adapted, and modified until the desired result is achieved. One of the greatest advantages of long experience in the field of intercultural communication and training is a history of trying—and sometimes deciding not to use—many of the methods that are already available, and, in the process, becoming intimately familiar with their advantages and disadvantages.

There is no substitute for getting all the experience you can in any way that you can (even disappointing experiences are opportunities for learning) and for maintaining a high level of curiosity and willingness to learn from colleagues and participants alike. This will form the resource bank from which you can draw when it is time to create your very own "other" method.

Reference

Storti, Craig. *Cross-Cultural Dialogues: 74 Brief Encounters with Cultural Difference.* Yarmouth, ME: Intercultural Press, 1994.

Field Studies: Individual and Group Trips, Expeditions, and Hunts

Michael Gottlieb Berney

Field studies are those training activities through which participants actively explore the environment of another culture. They may take place in a building, on a campus, around a city, or in the countryside. Participants may work in groups or on their own. The common denominator is that participants themselves gather information that the trainer later helps them analyze. As a tool for cross-cultural training, this method permits participants to practice adaptation skills at the same time as they collect data. This method thus builds skills as well as knowledge.

Background and Specific Contexts in Which Field Studies Have Been Used

The Peace Corps pioneered an in-country "live-in" in the 1960s to provide a dose of real-life experience. The current version is termed "fully integrated training," which emphasizes the need to integrate, rather than compartmentalize, training in technical skills, language, crossing cultures, and health and safety. When trainees arrive in a host country, Peace Corps trainers provide a basic introduction and then send them to a small village, where they live with families. A Peace Corps support person/trainer is stationed in each village where he or she acts as a mentor or coach, helping trainees build skills and adapt to the local situation. In other training designs, where trainees live with families yet train daily as a group, a critical element is the discussion following the experience: trainers reassemble the volunteers as a group to analyze ways to adapt successfully to the local society.

World Learning (formerly the Experiment in International Living) conducts a similar field study in the United States called Drop Off. Students in the two-year upper-level bachelor's program are driven to small towns in Vermont, New Hampshire, and Massachusetts and dropped off in groups of two or three to learn about the community and themselves. An orientation provides them with the basic objectives and suggestions for safety. For the twenty-four hours they are in the community they are given five dollars and a roll of Life Savers and are asked not to bring any other source of money. They are also given a letter of introduction and telephone numbers they can call if they want to be picked up early. Again, the organizers construct the experience so that participants will practice adaptation skills at the same time as they collect information. The real-life encounters allow the trainers to highlight actual skills the participants used and to involve the group in addressing problems they will confront when they go to another culture for a subsequent seven-month internship.

The U.S. Department of Agriculture has also used a fieldwork exercise with international participants arriving in the United States for a four- to six-week training course. The field trip begins to familiarize participants with Washington, DC, including living accommodations and the surrounding community. The purpose is to help participants build a bank of survival information and to introduce cultural observation as a process for obtaining information from the social environment. This exercise—briefer than those developed by the Peace Corps or World Learning—takes approximately fifteen to thirty minutes to assign; then the excursion requires two and one-half hours (with the participants having lunch during the exercise), and debriefing can take anywhere from one-half hour to an hour. This design was originally developed by Jim McCaffrey of Training Resources Group in Alexandria, Virginia.

At Miami-Dade Community College, International Student Services Center for North Campus developed a field trip program titled "Miami…See it Like a Native," using a grant from the National Association for Foreign Student Affairs and the Bureau of Educational and Cultural Affairs of the U.S. Information Agency. In this program, designed for international students in their first year of study, leaders take students to different locations and leave them to explore the environment. In some cases, participants receive assignments to collect specific information. A sample of the range of information the students are asked to collect can be found in Appendix A: *Calle Ocho* Cultural Treasure Hunt. The students also use public transportation to increase their skills in moving around the city.

Berlitz language centers have used scavenger hunts in their English-language training programs. Students who speak little English visit a neighborhood with a list of items that they are to collect (for example, a spool of thread; a small, self-fastening plastic bag; a cracker). To collect these items, students independently devise ways to approach individuals at their homes or on the street. The assigned task inevitably leads to interactions beyond the simple collection of items.

Important Considerations When Designing a Field Study

There are a number of questions to contemplate when designing a field study. The following list of design questions is derived from this author's experience while working for Meridian International Center's training division. Since the 1960s, Meridian had used a guided field trip as part of its orientation program for international visitors to the United States. Volunteers took groups of trainees to shopping centers to visit stores, laundries, and supermarkets. Then in the mid-1980s, Meridian stopped using guides in order to increase the impact of the training so that participants had to wrestle with these challenges on their own.

We used the following questions to design our field study. They suggest factors you will want to consider in designing your field study. Following each design question are Meridian's responses for the programs they conducted during my tenure from 1986 to 1988.

Participant Description

What were the characteristics of the participants? Participants were visitors to the United States. Some had come for the first time and spoke little English. No more than two or three came from any one country. Some appeared frightened by Washington, DC—the place as well as the people they met. A few may have lived or studied in the United States before.

What knowledge or skills did participants have for cross-cultural adjustment? Some had skills in adaptation from having studied in a different country. Some were aware of culture shock from friends or colleagues who had lived abroad. Others, perhaps led by watching television and movies to see this country as a place of violence, had such a high degree of fear that they may not have wanted to leave their hotel room.

What were their needs? They were in the United States for as little as three weeks or as long as a year. Most were in academic programs or visiting institutions where they were on their own, attending courses with graduate students, or perhaps meeting with officials. The contrasts that may have shocked them related to fundamental differences in values: informality versus formality; time and its control versus human interaction; equality versus hierarchy. This last difference may have been especially frustrating for older individuals interacting with much younger people in positions of authority. For a brief description of these value contrasts written for visitors to the United States, see Kohls (1984). For a description written for Americans going to other countries, see Kohls (1996).

What were their learning styles? These individuals, typically schooled in traditional systems, were accustomed to rote learning and lecture.

How did the answers to these questions affect the design of the program? An assessment of the participants coming to Meridian's orientation program led me and my colleagues to send people out in groups of four to five and to ask that each group operate as a team. Teams were comprised so that they were as diverse as possible, for example, mixing older individuals with younger and those who had been to the United States before with those who were arriving for their first visit.

The range of participant interests caused the exploration to take place on different levels: some might have been addressing basic security and logistic concerns, while others might have been looking from a macroperspective at how American society operated. As part of this team exercise, participants shared multiple perspectives on a variety of issues. Even if one participant needed to focus initially on how to order food in a fast-food restaurant, he or she later reflected on the experience of watching parents and children interact in that public setting and used that first-hand experience to deepen understanding of values and cultural assumptions in the United States.

Objectives

What knowledge and skills did the participants need? Meridian's objectives, based on the characteristics of its trainees, were for its participants to

❖ work as a team to answer the individual questions and concerns participants have about the city—to develop a strategy for exploring any new place,

❖ identify differences in behavior that may result from differences in values,

❖ practice a highly participatory style of learning to optimize learning and interacting, and

❖ gain confidence in their ability to be self-sufficient.

What were the design implications? Based on these objectives, participants were given minimal instruction when they started out. We emphasized the purpose of the exercise and introduced—or had participants who had studied in the United States explain—the individual-centered, self-starter style that can be found in most graduate institutions and social environments in the United States. The task was framed as an opportunity to try out (or be reacquainted with) that style of behavior.

Resources and Constraints

What resources were available? Meridian provided a staff member available by phone if someone got lost and a trainer who could facilitate the introduction and the debriefing of the field trip. In addition, staff created and reproduced workbooks for each participant.

How much time was there? In a week-long program, participants might go out and explore on Monday from 1:30-4:00 P.M., possibly Monday evening, and then used Tuesday from 8:30-10:00 A.M. for the analysis back at Meridian. Alternately, the field study could occur during a morning with time for discussion that afternoon.

What were the other constraints? Timing this activity soon after participants arrived in the United States increased the likelihood that problems, such as lost luggage, would distract them. During winter, visitors from warm climates in particular found getting around in the cold (let alone in snow or icy conditions) difficult. Status concerns ("We are not students of anthropology," stated one high-placed government official) made it particularly difficult for some participants to venture out on their own; some raised other concerns to resist the participatory exercise. Visitors from countries where men and women do not typically interact outside of the family had additional concerns. All of these issues required sensitivity on the part of the organizers.

What were the design implications? The participants had an entire afternoon and evening for the exercise so that they could truly investigate a bit of U.S. society. We planned to deal with resistance by noting the culture contrasts that had surfaced ("If you are saying that only a group of students would do this type of activity in your country, while we are asking that senior officials do it here, then maybe we have already found a difference between customs in our two countries," we might say). When we had a sick participant or one with lost luggage, we encouraged the team to incorporate a trip to the doctor or airport as part of its expedition.

Content

What information needed to be available in the field study? This question covered both what materials you need to provide in advance and what information individuals should be able to discover on their own.

Because a primary objective of the Meridian field study was for the group to answer the individual questions and concerns of participants, their questions and concerns suggested the sets of information that needed to be available. For example, if a particular group wanted to learn how to use the Washington, DC, transportation system, we provided maps and Metro instructions. Once they got to a Metro station, they were able to try out automated machines that issued tickets and obtain more information, both in printed form and through asking people for help (which some found to their surprise local folk freely offered once asked). If, however, people wanted to learn how men and women interact in the United States, we directed them to observe interactions in stores and in office buildings.

Because a further objective was for participants to generalize this experience to new places that they would visit, we hoped participants would collect information about how to gather information as well as data that are specific to Washington, DC. The literature they found was most likely Washington-specific, but experience—for example, it helped to initiate dialogue rather than wait for people to notice that you were lost—was often generalized to other locales.

To help participants identify the range of behavior among people in the United States, they needed to watch people interact in different settings. We anticipated that different teams would collect contradictory information, dramatizing that there are no simple or "right" answers out there. Noticing the complexity of social patterns also reduced stereotyping.

Location

Where did the field study take place? To learn about people and social interaction in the United States, the best sites were those where participants could ask questions, try out new behavior, and observe daily life and customs. Stores, banks, a neighborhood clinic, a fast-food restaurant, an outdoor cafe, and a shopping mall were all possibilities. To model learning that was centered on participants (rather than teachers or trainers), the trainer encouraged teams to travel between these places on their own, using public transportation or walking. Another suggestion was to compare two similar institutions, for example, a supermarket and a small grocery store.

Safety needed to be addressed up front. We explained that Washington, DC, like any city in the world, had some areas where it was not safe to travel alone at night. We pointed out the more traveled areas, stated that traveling as a team would itself address the issue of safety, and invited them to investigate what was safe and what was not as they moved about.

Instructions

How did we introduce the activity and what directions did we provide? Because one objective was for participants to take the lead, perhaps the less said, the better. The trainer needed to divide the group into small teams and introduce the objectives for the activity. As stated earlier, especially for participants of high status (and who valued hierarchy), framing the purpose was critical, and it helped to have them restate why they were conducting this study. From that point on each team developed its own strategy for gathering information. The trainer asked teams to collect available materials in sufficient quantities to share with other teams.

Letting teams self-select tended to yield more homogeneous groups with greater comfort. We thought that participants would better achieve field study objectives by forming more diverse groups so that teams would have a blend of perspectives and abilities. So a final part of our instructions involved dividing participants into the teams in which they would work.

Generalization and Application

How did we debrief the activity so that participants could gain insights into cross-cultural adaptation? When teams returned, either the same day or the following morning, the trainer had them work together to draw on newsprint what they observed. Each group reported on its observations. The trainer guided this process and asked people to interrupt with questions as the reports continued.

How did participants apply what they learned to their individual needs? After all teams shared their observations, the trainer asked the group to suggest general steps that they might take when they traveled to new locations (for example, "What would you do differently if you are on your own?"). He or she asked participants to list examples of behavior that differed from what they anticipated, which would lead into an ensuing presentation on cultural values in the United States that may have explained some of that behavior. The trainer also asked what participants learned that would help them during the rest of their stay in the United States.

Here it was particularly important that teams reported to one another rather than to the trainers, whom they may have viewed as authorities. By leaving some questions unanswered and encouraging dialogue, this analysis itself encouraged participants to maintain and continue their discussion and study.

Benefits and Costs to the Trainees

In contrast to most cross-cultural training methods in which participants practice skills in the classroom, a field study can permit practice through real-life encounters. Even if participants cannot explore the environment they will face, interactions in a challenging environment create a richness difficult to achieve in the classroom setting. In the classroom a trainer can talk about communicating with people from a different culture. Participants can study nonverbal and verbal cues and even practice interactions through role plays. A trainer can help trainees to understand the assumptions that they bring to such interactions. The field study, by comparison, lets participants discover how they respond to cross-cultural encounters. Somehow it all comes together for the trainees when they are "out there": in a village or part of town where no one speaks their first language, where the shopkeeper behaves in different ways from those to which they are accustomed, and when even making change for a purchase becomes a complex task. Outside the classroom, taking a break to use the lavatory may not provide an escape from cross-cultural training.

The disadvantages of the method are several: precisely because a field study occurs outside the classroom, trainers cannot control the experience, and experiences will vary from individual to individual. Real-life experiences may fascinate some people, while others may feel overwhelmed. As a trainer, you may struggle with conflicting urges to make this activity safe and challenging.

Outcomes for the Trainer/Training Program

What training institutions can provide participants is invariably restricted. Resources are limited, you may have only some of the materials you want, and you and your fellow trainers may know about only some of the experiences you want to share with the trainees. The field study removes many of these limitations. In selecting sites for participants to visit, you can complement what participants explore within the walls of the training institution.

From the perspective of the trainer, your focus shifts from providing an experience to deciphering one. The participants return to you having had personal encounters and having gathered knowledge first-hand. Your role is then to assist trainees to understand what they experienced.

At Meridian, the field study session survived other program changes. Though designed for a five-day program, Meridian trainers use the field study even in a two-day session, primarily because participants gain insights into things they previously would not have noticed. Carole Gaillard Watt, Meridian's past executive vice president responsible for orientation and training programs, borrowed a phrase from the French novelist Marcel Proust (1871-1922), who said that the real voyage of discovery consists not in seeking new lands, but in seeing with new eyes.

Comparison of the Field Study with Other Methods

The field study in its various forms is perhaps most like a simulation, which tries to model aspects of reality in a controlled environment. But, the field study switches the emphasis—there is perhaps greater reality and certainly less control. If trainees are exploring an area different from their final destination, they are to some extent engaging in role play. They try out some of the behavior they might use when they move to their destination.

Resources

For more information about the field study used in the "Discovering the United States" orientation and training program conducted by Meridian International Center, contact the Training and Visitors Services Division of Meridian, 1630 Crescent Place, NW, Washington, DC 20009; phone 202-667-6800.

References

Kohls, L. Robert. *Survival Kit for Overseas Living*. 3d ed. Yarmouth, ME: Intercultural Press,1996.

———. "Values Americans Live By." Washington, DC: Meridian House International, 1984. Article available in English and Spanish from the Meridian Training and Visitors Services Division.

Appendix A

Calle Ocho Cultural Treasure Hunt

List three tropical fruits used to make ices and ice creams.

1.

2.

3.

What is the name of the starchy plant in the banana family that is served both sweet and nonsweet?

4.

What is a *media noche*?

5.

To what, or whom, is the monument on the corner of 8th Street and 13th Avenue dedicated?

6.

What is the name of the park where dominoes is played?

7.

List the ingredients of a Cuban sandwich.

8.

9.

10.

What kind of merchandise is sold at a *ferreteria*?

11.

List the name of two *joyerias*.

12.

13.

What is a *cubilite*?

14.

What is *cortadito*?

15.

What is a frita and what is it made of?

16.

17.

What is known as *salsa* (in music)?

18.

What is the national attire for Cuban men and where can you buy it?

19.

20.

What would the basic dishes of a Cuban meal be?

21.

What is *guarapo*?

22.

From materials developed for the "Miami…See It Like a Native" program, contact Joel Fleischer, Coordinator, International Student Services, Miami-Dade Community College, North Campus, 11380 N.W. 27th Avenue, Miami, FL 33167.

Visual Imagery as a Training Tool

Fanchon J. Silberstein and Dorothy A. Sisk

"Seeing with the mind's eye" is a simple way of defining visual imagery, and psychologists often describe it as the language of the unconscious. Visual imagery can alter an individual's state of awareness, and numerous writers (Rudhar 1982; Ernst 1982; Sisk and Shallcross 1989; Schiffman 1980; Weisburd 1987) have chronicled its importance as a companion to creative thought, as a healing power, as a means of developing awareness, and as a way to expand rational thinking. We have used visual imagery as a training tool to assist participants in viewing their cultures more clearly and in understanding how personal assumptions and values affect multicultural interactions. To develop a better understanding and appreciation of visual imagery as a training tool, we present a brief history followed by specific procedures for putting it to use. We will identify several contexts in which we have used visual imagery successfully and discuss potential pitfalls and problems. Last, we will list resources to assist trainers interested in exploring its potential.

History of Visual Imagery

Early societies valued dreams and fantasies as products of visual imagery. These ancient peoples lived in a symbiotic union with nature, and their art displayed images of nature as a significant force. Today, many Eastern cultures and indigenous peoples continue to live in a similar relationship to nature.

As early as 200 B.C., writers described the purposeful use of visual imagery. The ancient scholar Patanjali (Sisk and Shallcross 1986) describes it as having three states. The first he called *dharana*, in which the individual focuses on a given place or object. In the second state, *dhyana*, the individual strengthens the focus of attention by using supportive gestures, such as hand movements or body postures. And in the third, *samadhi*, the individual experiences a union or fusion with the object and is not able to distinguish self from object. There is a sense of being absorbed into the object. To achieve the first state of dharana, many Eastern cultures use mandalas (simple or complex geometric forms, depending upon the purpose—see illustration on page 188) to center the eye or focus concentration. Psychologist Carl G. Jung (1983), in *Memories, Dreams and Reflections*, describes the imagery process, particularly samadhi, and champions the seeking of unity in mind, body, and spirit.

The ancient Greeks used principles of healing in which visual imagery cured disease. Today, physicians and patients still use visual imagery, particularly to control pain and to fight catastrophic illnesses. Some physicians now recognize the role images play in producing diseases as well as in healing them. This phenomenon represents a powerful example of the importance of visual imagery in modern life.

In summary, visual imagery has a rich tradition extending from our modern world back through time to ancient peoples who (as suggested by anthropologists) often made little distinction between sleeping and waking states or between visions and perceptions. The trainer who uses samadhi as well as the other two states of visual imagery can directly encourage participants to personalize their learning experiences and enrich and deepen the training effects.

Procedure for Using Visual Imagery

A design using four related guided imagery exercises to deepen cross-cultural understanding follows. However, before using visual imagery, there are several steps you need to take to prepare your group.

Step 1

Warm-Up. First, create a sense of belonging or community, build trust, and stimulate mutual interest within the group. One way you can build this community is by asking the participants to introduce themselves, to define their understanding of visual imagery, and to report on how they have used it. As they provide examples from their professional and personal lives, the participants expand their individual understanding of the technique and its merits. This warm-up time serves to reaffirm the many ways to use the technique and highlights similarities and differences in the participants' responses.

Step 2

History of Visual Imagery. Next, present a brief history of the technique, a simple working definition, and specific applications of visual imagery as a training tool. This type of discussion familiarizes the participants with the technique and provides an opportunity to ask questions. In addition, if individuals have concerns or fears they can identify and discuss them at this time.

Step 3

Agenda. Then share the agenda, including goals and objectives, of the visual imagery session. The goals are these:
1. To build understanding of self and others
2. To perceive similarities and differences in cultures

3. To try on different roles, ideas, and attitudes in a safe environment
4. To increase the ability to use visual imagery creatively

Listing the goals establishes a sense of orderly learning and purpose and shows respect for the integrity of the participants. In the body of the workshop, participants explore their understanding of themselves and others through specific training activities. We find that when participants fully experience an activity and process it so that the insights it offers are internalized, they are more likely to use visual imagery effectively. This type of active learning, compared with a more didactic approach, involves both the intellect and the senses and enhances personal benefits from the technique.

Many of our ideas for using visual imagery in training are derived from processes in Gestalt psychology, designed to help participants increase self-understanding. Images, ideas, and connections create a whole, or "gestalt." We will describe certain activities that were popularized by the Gestalt psychologist Fritz Perls (1958), who recommended a short relaxation exercise to increase the participant's receptivity to visual imagery.

Step 4

Relaxation. Introduce relaxation techniques in a simple manner, and for this and all visual imagery activities, use a modulated tone, which slows the process sufficiently to provide time for participants to create images. These images eventually contribute to the gestalt. For example,

> Think of a place where you can be quiet. This can be a real place or a place that exists only in your imagination. Sit or lie down, whichever is more comfortable or preferable to you.
>
> Now close your eyes and become aware of your breathing.
>
> Take several deep breaths and count slowly, from 1 to 7 on each inhale and from 1 to 7 on each exhale.
>
> Inhale 1-2-3-4-5-6-7. Now exhale 1-2-3-4-5-6-7.
>
> Concentrate on relaxing your entire body. Begin with your toes.
>
> First tense your toes, hold them that way, and relax. Now tense your ankles, hold them, and relax.

Continue this exercise by asking participants to tense, hold, and relax their knees, thighs, hips, buttocks, stomach, chest, shoulders, arms, hands, fingers, neck, head, and face. Following this process, ask them to notice changes in each part of their bodies as they concentrate on it. Relaxation exercises help participants to use visual imagery effectively; however, an experienced imager can become quiet by simply taking a few deep breaths or by imaging a quiet place or using a mandala such as the one on the following page to focus awareness.

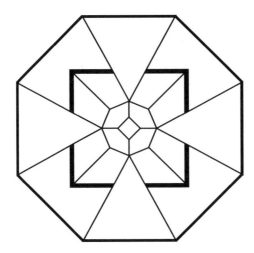

Zdenek (1983), in *The Right Brain Experience*, suggests that focusing on a mandala encourages the spatially oriented functions of the cerebral right hemisphere of the brain to dominate the logical, sequential, and rational processes of the left cerebral hemisphere. She suggests that participants focus on the center of the mandala and become aware of their body relaxing. We find that when participants concentrate or focus on a visual pattern for five minutes or more, their inner dialogue is gradually replaced by a quieting process that encourages visual imagery. When people are relaxed, you are ready to proceed with the first guided imagery exercise.

Exercise 1

Self-Understanding Activity

In the following activity, adapted from Fritz Perls' "Revisiting the House of a Friend," participants use imagery to build understanding of self and others. Give these directions:

> Think of a house that you might want to revisit.
>
> Choose a memory of the house that is not too distant or difficult for you to recall.
>
> Now, close your eyes, and be aware of what you see. What do you actually see?
>
> Is someone opening the door?
>
> Are there other people in your image?
>
> Try to accept the images as they appear without conscious editing.
>
> Allow yourself to go back to this remembered place. Notice what is there, and hold on to the pictures.
>
> As the pictures reveal themselves, you may find words linked to them.

Concentrate on the images. In a few moments, prepare to share the images if you so desire. Now, take one last look at the images. Try to see them in their totality.

Be aware of your feelings and at the count of 3 (1-2-3) move some part of your body. Open your eyes.

Encourage participants to share their images with another person or in small groups of three. Remind them to avoid interpretations by reporting only what they have seen. There will be time later to go below the surface. It is essential that trainees or participants draw their own conclusions. The trainer serves as a guide, stepping back when necessary. In facilitating the exercise and the processing, remind participants that if sensitive or damaging thoughts or images emerge, it is permissible to keep them private and that everyone will respect that desire.

Processing. Ask the participants to share insights from the exercise in groups of three or four. Participants are usually more comfortable discussing personal information and feelings in small groups. After fifteen or more minutes, bring the whole group together and pose a question such as, "Were you surprised by anything?" or "Did anything become more clear?" Point out similarities and differences in the participants' responses and note that different points of view provide new ideas and ways of looking at things. An understanding of one's self sets the stage for deepening cross-cultural understanding.

Exercise 2

Bridging between Internal and External

To understand, appreciate, and be sensitive to other cultures, the participant must work with images and experiences outside the self. The image moves from the interior landscape to an external, concrete experience. The following exercise aids in this process. (As with most visual imagery exercises, this should be preceded by a relaxation exercise. The participants are asked to close their eyes as the trainer introduces the instructions for the exercise. Remember to pause after each image that you introduce to allow time for inner searching and seeing.)

Now that you are in a relaxed state, concentrate your awareness on your country.

But as you picture it, observe that you are visiting before it was created as a nation.

What you see now is the land many years ago, before anyone lived there.

To see it fully, you must float above it, lightly as a bird. Look about you and observe the land itself.

What do you see? (Pause following each question to give sufficient time for silent reflection.)

What does the land look like? Are there trees? Rivers? Mountains? Deserts? What else do you see?

Are there animals?

Are there people?

How do they appear? What are they wearing? What do you notice about their appearance: hands, hair, eyes, height?

What are they doing? Are they working? Caring for families?

Do they seem happy? Sad? Serious? Lighthearted?

What might these people be thinking about?

What might they worry about?

When you are ready, open your eyes.

Shift in your chair and reflect quietly on how you feel and what you know.

Processing. Ask participants again to share their insights in small groups. Alternatively, ask the following questions of the whole group:

Would anyone like to describe what he or she saw? (land, people, etc.)

What were people doing? Feeling?

How did you feel going through this exercise?

What did you realize?

Record the group's comments on newsprint and use this information later in problem solving or in an introduction to other exercises. This exercise can be used to create a base for further exercises in cross-cultural awareness. One possibility follows.

Exercise 3

Cultural Understanding

Now, let's go back to your quiet, envisioning self.

Close your eyes again and concentrate on your breathing. Sense your back against the chair, your feet on the floor.

Return to floating above your country. Now, many years have passed, and you are looking at a familiar nation. As you float above, identify specific landmarks: mountains, rivers, plains, streets, buildings.

Because you are floating high above your country, you can still see the land as a composite, as a patchwork. You can see great distances just by turning your head.

Now find a town, a village, a farm, or another place to visit. Float for a few moments, decide where you want to go. Now gently lower yourself to the place you have chosen. You are in a special situation because you are invisible. Walk through the streets and on the roads or through the area you have chosen.

It is growing dark and people are assembling for the evening meal. Enter a house or dwelling and sit quietly with a family at their table. Listen to them. What are they saying? What do you notice? What brings them joy? What do they worry about?

When you are ready, open your eyes and sit quietly.

Processing. Ask participants to talk in groups of three (or with a partner) about their experience. Encourage the participants to go below surface appearances and look for relationships and meaning. Give them time to discuss their experiences and ideas and ask for feedback from individual groups. Conclude this series of three exercises by providing opportunities for participants to generalize from their experiences. The visual imagery exercises will have provided a wealth of material and insights. Ask such questions as, "What did you notice about the worries of the family in Exercise 3 that were peculiar to its culture?" "Would people from other countries be likely to have the same concerns?" After the processing you may ask the participants if they have ever had a cross-cultural interaction that enlarged their perception of family life in another culture. Family life is an example of an element of culture that the visual imagery exercises can bring especially well into focus. Other cultural elements will have emerged during the processing of these exercises that you may want participants to expand upon as well.

Training Contexts for Using Visual Imagery

Rudolf Arnheim (1969), philosopher and former professor of visual studies, says that when you want to think through an issue, you need a basis in imagery. He studied the relationship between thinking and seeing and concluded that images acquired early in life usually support basic learning and give us the basis for moving to higher levels of reasoning. This leads us to appreciate how fundamental the use of imagery is in solving problems and engaging in creative thinking.

Intercultural leadership training is one of the contexts in which visual imagery can be a powerful tool. We have used the exercises with multicultural groups to encourage them to focus on leadership in specific contexts. Imagery exercises, tailored for particular individuals and groups, help them plan, prepare, and take responsibility for many aspects of an intercultural experience. We have used these exercises in the following contexts:

❖ overseas relocation and reentry
❖ general cultural awareness
❖ culture-specific preparation
❖ orientation
❖ preparation of professionals to provide services to a multicultural population
❖ culture shock
❖ problem solving in specific settings
❖ empathy building

❖ perceptions of moral or immoral behavior in cross-cultural contexts

❖ goal setting

❖ ethnocentrism

❖ values clarification

The training context determines the learning goal and provides the audience for the visual imagery exercise. Here is a description of an activity that can be adapted to a variety of situations. A group of U.S. Department of Defense teachers was returning to big cities in the United States from small towns in Turkey and Greece. During reentry training, we asked them to picture the places they had lived abroad, concentrating on what was most important to them, including smells and sounds. We asked them to focus on their feelings about these things and to hold those feelings tightly in their right hand. We then asked them to float above the homes in which they would live in the United States, continuing to hold the important experiences from their overseas sojourns, bringing them to their lives at home. The concluding discussion focused on integrating overseas experience into work and domestic life in the United States. At the end of the exercise many people found fingernail marks in the palms of their right hand.

The setting, actual or imagined, for the imagery exercises should be relevant to the needs of the trainees. For example, when your goal is role rehearsal for work, select a setting in the workplace, even the office of the employer. If your goal is to help a group of anxious participants relax, suggest that they envision a secure place in which they can safely feel emotions. When participants can vividly recall feelings and feel safe to do so, they can be reminded that this is a resource they carry with them that can be utilized under other conditions. In the future, they can virtually return to situations simply by closing their eyes and calling forth their feelings.

Benefits to the Learner

Overall, in many training settings visual imagery will enrich other material and motivate participants to personalize and react to learning. The trainer, as guide, uses imagery exercises to call upon the best resources of each individual learner. Thus, these exercises empower learners, have an immediate impact on them in their present situations, encourage an increase in self-knowledge, and demonstrate respect and appreciation for the inner life. Exercises in visual imagery are also consistent with principles of adult learning. They encourage spontaneity, respect choice, call upon previous experience, and give opportunities for direct participation, both in the calling up of the imagery itself and later in the processing.

Resistance and Pitfalls

Most facilitators are familiar with the resistance of some participants to interactive training exercises of any type, and it is likely that some participants may be puzzled by or dubious of the use of guided imagery in particular. This reaction is understandable, especially if they cannot see the connection to other learning.

Resistance may diminish when you point out that visual imagery can be used as a type of quick problem solving. In other words, reframe the activity to emphasize its usefulness and explain it in more conventional, educational language. In any case, present the rationale behind the activity, and give individuals the choice to participate or abstain.

Though you may clearly understand the use of visual imagery, participants may need help in understanding its value in encouraging group development and in enhancing role plays, simulations, or problem-solving exercises. We believe cross-cultural success may be increased if a participant rehearses behavior by imaging different roles, ideas, and attitudes. The risk is minimal, since one is only imagining these different ways of being.

Some trainees may be uncomfortable with ambiguity or open-endedness. It is very important that the use of imagery be directly related to the training goals of the program and clearly guided by the facilitator. Later, when participants are more comfortable and accustomed to using visual imagery, it is desirable to drop some of the guidance and encourage participants to create their own imagery.

Visual imagery, as a training tool, deepens cross-cultural understanding and is complementary to other methods. It heightens learning and aids in developing content for case studies and role plays.

References

Arnheim, Rudolf. *Visual Thinking*. New York: Viking Press, 1969.

Ernst, M. "Inspiration to Order." In *The Creative Process*, edited by B. Ghiselin. New York: Mentor Books, 1982.

Jung, Carl G. *Memories, Dreams and Reflections*. New York: Pantheon Books, 1983.

Perls, Fritz. "Gestalt Techniques." Esalen Workshop, June 1958.

Rudhar, P. *The Magic of Tone and the Art of Music*. Boulder, CO: Shambhala, 1982.

Schiffman, Muriel. *Gestalt Self-Therapy and Further Techniques for Personal Growth*. Berkeley: Wingbow Press, 1980.

Sisk, Dorothy A., and D. Shallcross. *Intuition: An Inner Way of Knowing*. Buffalo, NY: Bearly Limited, 1989.

———. *Leadership: Making Things Happen*. Buffalo, NY: Bearly Limited, 1986.

Weisburd, S. "The Spark: Personal Testimonies of Creativity." *Science News* 132 (1987 November): 298–300.

Zdenek, M. *The Right Brain Experience*. New York: McGraw-Hill, 1983.

Resources

Dinkmeyer, Don, and Lewis Losoney. *The Encouragement Book*. New York: Prentice Hall, 1980.

Fagan, Joen, and Irma Lee Shepherd, eds. *Gestalt Therapy Now: Theory, Techniques, Applications.* Palo Alto, CA: Science and Behavior Books, 1970.

Gawain, Shakti. *Creative Visualization.* New York: Bantam New Age Books, 1982.

Jaffe, Dennis. *Healing from Within.* New York: Simon & Schuster, 1986.

Noddings, N., and P. J. Shore. *Awakening the Inner Eye.* New York: Teachers College Press, 1984.

Samuels, M., and N. Samuels. *Seeing with the Mind's Eye.* New York: Random House, 1975.

Sher, Barbara. *Wishcraft: How to Get What You Really Want.* New York: Penguin U.S.A., 1979.

Stevens, John O. *Awareness: Exploring, Experimenting, Experiencing.* Lafayette, CA: Real People Press, 1971.

Vaughn, F. *Awakening Intuition.* New York: Doubleday, 1979.

A Primer for Designing and Using Participant Training Manuals

Robert Cyr

Training manuals are more than just a text that accompanies the program. A properly designed training manual assists in structuring the learning process. It can help learners more clearly understand cultural concepts and analyze their meaning. The training manual can guide the pace of the learning, and after the course is over, the manual helps in reviewing and retaining what was learned.

Introduction

Training manuals are an important way to help learners follow lectures and discussions that are usually an integral part of cross-cultural learning. Training manuals record key learning concepts, usually in the order they are to be discussed, and often include case studies, exercises, and articles for background reading. They can be used in most kinds of intercultural training, with large groups or for one-on-one instruction, for short seminars or for training conducted over an extended period.

Yet, training manuals are not prepared and used as frequently as they should be, most often because trainers think they are too costly and that technical expertise is needed to produce professional-looking materials. In fact, since desktop publishing capabilities are now included in most word-processing programs, simple, well-designed, and effective manuals can be developed in-house by any organization, even those with limited staff and restricted budgets.

The first thing to do is determine which type of training manual best fits your needs. Then consider the following: content, page design, supplementary content (for example, case studies, practice exercises, and readings), type of binding, and a few other components such as the preface and table of contents.

This chapter provides a simple "how-to" primer for putting together and using professional-looking and affordable training manuals. While some costs are involved, they are minimal. And with some careful planning, creativity, and effort, you can produce a powerful training instrument.

Types of Manuals

There are two broad categories of training for which manuals are prepared: *instructor-led* and *self-guided*. Since most intercultural training involves a session leader or facilitator who provides key information and guides group discussion, the instructor-led manual is the more common. We will start, therefore, with a brief discussion of self-guided training manuals and then devote the majority of the chapter to instructor-led training manuals.

Self-Guided Training Manuals

Using Self-Paced Guides

Self-paced guides or self-guided workbooks need to be much more detailed than instructor-led manuals and are more difficult to develop by yourself. Fortunately, there are some good published guides available to help prepare sojourners or immigrants for adjustment in a host county or readjustment on their return home. Martha Denny's *Going Home: A Workbook for Reentry and Professional Integration* (1986) is a fine example, designed to be used over an extended period. According to Denny, we rarely have the opportunity to follow the growth of an individual and be available at the right time to provide guidance. On the other hand, the material in workbooks stimulates development through self-evaluation which stays with the person. Workbooks provide a framework for thinking about the most important issues and a structure for organizing experience.

Self-guided workbooks contain guidelines for dealing with frequently encountered problems. Worksheets, checklists, and exercises aim to stimulate values clarification, goal setting, and action planning. In this way individuals are encouraged to assess critical factors for decision making, personal growth, and intercultural adaptation.

Adults are not the only group to benefit from self-guided cross-cultural training. *Where in the World Are You Going?* (Blohm 1996) is a workbook filled with activities for children ages five to ten, which will make any family's overseas move more manageable. Children begin with exercises concentrating on themselves and their families and how they can help each other get ready for the move. These exercises give them an opportunity to examine their feelings and say good-bye. Next the workbook addresses the new country and how best to learn about it. Cultural differences provide perhaps the greatest challenge for children, and Blohm offers several exercises that tackle this head-on. Not unlike workbooks for adults, this one draws children into making decisions, learning more about themselves, and beginning the process of adapting to the new culture. It sets a standard for children's workbooks.

Although these manuals are intended to provide self-guided instruction, they work best in conjunction with individual counseling and group discussion. These support activities can serve to stimulate the discipline needed to progress through the workbook conscientiously and also serve as a feedback mechanism for values exploration and clarification.

Self-guided workbooks can also be used as an adjunct to instructor-led intercultural training: exercises can be assigned and reviewed later in class discussion. For example, the information on the cultural influences that make an American and how the world sees Americans in Robert Kohls' *Survival Kit for Overseas Living* (1996) can be helpful whether read on the plane going over or as an assignment in a training program. But when it is an assignment, you have the chance in a subsequent class discussion to explore the subject more fully, especially by bringing in the varied personal experiences with target cultures of the participants. Though focused on Americans, Kohls' work can also serve as a model for an exercise for non-Americans going abroad.

Here are some guidelines to help assure effective workbook utilization. Do a pilot test to determine its strengths and weaknesses. When distributing the workbook to individuals or groups, preview its structure and explain how each part affects the success of the overall process. Indicate as clearly and specifically as possible the benefits to be derived from conscientiously following the workbook process. Give a realistic estimation of the effort required to complete it. Describe potential roadblocks, and have trainees suggest ways the roadblocks might be overcome. Help the trainees set a daily, weekly, or monthly schedule for completing workbook assignments. Schedule individual counseling sessions to review progress. And finally, whenever possible, include group discussions with others who are experiencing or have experienced in the past similar cross-cultural problems and discoveries.

Instructor-Led Training Manuals

Instructor-led training manuals are intended for use in the classroom setting. They can be written in either of two styles: *narrative* or *skeletal*. The narrative form approaches the detail and comprehensiveness of a script. Manuals in this format frequently contain blocks of prose in paragraph form on the left side of the page, with the right side blank for taking notes. In the skeletal style the prose is abbreviated, as in outline or topical form.

The chief benefit for trainees in using the skeletal manual is that it encourages their active participation in the training by requiring more personal selection and interpretation of what they learn. The main benefit to the designer of the manual is that, with less detail, it is easier to develop initially and to revise when necessary.

There are benefits for the trainer as well. The skeletal form serves more as a cueing instrument than a script does and allows trainers greater flexibility and room for creativity in constructing activities and communicating ideas. Most of the subsequent discussion in this chapter pertains to the skeletal-form manual.

Page Content

How much information do you put on a page? Since the purpose of the manual is to provide only key points and to assist in taking notes, limit each page to eight to ten sentences or phrases. I leave enough white space between lines for trainees to write their notes from lectures and discussions.

Initially, I provided only a few key words or phrases under each topic heading—much like the bullet points in slide presentations—and indicated to trainees that they should complete the ideas through detailed note taking. But experience revealed that some participants took very few notes, and the usefulness of their manuals as a review tool was consequently greatly diminished. So in subsequent editions of the manual I provided key ideas in sentence form.

The reason to limit the number of ideas on a page to about ten is that it controls the length of class discussion, structures its direction, and provides a summary that can be easily reviewed, all of which helps keep training moving and on track.

Page Design

The type style of the page is one of the more important factors affecting the overall professionalism and quality of its appearance. A few years ago, the only way to get anything on a page besides the standard elite or prestige typeface was to go to an outside printer or use desktop publishing programs that were expensive to buy and difficult to develop proficiency in. Now every word-processing software program comes with multiple type styles and font options. I prefer *New Times Roman* in fourteen point. The font style is attractive and easy to read, and the slightly larger typeface makes it easier for trainees to locate information as they shift their focus back and forth between the instructor and the training manual.

Bold-print page titles and larger print for the content may not seem like dramatic innovations, but they are a far cry from the typewritten, stapled packets of handouts one sometimes received in intercultural seminars. And even if the text is no more than an easy-to-read replication of your newsprint pages, it saves trainees the time and distraction of copying this information. Many course participants have thanked me for that.

Here are a few more guidelines about page design:

❖ Decide between printing on just one side of the page or printing back-to-back. One-sided printing adds to clarity, since there is no print from the reverse side to show through, and the blank opposite side of the page can be used for note taking. On the other hand, two-sided printing is more economical.

❖ Avoid mixing type styles; most people consider it unattractive.

❖ Avoid using overly large type; it looks like a flyer.

❖ Do not mix horizontal and vertical page layouts.

❖ Always be consistent and strive for simplicity.

Training Manual Content

Whatever the design of your training, it can be incorporated into your training manual. While the program content is provided in the experiential exercises and readings, the structure of the program is revealed by the course schedule and section introductions. I use section introductions to help students focus on the content to be covered and the specific goals of the training.

Section Introductions

Section introductions are single pages at the start of each module, chapter, or other major division of your training manual. My introductions have three components: "Overview," "Why This Information Is Important," and "Training Objectives." The "Overview" briefly summarizes the main content of the section. "Why This Information Is Important" is a two- or three-sentence description of the significance of the content of the section. Under "Training Objectives," list two or three behaviors, activities, or actions the student will be able to accomplish after completing the section. Objectives begin with verbs, as in the following example:

After completing this section, you will be better able to do the following:
❖ Follow the correct protocol in exchanging business cards with Japanese business professionals

❖ Participate effectively in a Japanese business meeting

❖ Interpret the significance of silence as a Japanese negotiation tactic

Reading the objectives aloud in class at the beginning of a section helps focus the students—and the instructor—on the purpose of the training. Note that objectives avoid using such words as *learn, understand, know*, or *be aware of.* In preparing a learning objective, your initial notion may be that the goal of the teaching is to enable students to understand an idea or concept. At that point ask yourself, "Understand in order to be able to do what?" The answer to that question is the true objective of learning expressed in terms of behavioral outcomes.

Case Studies and Exercises

In my *Client Relations—Japan* program, I use case studies from Richard Brislin's *Intercultural Interactions: A Practical Guide* (1986). This book is an anthology of over one hundred critical incidents or mini case studies indexed by nation and underlying cultural issue. This kind of training device is frequently called a culture assimilator or intercultural sensitizer (see *Sourcebook*, Vol. 1, "Culture Assimilator"). Each problem is presented in anecdotal form with alternative explanations of the cross-cultural issues critiqued in a separate section. Other such books exist, and permission to reprint individual critical incidents can be obtained at little or no expense. All you really need to do is adapt them to the style of the manual.

There is a substantial body of instructional material available in the cross-cultural training literature (much of it identified in the two volumes of the *Sourcebook*), though some intercultural trainers prefer to develop their own case studies to save on expense or because they need to use more customized activities.

Various kinds of experiential and practice exercises can be included with instructions for carrying them out along with debriefing or processing questions. Again, make sure they are adapted to your manual's design format.

If you prefer to distribute exercises in class at the time they are to be used, prepunch with holes for later inclusion in the training manual binder.

Readings

Many trainers provide reading materials as part of precourse assignments or as information to be read later. These may include magazine articles, newspaper stories, or excerpts from books.

Unless the material used is very brief (200 words or less), copyright laws require you to obtain permission from the publisher and/or author before reproducing. It has been my experience that in most instances permission is granted at no cost or for a very reasonable fee. A short letter to the publisher specifying title, author, publishing date, and page numbers together with a description of your organization and the intended use of the material is all that is needed.

In their responses, publishers will provide the exact wording to use in your manual to indicate reprint permission has been granted. The law requires that you take the trouble to write to get that permission. Moreover, those permissions at the bottom of the page are an additional testimony to your research and the professionalism of the course.

Binders

It may seem like a minor aspect of the manual, but the binder cover can reinforce impressions about the sophistication and quality of your program. It is often said, you cannot tell a book by its cover; nonetheless, first impressions matter. Rather than a cover bearing just the printed title of the course and the name of your college or company, consider putting some time and creativity into the cover design.

I have produced a series of training programs for communicating and interacting with Asian clients. These have included *Client Relations—Japan, Client Relations—China*, and *Client Relations—Korea*. And for domestic clients, I developed *Client Relations—Today*. I wanted titles that were short, strong, and dynamic. What you call things affects how they are perceived. I knew at the outset I would be producing a series of related courses, so the first cover established a set of design themes that could be repeated with variations in subsequent manuals. I wanted this series to look interesting too. Here's how it looked:

Figure 1

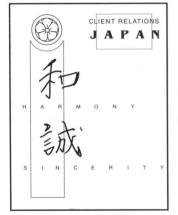  

We started with Japan, then with two subsequent volumes, we altered the lettering of the country designation, changed the style of the latticework, used Chinese or Korean words for the key concepts, and used a different second color. For the *Client Relations—Today* training manual, we could not use the oriental column as a design motif, but we kept the rectangular shape by placing a door frame behind a stylized silhouette of two people shaking hands.

To avoid excessively high costs in producing the design, either draw it yourself or approach the graphic arts department of a local college, as I did. Talented students are often eager for opportunities to develop samples for their portfolios. Payment should be appropriate but will not be on the scale expected by public relations or graphic arts firms.

Many professional printing firms will stamp your design on your binder covers, and some specialize in doing so. Our printer provided his own binders. We were surprised that the total cost of binders and imprinting was less than we were paying for binders alone. Previously we had been paying too much for unnecessary options such as inside pockets and the like, and our new printer gave a substantial discount on the cost of the binders because of the quantity we ordered.

Other Components

There are a few remaining items to consider including in your training manual.

Preface—A preface page indicates the overall purpose of your course, emphasizes a specific goal, indicates the research basis of your content, and may acknowledge special assistance you received in developing the program.

Table of contents—A table of contents lists the main topics and sections of the training manual and helps trainees to locate material for reference, review, or preview during class. Be sure to number the pages. It saves a lot of search time in class.

Overall course objectives—A page that lists your course objectives establishes at the beginning of the manual, as it does at the outset of the class, the expected outcomes of your training.

Course schedule—A course schedule page is useful when course topics follow a structured sequence of days and times.

Glossary—A glossary helps trainees understand, reference, and review key or repeatedly used terms.

Bibliography—A bibliography provides a list of readings for more information. Go over the list during class and comment on the particular usefulness of each book, periodical, or essay so participants can decide where to start in their subsequent readings.

How Many Pages Should You Include in a Manual?

Obviously, it depends. My manuals usually have about ninety pages of text, exercises, and case studies, and thirty to fifty pages of supplementary readings for a two-day program. But your training method and topic may require many more or far fewer pages.

Summary

Training manuals and workbooks are powerful tools for the intercultural trainer. They are particularly useful when they are customized to your particular subject matter and specific training needs. Think through how you might apply or modify the guidelines I have presented here. First creations, like first steps, are tentative and are the hardest. But improvements in your manuals will come about incrementally over time. The result is a more sophisticated, more professional, and, finally, more effective training program.

References

Blohm, Judith. *Where in the World Are You Going?* Yarmouth, ME: Intercultural Press, 1996.

Brislin, Richard W., Kenneth Cushner, Craig Cherrie, and Mahealani Yong. *Intercultural Interactions: A Practical Guide.* Beverly Hills, CA: Sage, 1986.

Denny, Martha. *Going Home: A Workbook for Reentry and Professional Integration.* Washington, DC: National Association for Foreign Student Affairs, 1986.

Kohls, L. Robert. *Survival Kit for Overseas Living.* 3d ed. Yarmouth, ME: Intercultural Press, 1996.

Cross-Cultural Dialogues

Craig Storti

Across-cultural dialogue is a brief conversation between two people from different cultures, during the course of which the speakers make statements which reveal or betray very different values, attitudes, or views of the world—in short, cultural differences. More specifically, what happens is that one of the speakers projects a value or an assumption about the other person's culture that is not accurate, and, as a result, the communication between these two people either breaks down altogether or is extremely confusing or frustrating. A well-constructed dialogue (see next page for an example) presents the cultural difference in such a way that it is not easy for the average participant even to see it (which is, after all, how most cultural conditioning is manifest, as entirely natural, unconscious behavior). When confronted with a series of dialogues in which they cannot see that anything in particular has happened, workshop participants are struck by the subtlety and depth of their own cultural conditioning and alerted to the fact that in dealing with people from other cultures, they may have to monitor their behavior more closely. What comes naturally to you may not be what comes naturally to me, and if you and I are going to live near each other, work together, marry each other, or just talk to each other, some adjustments may be in order.

History

The concept at the heart of the dialogue method, that people from different cultures have different values, assumptions, and so forth, is not new, of course. What was new (so far as this writer knows) was Alfred Kraemer's work, beginning in 1973 and described in another chapter in this book, creating a series of these conversations and using them with workshop participants to make them more culturally self-aware. Whether Kraemer's conversations have been used much in the format for which they were originally designed or whether the method has been imitated and used in other contexts, I cannot say. I came across Kraemer's work in the late 1980s, tried some of the dialogues out in a workshop I was then conducting at the Foreign Service Institute, and, greatly encouraged by the response of the audience, began writing and using my own dialogues regularly in workshops. As it happens, most of my work is with American audiences, and the dialogues, therefore, are between an American and someone from another culture. Any two cultures would do, of course.

While my dialogues, like Kraemer's, use conversational excerpts as what we might call the triggering device, there are at least two differences in how we use the method: his dialogues were on videotape, and his goal was to provide trainees with guided, intensive practice in uncovering one's own cultural conditioning. My goal, which encompasses cultural self-awareness, is also to dramatize subtle differences between cultures.

I subsequently proposed a book of dialogues to Intercultural Press; it found the idea intriguing and brought out *Cross-Cultural Dialogues: 74 Brief Encounters with Cultural Difference* in January of 1994. As a trainer and a writer, I remain deeply indebted to Dr. Kraemer for pioneering this wonderful concept.

Procedure

To understand how to use a dialogue, we first need to look at an example (from page 43 of *Cross-Cultural Dialogues*):

> Sarah: I was hoping we could have that meeting of the sales team tomorrow morning.
>
> Felice: Actually, my daughter has some kind of flu and I was going to take her to the doctor tomorrow morning.
>
> Sarah: I see. Well, let me check with Bob and see if he can sit in for you. Shouldn't be any problem. I'll let you know.
>
> Felice: Thank you.
>
> Sarah: Don't mention it.

In this exchange Sarah has at best surprised Felice and in all probability has offended her. Felice comes from a culture where the needs of the family will almost always take precedence over the needs of the employer. If a child is sick, the employee will of course attend to that emergency, and the employer, after expressing deep sympathy and asking whether he/she can be of any assistance, will do whatever has to be done at the workplace to contain the fallout (without making any mention of it, of course). For her part, Sarah comes from a culture where people try to keep their personal lives and their work lives separate and where family considerations should, whenever possible, not be allowed to interfere (as an American might put it) with work. This does not mean U.S. bosses are heartless and do not care if a child gets sick, but they expect the employee to work around his or her work schedule in sorting out family-related problems.

A typical dialogue, then, consists of a conversation like the one in the example, where two cultures have come up against each other and certain differences in behavior or values have left one or both parties not understanding or appreciating the other, with inevitable consequences, depending on the context. The differences are neither obvious to the speakers nor, in most cases, to the reader.

In a workshop, the participants—for example, a group of Americans about to be posted overseas for two years—are shown a number of these conversations and asked to figure out what cultural difference accounts for the breakdown in communication or understanding that occurs. In getting to the heart of the dialogue, participants thus discover how certain of their typical behaviors or attitudes are cultural, not universal, and may not travel well. Specifically, the activity would be carried out in the following manner:

Step 1. Explain to the group that now they are going to work on a series of dialogues or brief conversations between an American and someone from another culture and that during the course of these conversations the Americans wrongly project an American value or attitude onto the other culture. You might need to explain here that to project a value means assuming it to be true of another culture when in fact it is only true of your own. Owing to this projection, the communication either breaks down or results in a serious misunderstanding. Then tell participants that their task is to form groups of three or more, read the dialogues, and try to figure out what the American has assumed that is not true.

Step 2. At this point, before sending them off in their groups, it is very important to go over one of the dialogues with the whole group, to show them what you mean. Accordingly, you should select a dialogue, read through it, and then ask the group what went wrong or why the conversation did not go well. Sometimes they will be able to say, but in most cases, if the dialogue is good, they will not have seen any cultural content and will wonder what you are talking about. This is, in fact, exactly what you want to happen—and the whole point behind this concept; that is, people should read the dialogues and not see anything. If the cultural mistakes or assumptions being made in the dialogues are obvious, then participants will not identify with the mistakes and not believe that they would ever say anything like this (and hence need this training). It is because the dialogues are subtle, the differences not immediately apparent, that they work. For when a trainee reads a dialogue and sees no cultural content until it is pointed out, then that person has to admit that he or she could have said something similar in that situation. And the participant often feels that "I better pay attention." (In fact, people often come up after the exercise to say that they *have* said something very much like the exchange in a dialogue.) For this reason, you should either use tested and proven dialogues or take great care in developing and testing your own. The four essential points for writing an effective dialogue are explained in the notes at the end of this chapter.

Step 3. After you have done a dialogue with the entire group, then send participants off to figure out the rest on their own, warning them that the differences here are not obvious and they may have to read between the lines to understand what's happening. Seven or eight dialogues are usually enough to make the point; for this number, allow the groups 15–20 minutes to complete their discussions.

Step 4. After the announced time has elapsed, get everyone's attention (they can stay in their groups for this step if they wish) and ask them if they have figured things out. At this point, read each dialogue out loud or assign people to play parts. After you read each one, ask the groups what they concluded. In some cases, participants will either have figured the dialogue out or have gotten much of what you were looking for. In others, no one really has any idea (though they may make one or two feeble observations). In this case, go through the dialogue and explain what was happening.

You will need to deal with explanations that were not what you had in mind when you wrote the dialogue (or do not address the specific cultural point the author of the dialogues you are using had in mind). The best way to handle these alternative explanations is to say that you can see how someone might think that or that, yes, the dialogue could support such an interpretation, but can they see anything else? What you do not want to do is let go of any important cultural point the dialogue was intended to illustrate just because it may also illustrate another point (and you are reluctant to disappoint a group that is quite proud of what it has come up with). My experience has been that these alternative explanations, while often quite valid, usually are not as powerful as the point the dialogue was constructed to reveal. So acknowledge that, yes, dialogues are deep and can reveal multiple truths at deeper levels, but what you had in mind was....

Contexts

Dialogues are appropriate for almost any kind and length of training program and even for more formal, lecture-style presentations. In the latter case a dialogue can be projected on an overhead and either decoded for the audience or turned over to them for deciphering, all by way of illustrating cultural differences in real settings and real situations. What the dialogue technique teaches is that each of us is a deeply cultural being, that culture shows up in our most common behavior, and that therefore whenever we are interacting with someone from another culture, we can (1) expect their culture to come up and (2) expect that manifestations of our own culture may not be expected (at best), understood, or appreciated. Since these learning points are valuable for almost any potential audience of culture crossers, the technique has almost unlimited applicability. It is especially useful, however, with people who for one reason or another (usually a lack of experience) do not really believe that others are truly all that different from themselves. Such people may nod their heads and agree that, of course, we are all different, but they still leave the room and expect their Spanish taxi driver to act just like an American. However, once they are confronted with dialogues— asked, that is, to decode a few of these conversations—and fail to see anything at all in the exchanges, these same people emerge slightly humbled. Dialogues leave people who do not believe in culture with no place to hide.

While dialogues are especially useful for nonbelievers, they work well with any audience, including people with considerable cross-cultural experience. In some cases these people see scenes from their life recaptured in the dialogue; in others they find the explanation for something that happened once and was never understood; and in others they learn something they did not know about themselves or about another culture.

For the audience that is neither particularly naive nor highly experienced, dialogues do exactly what they were designed to do: teach people some deeper truths about their own culture—and a truth or two about selected other cultures in the bargain.

This latter point bears some elaboration. While the primary learning in a dialogue is an insight into one's own culture (American in the case of my book), it is not possible to discuss a dialogue without learning something about the culture of the other person in the conversation, if only that his or her culture is not like your own. If it happens that you are working with a group in which everyone is going to one country or is only interested in one particular country or culture, you could use a selection of dialogues which featured only that country as the other culture, which would then permit you to make some telling points about the target culture as well.

Dialogues work as well with non-Americans as they do with Americans. When the dialogue is written from an American point of view (the person who does not understand or who is projecting is the American), then the learning point with non-Americans is not how *I* behave and what some of *my* values are, but how *Americans* behave and what some of *their* values are.

Since dialogues necessarily contain some information about other, non-American cultures, they can also be used to instruct non-Americans in some of their own values and attitudes. I have not used them in this way very often, but on the occasions when I have, the non-American participants were surprised and delighted to discover themselves in the dialogues. Naturally, one runs the risk here of non-Americans disavowing or even strenuously objecting to the portrait you have painted of them (especially embarrassing in a mixed American/non-American group), but then that is an occupational hazard in our field.

Pitfalls

This brings us to some of the pitfalls of dialogues. It is possible that someone will object to the characterization you have made either of Americans or the other culture in the dialogue. This happens less than one might imagine, because the dialogues feature individuals (like Sarah and Felice above), so that the particular cultural characteristic is personalized. The response to make if you are challenged in this way is that of course not every American behaves like this but there is nevertheless this streak in our culture.

While one might expect to be hit with the generalization charge, that is rarely the case (at least in the dialogue itself, though you may lay yourself open to this charge depending on what you say *about* the dialogue). I handle this as follows: I point out that you cannot talk about culture without generalizing, but that generalizations should be treated with the respect they deserve. That is, while they are true of some of the people some of the time—generalizations always have a kernel of truth—and are true of cultures rather more often than that, every individual is a personal and unique variation on a cultural theme.

The most common pitfall is that people do not see the point you were looking for and explain the dialogue in some other way. As I suggested above, you can accept these alternate explanations (it usually does no harm), but you should make sure the point *you* wanted to make with the dialogue gets made. Needless to say, the explanation that "They're just not communicating" or "They have a communication problem" is not especially illuminating nor specific enough for our purposes.

Notes on Writing a Dialogue

I learned to write dialogues by trial and error, stitching a few together, trying them out on innocent bystanders, and reworking those that did not ring true. You can be saved the trouble by reading the text which follows, excerpted from an appendix to *Cross-Cultural Dialogues*, 133–36.

The dialogue concept is a flexible one; it can be used in any kind of training or other setting where the object is to make people aware of how other people are different from them.

For a successful dialogue, you need four ingredients, each of which is discussed below:

❖ The conversation must sound natural

❖ The difference or mistake must not be obvious

❖ The mistake must not be a result of some esoteric knowledge the average reader would never have heard of

❖ The conversation should contain clues to the difference (which one sees when they are pointed out)

The reader or workshop participant must identify immediately with the conversation; that is, he or she must instinctively feel that this is an entirely believable situation and an entirely likely verbal exchange. In the best dialogues, the reader feels that he or she has in fact *had* this conversation or something very much like it. To compose a good dialogue, then, be sure the situation you set up is believable and the language you use is how people really talk.

The success of this whole technique depends on people reading the dialogue and not seeing anything "wrong." As we noted, if the "mistakes" or cultural differences were obvious, people would not be having conversations like these. The reader must be convinced that these are not just the sorts of things that unaware, insensitive people might say, but that he or she could very easily have made these same remarks. And the only way to make this point is to construct the dialogues in such a way that nothing appears to have happened or to be "wrong" with these remarks. If the reader sees nothing wrong here, then he or she has to admit, "Yes, I could have said something like this. Anyone could have." And when the reader thinks that, you have him where you want him or her!

At the same time, the dialogue must not turn on some culture-specific information the normal reader would never have heard of, something to the effect that white is the color of mourning in India or you never wrap wedding presents in red in Paraguay. The reader or workshop participant should feel that if only he or she were a little more aware, a little more alert, the misunderstanding could have been avoided. But if the mistake hinges on a piece of esoteric information, then the reader could only avoid it by sheer coincidence, which means that he or she does not identify with the dialogue and can easily dismiss it as unrealistic. You must never give the reader or trainee an excuse to discount the dialogue.

Finally, the key to the dialogue should be somewhere within it. This is not to say that the explanation for what has gone wrong must be in the dialogue, but there must be some hint or clue which, if the reader could only see it, would tip him or her off to an impending (or unfolding) misunderstanding or faux pas. This gives the reader some hope that with a little practice and a new way of seeing, he or she might be able to start avoiding such mistakes. If cultural differences can never really be apprehended, then what's the point in knowing about them?

The actual writing of a dialogue is not as hard as all this makes it sound. Most of the dialogues in this book were triggered by a single observation and the first draft written in a few minutes. In most cases, though not all, the process was the same:

1. You think of or are otherwise made aware of a particular cultural value or attitude, either American or foreign.

2. You think up a concrete example of a situation where this value or attitude would come into play.

3. You imagine the conversation that would take place in that situation between someone who holds that value and someone who does not.

4. You polish and refine the dialogue as necessary to make it more natural, more subtle, a little humorous if possible, and a little surprising.

References

Kraemer, Alfred J. *Development of a Cultural Self-Awareness Approach to In-struction in Intercultural Communication* (Technical Report 73-17). Alexandria, VA: HumRRO, 1973. (Available through NTIS as document no. AD 765486).

Storti, Craig. *Cross-Cultural Dialogues: 74 Brief Encounters with Cultural Difference.* Yarmouth, ME: Intercultural Press, 1994.

Cross-Cultural Analysis
as a Training Tool

Albert R. Wight

Cross-Cultural Analysis (CCA) has proved to be one of the most effective exercises for cross-cultural training that I have encountered. Given a short program, I would select it over any others I have used. In a longer program, I would certainly include it as a major activity, perhaps the central activity of the program. It provides a foundation upon which other activities can build, and it is involving, meaningful, and personal. It allows participants to learn a great deal in a short time, not only about the other culture but also about their own culture, the interaction of the cultures represented, and about themselves and others as cultural beings.

History

Origin of the Cross-Cultural Analysis Exercise

Like so many cross-cultural training activities, CCA originated in Peace Corps training in the mid-1960s. By that time the Peace Corps had come to the realization that the traditional university information-transmission approach to training did not result in the understanding and change in behavior required for persons to live and work effectively in another culture (Harrison and Hopkins 1967) and was experimenting with a wide variety of other approaches to cross-cultural training, including outward bound, sensitivity training, and various experiential activities (Wight and Hammons 1970). The Human Resources Research Office (HumRRO—a contract research center), as a part of this experimentation, was developing its contrast-American role plays (Stewart, Danielian, and Foster, 1969). I was developing a program for Peace Corps training at Utah State University following the model of *management laboratory training* (Morton and Wight 1963), the term we used before *experiential* came in vogue.

In 1965 I was fortunate to receive a draft copy of Edward Stewart's landmark contrast-American paper, in which he contrasted typical American values and views with those of an unidentified contrast culture. I immediately recognized its value if converted into an instrumented, experiential exercise and incorporated in the laboratory training I was developing. It was thus first used in 1966 in Peace Corps programs at Utah State University (Wight 1969). It has been used since that time by myself and others in countless cross-cultural training programs, for many diverse groups. In many programs it has been the primary activity, the mainstay of the program. For the past twenty years, it has been used extensively in cross-cultural programs for business and industry.

Early Versions of the Cross-Cultural Analysis Exercise

The first CCA exercises were little more than Stewart's culture-contrast dimensions presented on a form that allowed individual participants to examine where the American culture, the other culture, and they personally would fall on a scale between each pair of contrasting positions on each dimension (see Wight and Hammons 1970). For example, Stewart's dimension "Ascription versus Achievement" might be presented as follows (after a brief definition of the terms is given):

> Instructions: Following is a series of contrasting values or cultural orientations on which American culture and the host culture might differ. For each pair of contrasting positions, indicate where you feel the American culture, the other culture, and you personally would fall on the scale between the two extremes by writing the appropriate number in the space provided on the answer sheet. (For example, a 9 would indicate "Strongly toward Ascription," a 1 would indicate "Strongly toward Achievement," and a 5 would be halfway between the two.) If you don't know, give it your best guess. Write your comments or a clarification of your position in the space provided.

Ascription   9   8   7   6   5   4   3   2   1   Achievement

The individual analysis was followed by group discussion of the individual responses and attempts to arrive at consensus on the differing positions of the two cultures being examined—the culture of the American trainees and the culture of the host country. The host culture was represented in the exercise and in follow-up discussions by language teachers in the training program. Returned Peace Corps volunteers also participated, to share their perspectives from their experience in the host culture.

Recent Refinements

Over the years, the dimensions have been expanded and refined to better delineate the critical differences in beliefs, attitudes, values, assumptions, expectations, and behaviors between cultures. CCA has been used primarily in programs with North Americans preparing to live and work in other cultures, but it would be appropriate for use with persons from any culture. In addition to my own work with the exercise, Michael Tucker, Gary Wederspahn, George Renwick, and Steve Rhinesmith have been the primary contributors to its development.

As the dimensions of the exercise have evolved, especially with the continuing refinement and definition of fundamental differences between cultures, they have become more specific and concrete than those presented initially by Stewart in 1965. Programs for business and industry now include dimensions related to cultural differences in managerial and organizational philosophy and practice (such as "Top-Down Decision Making" versus "Bottom-Up Decision Making") along with social and interpersonal dimensions, such as "Conciliatory" versus "Unyielding." (See Appendix A for additional examples of themes or dimensions used in Cross-Cultural Analysis.)

Comparison with the Culture-Contrast Method

In some respects, the CCA is perhaps more similar to the culture-contrast method than any other. Like the culture-contrast method, it analyzes critical differences between cultures, but it differs in that the focus is on the cultures as they have been internalized and interpreted by the participants from both cultures, not as they have been defined by an observer or expert. Unlike the culture-contrast method, CCA is not dependent on a highly skilled actor or trainer. The culture-contrast method is a one-on-one role-play situation, whereas the CCA is an individual activity followed by group discussion and analysis.

The culture-contrast method makes use of an actor who plays the role of a person from a hypothetical contrast culture. The American is not playing the role of another person but is himself or herself in the session. The stage is set, but the American is not told to behave in any particular way. His or her behavior is whatever comes naturally in the session. The actor reacts to whatever the American says or does, but usually differently from what the American might expect of someone in that situation. The content is what develops in the session and is understood or clarified as it is discussed following the session.

If time were available for each participant to go through the role play, this would be a very involving activity for each person. Considering the time constraints of most training programs, however, this is not possible. Usually one or two participants are involved in the role play, with the other participants as observers. The activity is not as effective, of course, for the observers.

In the CCA, all participants, from both cultures, are involved in the analysis and discussion. No one is role-playing. Neither culture is a hypothetical culture. Both cultures are real, and the participants are living examples of the two cultures they represent and of the diversity found within each culture.

The two exercises do not conflict with one another. They are complementary and could be used in the same program. If used in the same program, it would be best to precede the CCA with the culture-contrast role play and save the discussion for the CCA exercise. The CCA discussion would help explain a lot of what was happening in the role play, taking the analysis to a greater depth and expanding on the dimensions examined, with a focus on the particular culture rather than the hypothetical contrast culture. You would have to decide whether the role play should be with someone representing a hypothetical contrast culture or the actual culture the trainees were preparing to enter. A variation is to follow the CCA with role plays that require the participants to apply what they have learned.

Description of the Cross-Cultural Analysis Exercise

Objectives

The purpose of CCA is to involve participants in the identification and intensive analysis of fundamental characteristics of their own culture and the culture they are preparing to enter, characteristics that are likely to create problems or misunderstandings between persons from the two different cultures. Objectives of the exercise are these:

❖ Understanding fundamental differences in beliefs, attitudes, values, assumptions, expectations, customs, and behavior between one's own culture and the other culture

❖ Understanding the consequences of the identified cultural differences, particularly with respect to expectations, perceptions, feelings, and responses of persons engaged in cross-cultural interaction

❖ Understanding oneself as a product of one's own culture and others as products of their own cultures

❖ Ability to interpret behavior of persons from the other culture and to predict reactions (one's own and others')

❖ Ability to modify one's own attitudes, expectations, and behavior in accordance with the requirements of the intercultural situation

❖ Acceptance, tolerance, and appreciation of cultural differences

❖ Increased self-awareness

Participants sometimes have difficulty accepting "understanding their own culture" as an important objective, but the exercise helps them realize the extent to which they are products of their own culture and the implications for their effectiveness and satisfaction in another culture. As they hear the perceptions of and reactions to their culture discussed by persons from the other culture, they begin to recognize that their cultural baggage contributes as much if not more to their cross-cultural problems than their lack of knowledge of the other culture. They discover that much of what they had assumed to be universal in human behavior is in reality culturally determined and that many of their own attitudes and much of their behavior is unconsciously determined by unrecognized cultural conditioning.

Structure of the Exercise

The basic structure of the exercise has not changed since it was first developed. It consists of an individual activity, followed by a small group activity, then a general discussion (see "Conducting the Cross-Cultural Analysis Exercise" in this chapter).

The Role of the Participant

The CCA exercise was designed to be experiential, based on the participant's experience—the unique, personal way in which the individual participant encounters, perceives, interprets, and reacts to the events and content of training. This is in contrast with traditional training, which is based on the trainer's, or expert's, selection, interpretation, and delivery of the content.

The exercise involves participants actively in their own analysis of content, arriving at their own conclusions, and examining implications and applications. It does not give them expert opinion or advice. It is made clear in the exercise that the participants, both trainees and resource persons, are the experts on their own culture. It is their experience and their interpretation of that experience which is of interest, not the results of a survey or the opinions of outside experts. The conclusions and decisions regarding implications are theirs, not the trainer's. It is assumed in experiential training that this personal involvement is much more likely to result in personal understanding, acceptance, ownership, commitment, and change.

The Role of the Trainer

Your role as the trainer is not presented to the participants as that of an expert. You are a process facilitator, providing structure and instructions, guiding the participants through the exercise, watching the time, asking questions, ensuring participation if necessary, summarizing, and providing theoretical input (in small doses) or models, if useful for clarification. You do not tell the participants what they should do (other than structuring the activity) or what they should think. It is often better if you do not enter into the discussion but act instead more as an observer, allowing the participants to manage their own interaction, which they are quite capable of doing with the instructions provided. You are also a learner, since each group of participants is different and is likely to bring a unique interpretation or a new twist to a particular dimension that contributes to deeper understanding. Your skill is in structuring and facilitating the activity for maximum participation and in the preparatory work, that is, in conducting research and/or recording your observations, selecting the dimensions, and preparing the instruments.

The Instruments

The CCA exercise is "instrumented" in that it depends on a set of materials more than on the skills of the trainer. Although it is always desirable for the trainer to have substantial cross-cultural experience, with the instrumented approach you can conduct the exercise quite effectively without having had personal experience in the target culture, since you are not expected to be the expert. You do not have to present the dimensions verbally or define them, since this is done by the instruments. The instruments present a number of dimensions on which the cultures are expected to differ and clarify the distinction between each pair of contrasting positions on each dimension. They also provide instructions for both the individual work and group discussion.

For each dimension, the instruments present two *possible* orientations that might be held by persons from different cultures; not presented as truths or even as accepted differences in orientation of the particular cultures being compared. This lessens the likelihood of having someone challenge the orientation as not being representative of one of the two cultures in the program and taking valuable time away from the exercise. Another reason for not presenting the orientations as true, verified, or accepted (by experts) differences is that one of the metagoals of the exercise is to wean participants away from dependence on experts to a self-examining, critical reliance on their own feelings, perceptions, and judgment. A third reason is to help participants develop an orientation toward using people from the other culture as cultural informants and to develop the skills for doing so.

A different set of instruments is prepared for any two given cultures, which includes those dimensions that best represent the important, fundamental differences between the two cultures in the view of the person or persons developing the exercise. In Stewart's monograph (1965), detailed descriptions of contrasting orientations regarding given dimensions were provided, one position being that of the "typical" American and the other the contrast American. The contrast American was not any particular culture; it was what Stewart found to be a common orientation among many cultures (primarily Third World), which he felt to be in contrast to the typical American position.

Developing Cross-Cultural Analysis Materials

Some Resources

Stewart's culture-contrast materials are a good place to begin, since this is where it all started. Using his concepts as a base, you can draw on your own experience in the two different cultures to identify the critical differences between them. You should expand this through discussions with others or by reading analyses of the two cultures in the literature. Many such analyses are available. The InterAct series, edited by George Renwick for the Intercultural Press, are an excellent example. Each Interact analyzes differences in values, attitudes, and behavior between Americans and nationals from specific other countries, discusses how these differences influence working and personal relationships, and offers guidelines for more effective interaction.

With a culture where you do not have personal experience or a ready-made analysis to draw upon, you can compile a large number of contrasting dimensions from the literature on the other culture. You should then discuss the collection of dimensions with cultural informants to select and define a subset that would be most appropriate for the specific cultures being compared.

The Dimensions

In selecting dimensions, it is important to choose those that you have reason to believe do in fact represent important differences between the two cultures. There is no point in wasting time on dimensions where the differences are of little importance. Some differences might be subtle, but if important they should be included, since small or poorly understood differences can lead to major misunderstandings. The subtleties can be identified and clarified in the discussions and will lead to insight and understanding that might not otherwise be achieved.

Very often you will find a lot of similarity between different dimensions. If it appears there is too much redundancy, eliminate some or combine them in some way, but use caution; though similar, each separate dimension might shed additional light on important differences. Regarding the number of dimensions to include, as with the Critical Incidents exercise (to which CCA is similar; see *Intercultural Sourcebook*, Vol. 1), it is better to have too many contrasting dimensions than too few. Select several to give adequate coverage to the important differences between the two cultures, based on your judgment and the judgment of your informants.

Content of the contrasting dimensions depends on the nature of the program. It would be counterproductive to include management and organizational dimensions in a program for exchange students, for example. These are essential, however, for someone preparing to work with an international company in another culture. Social dimensions are important for any group, regardless of the nature of their assignment.

The particular sequence of presentation of the contrasting dimensions in the activity is not of great concern, but it is best if the exercise progresses in some way that makes sense. It can be disconcerting if the discussion appears to jump around in a random or illogical fashion. More obvious differences are better in the beginning, with more subtle differences presented later, after the participants have gained some experience in analysis and the discussion is flowing. It is better if dimensions that are similar or in some way related are grouped together.

Conducting the Cross-Cultural Analysis Exercise

Your introduction to the exercise should be brief. State what the exercise is, its purpose (perhaps giving objectives similar to those presented earlier), and its structure.

Resource Persons

The exercise should always be explained and the materials given to the resource persons to review prior to the training program. They need time to think about the cultural dimensions, and they also need to understand the experiential nature of the program and what is expected of them, that is, what their role is. It is important to dispel the notion that they will be expected to be instructors or to lecture on their culture. Explain to them that they will be expected to bring their views, their understanding, and their experiences to the discussions, and that they may disagree among themselves.

Individual Session

Following the brief introduction, hand out the worksheets (instruments) for the individual activity. Review the written instructions (see Appendix B) to make sure everyone understands them. The instructions ask the participants to decide the extent to which the statements that are provided accurately describe the position of their culture and the other culture on each dimension, and to complete the questionnaire accordingly. (I usually use one sheet of paper for each dimension, followed by the questions, on the same sheet, for that dimension.) Participants are told that they may modify the statements to reflect more accurately the positions of the two cultures as they understand them, if they feel it is necessary. It is also worthwhile to ask them to indicate where they fall individually with respect to the different positions, thus revealing the extent to which they feel they are like a typical person from their own culture. Since few people feel they are typical, this allows them to examine and later to share with others how they see themselves with respect to each dimension.

The individual work is best done as homework, if it fits the program schedule, or as "prework" prior to the training program. If neither is possible, time for the individual work must be provided in the program. One problem is that some participants will take much longer to complete the work than others. Try the exercise on several people ahead of time to determine how much time should be allowed for the average participant. It is best not to have the entire group wait for slow readers to finish. Participants should be advised to read quickly and to write very brief responses to the questions. When it is time to stop, ask those who are not finished to read through the remainder of the dimensions quickly without taking time to respond to the questions. They can formulate their responses during the discussion.

Group Activity

If the number of participants is small enough, and you have sufficient resource persons, you might have them remain in one group. If there are more than twelve to fourteen participants, and if sufficient resource persons are available (at least two per group), it would be better to break into small groups. These discussions have been conducted with more than thirty persons in the group, when a small number of resource persons was available, but this is not a desirable situation and requires more skill and active involvement of the facilitator. Ideally there would be an equal number of resource persons and trainees. If there is only one group, it is best if you stay with the group, but avoid being trapped into playing the expert role. If there is more than one small group, and resource persons are in the groups, it is advisable for you to visit the small groups as an observer and timekeeper. In the summary discussion, you can then report any observations you might have made.

A variation when you have a large number of participants and an insufficient number of resource persons is to have the trainees go through the exercise in their small groups and then have the resource persons review the exercise in their own separate group. It would be best for you to be with the resource persons, unless they prefer to discuss in a language you do not understand. These discussions are followed by a general *summary discussion* where the small groups share their conclusions as they normally would, after which the resource group shares its conclusions and reacts to the reports from the small groups.

The instructions provided for the group activity (see Appendix C) ask the participants and resource persons to compare individual answers to the questionnaire and then attempt to arrive at a consensus on what is typical in each culture on each dimension, which, after a wide-ranging discussion of values and orientations within each culture, they are usually able to do. This is a very involving activity for both trainees and resource persons, normally resulting in substantive cross-cultural insights. The resource persons, who had not thought of themselves as learners in this activity, become every bit as involved as the trainees.

Summary Discussion

With one small group, the summary discussion can be held at the end of the group activity. With more than one group, you should hold a final large group session in which the small groups report on their deliberations and share their conclusions. The summary session requires less time than the small group activity, since most of the sharing and discussion will have taken place in the small groups. It covers the highlights and allows groups to discuss with other groups or with resource persons questions that were not fully resolved in the small groups.

If you are facilitating a discussion full-time (rather than floating among several groups), it is useful for you to record characteristics of each culture on a separate piece of newsprint as they are identified, so that you can then review and compare the lists during the summary discussion. If the small groups meet separately, participants can brainstorm the lists during the summary session. I usually reproduce the lists and give them to each participant following the exercise.

Final Activity

It is useful at the end of the summary discussion to ask each participant to study the two lists and put him- or herself in the position of someone from the other culture. Then give instructions such as the following: "Imagine you are someone with the characteristics you see listed. Now imagine that you are confronted by someone with the characteristics on the other sheet. How would you feel about that person?" Record the responses as they are given. This can be a very revealing activity.

Supplemental Activities

The Iceberg Presentation

A good introduction to the CCA exercise, which I borrowed from Gary Wederspahn (I am not sure where he got it), is the iceberg. Prior to beginning the CCA exercise, ask participants to share what words come to mind when they think of "culture." Write the words on the board or newsprint as they are given, but place them in the following manner: Write those things that are readily observable—for example, clothing, behavior, and habits—in the center toward the top of the board or sheet. Write those which are not directly observable—such as beliefs, values, attitudes, and expectations—in the center, lower on the sheet. Write such things as education, traditions, customs, language, politics, geography, and the like on the lower part of the sheet to one side or the other. These latter are influences from the culture on the individual, whereas the center is reserved for aspects of character and personality *within* the individual which are more or less shared with others in the same culture. When the brainstorming is completed, draw the iceberg shape around the list, as in Figure 1, and a horizontal wavy line, representing the waterline, below those cultural aspects that are observable. It is immediately apparent that there is a great deal more below the surface (much of which may be unconscious) than above the surface—the tip of the iceberg. Make the point that the purpose of the CCA is to develop a better understanding of what lies beneath the surface.

Figure 1. Iceberg Model of Surface and Subsurface Cultural Aspects

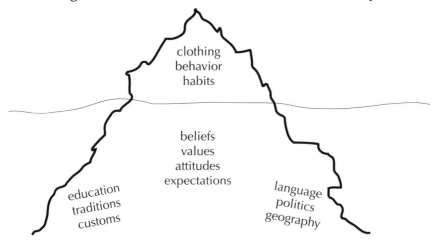

The Normal Distribution Presentation

Sometime during the activity, usually in the summary discussion or earlier, if everyone remains in one group, a brief presentation on stereotyping is worthwhile. It is best in response to a question raised or to elaborate on a point made by the participants regarding the risk of stereotyping. I draw two overlapping normal, bell-shaped curves to represent the position of two cultures on any given dimension. The curves illustrate the fact that the majority of the people in one culture

Figure 2. Bell-Shaped Curves Illustrating the Difference between Cultures X and Y for Dimension A

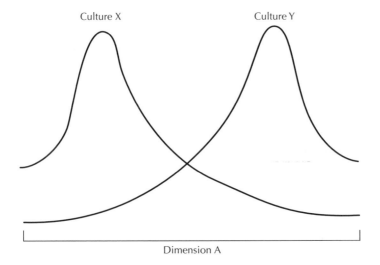

will be different from the majority of the people in the other culture but that there is variability within each culture. Some persons in one culture, at one extreme of the normal curve, will be more like the average person in the other culture than the average person in their own, and vice versa.

There is a wide range of differences on any given dimension within each culture. These might be individual differences, or they might be related to social status, education, occupation, religion, region, and so forth. The curve may be higher or lower (flatter) as well, indicating greater homogeneity or heterogeneity within the culture. It is good to make the point that no culture is static; we are dealing with cultures in transition. Our own culture and the other culture are continuously changing. But in spite of this complexity and the differences within cultures, there are normative differences between the cultures that are important to understand if we are to be effective in living and working with persons from that culture.

Conclusion

Cross-Cultural Analysis allows an intensive examination by participants of two or more different cultures. Although it consists primarily of analysis and discussion, it is not an academic exercise. Participants do not examine culture in the abstract or study what the experts say about the cultures being examined. They analyze and compare how they and others from their culture and the other culture think, feel, and behave—their beliefs, attitudes, values, customs, and assumptions— and how they and others react to the cultural differences revealed. It provides the basis for continued learning through encounters with the other culture and prepares the participant for more effective interaction with that culture.

References

Harrison, Roger, and Richard Hopkins. "The Design of Cross-Cultural Training: An Alternative to the University Model." *Journal of Applied Behavioral Science* 3, no. 4 (1967).

InterAct series. Yarmouth, ME: Intercultural Press.

Morton, Robert B., and Albert R. Wight. *Proceedings Manual for the Organizational Training Laboratory.* Sacramento, CA: Aerojet-General Corporation, 1963.

Stewart, Edward C. *Aspects of American Culture Assumptions and Values that Affect Cross-Cultural Effectiveness* (draft). Alexandria, VA: HumRRO, 1965.

Stewart, Edward C., Jack Danielian, and Robert J. Foster. *Simulating Intercultural Communication through Role Playing* (Technical Report 69–7). Alexandria, VA: HumRRO, 1969.

Wight, Albert R. *Trainers Manual for an Instrumented Experiential Laboratory for Peace Corps Training.* Washington,DC: Peace Corps, 1969.

Wight, Albert R., and Anne Hammons. *Guidelines for Peace Corps Cross-Cultural Training.* Center for Research and Education, Estes Park, CO, 1970. Produced under Peace Corps contract.

Appendix A

Examples of Themes or Dimensions
Used in Cross-Cultural Analysis

1. Attitude toward Friendship and Commitment

A. In some cultures: People value being friendly. Having a wide circle of friends is important, but it is relatively easy to move in and out of relationships. Deep commitments to others are rare.

B. In other cultures: Strong loyalty to a small number of close personal friends is the rule. Friendship is based on mutual trust and dependability. Little effort is made to be friendly toward people in general.

2. Attitude toward Openness

A. In some cultures: People value their privacy. They share only superficial information with others, unless they are close relatives or friends. They do not intrude into the privacy of others with embarrassing questions.

B. In other cultures: Privacy is not valued. People know everything about their friends and neighbors, readily share personal information, and ask questions regarding intimate details of others' personal lives.

3. Attitude toward Confrontation

A. In some cultures: Confrontation, getting facts on the table and dealing with them openly, directly, and honestly, is important in business or work relationships. There should be little concern for feelings when you have a job to do.

B. In other cultures: It is important to use tact and diplomacy, showing concern for others' feelings in business or work relationships. It is rude to confront problems directly or bluntly.

Note: These normally appear on separate pages, with related questions and adequate space for answers.

Appendix B

Cross-Cultural Analysis Instructions

Purpose

The purpose of the following activity is not only to help you learn more about the other culture but also ways in which it differs from your own. In doing so you will probably learn something about your own culture as well. Most people take their own culture for granted. They seldom, if ever, think about it and are not able to describe it until they can compare and contrast it with another culture. When they examine their own culture against another, they discover that much of what they thought was human nature is actually culturally determined and varies from culture to culture. Understanding the differences between your culture and the other is perhaps the best preparation you can receive for interacting with the other culture. You achieve a better understanding of the differences in values, perceptions, attitudes, and expectations as well as reactions that are likely to occur with respect to the various themes presented in the activity.

Instructions

The exercise is first to be completed *individually.* On each of the following pages, you will be presented with a theme with respect to which there may be significant differences between your culture and the other culture. Two differing orientations or attitudes relating to this theme will be given for your consideration. These are not necessarily meant to represent the position of either your culture or the other culture but only as examples of possible differing positions.

After reading the examples, you will be asked to write, in the space provided, the position of your culture and the other culture with respect to that particular theme. If you are uncertain of the position of the other culture, give it your best guess. This is not a test of your knowledge, but a measure of attitudes that can throw light on your likelihood of success in interacting with people from another culture. You will be given an opportunity to compare and discuss your answers with those of others from both cultures later.

Please work quickly. Write brief, not lengthy, descriptions. These are primarily for your use in the discussions.

Appendix C

Cross-Cultural Analysis

Group Discussion

When everyone has read the cross-cultural analysis materials and answered the questions, you are to discuss each page as a group. The objective is to arrive at agreement on the central position of both cultures on each dimension or on variations that might occur within each culture. The purpose of the exercise is to identify the significant differences in beliefs, values, assumptions, attitudes, expectations, customs, and behavior between the two cultures.

The participants are to give their views of their own culture first, followed by their assumptions regarding the position of the other culture. The resource persons will then give their perceptions of the participants' culture and how it differs from their own.

Make certain that everyone has a chance to be heard and that all views or perceptions are examined. You might also want to share information about where you are personally with respect to each dimension.

A Method for Developing Deep Cultural Self-Awareness through Intensive Practice: A Retrospective

Alfred J. Kraemer

Writing in the context of the study of international relations, the political scientist Kalevi J. Holsti (1977) reminded us that even the most objective scholars are partly prisoners of their experiences, the values predominant in their society, and the myths, traditions, and stereotypes that permeate their nation and environment. The work I shall describe was an effort to develop and implement a method that would help trainees come out of this prison.

Background

Some twenty-five years ago I was faced with the task of developing a training package (training concepts and materials, detailed instructional procedures, and an evaluation instrument) that could be incorporated into the training programs for government personnel being prepared for international assignments, and that would make the training more effective.* These programs were called area training or area studies programs. Much of what was done in these programs is now often called intercultural training.

The training was not intended to stand by itself, but was to be integrated with the other components of these programs and to be conducted whenever possible by in-house trainers. The programs lasted at least one week, therefore two days (15 training hours) were considered appropriate for the intercultural training com-

---

* The training discussed in this paper was developed by the author while he was a senior staff scientist with the Human Resources Research Organization in Alexandria, Virginia. The work was originally described in much greater detail in several reports (Kraemer 1973, 1974, 1978). This paper contains additional observations and insights derived from the author's experience in conducting and disseminating the training. Acknowledgments are contained in the original reports, which also contain the scripts. The tapes are no longer available, though two of the reports are available from NTIS.

ponent. It was envisioned that the training would eventually also be useful in programs for trainees who would work with people of various cultural backgrounds, such as U.S. officials assigned to multinational groups.

The objective of the training was to develop the trainees' cultural self-awareness, defined as their ability to recognize relatively subtle manifestations of their own cultural conditioning. This definition implies a much deeper level of cultural self-awareness than can be achieved by instruction designed to get trainees to "know their own culture," which usually meant familiarizing them with anthropological and sociological generalizations about their culture. The objective had emerged as a result of extensive preliminary research, which included an examination of other training development efforts being pursued at the time and a determination of the common weaknesses of ongoing programs conducted by (or for) various government agencies.

One of the common weaknesses of the programs I examined was the absence of any training that would prepare trainees for the inevitable difficulties in intercultural communication (apart from those due to their inadequate foreign language skills). Program managers believed they were doing just that by providing trainees with as much information (through lectures, readings, films, and discussions) about the host country, or the regions where it was located, as time would permit. This approach was potentially useful to the extent that trainees would remember this information on the job (assuming they had actually acquired it in the first place). By itself, however, it could not be expected to provide trainees with any of the skills needed for one of the most difficult aspects of working with people of another society—preventing misunderstandings due to differences in cultural assumptions and values, or diagnosing and correcting them when they could not be avoided. Since these programs did not include a determination of the extent to which the trainees had actually learned what they were supposed to learn, program managers could remain comfortable in the belief that the intended learning had in fact taken place.

Several trainee characteristics had to be taken into account. In some programs all trainees would be assigned to the same country. In others trainees would be going to various countries in the same region. And then there were programs in which the trainees were going to a variety of geographical destinations. More often than not, the trainees were not novices. They either had prior intercultural experience or they were in comparatively long programs and would have received other intercultural training prior to the training described here.

Once I began working on the project, it quickly became obvious that the same method (to be described later) could be used in the development of domestic versions of the training—for professionals working in the United States. And, in fact, not long after the completion of the project, one such version was developed for educators (administrators, teachers, and counselors). Although the content of the materials is different, the objective, the training concepts, and the instructional procedures are the same in both versions. A summary account of the work involved in these projects begins with the conceptual framework.

Conceptual Framework

It is virtually impossible for anyone to communicate with other people without making assumptions about them. We may make these assumptions knowingly or, more commonly, without being aware of making them. Ease of communication is determined in part by the extent to which the assumptions are correct. We may recognize that false assumptions are interfering with communication. Sometimes we discover later that this has occurred. Often we never become aware of it.

The more we know about other persons, the less we have to assume about them. When our knowledge is limited, we tend to fill in the gaps. Two psychological processes help us do that: stereotyping, when we attribute characteristics to people that we believe are shared by the members of the groups to which we think they belong; and projection, when we assume that their thinking in a given situation is similar to what our own would be if we were in their place. The training I developed focuses on the latter.

Projection

Projection involves assumptions that can be traced to a variety of factors that influence our thinking and behavior, such as age, gender, occupation, level of intelligence and education, situational constraints, and cultural background. The more persons in an encounter differ in these respects and the less they know about each other, the more likely they are to make false assumptions about each other.

Participants in intercultural encounters are often similar in many respects, making differences in their *cultural background* the most important factor contributing to false assumptions. When assumptions derived from one's own cultural conditioning are made (knowingly or implicitly) about people from another culture, we may call this process *intercultural projection*. Of course, there are many instances when intercultural projection causes no difficulty because the assumptions are based on common aspects in the cultural background of the participants. However, in order to determine if one's culturally conditioned assumptions are warranted, one must first be able to recognize them for what they are.

The following incident provides an illustration. The setting is a principal's office in an American high school, where many students are the children of refugees from Asia and Latin America. The father of one of them has come to visit the principal. He had been a writer before bringing his family to the United States. It is midafternoon and classes are just about over. During the conversation between the two men the janitor enters the office to empty the wastebasket—a routine occurrence at this time of the day. To get to the basket he steps between them, and in doing so, he momentarily interrupts their conversation. He says nothing, and the principal does not speak to him except to say, "Take it easy, Joe!" as he leaves. The father appeared taken aback by this seemingly trivial occurrence, and the principal, knowing that the father had only recently come to this country, explained that this was routine, that the janitor always came in at this time to empty the wastebasket. To no avail. From that point on, the conversation deteriorated, and the father soon left.

Could intercultural training have enabled the principal to avoid the misunderstanding that occurred here or, at least, to correct it after it occurred? The principal's task of diagnosis is considerably more difficult than it may appear. If you find it easy to identify the causes of the misunderstanding, do not assume that you could have done so immediately, had you been in the principal's place. Retrospective diagnosis is usually much easier than on-the-spot diagnosis.

Training methods that attempt to prepare trainees for specific incidents can alert them only to a minute fraction of all of the possibilities. Note that the principal's reaction to the janitor's interruption was as routine as the latter's behavior. For these reasons it seems unlikely that any kind of short-term intercultural training (even a program that included the present approach) would have enabled the principal to *avoid* the misunderstanding. It seems more fruitful to consider what kind of training would have enabled him to *diagnose* it, so that he could have attempted to deal with it.

The principal would have been in a better position to diagnose the difficulty had he been able to recognize how his own cultural conditioning manifested itself in the situation and what implicit assumptions it caused him to make about the father. Preferably, he should have been able to do that quickly enough to deal with the misunderstanding before the father's departure, but even later diagnosis would have been helpful. It would have enabled him to go over the matter in his next conversation with the father. I leave it to the reader to consider ways in which the principal might have cleared up the misunderstanding before the father's departure. Of course, there was intercultural projection on the father's part too, but the concern here is only with preparing the principal for intercultural encounters, not the father.

The relevant manifestation of the principal's cultural conditioning was his lack of annoyance with the behavior of the janitor. Although the janitor obviously has a low status in the school, the principal does not expect him to show any deference when he comes to empty the wastebasket. This is but one of the innumerable manifestations of the relatively egalitarian nature of American society. In the eyes of the father the behavior of the janitor probably called for a strong reprimand. When none was forthcoming, he most likely felt slighted, if not insulted. In any case, the principal's behavior must have seemed very odd. Intercultural projection occurred when the principal implicitly assumed that the father's reaction to the janitor's behavior was similar to his own. Note that the principal would not have reprimanded the janitor even if he had thought that this was what the father expected (the janitor belongs to a union!). It is one of those instances in intercultural encounters when it is very difficult to avoid misunderstandings.

It is useful to distinguish between spontaneous and planned interactions. For spontaneous ones, cultural self-awareness as a diagnostic tool cannot be put to use until after a difficulty has been noticed. For planned interactions, however, it can be helpful in advance. Suppose, for example, that the principal planned to give a talk to a group of immigrant parents, in order to influence them in some way, and prepared an outline of what he would tell them. By examining the ideas underlying his planned remarks to identify manifestations of his own cultural conditioning, he could discover implicit assumptions about his audience that might not be warranted.

Intercultural projection probably occurs in the thinking of people of any culture. Here is an example involving a Ukrainian poet who visited American universities on a lecture tour. Upon his return he wrote an article about his experiences in which he complained that "attempts to please an American audience are doomed in advance, because out of twenty listeners five may hold one point of view, seven another, and eight may have none at all" (Korotich 1977, 47). You may want to analyze this classic example of intercultural projection.

Intercultural projection can occur without actual intercultural encounters. It may manifest itself whenever a person of one culture describes, interprets, or reacts to the behavior of people of another culture. Many astute observers of international politics are aware of the phenomenon. For example, Kennan (1977) noted, "There is a tendency among Americans to assume that anyone who finds himself victimized by, or in opposition to, a given dictatorship or authoritarian regime is ipso facto a fighter for freedom, devoted to the principles of liberal democracy.... American diplomatic history affords one example after another of this naive assumption" (45). And Jervis (1976) observed that "often without realizing it, most [political] decision makers draw on their knowledge of their own political systems in their efforts to understand others" and that their "predispositions are most influenced by those domestic practices that are so deeply ingrained throughout the society that people do not realize the possibility of alternatives" (283).

Even cultural anthropologists will testify that years of intercultural experience do not necessarily help them avoid the kinds of difficulties alluded to here. Said one of them, "I did have to put up a strong fight with myself to keep from interpreting what was going on as though the Japanese were the same as I. This is the conventional and most common response and one that is often found even among anthropologists" (Hall 1976, 54).

The foregoing observations confirmed the conclusion I reached during preliminary research: developing cultural self-awareness within the time constraints of training would be very difficult.

Barriers to Developing Cultural Self-Awareness

Cultural versus other influences. The manifestations of a person's cultural conditioning (one's own as well as someone else's) are difficult to recognize because they are usually embedded among the manifestations of the many other influences that have shaped the person, such as class, profession, and gender.

Imagine, for example, that after observing the classroom behavior of a college professor for an hour, you were asked to identify the various verbal and nonverbal manifestations of the professor's cultural conditioning. Suppose you were asked to identify the manifestations of *my* cultural conditioning that are surely contained in these pages, or the manifestations of yours in your reactions to what I have written.

Resistance to cultural explanations. Developing the cultural self-awareness of *American* trainees is especially difficult because one of the manifestations of their cultural conditioning is the belief that—unlike people in many other cultures—*they* are not (or could avoid being) subject to cultural influences! As a result they tend to resist cultural explanations of their thinking and behavior and can readily come up with what they believe to be more plausible alternatives. Exceptions are the stereotyped characteristics of American culture they may have been exposed to such as "Americans want to get down to business," "Americans are competitive," "Americans believe time is money." But even the trainees' ready acceptance of these kinds of generalizations does not imply that they would find it easy to recognize subtle manifestations of the characteristics, especially in themselves. (I use the term *American* to refer to members of what is sometimes called the mainstream culture of the United States as well as to individuals of various ethnic backgrounds who have become acculturated to this mainstream.)

Ability level. Another difficulty in the development of cultural self-awareness through training stems from the varying ability level in any given group of trainees. The present training is not for beginners, that is, individuals who do not already have a certain level of understanding of cultural differences. In fact, years of experience with all sorts of trainees suggest that those who seemed to need it the most tended to benefit the least, because they had not first received more elementary training. Unfortunately, consumers' understanding of intercultural training has not yet reached the point where they see a need for separating trainees according to their existing ability levels, as is the case in foreign language training.

The Training Method

The conceptual framework and the foregoing considerations led to a training method whose main features can only be summarized here. The method was developed over a lengthy period during which other models were explored and revised or discarded. The essence of the method is that it provides trainees the opportunity for intensive, guided practice in recognizing subtle manifestations of their own cultural conditioning. There seems to be no valid reason for supposing that this ability can be developed in a training environment without such practice. Of course, it might be acquired during lengthy intercultural experience.

The training format is a small group exercise in which trainees are shown video recordings of brief, staged segments of conversations, in work settings, between an American and a host national in an imaginary, "non-Western" country. The Americans involved are a foreign service officer, army officers, Peace Corps volunteers, and an oil company executive. In the educators' version Anglos and Hispanics are interacting in a public school in the United States. (Throughout the rest of the narrative I use "Americans" when I refer to the original training, and "Anglos" when I refer to the second version.)

The roles are played by actors and the dialogue follows a script. The segments appear to be excerpts from ongoing conversations, but only the excerpts were written and produced. The content of the dialogue often appears to be trivial—intentionally so. In actual intercultural encounters the damaging effects of one's own cultural conditioning often seem to occur in what appear to be trivial aspects of conversation.

Stimulus Material

Excerpts. Each excerpt contains at least one manifestation of the cultural conditioning of the American (or Anglo). When there are more than one, they vary in their degree of subtlety.

Sequences. The excerpts are arranged in sequences of up to seven excerpts, and each sequence focuses on a particular cultural influence, for example, the tendency to believe that there is usually a best way of doing something. Each of the Americans (or Anglos) appears once in each sequence and exhibits a different manifestation of the cultural influence with which the sequence is concerned. There are twenty-one sequences in the original version and fourteen in the educators' version.

Task

Trainees view one excerpt at a time and attempt to identify—*in writing*—the cultural aspects of the thinking of the Americans (or Anglos) as it is reflected in what they are saying or, sometimes, not saying. The trainees' task is to discover the common cultural influence that manifests itself in all the video excerpts of a given sequence. By varying other aspects of personality from excerpt to excerpt in a given sequence, the structure of the exercise helps trainees to focus their attention on the *cultural* aspects which they might otherwise hardly notice. The exercise thus involves each trainee in an intensive, continuous task of analysis and synthesis.

Some of the cultural dimensions represented in the video recordings are as follows:

❖ How the self is defined
❖ How social encounters are perceived
❖ Attitudes toward incurring social obligations
❖ Attitudes toward gender-linked role differences
❖ The degree to which class and status differences are emphasized
❖ The importance of competition between individuals as a motivating factor
❖ The extent to which certain events or conditions are seen as "problems" calling for "solutions"
❖ The degree to which one's thoughts and spoken words about possible events are believed to influence the occurrence of these events
❖ The relative importance of obligations to society and personal obligations

This partial list conveys the level of abstraction used for constructing the sequences of excerpts. Lists of cultural dimensions are, by themselves, of little or no training value. It must also be noted that any given cultural dimension is rarely independent of other cultural dimensions.

Constructing the Dialogues

Some of the criteria for constructing the dialogues were these:
a. Each excerpt had to make sense without introductory narrative.

b. What the host national (or the Hispanic) was saying had to provide a clue (in most excerpts) as to the cultural aspect of what the American (or Anglo) was saying. (A clue is something that trainees perceive *they* would be very unlikely to say if they were in the other person's place. Such an utterance is a clue because it is the trainees' own cultural conditioning that causes it to be perceived that way. Thus, when excerpts seem very difficult, trainees can use the clues by asking themselves, "What is it about me that makes it very unlikely that I would say that?") In a number of excerpts a good clue was deliberately placed near the end of the dialogue so that the trainer could vary the difficulty of the exercise by either including or omitting that clue.

c. What the Americans (or Anglos) were saying had to be perceived by most trainees as something they themselves could easily be saying under the circumstances, thus enabling them to identify with these individuals. In short, their viewing of the recordings had to be something of a self-confrontation—more precisely, a confrontation with the cultural aspects of their personality.

The following three excerpts illustrate how these criteria were taken into account. They are taken from the educators' version of the training (Kraemer 1978). The conversations take place in an American high school. In the first example the setting is the teachers' lounge, where an Anglo teacher and a Hispanic teacher are in midconversation:

> Mrs. Ramirez: Yes, I'm sorry I couldn't come to the party. Did you enjoy it?
>
> Mrs. Jones: Oh yes. I met so many interesting people there. There was one woman who used to be an English teacher, but now she is high up in the Office of Education. And, oh, there was another man who works for IBM as a computer engineer, and has just been assigned to the Paris office.
>
> Mrs. Ramirez: Hmmm!
>
> Mrs. Jones: And, let's see, I talked for a long time with another gentleman who would never tell me what he was doing. I called him the mystery man.
>
> Mrs. Ramirez: Why did you call him that?

Mrs. Ramirez's question at the end is intended as the clue that the trainer may use to control the difficulty of the excerpt by stopping the tape either before or after the question. Note how the difficulty increases when the question is left out.

In this example the Anglo teacher's cultural conditioning manifests itself in her way of describing the people she met at the party and in her inability to describe a man because she could not find out what his occupation was. This reflects the tendency of Anglos to define people (including themselves) in terms of their activities and achievements. Another Anglo teacher would not have asked Mrs. Jones why she referred to the man as the "mystery man."

Note how the criteria for constructing dialogues were taken into account in the remaining two examples. The manifestations of the Anglo's cultural conditioning in these examples are not identified so that you may practice doing it yourself, thus getting some feel for the exercise. If you wish to do so, complete the following sentence in each case: The cultural aspect(s) of the Anglo's thinking is (are)....

In this example (taken from a different sequence) the setting is a classroom, where an Anglo teacher and a Hispanic student are standing near the teacher's desk, in midconversation:

Yolanda:	Also, I want to return your book, Mrs. Wilson. Thank you very much for lending it to me. I read some of the poems.
Mrs. Wilson:	Did you like them?
Yolanda:	Oh, yes. They are beautiful poems. But I had to use the dictionary.
Mrs. Wilson:	Oh, well...I tell you what, Yolanda...why don't you keep the book. It will help you improve your English.
Yolanda:	*(very excited)* You're giving it to me, Mrs. Wilson?
Mrs. Wilson:	Yes. Read the rest of the poems when you have the time. And...well...it's...you know, it's all right. I got it at a convention, I think. The publishers are always giving away books.

The setting in the last example (taken from a third sequence) is a conference room, where an Anglo teacher is in midconversation with the mother of one of her Hispanic students:

Mrs. Campbell:	And your mother has been living with you for some time?
Mrs. Romano:	Yes, she has been living with us for some time now. Before, she used to live with my brother, but he went into the Army. And now she's with us. But you know, she is very sick, and we take care of her. She cannot move. She is supposed to be in bed. Well, she can sit up, but can't go out by herself, you know. And she has to take medicine. But that really doesn't help much. And you see, now I don't have much time for my children.
Mrs. Campbell:	I understand this perfectly. We had a similar situation in our...you know...in our house a few years ago.
Mrs. Romano:	Was your mother sick?

Mrs. Campbell:	Yes, and also she was…she was just getting on in years. She had an operation, you know, and she never really recovered from that. She was very weak and just needed a lot of care and attention. I had to spend a great deal of time with her myself. So, you know, I understand. But fortunately, you know, we found a very good situation for her. We found a very nice place. It's not the usual kind of nursing home. She gets wonderful care and attention there. Have you ever thought of something like that?

The mother's reply—a good clue—has been omitted here. In addition to omitting the clues, the instructor can increase the level of difficulty of the exercise by skipping the easiest excerpt in a given sequence.

Some Aspects of the Instructional Procedure

Concepts

The task confronting trainees during the exercise is highly unusual. They must learn to observe interactions between two people in what is for most a completely novel way. For this reason they must first be introduced to some of the concepts associated with the task. (This is best done by the use of examples.) The concepts, some of which have been discussed earlier, are cultural conditioning, latent content, subtle manifestations of cultural influences, implicit assumptions, and projection or projected cognitive similarity. Introduction of other concepts is deferred to later stages of the exercise. The trainees' understanding of all the concepts is gradually developed as the exercise progresses.

Structure

At the beginning of the exercise the structure of the video recordings and the nature of the trainees' task of analysis (of excerpts) and synthesis (of a sequence) are explained, and they are given the rules they must follow. These concern such matters as inappropriate responses (for example, criticizing the people shown in the recordings), what to write when they are unable to find what they are looking for, how to use the clues, reading their responses as they wrote them when called upon to do so, and when to ask questions other than procedural ones.

For each excerpt trainees are asked to complete this sentence: The cultural aspect(s) of the American's thinking is (are)…. [In the second version of the training: The cultural aspect(s) of the Anglo's thinking is (are)….] Some trainees may resist the requirement that their response be in writing or may find it too difficult. But the requirement is important. If a response is not written down, it is likely to change when the trainee hears the responses of others. When that happens, the trainee is deprived of the benefit of feedback to the original response.

Feedback

The nature of the trainer's feedback is governed by the rule that it must be helpful only to the point of enabling trainees to develop the synthesis of a sequence on their own. Therefore, no responses to individual excerpts are labeled right or wrong. They are either appropriate (if they focus on cultural content) or inappropriate (if they do not). Since many excerpts contain manifestations of more than one cultural influence (in the interest of plausibility), an appropriate response does not necessarily contribute to the synthesis of a sequence and may have to be revised in the light of the responses to the other excerpts in the sequence.

An effective way of relating the exercise to the trainees' real-life experience is to draw their attention to subtle manifestations of their cultural conditioning in their responses to the dialogues and in their interaction with each other and with the trainer. This requires a high level of cultural self-awareness on the part of the trainer.

Trainees may come to the training with some firmly held ideas that have to be dispelled. A good example is the idea that one should display empathy with members of another cultural group, particularly those seen as less fortunate. But in intercultural encounters empathy (in the sense of putting oneself in the other person's shoes) amounts to intentional intercultural projection. It may create the very difficulties that cultural self-awareness is intended to prevent. The display of empathy is therefore likely to be helpful only in those instances where our knowledge of the other culture allows us to assume that a given situation looks the same to its members as it would to us, if we were in their place.

Resistance

Perhaps the most difficult task facing the trainer is dealing with resistance to the training caused by the fact (discussed earlier) that the trainees' cultural conditioning tends to deny the fundamental idea they must come to accept in the course of the exercise—that what they think and say and do in most situations is, in part, the result of influences over which they have no control. Some trainees may find the idea very threatening, and trainers must help them come to terms with the contradiction.

Perhaps the use of computer-assisted instructional techniques and interactive video technology could overcome some of the difficulties trainers face in working with groups of trainees who, at the start of the exercise, differ widely in their level of cultural self-awareness and in their aptitude for developing it further.

Evaluation

Training developers must always ask themselves several questions about a new training method, for example, to what extent does it bring about the intended learning? The question is not always easy to answer. In the present case it meant determining to what extent trainees have learned to recognize the subtle manifestations of their cultural conditioning. No instrument for measuring that ability was available, and one had to be developed. Details of its development (including its validation) and of the evaluation of the training can be found in the instructor's handbook (Kraemer 1974). This was done in connection with the first version of the training.

The evaluation instrument consists of twenty-eight statements, each of which includes four items of information about a person (or persons) whose nationality is unknown. Respondents are asked to indicate which of the four seems the best available clue that the person(s) could be American. Here are two examples:

> In a discussion of the psychological characteristics of older children, a psychologist writes the following statements:
>
> a. "Sexual emotions are not a new experience to them."
> b. "They are influenced by their parents' values, often without being aware of it."
> c. "During puberty they undergo important psychological changes."
> d. "They often become a problem to their parents because they are a problem to themselves."

Which of the four items is the best available clue that the psychologist could be American?

> A newspaper reporter, describing the scene of an accidental collapse of an apartment building, writes:
>
> a. "Many people in the crowd shook their heads in disbelief."
> b. "Police tried to keep people from getting close to the rubble."
> c. "A few people seemed to be looking for relatives among the victims."
> d. "In the crowd one man could be seen weeping openly."

Which of the four items is the best available clue that the reporter could be American?

In order to avoid any bias resulting from conducting the evaluation myself, it was carried out by senior staff members of two participating organizations, the Foreign Service Institute and the U.S. Army Command & General Staff College. These trainers had first gone through the training themselves. They could conduct only an abbreviated version of the training (lasting less than half as long as the complete version) because of time constraints on the trainees. (No organization could be found where trainees could be made available long enough for an evaluation of the complete training.) Two out of three groups of trainees who participated in the evaluation scored significantly higher statistically than comparable groups who had not received the training, but the difference was small. Trainee satisfaction with the training was high.

The effects of the training are likely to diminish over time, unless trainees continue to practice. This is best done during and after intercultural encounters. But even without such opportunities, there are plenty of occasions to practice one's ability to recognize cultural influences in one's own thinking. The pervasiveness of these influences assures frequent manifestations of their effects. At the very least, the training teaches participants how to look for these manifestations.

Dissemination

At the start of this project it was envisioned that the training would be disseminated mainly by having it conducted by the user organization's own trainers for whom an instructor's manual would be prepared. Toward the end of the project, however, as I conducted numerous experimental versions of the training, it became apparent that the development of cultural self-awareness was a much more difficult task than I had anticipated and that this method and its objective were too advanced for individuals who did not already have a certain level of understanding of cultural differences. It also became clear that the in-house trainers would have to be trained in how to conduct the exercise. Many seemed unfamiliar with the psychological processes involved in intercultural communication as well as the psychological processes trainees experience as they go through the exercise. Thus, there were two approaches to implementation. The preferred one was to train trainers of the user organizations and attempt to have the training institutionalized. The other approach, far less desirable, was for me to conduct the training initially and then find in-house trainers who might be qualified to conduct it and who were interested in doing so. In either case, trainers would first have to experience the exercise themselves.

Various difficulties were encountered. Only a few will be mentioned here. Perhaps the most frustrating one resulted from the discovery that people in administrative positions who had to ensure that some of their personnel were prepared for intercultural work had a much lower than expected level of cultural self-awareness. They usually had some intercultural experience and readily agreed with the proposition that "cultural self-awareness" (which to them meant something vague like "knowing your own culture") was indeed important. To explain the conceptual framework and describe the exercise to them, I would show them a few of the videotaped dialogue excerpts—some of them only had time to look at two or three.

The excerpts selected for this purpose were of an intermediate level of difficulty, but they often produced only a blank stare on the face of the viewer. Of course, one could always explain the cultural content beforehand, but that would cause the purpose of the videotaped material to be perceived as providing illustrations of points to be covered in the training rather than stimulus material designed to create a certain mental process in the trainee. "We're already covering these cultural differences in our training" would be a typical response in these cases. "Covering" cultural differences is, of course, not the same as developing the trainees' ability to recognize their subtle manifestations. The dilemma was that in order for these administrators to appreciate the need for the training, they first had to go through it themselves. Fortunately, there were exceptions.

Then there were difficulties with trainers. Some were very anxious to use the video recordings but saw no need for learning how to conduct the training. It seemed obvious to them—you simply show the dialogues to the trainees and facilitate group discussion as you go along. They seemed totally unprepared for the idea that training in a complex cognitive skill required that each trainee be given intensive, guided practice in the skill to be learned. The idea seems self-evident in training programs for many other activities that require complex cognitive skills, such as medical diagnosis, architectural design, piloting an airplane, playing bridge, psychotherapy, and speaking a foreign language. Somehow the idea has not yet permeated the field of intercultural training. Fortunately, here too there were exceptions.

Over the years bootlegged copies of the video recordings have turned up in many places (the tapes are no longer available), but there seems to have been little interest by their users in actually employing the training method or using the recordings with any other approach that would give each trainee intensive, guided practice. The temptation to use shortcuts to speed up the training is always present, as is the temptation to avoid any procedure that might result in trainee resistance. I understand that in most cases the users selected portions of the recordings to serve as teaching aids—as critical incidents to be discussed or as convenient illustrations of a cultural difference.

Of course, the method is not suitable in cases where the entire intercultural training (which must deal with many other aspects of the trainees' intercultural work) lasts only a few days or less. For the managers of such programs there is a film that "will stimulate cultural self-awareness" and "prepares individuals for cultural adjustment and effectiveness in a foreign environment"—in twenty-eight minutes![†]

Concluding Comments

One may wonder why intercultural training of several hours or a few days is taken seriously by trainees, when they would scoff at foreign language training of such short duration. There is a good reason. When you have participated in brief foreign language training you are acutely aware of how limited your learning has been and of the specifics of your remaining ignorance. For example, you would know that you are unable to carry on a conversation beyond the most simple pleasantries, or are unable to read a novel or write a commercial letter, or are unable to understand what is being said in a play or a movie. This awareness has great specificity. When you are trying to use the language, you are immediately aware, for example, of what words you do not know or of your difficulty in spelling a word. The reason we can make these judgments so readily is simple. We can easily compare our skills in the foreign language with those we have in our own.

Trainees completing brief intercultural training cannot make the same kind of comparison between what they have learned about the other culture and what they know about their own. Most of their knowledge of their own culture is subconscious and therefore unarticulated—they are unaware of the pervasiveness of their own cultural conditioning. Furthermore, they may implicitly take for granted that aspects of the other culture not dealt with in their training are probably simi-

---

[†] The quoted statements appear in an undated advertisement for a series of films entitled Going International, produced by Griggs Productions. The statements are intended to tell the prospective user what one of these films (running time: 28 minutes) will accomplish.

lar to comparable aspects in their own culture. For these reasons shortcomings in their intercultural training are unlikely to become apparent to them before they experience the other culture.

Organizations where more time is devoted to intercultural training are the exception. (The U.S. Peace Corps is a good example.) Perhaps someday the managers who allocate funds for the intercultural training of their personnel will wonder why it should take two weeks to train a bartender and several weeks to train a pastry baker but only a few hours or days to develop the ability to work with people of another culture. Until then, the observation by Harry C. Triandis that intercultural training "is now where medicine was in the nineteenth century" will remain true (1985, 1).

References

Hall, Edward T. *Beyond Culture*. Garden City, NY: Anchor/Doubleday, 1976.

Holsti, Kalevi J. *International Politics: A Framework for Analysis*. 3d ed. Englewood Cliffs, NJ: Prentice-Hall, 1977.

Jervis, Robert. *Perception and Misperception in International Politics*. Princeton, NJ: Princeton University Press, 1976.

Kennan, George F. *The Cloud of Danger*. Boston: Little Brown, 1977.

Korotich, Vitalii. "Taming a Desert of the Mind." *Atlas*, June 1977.

Kraemer, Alfred J. *Teacher Training Workshop in Intercultural Communication: Instructor's Guide*. Alexandria, VA: HumRRO, 1978.

———. *Workshop in Intercultural Communication: Handbook for Instructors* (Technical Report 74-13). Alexandria, VA: HumRRO, 1974. (Available through NTIS as document no. AD 782196.)

———. *Development of a Cultural Self-Awareness Approach to Instruction in Intercultural Communication* (Technical Report 73-17). Alexandria, VA: HumRRO, 1973. (Available through NTIS as document no. AD 765486.)

Triandis, Harry C. *Cross-Cultural Psychology as the Scientific Foundation of Cross-Cultural Training*. Paper presented at the plenary session of SIETAR International, San Antonio, TX, May 1985.

Culture Heroes in Intercultural Training

Edward C. Stewart and Jun Ohtake

Many intercultural training sessions focus on surface culture—those aspects of a culture that are readily observed—but seldom explore the deep thoughts and feelings that form basic patterns of behavior. The challenge is to establish the links between these patterns of behavior and deep concepts. Based on our analysis, we propose *cultural identity* as the key idea for solving this puzzle. Identity is a deep concept that incorporates emotions and beliefs and reflects membership in a sociocultural group. In developing our training method, we chose to use heroes to gain a more concrete understanding of cultural identity. Through the vehicle of the hero, we can achieve understanding of the practical consequences of how we act and communicate with our foreign colleagues.

The culture heroes training method plunges below the surface to focus on values and feelings; it engages the emotion of cultural identity and of belonging as well as the social difficulties of cross-cultural communication. An example of the power of cultural identity is the culture shock experienced by individuals in the absence of the familiar ways of their home culture, which leads to mistrust and suspicion of even close colleagues. We learn our identities from our immediate cultural milieu, from role models such as parents, contemporary heroes, and even historical figures. One of the ramifications of this process is that a broad concept, such as identity, is required if we are to examine deep culture in our quest to establish good working and personal relations across cultures.

Ways have to be found to join thinking and feeling in the training experience to foster deep intercultural learning. We discovered that for Americans—but even more so for other nationalities—the examination of the culture hero, in which emotions and purposes were personalized in an ideal figure, was a natural approach to achieving that goal. The general American tendency to disassociate thinking and feeling often turns intercultural communication into an abstract and empty exercise. To analyze human conflict by separating technical interests from human relations is to become captive to the social quicksand of thought.

We chose to name this training exercise "Culture Heroes" rather than "Cultural Heroes" for a very specific reason. Our understanding of "cultural heroes" is that it refers to those who stand for, defend, or represent their culture. Our choice of phrase conveys a different nuance of meaning: "culture hero" implies that societies have a concept of what a hero is and that heroic attributes differ from culture to culture.

In the training exercise, the intent is to select someone whom people see as a hero in the culture, whose career or whose life reveals configurations of the culture. A culture hero who does that may or may not represent the dominant cultural values, especially in a society with large ethnically different populations divided sharply along ethnic lines, but that can nevertheless be just as revealing and take us just as deep into an understanding of cultural differences.

We will begin by describing the background for development of the exercise and instructions for conducting it, then offer guidelines for discussion. This will be followed by examples of American and Japanese heroes as they can be used in the exercise and can serve as a guide to interpreting culture hero choices. For the person wishing to use this exercise in an instructional or training context, we suggest you familiarize yourself thoroughly with this description of it and then discuss it with Japanese and American cultural informants (or informants from other cultures if the exercise is adapted). Trainers and educators using this exercise need to know the selected cultures well to be able to use it.

Background

The culture heroes method has its roots in research. The exercise began as an inquiry into human aggression and cultural memories of war. The idea we had in mind was to analyze the exploits of mythical and legendary heroes who had fought in historical battles and whose deeds had been preserved either in literature or in holy writings. The criteria used to select battles for inclusion in the inquiry were that their heroes had accepted the ethic of heroic sacrifice to their nations in war and their deeds had primed the imagination and fantasy of their own people.

Among those selected, Westerners are familiar with David in the Bible and Achilles in Homer's *Iliad*. Japanese know Yoshitsune, Atsumori, and Kumagae in *Atsumori*; while the vast subcontinent of India still resonates with Lord Krishna and Prince Arjuna in the *Bhagavad Gita*. We concentrated on Japanese culture because of its sharp contrast with American culture, and we can gain insight into *each* culture by contrasting it with the other. It was in this process that we began to grasp the significance of identity formation, which led us in a new direction. This occurred because the role and meaning of the hero in Japanese society eluded the Western mind, which is accustomed to aggressive heroic deeds such as those of David and Achilles. The Japanese paradox of the hero's "nobility of failure" (achieving nobility in the act of failing) impelled us to define the inquiry more broadly, abandon aggression as the sole subject, and adopt the more general concept of identification to understand the power that hero figures have to influence others.

The distinction between Japanese and American notions of surface and deep culture, perhaps more than any other idea used in training and teaching, explains the difference between Japanese and American cultures. Using Japanese and American cultures as points of reference for interpreting the meaning of heroes, we adopted the *cultural trilogy* (Stewart 1996) as our theoretical framework. We present the trilogy here at its first mention; however, we will discuss it in greater detail later in the chapter.

Figure 1

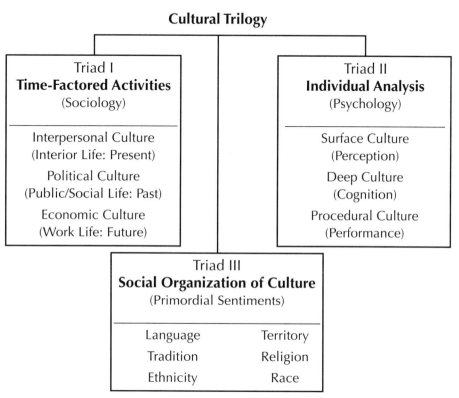

The culture's sense of belonging, power, and achievement are expressed within the first triad, Time-Factored Activities. The concepts of surface and deep culture are found within the second triad, Individual Analysis. The emotional dimensions of identity are embedded in the primordial sentiments of the third triad, the Social Organization of Culture. This armed us with a framework and interpretation which seemed natural to the Japanese and acceptable to Americans and other Westerners, and we could pass it on to trainers via the culture heroes exercise.

Ways of Using the Culture Heroes Exercise

As a learning activity, the culture hero has been used in three different ways in Japan; first, informally, as a topic of conversation. In our experience, Japanese students as well as professional people gravitate naturally to the subject. Usually, you can introduce the idea directly by saying, "I am conducting research on Japanese heroes and would like your selections and comments." On occasion, we have had the experience of meeting someone months after a conversation on heroes and being asked spontaneously how the research is progressing.

The second way we have used the hero theme is in presentations or guided discussion situations, such as those which take place during professional conferences in groups ranging from several to thirty people. Usually we begin with a few words on the difficulties of cross-cultural communication and express our interest in developing simple ways for improving understanding across cultures. At this point we introduce the subject of heroes and ask each member of the group to think about selecting a hero, giving the participants three criteria for making the choice:

❖ The hero should be someone with whom the person selecting feels a real and very strong identification—a role model.

❖ The hero should be well known so that the selection communicates something about the culture. That is, the participant's choice should not be idiosyncratic.

❖ The reasons for selecting the hero should not be so culturally specific that the choice makes no sense to someone from another culture.

The criteria for selecting heroes are flexible, serving as guides rather than rules. Once the participants have selected their heroes, we ask each one in turn to identify his or her choice and give reasons for the selection. Then we guide the discussion along some of the lines presented later in this chapter.

The third way we use the culture hero theme is in the structured training session described next.

Conducting the Exercise

In these guidelines for conducting the exercise, we will offer observations about (1) the process of selecting heroes, (2) the meaning of choices for the individuals making them, and (3) the processing of the results of the exercise.

The Selection of Heroes

Point out that you are using the idea of the culture hero as a training tool, phrasing your introductory remarks according to trainee interest. It is important, however, to get across that there are two levels of hero: personal and cultural. By personal hero we mean some living or historical person who has provided you with an image or model that influenced your thinking and your emotional development, helped form your beliefs, guided how you behaved, and influenced how you have led your life. By culture hero, we mean a hero who is known by all or most people of your society and is accepted as a member of the reference or home culture of the trainees. Remember, you are looking for a *culture* hero.

After describing the two levels of heroes and presenting the criteria for selection, ask participants to write down their individual choices. If the group is five or fewer, discuss the individual choices with the whole group. If more than five, divide them into subgroups and ask them to agree on a single hero to report to the full group.

The Meaning of Choices

Once the heroes are selected, you should lead a discussion to reveal the nature and meaning of the choices. One way to enhance the learning is to ask the participants to recount the stories of their heroes. It draws more meaning from the selection process and can help move the discussion to deeper levels. Keep your observations and questions concrete and relevant to the trainees.

In writing the questions listed below, we had the results of three training programs in mind. In one of these training sessions of predominantly Japanese participants, the trainees chose Yoshitsune and Admiral Yamamoto. In a second program of mainly Westerners, the groups chose the two great advocates of nonviolent resistance, Martin Luther King Jr. and Mahatma Ghandi.

These questions should work as well for other choices, but take care to let the discussion evolve in directions relevant to the selections of the participants.

Questions about the Hero

❖ How would you describe the mission, the work, or the message of the hero with whom you identify?

❖ What are the successes and victories for which the hero is known?

❖ What obstacles, difficulties, and opposition did the hero confront?

❖ What are the defeats and failures which contributed to or detracted from the hero's reputation?

❖ Is the hero admired for nobility in defeat and failure?

❖ What kind of fortitude and courage did the hero show?

❖ Is the hero admired for personal integrity and dedication to cultural beliefs when confronting adversity?

❖ What was the nature of the forces opposing the hero and the character of adversaries or enemies confronting the hero?

❖ What are the weaknesses, shortcomings, or disgraces attached to the hero?

Questions Related to the Life of the Individual

❖ What has the role of the hero been in your own thoughts and feelings?

❖ Do you remember the time and circumstances in your life when you first became aware of the hero?

❖ How would your thinking and feelings be different if you had never heard of or learned about the hero?

Questions Related to the Social Life

❖ Who helped, competed with, or opposed your hero? (This places the hero into context.)

❖ In what ways is the hero mute or silent about your culture?

❖ In what ways do you consider the hero a good communicator and representative of your culture?

In closing the discussion, be sure to place the heroes in relation to other culture heroes and identify them with appropriate cultural movements. This will help end the training session on a cross-cultural note.

Guidelines for the Discussion of Chosen Heroes

For the culture heroes discussion, you are going to need a lot of background on cultural differences and the process of identification. The questions you ask should lead to perceptions of identity and belonging, and should clarify the sense of achievement and power in the culture. These comprise the essence of the hero—what he or she has done, what kind of personal qualities he or she embodies, and what his or her relationship is to the culture. You can use the cultural trilogy (see Figure 1) as a template to help you guide the discussion and analysis to reach the core learning opportunity provided by the culture heroes method. Since the elements of the cultural trilogy are reflected in the trainees' culture and make sense in other cultures as well, this allows you to generalize across cultures during the discussion.

One can plot the meaning of the differences between any two cultures by analyzing heroes according to the cultural trilogy. However, in most cases every element will not pertain to a specific hero. You need to select those concepts in the cultural trilogy that best explain the reasons why members of the culture identify with the hero—why the hero has achieved a cultural identity in that society.

We believe the cultural trilogy bridges the chasm separating American (Western) and Japanese culture. So the first thing we will describe in our quest to better understand the deep cultures symbolized by Japanese and American heroes is the components of the cultural trilogy.

Triad I: Time-Factored Activities

In Japanese culture, the emphasis on rhythms of daily life is extraordinary. Without the mediation of personalized figures, living or at least symbolic, most Japanese find it difficult to empathize with large groups. For example, a member of a large company like Toyota does not see him- or herself as an employee of Toyota so much as a member of his or her working group or cohort. The reality of lifebuilding activity (public life) for the ordinary Japanese is one that embodies a high point of existence but at the same time is closely attached to the uneasiness of lifekeeping (interior life). The down-to-earth, socially oriented hero decreases the uneasiness of the interior life and interpersonal relations, thereby raising the hero's credibility. The main function of Japanese heroes seems to be to integrate interior, work, and public life into a seamless web from the vantage point of interpersonal culture.

The concept of time-factored activities helps build our understanding of the culture hero in Japan. Without this element we would not be able to grasp the Japanese concept of power and the influence that inter- and intrapersonal rhythms have had on Japanese heroes. We think of them as time-factored activities because they occur in time rhythms such as weeks, months, or years. Perception of time rhythms can be imposed from the outside or be part of one's interior life.

Table 1 charts time-factored activities in terms of variables that can differ across cultures. *Culture* within our system refers to levels or aspects of life. *Formal activity* denotes the events (lifekeeping, lifemaking, or lifebuilding) taking place, and the *informal name* locates the activity in the person or the world. *Time form* and *time orientation* link the cultural activities to time factors.

Table 1. Time-Factored Activities

Culture	Formal Activity	Informal Name	Time Form	Time Orientation
Interpersonal	Lifekeeping	Interior Life	Cyclic	Present
Economic-Technical	Lifemaking	Work Life	Linear	Near Future
Sociopolitical	Lifebuilding	Public Life	Episodic	Past

Interpersonal Culture. Interior activities refer to physiological needs such as those satisfied by food, drink, sleep, physical comfort, and shelter. By necessity, interior activities become routinized and require little judgment or forethought, and their pursuit typically occurs in the social context of familiar and trusted people. The impression of time is cyclic, and the temporal orientation is the present. In strange surroundings or in times of danger, the routines of interior patterns are disturbed and we become preoccupied with reinstating them.

People generally are not willing to live with a minimal satisfaction of their basic physical and social needs. In addition, our daily and weekly rounds of activities minister to power, social belongingness, and achievement needs. The repetitive cycles of interior life lack direction and meaning until we elaborate the material necessities of interpersonal culture and invest performance with symbolic meaning. Food is not served haphazardly; it is prepared and cooked—in this case among Japanese in earthenware pottery and eaten at convivial dinners, typically in the company of family or close friends and companions. When food is prepared in exotic ways and served on chinaware at commemorative banquets, it ministers to the need for social belonging. Interior activities provide the logistics of action for other cycles of activity which are more abstract and recur in longer periods of time. These may be regular days for shopping, for visiting friends and relatives, and for recreational or hobby-related excursions.

Economic-Technical Culture. Many activities occur in time rhythms of weeks and months, which are superimposed upon interior rhythms. Time is linear and orientation is to the near future for work events and things related to careers. In schools, the actions of both instructors and students are governed by rhythms of time in months and years. Routinizing life at the level of economic-technical culture typically requires training, since it does not happen as naturally as at the level of interpersonal culture. At this level, planning, decision making, and evaluation (among other activities) gain in significance. Economic cultural events are those associated with work and employment in which individuals are interacting with colleagues, associates, and friends.

Sociopolitical Culture. The temporal orientation for the third rhythm of activity, public life, is first toward the past and second, toward the future. Time is no longer cyclic or linear, but episodic; commemorating fixed dates, events, or periods of time from the points of view of the individual and the nation. Episodes or events related to birth, marriage, anniversaries, promotion, retirement, and death mark the sociopolitical life span. Birthdays of national heroes, religious holidays, and days set aside to commemorate special groups and famous historical events are symbolic markers of the public life of the nation and of its people and contribute to the social and political dimensions of the identity of the individual.

Observations about the time rhythms of activity (cyclic, linear, episodic) led to the insight that interpersonal values (part of the cyclic and present-oriented rhythm) are dominant in Japanese culture and project to the other two rhythms as well. The question is, how are the three rhythms integrated into distinctive patterns? Undoubtedly all societies use the same mechanism, but each in its own way.

In Japan, power in all of its symbolism comes to a peak in sociopolitical culture in the form of the Emperor as a symbol of benevolence and of the nation. At the more mundane level of daily life for the people, a forceful power figure faces a difficult situation. The true Japanese power figure is one who has taken the right steps in the right manner toward the right things and has been accepted by the elders and/or by the group, much like an apprentice in the older Buddhist sects. He or she who is elected is seldom popular and, in any case, usually lacks power. Power in Japanese culture is primarily invested in the prerogatives of belonging and being. The Japanese power figure faces the difficult task of choosing between leadership and conformity which is rarely crystal clear.

For the Americans, both the relative concentration on economic-technical culture and a powerful action orientation are associated with the propensity of American heroes to take action. Western heroes are largely noted for what they did, how they did it, and why they did the deed. Although heroic deeds are part of all heroes, the *consequences* of heroic actions apparently are more important for the Westerner. It is important that they succeed. In contrast, the Japanese hero leans toward states of being. He is noted for who he is and how he became what he is. For the Japanese, it is purity of heart and sincerity of intentions that matter. The individualism of the Japanese is asserted in purity and in rituals such as those at the time of death.

Triad II: Individual Analysis

If Time-Factored Activities might be called the sociology of a culture, then the Individual Analysis could be called the psychology of a culture. Both the sociology *and* the psychology of a culture are necessary for our understanding of deep culture.

Surface Culture: The "What." The metaphor "surface" suggests the perceived features such as the sounds of the language, nonverbal expressions, way of dress, artifacts, art objects, and many other events and objects that qualify as the "what" of a culture. Perception brings these people, items, and events to the individual as images, sounds, smells, and feelings. For example, visual perception is one of the sensory modes used to construct an object. The *haniwa* sculpture of a samurai warrior sits firmly on the shelf as an object that is neither dispersed in space nor experienced inside the perceiver's body. Vision, hearing, and touch are object-centered sensory modalities easily understood as belonging in surface culture. Pain, on the other hand, is mysterious and difficult to understood as an integral part of surface culture.

In the inquiry of the cultural memories of war, we had frequent occasions to confront pain. Achilles, the ancient Greek hero in Homer's *Iliad*, ignored pain, treating it as an abstraction. However, Kumagae and the other samurai were very sensitive to pain and suffering, treating them as concrete experiences. These disparate reactions indicate the enigmatic nature of pain and also the cultural difference in handling it. Like vision, hearing, and touch, pain is an integrated and unitary perceptual modality (Geldard 1953, Zborowski 1969), but a quixotic one different from the other senses (McConnell 1986). It is a subjective and powerful human experience with a perceptible and distinctive range of negative somatic sensations.

The consequence of pain physiology is an experience that is primarily aversive and private. The more the individual suffers from pain, the greater is the sufferer's sense of being alone. Pain is internal, not external. That is, it constructs no objects and has no cognitive forms, only feelings of intensity described as temporal, spatial, pressure, thermal, and other internal properties (Melzack and Wall 1988). Any symbolic content of pain is learned and, therefore, cultural. In contrast to perceiving an externalized object, the experience of pain takes place in the interior of the body. The objectless quality and the privacy of pain—especially when intense—can drive out all conscious thought and feeling and grant free rein to the imagination to invent instruments that explain the causes of the pain (see Scarry 1985, 161–80).

From the viewpoint of our interest in culture, the experience of pain is largely understood as suffering, emotions, feelings, and anxiety rather than the sensory experience of pain itself. Since emotions and feelings play such an important role in the story of every culture hero, it is worthwhile to elaborate the impact of emotions on behavior and to illuminate the connection between emotion and pain, aggression, prejudice, and war. Using a behavioral criterion of universal facial expressions, Ekman, Friesen, and Ellsworth have identified six basic emotions: happiness, sadness, anger, fear, disgust, and surprise (1972). Fear and anger are the emotions so often found in heroes.

When fear is great and the frightened one freezes, the body closes in upon itself, the skin pales, the limbs and torso become clammy and cold. The feeling of fear impels the individual to look outside for help, but at the same time the outside world appears to have gathered against the individual. There seems no rational escape from the causes of fear—real or imaginary. The powerlessness of fear makes the individual vulnerable to anger, an energetic emotion that shoves fear aside.

In the American folk mind, anger has a cognitive structure and also a narrative of danger. The angry person runs the risk that the container of anger will boil over or explode. It is believed that an explosion may be prevented by using sufficient force and energy to contain anger, but when anger increases past a certain limit, the pressure explodes and the person loses control (he blew his stack).

Recognizing the danger inherent in anger, whereby perceptions are distorted, the angry person views anger as an opponent in a struggle (she fought back her anger). When anger focuses on danger to others, there is a widespread metaphor in Western culture that passions are beasts inside a person. Slaying the angry beast who is besetting others is typically seen as a heroic act.

> ...there is a part of each person that is a wild animal. Civilized people are supposed to keep that part of them private, that is, they are supposed to keep the animal inside them. In the metaphor, loss of control is equivalent to the animal [on the] loose. And the behavior of a person who has lost control is various passions— desire, anger, etc. In the case of anger, the beast presents a danger to other people. (Lakoff 1987, 492)

Deep Culture: The "Why." The metaphor "deep" suggests concepts that underlie and give meaning to surface culture. Deep culture involves abstract ideas about things, people, events, logic, and facts that are separated from context, time, and space. An example illustrates the difference between deep and surface culture.

Some years ago, a young woman and friend of the senior author was going through a difficult period in her life and was suffering from a deep depression. She was directed to a psychiatrist whom she liked and decided to enter into therapy. After some weeks of treatment she felt quite satisfied with the psychiatrist and developed a strong attachment to him. One day, she was shopping in a supermarket when she noticed a man pushing a cart with some groceries in it, coming down the aisle in her direction. He attracted her attention, since he seemed vaguely familiar. Suddenly, as he approached her, she recognized him as her psychiatrist. She was startled and before she could contain herself she blurted out, "Do you eat too?"

How do we explain her amusing but strange reaction? First, her acquaintance with the psychiatrist was from the therapy sessions conducted in the psychiatrist's office. The situation (office) and event (therapy session) were a restricted context. She had formed an intense attachment to the psychiatrist, so in her mind and emotions he existed only in her space and time. The strength of her feelings and emotions did not attribute to him an existence in his own interpersonal time, space, and activities. Meeting him in the context of the supermarket compelled her to revise her concept of him to that of a human being, a male, who was a psychiatrist (professional) but who also had a personal life. Much of her confusion derives from the intensity of the interpersonal patterns of therapy sessions which interfered with her ability to go beyond a specific time, place, and context. Had she previously asked herself deep culture questions such as What is a psychiatrist? What is therapy? and so on, she most likely would have recognized him immediately. The answers to these questions are the thoughts and abstractions of deep culture.

Deep culture is distributed among all members of a community and is detached from any utility in real time or space, although it motivates both the surface and procedural manifestations of a culture. When individuals become more conscious of their deep culture, they are better able to communicate with and understand individuals who have different cultural backgrounds.

For Japanese, deep culture is an underlying axiom. It is even a truth with a divine spark. The word *shinri* (truth) captures both the spiritual meaning and the logical reasoning of truth. The Japanese accept the diverse nature of the surface culture and of the bridge leading to deep culture, but they disguise the bridge and conceal deep thoughts and feelings in human relations that appear as procedural culture. From the outside, deep culture may seem nonexistent. The Japanese believe human nature resides in the underlying truth of deep culture. They disguise and hide the negative aspects of human nature in the labyrinth of human relations, while on the surface, in procedures of communication, they insist on politeness and social manners. Deep culture is understood and could be described but not explained. Surface, deep, and procedural cultures exist as a seamless web of human relations that resist analytical parsing into separate components. On the other hand, grasping this abstraction can help us understand other cultures as well as the Japanese.

To Americans, this seems to be an escape or abandonment of effort. Americans also consider human nature as deep culture, but unlike Japanese who disguise the negative aspects of human nature, Americans deal with it in surface culture in an effort to openly change its negative features, a procedure that seems trivial and pointless to Japanese.

Original sin or pure evil opposite pure good does not exist in Japanese culture. The acceptance of evil, as in Western (Christian) cultures, does not appear natural to the Japanese. An underlying benevolence symbolized by a divine figure always pervades their mental landscape. Sometimes the benevolence of human nature is reflected in figures such as the Emperor, but many Americans hold a view of the Emperor different from the Japanese benevolent view. Some Japanese believe the Emperor is merely the most prominent reflection in a pool of more complex and abundant benevolent forms.

The concept of yin and yang, where dark and light complement each other, seems to suggest that Japanese culture does indeed include good opposing evil. But actually the same context allows room for both poles to form a strange symbiosis. Although they never blend, there is the curving intrusion—the point of light and dark in its opposite. Therefore, unlike the Western hero, the Japanese culture hero does not convey an image of pure good versus pure evil, but a portrayal of the whole, combining both and accommodating conflict between goodness and honesty on one side and cultural gaps and a social code of ethics on the other.

Procedural Culture: The "How." The third aspect of the psychological analysis of culture provides deep culture with more context and a synthesis between the surface and deep cultures. Procedural culture combines surface and deep culture in the individual and community by bringing task orientations, contextual intentions, and goals into individual experience. Procedural culture involves activities and processes occurring in real time. These activities and processes include, for example, communication, problem solving, negotiation, and decision making. Procedure is at the core of culture; the recipe for how to do things.

The Japanese stress procedural culture and its survival component. Both in religion and in knowledge, the Japanese concern is more for what has to be done and for the style of doing it, less for beliefs or logic. For example, the original Japanese religion is Shinto. To be Shintoist is to do Shinto things, not to hold Shinto beliefs—of which there are few.

Another example of the differences between American and Japanese procedural culture resides in their approaches to conflict and methods of persuasion. Americans prefer to use logic and reason as tools, with values, beliefs, and passion as drives. Japanese rely on harmony, passion, beliefs, and values as tools, with logic and rationale as drives. The American conquest of conflict, reaching for the utmost truth, seems trivial to a Japanese. For their part, the Japanese tend to resolve conflict by accepting it. First, the Japanese must reach a consensus with the opposing party regarding the existence and nature of the conflict. Then they must accept it as it is and find a compromise reaction to the conflict. It is a long and redundant process, but its goal is to reach an agreement which both sides can value. For the American, this would not be accepted as a true resolution. Compromise amounts to "giving in," giving up one's own interest or demand. For the Japanese, compromise is an act of benevolent acceptance. If one party does not respond with benevolence, that party is considered childish, selfish, and inconsiderate.

Triad III: The Social Organization of Culture

The primordial sentiments have greater meaning for Japanese culture than for American culture. The primordial sentiments in Triad III—language, tradition, ethnicity, territory, religion, and race—make up the content of cultural identity. In Japanese society each primordial sentiment contributes to the cultural identity of an individual. In regard to the social organization of culture, Japanese stress harmony as the goal in society and generally accept benevolence as the attribute of authority.

The growth of identity in America has followed a different course. American national identity has its roots in the eighteenth-century American struggle for independence and democracy. The content of American identity was determined primarily by democratic civil values in interpersonal culture and the value of equality in deep culture. With the exceptions of race and religion, the influence of the primordial sentiments was overshadowed by civil values. The inspiration for American national identity came from rugged individualism and the conquest of the wilderness. Americans built their identity through the process of identification with the interests, rights, and opportunities of individual citizens rather than encumbering identity with the baggage of the past, of family, and of culture as contained in the primordial sentiments.

In regard to the feelings of identity, during colonial days Americans acquired the sentiment of effort-optimism and the belief in the future. Keeping in step with the ethos, American entrepreneurs developed principles of efficiency in deep culture and of time control in procedural culture. Efficient operations were implemented in work life, becoming famous as the American assembly line geared for mass production. But efficiency soon collided with the emotions of workers and managers. The expression of emotion was seen as a spoiler of efficiency. In the nineteenth century, an assault was launched to banish emotions (particularly anger) from the workplace. By the twentieth century, the culture of efficiency had spread through American interior and public life, curbing emotions and building a deep theory of efficiency enshrined as the philosophy of pragmatism.

Although the Triad III emotions of cultural belonging and the powerful senti-ments of identity and uniqueness are important for understanding Abraham Lin-coln, the American leader, and Kumagae, the Japanese hero, in both Japanese and American cultures the relations between emotion, primordial sentiments, and iden-tity are too complex and extended to be treated fairly here. Hence we decided to limit the use of Triad III when we plot our two interpretations of identity in an American hero and a Japanese hero. We shall begin with the American hero, since the cultural implications of Lincoln's culture heroism are episodes in Ameri-can history. Interpretation will be more direct. The meaning of Kumagae will be interpreted in a more complex and profound way, incorporating mythological and aesthetic principles in the representation of Japanese culture.

Lincoln: An American Culture Hero

Memories of Lincoln are inseparable from the social-political events of the times. As the American president and commander-in-chief of the Union forces during the Civil War, he naturally became a political hero. Lincoln was controversial to opponents, but after his death—less than a week following Lee's surrender to Grant—his reputation rose above the political turmoil. From the distance of the present, Lincoln is revered as the emancipator of the slaves, abolisher of slavery, and preserver of the Union. He is firmly established as a culture hero in addition to historical hero. Why?

Since the founding of the republic, Americans have been entranced by the occupant of the White House. From the beginning, they turned their backs on the pomp and circumstance of Europe's reigning monarchs and saw the president not only as having executive authority but also as the representative of Americans as a people committed to individual initiative and equality in human relations. Lincoln's stature as a culture hero is neither technical nor political, but interper-sonal, and it derives from his actions, the impact of his words, and the material-ization of his values and thoughts on the nation's scene.

Lincoln had a clever mind that projected a somber intelligence and a wry sense of humor. He was a tall, ungainly man of homespun appearance and was usually dressed in unkempt clothes. His disheveled appearance clashed with his position as president. The contrast between his spectacular facial features, unruly hair, and framing beard created the impression of a carved, craggy face: people around him responded to that face, feeling that they had always known him and could trust him. He had the capacity for putting the issues of the moment and the sentiments of the time into words. It was difficult to imagine him as a tricky poli-tician or as a deceiver. He was an individualist and he was competent. As resident of the White House and with his character and personal qualities, he embodied American cultural ideals.

Cultural Analysis

Lincoln was a humble man, free of arrogance, who never sought revenge. He appealed to the deep abstraction that the Union must be preserved. To reduce hate and discord, he delayed proclaiming emancipation and implementing enforcement as long as possible. At the end of the war, he urged a profound forgiveness for the South.

He was on the right side, the war was won and peace established, perhaps, with less recrimination between North and South than in any other comparable modern war. The enormous battle casualties left Americans with a sense of loss, which estranged them from warfare as a way of life. Lincoln's assassination by an actor, a few days after the armistice, spared him from the dirty work of reparations and reconstruction. Americans remember his death as a deep loss—unnecessary and undeserved—symbolizing perhaps the sense of loss of Federal and Confederate soldiers killed during the war. His life ended, but his words lived on as did the consequences of his actions. The sense of loss from his death was needed by the nation to justify a true reconciliation between North and South, black and white. Lincoln is a great American culture hero explained by the deep sentiment that the sacrifice of his life saved the South for the Union.

Kumagae: A Japanese Culture Hero

Kumagae appears as the hero in the ballad *Atsumori*. It is a type of ballad-drama known as *kowaka*, descended from medieval times and performed in remote villages of Kyushu. The drama deals with a traumatic experience, the conversion of a high-minded but worldly man from his mundane life to a life of religious blessedness. The story begins at the battle of Ichinotani, A.D. 1148, fought next to the seashore, near Kobe, on the island of Honshu. Warriors of the Genji clan launched a daring attack down a mountainside against armed forces of the Heike clan. The Genji clansmen, led by Yoshitsune, their scion and legendary hero, inflicted a disastrous defeat upon the Heike forces, who fled to their vessels waiting offshore.

Atsumori, a young courtier of the Heike clan, renowned for his skill as a flutist, spent the night before the battle in the inner palace, but with the defeat, Atsumori, among the Heike forces in flight, attempts to make his way to the Heike vessels and escape. He reaches the beach, but before plunging into the surf, he discovers that his transverse flute, carved from Chinese bamboo, has been left behind. He wheels his horse around, races back to the inner palace, and retrieves the flute. Once more he rushes to the beach, but to his dismay, the Heike vessels are pushing far out to sea. Atsumori slackens the reins, allowing his horse to run free, but before he can escape from the site, Kumagae, a redoubtable Genji warrior, overtakes and challenges him to combat. Failing to escape, Atsumori gallantly accepts the challenge, but in combat he is no match for Kumagae, who easily throws him down. The Genji warrior tears off Atsumori's helmet, draws a blade from his waist, and is about to sever Atsumori's head when Kumagae, blade in hand, hesitates to glance at the pitiable face of Atsumori, a lad who is maybe fifteen years old. Atsumori's youthful appearance reminds Kumagae of the contrasting looks of his own son, who is homely and barbarous. The warrior is moved by benevolence to spare the youth's life. He helps him to his feet, lifts him up onto his horse, and both ride off to the west.

Unknown to Kumagae, the Genji leaders (perhaps Yoshitsune and others in close attendance) observe the combat and the benevolence of Kumagae from a position above on the crest of a hill. Suspecting Kumagae of treason for sparing a foe, the observing party rides in pursuit of Kumagae. Kumagae perceives that he is being chased and will be caught, and he knows that both he and Atsumori shall die. Vowing to pray for the soul of the youth, he seizes him tightly and both plunge to the ground. Kumagae quickly strikes off the young courtier's head and holds it high as he weeps helplessly.

In the events that follow, Kumagae repents his deed and the code of the samurai. He carries the head of Atsumori to a Buddhist monk (bonze), who conducts memorial rites. Kumagae watches the young flutist's head vanish in smoke and impermanence. Placing the ashes in a bag, Kumagae ties it around his neck and always carries it with him. After joining a Buddhist sect, he changes his name to Rensho and sets out on a journey to Mount Koya. He approaches and enters a famous Buddhist shrine, the Cloister of the Interior. There he deposits the ashes of Atsumori and completes appropriate rituals.

A hero of the spirit, Kumagae dies from natural causes long after the battle of Ichinotani. Atsumori's death on the seaside is the cause of Kumagae's apostasy and life of redemption as Rensho. In this ballad both Kumagae and Atsumori are complex mythical figures who engage the spirit, aesthetics, and morality. But Yoshitsune, commander and victor at Ichinotani, is not even named in the ballad. At best, he appears as a shadowy figure—perhaps he was one of the horsemen on the crest of the hill whose power displaced the benevolence of Kumagae. Neither one of the two principal figures—Kumagae or Yoshitsune—emerges in a Western heroic mold of power or aggression. Other ballads tell us that years later, Yoshitsune ends his days as a fugitive and dies by his own hand to avoid the disgrace of capture and execution. It is meeting his bitter fate—the nobility of failure—that in Japan makes him a hero.

Cultural Analysis

The trauma in *Atsumori* is the deep sadness of the destruction and death of war. Analyzing a hero from a ballad to interpret culture and cultural differences is not capricious. The primordial sentiments of tradition and language occupy a position in the Japanese sense of reality quite different from the American view. The Japanese modes of expression in poetry, mythology, and communication generally have three pronounced tendencies (Wells 1968, 14–23).

First, *form is dominant over substance*. The qualities of artfulness, refinement, and craftsmanship are of the highest order and act to diminish deep emotions and to ritualize profound ideas. It is procedural culture which is important and not deep culture, which remains concealed and elusive.

The second tendency is to *focus on perceptual reality*. Although the Japanese are among the foremost masters of audacious stylization, likewise they are masters of the keenest realism, and their observations are unsurpassed for accuracy (Wells, 15). The sharp Japanese eye detects not only the universal but also the particular and circumstantial. The Japanese vision is aesthetic and visual rather than philosophical, and is dedicated to sentiments of place and context (Wells,

14–16). For the Japanese it is the particular perceiver and the concrete entity that have meaning.

The third pronounced tendency is to view *art as a reshaping of experience*. Drama by its very nature is artificial, but it is also naturalistic (Wells, 17). The implication of the principle is that the artifices of drama and poetry do reveal the truth and represent reality.

In the *Atsumori* ballad, Kumagae spies Atsumori at the end of the battle while seeking a nobleman for a duel. All the warriors he has killed in the battle have been of humble birth, like himself. His samurai's ambition has been unquenched, but the sight of Atsumori—who conveys the appearance of a nobleman—alerts his competitive warrior's instinct. Once he defeats Atsumori and recognizes his foe is a child who reminds him of his own son, he spares his life out of benevolence. But the act of compassion is observed by his commanders, who interpret his kindness as treachery and a violation of the samurai code. When Kumagae realizes that he is pursued and will be caught and killed, he does not deny or resist the confrontation with the samurai code and beheads Atsumori. His genuine grief is the main point of the ballad. But the reality of life and of being a samurai cannot be challenged. His grief is more sadness and despair than it is guilt. Whatever one's feelings and emotions are, they must be adapted to the social-political culture. In this case, Kumagae's deep emotions and thoughts must be ritualized and relieved in the procedural culture as Rensho, the Buddhist monk. The need to belong and to pursue the rituals of the group supersede the deep values and sentiments of the individual in Japanese culture.

Interpreting Culture Hero Choices

Cultural identity is an intellectual concept you can use to guide your trainees to a discovery of cultural insights.

For Americans, *identification* plays a central role in selecting heroes, as charisma makes the hero become one with the individual. Freud defined identification as the psychological process in which another person stands for the self. The hero provides a figure with whom one can identify, which integrates private fantasy with the external demands of life. The simplest case of identification is that in which the self incorporates an object from outside into one's self. This has several distinct features. It is intense and it may involve different areas of the person's life. For example, you may identify with one figure in sports but identify with quite a different person in your work.

Another feature of identification is that the personal image one holds of others acts as a filter for perceiving them. The image of leader, for instance, often reflects the wishes and needs of the individual rather than what the leader is actually like. The idealized image is projected on the actual leader.

Finally, people most frequently think of identification as a positive emotion based on the hero's admirable traits or achievements, but it is also possible for people to identify with those who are villains or those they hate, that is, antiheroes (McIntosh 1969, 74). An example might be Adolf Hitler, in the sense that his quest for power succeeded for a while. Consider what might have happened to his reputation had he died in 1936 or 1937, shortly after he came to power.

Identification is a social process characteristic of Europeans that is diminished among Americans, for whom the core dimension of human existence is individualism. The separation of the self-concept from the social realm of society makes American culture probably the most individualistic in the world. As a result, one of the basic lines of interpretation for the hero exercise lies in the degree to which the choices of the American participants reflect or contradict the radical individualism of their culture.

The Japanese have two orientations toward heroes that are reflected in the two words they use when talking about them. In one study on Japanese heroes undertaken by the authors, Japanese subjects of all ages used a Japanese word, *akogare*, which is closely related to the meaning of the hero, yet distinct. The word *hero*, on the other hand, is most often translated as *eiyu* and is defined as a person with superior talent or with superior bravery (Sanseido 1979).

The Japanese live in a hierarchical society in which the individual learns to regard elderly citizens as social symbols that integrate the group (Lebra 1976, 2–9). These and other values of Japanese culture allow us to interpret the meaning of akogare and of eiyu. An important difference between the two concepts is reflected in the way they were used by our subjects in the empirical study of the hero in Japanese society. Conceptually, akogare is admiration that is real and can be felt by anyone, and it can lead to romantic notions not unlike those found in fan clubs. The hero (eiyu) is a model which the subjects felt should be portrayed, but not copied, for it is absolutely impossible to become anything like the figure.

Emotions and feelings regarding eiyu remain in the realm of fantasy. For younger Japanese, akogare can be felt between members of the same sex; the hero (eiyu), however, can only be a male (which reflects the male orientation in Japanese society). The difference in the way Japanese apply akogare and eiyu indicates that the akogare reference is to interior activities, while eiyu applies more to work and perhaps holds some public nuances. This split appears to parallel the major distinction in Japanese perception between *honne*, the emotional and dynamic center of the personality, and *tatemae*, the external social facade.

Need of expression is also separated into two parts. The personal need of expression, which—like tatemae—is closer to reality and is therefore accessible, is reflected in the concept of akogare; while the "ultra-real" and impersonal need of expression—the deeper dynamics of honne—is reflected in that of eiyu.

> Japanese myths present a dislocation of time...the hero returns after his mythic journey to find that everyone in his village has aged terribly; the proof of his experience is the proof of his own identity (when he reveals knowledge or characteristics that no one but he would have, and that are accepted as "historically true" by surviving villagers) and the fact that he has not aged (as he would have done had he stayed in this world) (O'Flaherty 1980, 105).

Thus the mythic hero links the supernatural and the people in their daily lives. The Japanese hero often goes against the absolute and undefeatable, and his efforts are to no avail. Japanese value the grit of the hero in his defeat. Ivan Morris

(1975) argues that the quintessential Japanese hero must rise very high in the arc of success, then plummet to the depths of failure before he is accepted as a genuine hero. Japanese empathy picks up the hero in his defeat with a profound and solemn faith in his effort. It represents the Japanese urge toward individualism, the emotional center of honne. At the same time, the failure reinforces the social norms of tatemae, which in Japanese culture must always prevail as the natural state of affairs.

In either case, the hero must become someone who has done something that others feel has positive meaning and value. At a general level, the hero must confirm that our deepest values are true and real, for example, individualism for Americans and the right state of being for Japanese. Even in going against the grain, the hero must be life-affirming and oppose whatever is life-denying (Criner 1988, 545). Consequently, the hero must have an enemy of a sort, which could be a nine-headed dragon, an emotional desire, or even an internal struggle. The enemy, or struggle, does not have to be physical or even real. It can be an ethical or moral issue arising in the relationship between itself and society.

The hero holds an ideal or philosophy, a given set of values that is sentimentally correct. These are similar to the orthodox Western view, but the sentiment involved is of a different nature. The Japanese hero must have character, and there is an element of innateness in him which is not shared to the same degree with Western heroes. The Japanese hero depends more on emotions than on physical deeds and is enmeshed in fate, while the Western hero is swept along by destiny and has a hand in directing it.

Inquiry along these lines is likely to be particularly fruitful when debriefing the hero choices of the Japanese participants. Using our deep culture analysis and interpretation of culture heroes helps identify and sort out some critical differences between Japanese and American cultures. The development of the culture heroes method, using the framework of the cultural trilogy, serves as a map for trainers who do not know the territory they are entering.

Final note: Clearly it has been necessary to describe this exercise using the cultures in which we have had experience. However, we urge you to adapt it to other cultures. The effort may call for some research and a bicultural training team, but the training results will be rewarding.

Conclusions

This analysis of Japanese and American culture from the point of view of the hero introduces, among other things, an emotional factor into cultural insight. Like the Emperor, many leaders in Japanese groups aim to generate benevolence and build harmony. They avoid conflict, decisions, or actions that may impair their ability to conciliate or reconcile. This view of leadership is centered on lifekeeping (internal life) values which eventually impart their tone to lifemaking (work life) and lifeleading (public life) rhythms. In the business world, organizational culture is typically explained as the philosophy and precepts of the founder or the president of the company (often regarded as a corporate hero). Managers and workers of even highly successful industries seem preoccupied with survival—indeed the entire country shares that concern. The hero in Japanese culture is the figure integrating the rhythms of activity from the perspective of lifekeeping and in definitely nonheroic ways.

In American culture, heroes perform deeds and accomplish. In fact, corporate heroes often serve as role models in the careers of executives on their way up. Lifemaking rhythms loom larger than in Japan. American thought and concepts display more flexibility than Japanese in moving back and forth between the three rhythms of activity. Where Japanese may use symbolism, imagery, proverbs, or heroes, Americans will use dry and abstract analysis. This more abstract quality is clear in the American perception of aggression and power. As a consequence, American heroes are likely to exert a rather different influence on their followers in comparison with Japanese heroes.

The culture hero is a most effective tool for bringing forth innermost values, but these values may not reflect the current sociopolitical culture of the Japanese in their own context. Therefore, as a cross-cultural trainer you should be prepared to appreciate the emotions of the Japanese becoming poised between the individual and the cultural community, but yielding to tatemae, as did Kumagae.

Concepts which go below the surface in understanding Japanese and American culture can produce startling insights in training. Once participants have seen the model and experienced the process of using the hero as the core for the analysis, they can begin to grasp the deep complexity of cultures and are often eager to undertake further analyses centering on other topics. Be prepared!

References

Criner, L. "The Hero and Society." *The World and I.* New York: News World Communication, 1988.

Ekman, Paul, Wallace V. Friesen, and P. Ellsworth. *Emotion in the Human Face.* New York: Pergamon Press, 1972.

Geldard, Frank A. *The Human Senses.* New York: John Wiley, 1953.

Homer. "The Odyssey." In *The Iliad of Homer and The Odyssey,* translated by Samuel Butler, 1–179. Chicago: *Encyclopedia Britannica,* 1952.

Lakoff, George. *Women, Fire, and Dangerous Things.* Chicago: University of Chicago Press, 1987.

Lebra, Takie S. *Japanese Patterns of Behavior.* Honolulu: University Press of Hawaii, 1976.

McConnell, James V. *Understanding Human Behavior.* New York: Holt, Rinehart and Winston, 1986.

McIntosh, Donald. *The Foundations of Human Society.* Chicago: University of Chicago Press, 1969.

Melzack, Ronald, and Patrick D. Wall. *The Challenge of Pain.* London: Penguin Books, 1988.

Morris, Ivan. *The Nobility of Failure.* Tokyo: Charles E. Tuttle, 1975.

O'Flaherty, Wendy. "Inside and Outside the Mouth of God: The Boundary between Myth and Reality." *Daedalus* 109, no. 2 (Spring 1980): 93–125.

Sanseido. *Sanseido's Daily Concise English Dictionary.* Tokyo: Sanseido Press, 1979.

Scarry, Elaine. *The Body in Pain.* Oxford, UK: Oxford University Press, 1985.

Stewart, Edward C. "A Triadic Analysis of Culture." *Intercultural Communication Studies* 9 (1996): 1–30.

Wells, Henry W. *Ancient Poetry from China, Japan, and India.* Columbia, SC: University of South Carolina Press, 1968.

Zborowski, Mark. *People in Pain.* San Francisco: Jossey-Bass, 1969.

Resources

Campbell, Joseph. "The Historical Development of Mythology." In *Myth and Mythmaking,* edited by Henry A. Murray, 19–45. Boston: Beacon Press, 1968.

Fisher, Roger, and S. Brown. *Getting Together: Building a Relationship that Gets to Yes.* Boston: Houghton Mifflin, 1988.

Gleitman, H. *Basic Psychology.* New York: W. W. Norton, 1987.

Janis, Irving, and Leon Mann. *Decision Making.* New York: Free Press, 1977.

Mouer, Ross, and Yoshio Sugimoto. *Images of Japanese Society: A Study in the Structure of Social Reality.* London: Routledge & Kegan, 1986.

Ohtake, Jun. *The Hero in Japanese Culture.* Senior thesis, Tokyo: ICU, 1989.

Snell, Bruno. *The Discovery of the Mind.* Oxford: Basil Blackwell, 1953.

Stearns, Carol Z., and Peter N. Stearns. *Anger.* Chicago: University of Chicago Press, 1986.

Stewart, Edward C. "The Primordial Roots of Being." *Zygon* 22, no. 1 (March 1987): 87–107.

———. *Cultural Memories of War.* Manuscript, 1983.

Stewart, Edward C., and Milton J. Bennett. *American Cultural Patterns.* 2d ed. Yarmouth, ME: Intercultural Press, 1991.

van Wolfenren, Karel. *The Enigma of Japanese Power.* New York: Alfred A. Knopf, 1989.

Overview of Area-Specific Training

Sandra M. Fowler,
Monica G. Mumford, and V. Lynn Tyler

Area-specific training seeks to enable individuals to develop essential attitudes, workable knowledge, and adaptive skills for interacting with particular peoples and systems. Being the representative of one's own culture becomes sobering at times. Being foreign requires confidence, and area-specific training can help enhance that confidence. Many people have accepted the challenge of living and working in other cultures because they have the personality, skills, and desire to help people in particular parts of the world meet certain challenges. As you would use a map to locate yourself in unfamiliar territory, cross-cultural training can help guide you through unfamiliar interactions. Maps are neither the territory nor the situation—any more than training is the actual experience. But both maps and training provide guides to interacting successfully with people in or from a specific area or region other than your own.

Background

According to Landis and Brislin (1983), cross-cultural relations basically rest on three historical supports: religion, war, and commerce. "History, with its blessed ability to ignore unintended consequences of events, does not record the first intercultural expert. Surely, he followed the invasion routes of the ancient world." Religious missionaries provided "a second source for today's cross-cultural trainer.... Behind the armies and the priests came the traders and merchants.... The need of the modern multinational corporation to have personnel trained in intercultural relations is not, in principle, any different from the trappers of the Hudson's Bay Company who had to learn and accept Indian customs and folkways" (1).

In any case, people have needed for century upon century to know about outsiders—other families, clans, tribes, nations, regions, continents. Perhaps in the future we will need to know about the populace of other planets and galaxies.

In the meantime, we are challenged today by many of the same problems faced by both early hunters and gatherers of accurate information and old-time designers of effective learning experiences.

Traditionally, area-specific training has comprised the following categories or systems:

❖ *Geographic.* This category refers to countries or regions such as Africa, North and South America, Asia, Europe, Oceania, the Pacific Rim. This sometimes is expressed as the East, the North, the South, or the West.

❖ *Political.* Types of national and local governments fall into categories such as democratic, communist, fascist, independent, socialist—with variations and combinations. Global and/or area political systems are sometimes referred to as East-West, First, Second, Third, or Fourth worlds.

❖ *Economic.* Major, minor, region, classes, status, rural, and urban fall within this category. The terms sometimes applied in this category are developed, developing, underdeveloped, undeveloped, and the like.

❖ *Topical.* Ways of thinking, feeling, behaving, and communicating in and between cultures—each having recognizable patterns, language, and at least partial documentation or shareable perception—fall within this category. Terms we hear: advanced, backward, cosmopolitan, global, neutral, or scientific.

L. Robert Kohls proposes seven categories of factual background data in his chapter. His list expands the traditional categories. In addition to geographic, political, and economic, Kohls adds four categories: historical, religious/philosophical, social, and aesthetic (and omits topical).

Definitions and Description

Definitions depend on the people and the issues involved. Definitions are not always agreed upon, and reading through the newspaper is one of the best ways to realize that words are often used loosely, without rigorous attention to the definitions. As cross-cultural professionals, we need to be specific about the meaning of the words. Definitions can help us focus our training and help our trainees understand the differences.

Area-specific training can be said to differ from culture-general training almost totally in its focus on a specific culture—its values, norms, assumptions, patterns of behavior, language, communication patterns, and ways of thinking—as well as its many other aspects, superficial as well as deep. Area-specific and culture-specific are used synonymously. However, the appropriate term to use is *area-specific* when trainees are being prepared to go to another country. When trainees are being trained to interact with another culture found within their organizations, communities, and homes, *culture-specific* is the more appropriate term.

General-area training uses various methods to help trainees sort through specific principles which identify and enhance potential interactions between themselves and representatives of their target culture. General-area training often includes sample or hypothetical area-specific incidents or cases. These can be presented during training using such methods as culture assimilators, case studies, critical incidents, or lists of social indicators.

Country-specific training, such as the training described by George Renwick in his chapter on China, features representative information regarding the cultures within the country. The knowledge and skills addressed during training are maps of the patterns of behavior people most regularly follow locally, such as hosts with visitors or partners in a negotiation. Good country-specific training will be practical, ethical, and efficient and will concentrate on intercultural interaction.

Cross-cultural usually implies persons crossing into a culture different from their own. Examples might be a Tongan female student attending a West European university or an American male conducting business in Beijing. The focus is on the learning needs of the person doing the crossing into the other culture. Another term, *transcultural,* implies a similar focus.

Intercultural indicates interaction between distinct people. Intercultural interactions may occur at home or abroad in multiple circumstances and contexts. Dealing with ideas, feelings, and behaviors beyond one's own is interculturally consequential and elicits various changes both in oneself and in the other people involved—usually in notable ways. The intercultural focus is on the learning needs of all parties involved in the interaction.

Goals of Area-Specific Training

Many culture-specific trainers try to create integrated explorations so that trainees discover what proves most useful for positive experiences while overcoming biases and allaying fears. These explorations integrate knowledge and feelings concerning other people. Trainers emphasize learning what is and is not available for practical use at particular times, in particular places. They use patterns to simplify what otherwise would be too complex. For example, trainees practice analyzing what attitudes are being demonstrated when people of the target culture behave in ways that appear unusual and learn to recognize underlying attitudes in particular situations. Although the goal of area-specific training is always to build expertise in interacting in a specific area of the world, there are many less obvious goals that can be addressed.

Choices. A common reaction to culture-specific learning is denying that one will have to change in the other culture. Perhaps dressing differently or eating local foods is acceptable, but there can be much resistance to adapting in deeper or less comfortable ways. One of the goals of area-specific training can be to encourage trainees to understand the consequences of choosing to make only a superficial adaptation to the region in which they will be living and working. For example, trainers often highlight varying cultural values. These manifest themselves in other cultures as "oughts" and "shoulds." Trainees must think these through, know how they feel about them, try to accept them as "coulds" and "woulds" in their own lives, and make choices accordingly.

Outcomes. Intercultural satisfaction comes most often in mutually beneficial encounters with people and situations. Training can prepare trainees to maximize the potential for expected outcomes. To do this, designers of area-specific training use models and methods to propose guidelines for those who want valid and reliable knowledge that will lead to the desired outcomes in specific real-life situations. Area-specific trainers must keep in mind that the participants' own backgrounds help dictate what is perceived to be useful and acceptable in specific circumstances and with certain people. When area-specific training is off the mark, its goals will not be perceived as useful—or worse, it can have unfortunate consequences.

Meaning. Just as in other intercultural training, a goal of area-specific training is to make experience an exploration, a continuing search for shareable meaning. The meaning we attribute to behavior in a different culture derives from the comparative meaning we would give it in our own culture. This is cultural baggage that is usually impossible to leave home. Area-specific training provides tools for validating meaning in the other culture. Individual explorations, with trainer assistance, entail vicarious think-through, feel-in, and behave-as-if experiences. Trainees need sufficient opportunities to practice culture-specific patterns in order to understand and appropriately interact with different culture-specific principles. The more they practice, the better they will be able to accurately attribute meaning in the other culture.

Issues Challenging Area-Specific Training

Many challenges face area-specific trainers. Perhaps the most salient challenge concerns the concepts and process of learning how to learn. No trainer can lead by the hand or push from behind when the trainee is actually on-site (in-country). Keeping in mind that we are helping the person become self-sufficient and independently capable in a given culture, we need to deal with the following issues firmly and sensitively.

No one can learn, or is able to deal with, all the needed facts—even in one's own area or culture. Times, behaviors, values, and circumstances change. Feelings sometimes (often) override facts. What is apropos for local people may not be so for visitors. How does one decide when to use one's own or local customs—or not to? The people who design area-specific training seek answers to such questions and appropriate responses for each region of the world.

People need to develop an ability to distinguish the personal from the cultural, not an easy task, since cultural differences often masquerade as idiosyncrasies. And what seems to be a personal quirk can turn out to be an important cultural norm. Sojourners need to understand cultural nuances, variances, and the similar yet differing needs found in people within the varying cultures in which they will be living and working.

There are limits to how much information can be processed, and how well. That forces area-specific trainers to consider pacing and sequencing information for maximum comprehension and retention. One solution is to help participants learn how to learn with classroom activities and homework assignments that address specific aspects of the target culture.

Situations may arise, such as natural disasters or political coups, that make area-specific training outdated or unusable, no matter the ability, willingness, and readiness of trainees. Area-specific training designers have to prepare trainees to answer the challenge of the unexpected and must help them cope, arming them with options appropriate for a specific region or political or economic system.

Area-specific experts have found that the best area-specific training builds on life experiences, since life is a constantly evolving series of specific intercultural opportunities (old with young, male with female, and foreign with familiar). People tend to learn from these experiences—or to avoid them. The more satisfying these experiences are, the more trainees will understand and accomplish. Each of us can become both teacher and learner. As we prepare and profit from area-specific training, we are better prepared to enable others.

These learning-how-to-learn issues challenge intercultural trainers because of their widespread implications. They affect design, methods, and resources—indeed, every aspect of the training process.

Area-Specific Compared with Other Types of Intercultural Training

Most area-specific training programs tend to be strengthened with the use of a variety of methods. In fact, most area-specific training uses all the methods described in this *Sourcebook*. However, there is perhaps a greater emphasis on reliable resources in area-specific training. People are the major source of timely and applicable culture-specific information. The people you seek out to provide workable, culture-specific information are cultural brokers, mentors, or informants. The challenge in area-specific training, in comparison with culture-general training, is finding people with up-to-the-minute information to bring to the training session and teaching trainees to find similar experts in the culture where they will be living and working. Area-specific training is more like other types of intercultural training than it is different. There is always more to discover than there is time available and more to assess about people and their culture than is feasible.

Information: Sources and Resources

The first step for any trainer is to locate reliable sources of area-specific information, but that is not all. The key is to learn how to validate your data, then teach your trainees how to use it. This is no time for secrets. Whatever information-validating process works for you, your trainees deserve to know how to replicate the same process or develop an even better one. Three things your trainees must know about using sources and resources are (1) how to find and work with mentors and informants, (2) how to validate information, and (3) the absolute necessity to suspend judgment until information has been validated.

Since the foundation of culture-specific training is information and its effective use, trainers who conduct such training must develop a sixth sense about their resources. The reason is that certain resources produce success, while others often fail. Area-specific information appears in print and other media, but most often it is learned through word of mouth, patience, and common sense. It is possible to obtain data, be trained in its use, and find it does not work in particular situations. All the pertinent realities of a situation are rarely apparent. So people are left to make decisions, behave in certain ways, solve problems, negotiate contracts, and learn how to resolve conflicts with insufficient or ambiguous data. Unfortunately, cultural awareness in itself may or may not limit mistakes.

Critical events could compel redefinition of appropriate behavior: Who does what, when, and under which conditions? What succeeds? What fails? Why? How can you recover if necessary? Your trainees need to know how things are done, how the above questions are answered in their target culture. How is a sensitive, knowledgeable foreigner expected to handle the situation? For example, a person may be well trained in decision making, but only for given situations. Gift giving may seem to be a simple exchange, but it is situationally significant in certain cultures. What does it mean when a gift is wrapped in a given way? Does one accept gifts with jests or shyness? Do you unwrap the gift in front of the gift giver or later in private? How can you be sure? How do you respond—with returned favors or not? Is protocol the same throughout the region?

People who develop skills in area-specific training are able to respond acceptably to such queries. They learn how to do an information assessment with such analytical questions as these:

❖ How accurate is my perception of what is being expressed? If inaccurate, what next?

❖ How reliable are the cultural informants (that is, are their perceptions verifiable)?

❖ Who benefits from sharing this information with me? What are the cultural informant's ethical constraints?

❖ If only naive, inexperienced cultural informants are available, how can one validate what they portray as facts? What information is acceptable? Which is out-of-date?

Sometimes situations require accepting insights gained on the spur of the moment from trustworthy locals rather than from foreign experts. Even longtime culture specialists are naive in some fields and at various levels of information use. A taxi driver may have more insight on certain subjects than a college professor. Trainees must have the confidence to use their human intuition, trust (or distrust) rational thought, suspend judgment until reliable help is available, and take necessary risks. Experienced trainers help people understand and meet their needs for uncovering valid, reliable information once they are in-country or for dealing with a specific culture—at home or abroad.

Criteria for information provided in area-specific training depend much on the results of your needs assessment. You can use the following scale, which measures the level of importance of information, to prioritize your information gathering:

+++	Must Have
++	Good, Nice to Have if Available
+	Interesting
0	Unessential or Unknown
-	Useless but Harmless
--	Spurious, Deceptive
---	Misused, Harmful

The goal, of course, is to make sure trainees have or learn how to get and process all the "must have" information. Consistently having reliable and applicable information helps avoid confusion and offense in area-specific encounters. Interactions succeed most often when intercultural sensitivity is matched with needed facts, guided preparation, and experience.

Example: Culturgrams

Sometimes it is helpful for people to be oriented via a brief introduction to an area or country. This can be a launching point for what may become an intense, in-depth exploration. Examples of a useful introduction to specific cultures are Culturgrams, produced by the David M. Kennedy Center for International Studies at Brigham Young University. Because they were originally designed for church leaders who were to receive a 15-minute briefing about the people of each country to be visited, only a limited amount of cultural data is presented.

Culturgrams were never intended to be the only information a sojourner would receive. An expanded Experiential Learning Aids series was created using cultural assimilators and the like. By the 1990s, Culturgrams were available for nearly half the nations of our world, with some countries requiring several different ones to give adequate representation. A professional staff continues to expand the series and provides significant updating.

There are also Culturgrams, prepared in more detail than the typical guide, for visitors to the United States. These have been translated into Chinese, French, German, Italian, Japanese, Polish, Portuguese, Russian, and Spanish and are often used in training programs for guests. By 1990, other intercultural series, such as the Infograms *Coming Home Again, Families Moving Abroad, International Travel and Law,* and *Taming Travel Stress,* were available.

Culturgrams were devised as simple "people maps" for understanding and possibly interacting with those with differing customs, courtesies, and lifestyles. As four-page briefings, they encourage personal insights for active participation in another culture. An impossible requirement? Such validated information may be all that is readily available and up-to-date for general orientation. Area-specific trainees need to respond to such questions as:

❖ What are the general purposes of the interactions for readers who will be somehow involved with this culture?

❖ What can be quickly learned about specific people and their circumstances? By whom?

❖ What should be learned from them and from one's own experiences? Why? What should be avoided?

❖ What can be usefully learned while interacting with these people? How?

Tested writer guides and notes for contributors and reviewers give consistency to the Culturgrams. An effective method in area-specific training is to ask trainees to develop their own kind of Culturgrams. This introduces them to resources, techniques for gathering data, and critical thinking. Topics suggest a basic yet wide coverage of people-centered area specifics:

Attitudes/Values	History/Government	Recreation/Leisure
Communication/Language	Holidays/Rituals	Religion/Philosophy
Courtship/Marriage	Housing	Resources
Development	Land/Climate	Social Class/Security
Diet	Meetings/Interviews	Transportation
Education	Particular Needs	Visiting
Family/Relationships	Personal Appearance	Work/Business
Greetings/Farewells	Population	Other (_____)
Health	Public Address	

Trainees developing their own Culturgrams need to take *context* and *situation* into account. The following questions help trainees focus on the context for their data:

1. Which similarities of thought, feeling, and action are vital between readers and the people(s) of the specific culture being described? Why? When can they be appropriately used?

2. How do specific interacters think, feel, or act differently? When? With whom?

3. How can important gaps be bridged to prevent offense or confusion? By whom? If not, what then?

4. How do local people expect visitors to act? What is acceptable? When? Why?

5. What trends and changes in specific culture markers or codes need to be dealt with? When? How?

6. What are the greatest immediate and long-range needs and concerns of this people? Who is trying to help? How could others help?

Culturgram authors and reviewers must be very selective about the information they use, as must trainers. This is the challenge for all culture-specific training—whether for a few minutes, a week, or even a year. It should help people answer these questions: In given circumstances, do I behave *my* way, *your* (our host's or someone else's) way, or *our* way (a new and significant way that is mutually beneficial)? When? How? With whom? Why?

Using Specific Resources

People: The Ultimate Resource

Situations and settings include the people who interact in them, but people frequently seem to understand little about themselves. Be prepared with questions that help clarify understanding and meaning, optional approaches, and a sense of what does not work in given situations. You can get the information you need if you press your resource person to be specific.

People often express concern when they hear or read variations in details and perceptions. This is a prime challenge in culture-specific training: reconciling these differences and using contrasting viewpoints to focus on the richness of a culture rather than trying to find "the truth." You can encourage trainees to find and follow real-life explorations everywhere.

Principles of public and private practices. Trainees need to find a cultural broker who can help them learn the principles for identifying what does or does not work in public or private situations in their target culture. These principles provide helpful clues for assessment and act as guides for learning the ways in which public and private practices vary. This is important information to have, since area-specific norms, mores, and practices can account for specific behavior in distinct situations—public more than private. Examples of private and public practices are initiating or stopping specific events (like how to begin or end a business meeting), expressing affection, negotiating, and recognizing others.

To use or refuse but not to abuse. Cultural brokers are also essential for identifying what not to do and why. What is *not* said in given situations (such as in gift giving and exchange) may be important. Cultural brokers can explain what is considered abuse (of feelings, things, privileges, and so forth) in their culture. Each courtesy and preference is both person- and area-specific and consequential. Choices always entail a cost and bring positive or negative consequences. Any "dos and don'ts" should pertain to specific critical situations you need to explore and resolve. Refuse information from cultural brokers whose information cannot be validated. Be careful to treat your cultural brokers with sensitivity, and do not abuse their kindness.

Area-Specific Print Materials: Books and Beyond

The references and resources that follow this chapter are generally available to area specialists. Priority resources are the people with whom you and trainees should interact to learn first-hand about the relevant country, culture, area, or region. Any list you use always requires personal validation and possible alternatives.

Considerations

Balancing Data with Wisdom

Area particulars usually change as situations do. People's abilities, attitudes, and expressions change in the process of living. Familiar settings appear different under pressured conditions and tempering influences. New skills and sensitivities are susceptible to modification through various intercultural experiences, interpretations, and resulting situations. Trainees must leave the training session knowing that they should constantly reappraise what they know, so it is situationally useful.

Avoiding the Magnetism of Expedience

Trainers who are in a hurry to deliver a training session and fail to update their information or models are taking the expedient path. This can be to the detriment of their trainees, who trust that the information they receive in training is accurate, timely, and pertinent. Snap judgments concerning area-specific insights may mean that critical and applicable facts are left out. One's own values change, however slightly, because intercultural events modify feelings. To deal successfully with the unknown, one uses courage, humor, patience, wisdom, more patience, and humility—one is always a student!

Kohls and Tyler felt constrained to include only what could be truly useful when they developed *A Select Guide to Area Studies Resources* (1988). They found both too much and too little of some kinds of data as they fought the magnetism of expedience.

Individuals, Institutions, Initiatives

Experience with other people invariably occurs at the individual level, even when institutional initiatives predominate. People who design area-specific training have to assess what relevant organizational requirements are, what the special initiatives are (for example, sales, time requirements, volunteer activities, or zeal), and what the trainee capabilities are. Although behavioral patterns may seem similar, these patterns (such as how individuals feel, think, or act under given circumstances) are culturally determined. Apparently similar patterns may really be quite different and not necessarily bad or useless.

The same is true within organizations. Institutions are made up of culturally varying individuals, each with distinct abilities, desires, and responsibilities. Flexibility is always required in the use of resources to meet particular needs and make things work. New solutions to old problems are often needed, as are old ways to resolve innovative concerns.

Sourcebooks, Reource People, and Sources Unanticipated

Print materials are often outdated by the time they are distributed—though principles and reference points may carry over. People sources can be preferable to print sources, especially to verify area-specific, broad-use analyses. Those who have been there, know they need to focus on past, current, and future situations and the people involved.

Global Action Networks is one example of a useful resource aid. It is one of several fine reference publications of the Union of International Associations. With companion volumes, this book features thousands of area-specific nonprofit organizations and individuals who identify, describe, and work to resolve common human problems.

SIETAR International (International Society for Intercultural Education, Training and Research), with its global membership, offers a referral directory so you can locate a member who is likely to know much of the information you need about a specific area. The Intercultural Press is an immediate source of area-specific resource aids and selected tools for training. In addition to resources found throughout this *Sourcebook,* there is the above-mentioned *Guide to Area Studies Resources,* which, though older, is still one of the best resources for models and methods and is still current for identifying and working with specific peoples and systems. Books available from the Intercultural Press (the InterAct series in particular) and Sage Publications, information on the Internet and other electronic systems, and basic refresher courses in book form, such as Seymour Fersh's *Learning about Peoples and Cultures* (1979), offer essential insights.

Outcomes and Benefits

Culture-specific training increases one's ability to avoid negative biases, simple ignorance, and inappropriate behavior in given situations. To succeed in or with another culture, trainees can—and must—learn to act appropriately so they may interact effectively.

Knowing how to behave locally often creates an opportunity to become integrated into the community. Effective and affective training helps people recognize and respect the specific protocols that require either behaving as do members of one's own culture or as culturally distinct others do. Training helps people avoid "going native" and becoming unacceptable to host and home. Training can also help people avoid maintaining idiosyncrasies, carrying self or home labels as if they were universals.

Appropriate behavior varies from area to area, from people to people. For example, honest apologies or gracious recognition can be expressed in ways that convey personal biases, misconceptions, ignorance, or well-trained skills and good manners. Culture-specific training teaches participants how to discover proper patterns for a particular behavior. This may take awhile, but the rewards are great.

Trainees who are ready for intercultural experiences receive such compliments as "You are certainly knowledgeable." It is a tribute to be accepted and complimented in this way. Despite the compliments, learning has not ended. New explorations and reorientation are essential to respond to questions not yet posed. Proper responses bring the thrill of adventure and discovery.

Singular Satisfactions and Situational Success

Training can enable people to feel and act beyond their own usual boundaries—it globalizes their experience. While total success is not always feasible, it is possible to rectify offenses and overcome confusion. Culture-specific training helps people know how to do this properly with the people in their new culture. It would be nice to become so expert that cultural change and difference are never bothersome, but that is not realistic. Situational success makes us enjoy what works well; we then can try to replicate culturally appropriate behavior. Each singular satisfaction is its own training reward.

References

Culturgrams and Infograms. David M. Kennedy Center for International Studies, Brigham Young University, Provo, UT.

Fersh, Seymour. *Learning about Peoples and Cultures.* Evanston: McDougal, Littel, 1979.

Global Action Networks. Union of International Associations Publications, 1050 rue Washington 40, 1050 Brussels, Belgium.

Kohls, L. Robert, and V. Lynn Tyler. *A Select Guide to Area Studies Resources.* Provo, UT: David M. Kennedy Center for International Studies, Brigham Young University, 1988.

Landis, Dan, and Richard W. Brislin, eds. *Handbook of Intercultural Training,* vol. 1. Elmsford, NY: Pergamon Press, 1983.

Resources

Graphic Arts Center Publishing Co., PO Box 10306, Portland, OR 97210. (Ask for Culture Shock Guides to Customs and Etiquette.)

Human Relations Area Files. (Available from most major university libraries; dated and primarily anthropological; still useful.)

Intercultural Press, PO Box 700, Yarmouth, ME 04096.

Sage Publications, PO Box 5048, Thousand Oaks, CA 91559-9924.

SIETAR International (International Society for Intercultural Education, Training and Research), PO Box 467, Putney, VT 05346.

World Book Encyclopedia of People and Places. World Book, 525 W. Monroe Street, Chicago, IL 60661.

Conceptual Model for Country/Area Studies

L. Robert Kohls

Country (or area) studies information—which amounts to most of the "hard" content of country-specific training programs—has often been the least interesting, least involving part of cross-cultural training. It needn't be so if the trainer uses a wide variety and imaginative sequencing of training activities to get the information across.

History

Country studies and area studies have perhaps the most ancient origin of any of the methods included in this entire book. At least from neolithic times, people have been much more peripatetic than was once believed. Herodotus, from the fifth century B.C., was probably the first identified intercultural practitioner. Others who engaged in historic cross-cultural interactions were Josephus, Ptolemy, Marco Polo, Ibn Khaldun, and Matteo Ricci. The explorers of Europe's Age of Discovery—Christopher Columbus, Vasco da Gama, Hernando Cortes, Ferdinand Magellan, and Francisco Pizarro—to name only a few, caused interaction among cultures. During their unusual power exchanges they had to notice the cultural differences—while taking advantage of their own technological advances. In any case, we would not now consider either their means or their ends to have been "intercultural" in nature, at least not according to the "rules" of the field today.

Much more recently in the United States, the area studies component, lodged comfortably in the ivy-covered halls of universities, was one of several forerunners of the interdisciplinary field of intercultural communication. Area studies, along with language learning, were the major approaches used through the early 1960s to prepare people for overseas assignments.

In the late 1960s, the more humanistic influences of sensitivity training and the encounter group movement made their influences felt in intercultural training, thus shifting the emphasis from the content-heavy approach of area studies to the psychological processes of the individual being trained, which moved trainers to the opposite extreme, where they often became reluctant to give any specific information about the other culture at all. They were interested in producing people who could learn how to learn or get the most out of the experience rather than people whose heads were full of isolated facts.

Neither extreme worked very well. Fortunately, the field has matured a great deal from those early years. According to Hoopes (Hoopes and Ventura 1979, iv), cognition and experience have been joined effectively in the training process, as seen in the diagram below, which illustrates the evolution of cross-cultural training approaches.

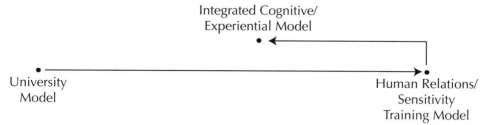

With the creation of more experiential training approaches in the mid- and late-1960s, area studies went into a decline. As the "culture-specific versus the culture-general" argument of the late 1960s and early 1970s heated up, the eclipse of area studies continued. Then, as that argument was resolved in favor of a combination of both approaches, area studies have been revitalized.

The term *area studies* occurred by accident of birth. Since the subject matter developed in academic departments (such as the departments of Latin American studies, Middle Eastern studies, and the like), people began to refer to this endeavor as area studies. This training approach was adopted by the practitioners of intercultural relations, but the focus was on preparing people who would be based in one country. So even when applied to one country, we generally use the term *area studies.* Had this kind of training originated in intercultural relations, everyone would probably refer to it as "country studies," even when applied to an area. My preference is to acknowledge both; hence country/area studies.

Procedure

This section has been divided into three subsections: preparing area studies information, presenting the information, and sequencing it.

Preparing Area Studies Information

The principal concern in preparing area studies data for an intercultural training program is not to overlook any relevant material. One can, of course, choose to eliminate a certain piece of information, but it should be a considered choice. Do not simply skip over it. For that reason, I have tried to err in the direction of listing too many rather than too few items. Based on your needs assessment, you, as trainer, are in the best position to pick and choose what to include and what to eliminate.

In developing the area studies portions of intercultural training programs, you will find the seven broad categories listed below to be helpful in making sure you have covered a country (or area) and its culture thoroughly.

1. Factual Background Data

Historical	Religious/Philosophical
Geographic	Social
Political	Aesthetic
Economic	

This kind of information can be collected by doing research in any adequate library facility. It is the most basic and least useful of the seven categories. You must be very selective in choosing what to include and what to eliminate—so that you do not end up overwhelming your trainees with too much data, such as the average annual rainfall of country X (unless they are going to an area where the quantity of rainfall is so utterly different from what they are used to that the information becomes quite practical).

2. Deep Cultural Programming

These are the enculturation processes, similar to the software in a computer, that individuals learn so early that they become the "normal" way of operating. People come to regard them as universal rather than culture-specific.

Beliefs	Norms
Attitudes	Values
Behaviors	Cultural assumptions (belief systems)
Customs	Cultural taboos/Social dos and don'ts/
Traditions	Topics to be avoided
Holidays/Ceremonies (births, mar-	Nonverbal communication (gestures)
riages, funerals, etc.)	Cognitive styles (thought processes)
Personality traits	

This is both the most valuable and the most difficult information to obtain. There are few books to turn to for help, and national informants are no more expert regarding their own culture than the average citizens of any country would be in expounding on their values or cultural assumptions. National informants are very useful in culture-specific training, but you must exercise caution, because most people of the world have very clear stereotypes of the strengths, and especially the weaknesses, of their countrymen and -women, especially those in regions of their country different from their own. Since you will not want to support their negative stereotypes, you must be aware of what they are, as they will often be expressed in subtle, indirect ways.

3. Business Practices

If the trainees are managers of multinational or global companies, naturally the category of Business Practices would be expanded to assume greater space in the program as a whole. In such cases, I start with a greatly expanded business-oriented topic list centered on the specific practices of the target country.

Workforce

Natural resources

Major exports

Major imports

Major trading partners

Transportation systems

Communication systems

Energy systems

Number of national holidays

Affiliation with international organizations

Recruitment procedures

Initial job assignment(s)

Training

Job rotation

Performance evaluation

Promotion

Salary and compensation criteria

Incentive systems

Job assignment and reassignment

Welfare

Employee layoffs

Retirement

Labor relations/unions

Internal structure of local corporations

National labor laws

Tariffs and duties

Import quotas

Export commitments

Limits on expansion

Price controls

Financing restrictions

Restrictions on nationality of management

Foreign ownership limitations

Local sourcing requirements

Nationalization and expropriation

Local manufacturing requirements

Interaction with the bureaucracy

Local environmental restrictions

Capital repatriation restrictions

Dividend remittance restrictions

Abrogation of royalty rights

Restrictions on spouse working

In addition, up-to-date evaluations of the political and economic risk factors as well as terrorism and security considerations (if applicable) should be included in a well-rounded program.

Any material which focuses on business practices in the target country should be presented by a person who has recent work experience in that country and who comes from the same culture as the program participants. The reason for this is simply that such a person has the experience of both the sending country and the receiving country and can see immediately where the expectations of the two systems are in contrast and/or conflict.

4. Logistical Information for Living on the Economy of the Country

What to take with you (and what can be obtained there)

Setting up a household in-country

Living off the local economy

Visa and passport requirements

Residence and work documents

Housing

Utilities

Electric current

Mail

Telephone, cable, electronics systems, and the like

Transportation

Banking

Insurance	Establishing a daily routine
Schools	Where to buy necessary items
Religious facilities	Exploring the host city and its resources
Health facilities	Entertainment/Leisure activities
Currency	Mutually supportive family behaviors
Legal holidays	Making contacts for children
Support systems	Maintaining old ties back home
Making friends	Security and terrorism issues (if relevant)

The material in this section, too, needs to be presented by people (of both sexes) who have recently returned from living in the city, area, or country to which the trainees are being assigned.

5. Famous People and Places of the Country

Heroes and others   Historic and scenic sites

This portion of the area studies program looks at the people and places that are part of the historic and cultural heritage of the host country. The importance of this information should not be overlooked. Consider, for example, that Americans would think it inexcusable, and a serious lack in the person's education, if a foreign visitor came to the United States without knowing who George Washington and Abraham Lincoln were. Yet Americans often go to other countries without the slightest idea of who their "Washingtons" and "Lincolns" are.

It is also important to know who the present-day president or prime minister of the country is and the names of the leading political opposition parties and leaders.

6. Problems Faced by the Country

Likewise, it is important for trainees to know the current economic, political, social, developmental, and environmental problems of the host country. While doing such research, be as objective as possible. Look at the issues in each problem area from the point of view of the people of that country as well as from your own perspective. It helps to understand as fully as possible the complex realities and interrelationships of the local situation.

If you do a thorough research job in this area, you may find twenty or thirty serious problems. Your trainees will need to know what these problems are and how the citizens of country X view them.

7. Integration Problems Faced by Foreigners Living in the Host Country

The consistency of most expatriate complaints is amazing. Consequently, the number of informants from whom you collect these items does not need to be very large. The information can be collected in-country and then presented by any staff trainer. In other words, it does not necessarily need to be presented by someone with recent in-country experience, but the information itself should have come from such informants.

The point should be made that the problems the expatriates are complaining about cannot be fairly blamed on the host country culture. The citizens of the country are rarely bothered by these same things. Rather, the problems derive from something brought into the country by the expatriates themselves—their different values, customs, expectations, and so forth.

In addition to describing the issues and situations to which the expatriates are reacting negatively, it is helpful to collect and disseminate information on what has been found to be useful in dealing with such problems.

Presenting Country/Area Studies Information

I share the bias of most cross-cultural trainers that training sessions should always be as experiential as possible. I also share the belief that a hands-on experience in the classroom is almost always superior to a lecture. This philosophy, to which most trainers subscribe, begins to break down, however, the closer one gets to what might be defined as the area studies component of a cross-cultural training program. Here, trainers who are ordinarily very creative often resort to formal lectures for their presentations.

The problem stems from the fact that lectures can always pack in more concentrated information in shorter periods of time than is possible with any experiential exercise. One alternative approach is to provide only a broad outline, then assign trainees the task of gathering their own information by themselves, using the written outline in this chapter as a guide for collecting the data.

Of course, lectures or lecturettes are still useful when they are not overlong or scheduled at times when the trainees are most likely to fall asleep. They should not be eliminated, but should be creative. Think of other ways to convey culture-specific information too. A question and answer format works well, or try having the trainees interview an expert (perhaps a host country national) who has knowledge of the country from having lived there fairly recently. Also, consult Thiagarajan (1985) for twenty-five other ways to improve a lecture.

Films and slides are useful too. And, of course, case studies and critical incidents can convey considerable amounts of culture-specific information. Prepared handouts are always helpful. So are vignettes videotaped from target-country soap opera programs, when you have access to them and when trainees have become fairly fluent in the language of the country. These videotapes are excellent for pointing out similarities and differences of actions, gestures, and other nonverbal cues.

Another effective method is to develop fairly exhaustive lists of cultural items for both cultures—the country the person is leaving and the country to which he or she is going—then pair natives of both countries for a series of training sessions which work from the lists. For example, put together an American going to Japan with a Japanese coming to the United States. The American and the Japanese use the two lists to explain aspects of both their cultures to each other, alternating in the role of teacher and learner. Make sure they understand they are free to move about the list as they like, stopping to ask about and explain items that are most appealing to them.

The following list suggests items to explore about Japan, but one could prepare a similar list for any country.

Things I Would Explore with a Japanese Cultural Informant, Become Expert in, or Collect in Japan

Flower arranging

Haniwa figures

Japanese gardens

Ceramics (especially teacups and saki bottles)

Buddhist paintings

Proverbs

Tea ceremony

Gagaku music

Buddhism (especially Zen)

Biwa (Japanese lute)

Shinto religion

Kabuki (traditional Japanese theatre)

Brush making

Bunraku (puppet theatre)

Fortune-telling

Sumi painting

Geomancy

Go (game)

Oriental Zodiac

Pachinko (pinball machine)

Origami (paper folding)

Chinese herbal medicine

Handmade papers

Cormorant fishing

Sumo wrestling

Ofuro (Japanese bath)

Kyudo (archery)

Sericulture (silk)

Kendo (fencing)

Geisha

Judo

Sashimi (raw fish)

Aikido (martial arts)

Pearl culture

Karate

Department stores

Cooking

Shopping arcades

Traditional festivals

Woodworking tools

Paper kites (hand-painted)

Bonsai trees

Noh masks

Hanko (seal stamps)

Buddhist sculpture

Tansu (wooden chests of drawers)

Architecture

Plastic food models

Buddhist temples

Bonkei (miniature tray scenery)

Shinto shrines

Toro (stone lanterns)

Folk toys

Tattooing

Acupuncture

Contemporary package designs

Calligraphy

Contemporary posters

Paper lanterns

Robotics

Momoyama folding screens and sliding doors

Yamato-e (narrative scroll paintings)

Momoyama castles

Novels (translated into English)

Oiled paper umbrellas

Woodblock prints (old and modern)

Tsuba sword guards

Folding fans

Menuki metal fittings on swords

Obi sashes

Netsuki charms

Lacquerware

Soroban (Japanese abacus)

Swords

Temple seal stamps

Haiku verse

Kokeshi (dolls)

Comic books

Talismans and good luck charms

Modern movies

Gift-wrap ornaments

Noren (entrance curtains with calligraphy)

Ryokan (Japanese inns)

Fish kites

Electronic music

Children's games

Massage

Wooden and horn combs

Baseball

Inro (medicine cases)

Meditation

Geta (wooden shoes)

"Living National Treasures"

Moe (family crests)

Rubbings of relief sculpture

Meishi (business cards printed in both English and Japanese)

Gyotaku (fish prints)

Koto and samisen (musical instruments)

Shinkansen (bullet trains)

Onsen (hot springs)

Bambooware

Raku, Bizen, Shino, Imari, Iga, Oribe, Karatsu, Kutani, Kakiemon, Yatsushiro, Seto, Shigaraki, Nabeshima, and Tamba (ceramicware)

Baskets, lacquered baskets

Matchbooks and boxes

Saki kegs (wine casks)

Mukimono (food garnishes)

And this is only the beginning....

Sequencing Country/Area Studies Information

Sequencing is important from two perspectives: (1) the sequence or order within the culture-specific component in which you present the information and (2) the order within the overall program in which the culture-specific component appears. There is no need to present the culture-specific material within the seven broad categories in the same order presented here; there is no single preferred order. It may help hold interest if one moves around within the seven categories. However, many inexperienced trainees are so concerned with logistical issues— what can I buy there and what should I be sure to take with me—that until those questions are answered, they can hear little else. Consequently, give people an opportunity at the beginning to raise their immediate concerns, and respond carefully and thoroughly to their questions so they will be ready to move on to the other important issues on your area studies list.

Where the area studies component should fit into a cross-cultural training program is not so open to whim or personal preference, however. The culture-specific versus culture-general debate had resolved itself by the late 1970s in favor of a need for both components plus one additional one: awareness of the society into which the trainees were initially enculturated, that is, cultural self-awareness.

Today, most trainers prefer to begin with culture-general, awareness-raising learning experiences and information, then move to looking at the participants' own culture as a culture, and then, finally, examine in depth the target country's culture, emphasizing in particular those aspects of it which are the most different from the trainees' own culture. (The similarities may be more appealing to most people, but since they are less likely to give us any trouble, we do not need to spend as much time on them as on the differences.)

From the above sequencing, it can be seen that the area studies component has become the final (and usually the most extensive) part of this kind of training program.

Contexts in Which Country/Area Studies Have Been Used Successfully

The typical context for area studies is a program for people who are moving to a new culture to work and live. These can be private citizens who have chosen to go overseas or government officials or military members assigned to an overseas post. Motivation for training varies between people who *choose* to go overseas and those who are *assigned*. In any case, participants are usually salaried employees and family members being sent by a corporation or agency and destined for one specific location. It was not too long ago that family members would not have been included in the training. When families are part of the program, care must be taken to design training for their special needs.

You may run into a situation where the trainees are not all going to the same place. Then you need to be creative, using homework assignments and class time for people to gather and integrate culture-specific information into your models.

There are some cases where culture-specific training is required for people not leaving their own country; for example, host families for foreign exchange students, corporate hosts for an international conference or meeting, or a merger between a domestic company and a foreign corporation.

Considerations for Using Country/Area Studies Information

As with most subjects, potential pitfalls and problems are legion. I will concentrate on what I believe are the four most common problems in conducting country/area studies training.

Failure to Validate Data

Contrary to common belief, not everything in print is true. Country/area studies data need to be checked and verified. This does not mean that every single fact needs to be checked, but some effort should be expended to check on the reliability of the source itself and perhaps on the most critical individual elements on which the effectiveness of the training depends.

Failure to Keep Data Current

Information changes rather quickly, and old data or old pictures do a disservice to people who consider you to be the expert on their target country.

The Tyranny of the Lecture

Because lectures are often boring, some people avoid them like the plague. On the other hand, some people overuse the lecture, because nothing else can pack as much information into a specified time slot. It takes from two to four times as long to convey the same amount of information through experiential exercises, and time is always too short. Both overuse and underuse are equally wrong, and in both instances it is the trainees who are the losers.

I recommend the use of lecturettes instead of longer lectures. It also helps if the lecturer is lively and humorous. Remember to intersperse lectures or lecturettes with experiential activities of the kind found in the pages of this *Sourcebook*. Indeed, lecturettes and exercises can sometimes be woven so seamlessly together that the participants can hardly tell them apart. Finally, use the suggestions for presenting country/area studies information on page 278 in this chapter.

Trainees' Demands for a List of Dos and Don'ts and Nothing More

Most trainees would be delighted with a short list of dos and don'ts for country X—and nothing more. This frustrates trainers who know how difficult it is to remember information presented this way, are aware of trainees' inability to deal with situations not on the list, and recognize that dos and don'ts do not allow for exceptions to the rule. So these trainers categorically refuse ever, ever to give such a list. Admittedly, well-done dos and don'ts lists are rare. I personally do not object to giving such lists, when they are carefully constructed, if those lists represent only a small fraction of the material covered and if they are given out at the optimal time (somewhere near the end of the training program).

As an example of good lists, I recommend those in Elizabeth Devine and Nancy L. Braganti's *Traveler's Guide to Asian Customs and Manners* (1986). This book covers fifteen Asian countries. (Be careful: there is another book by different authors but with exactly the same title.)

Resource Material

It is impossible for this chapter to provide the reader with complete and up-to-date bibliographies of the world's nearly two hundred countries. However, over the years I have learned to build a good bibliography for a specific country or region—given a good library and a good photocopy machine—in about two days' time. This is how you do it:

Start with the latest edition of the appropriate regional area studies bibliography produced by your Department of State, Foreign Ministry, or the like. In the United States, these are produced by the Area Studies School of the State Department's Foreign Service Institute (FSI), Center for the Study of Foreign Affairs, Arlington, Virginia. There is one for each region of the world. (Their only drawback is that they are never absolutely up-to-date.)

Next, go to a good library (where you have access to the stacks) and look at all the books they have on country X. Try at least three libraries, if there are good ones in your area.

Also look at the bibliographies in all of these books. Of course, they may not all have bibliographies, but when you finally find the right one, you only need one. This will provide you with recent books on country X to add to the basic bibliography of books you have gleaned from your diplomatic source or the FSI's regional bibliography.

Whenever possible, ask one or two country experts to critique your newly prepared bibliography and add their suggestions.

A Select Guide to Area Studies Resources (1988) by L. Robert Kohls and V. Lynn Tyler contains area studies and country studies information which is not readily available elsewhere. I consider it a guide to "generic area studies materials." These are books and other resources which provide information on all the world's countries but which are, for the most part, not separate volumes on individual countries. The books and other resources listed in this *Select Guide* will provide you with a wealth of information, much of which you might be unaware of otherwise.

The categories of resource materials contained therein are databases, books and other print media, films and videos, slides, microfiche, maps, public services, institutions, and libraries.

In the United States, there are several other significant resources. There is a great deal of controversy (so much so that one could make the argument that we are describing a single model with several slight variations), but the variations which do appear are significant. There is insufficient space to describe them fully here, but interested readers can track down the examples mentioned and examine them in greater detail.

The Country Handbook Model. Formerly Area Handbooks (now Country Study of…), these volumes, covering a large number of individual countries, have been written for the Department of Defense and are distributed to the public through the U.S. Government Printing Office. They are developed entirely from secondary sources.

The Foreign Service Institute's Country Profiles Model. These photocopied, in-house publications of the Overseas Briefing Center of the U.S. State Department's Center for the Study of Foreign Affairs provide a large amount of useful information, though they vary greatly from one another. Most have been prepared by foreign service officers' spouses.

The InterAct Model. George W. Renwick is the editor of a growing number of books which analyze the ways in which Americans and the nationals of about a dozen specific countries or regions interact, focusing especially on the points where cross-cultural difficulties occur. The InterAct series is published by Intercultural Press.

The Culturgram Model. These are the most widely distributed of all the publications discussed in this chapter. They are also, at four pages, the shortest in length. Produced by the Kennedy Center for International Studies of Brigham Young University, they provide more of the people-relating information than the Country Profiles and Country Handbook models. A manual on how to prepare a Culturgram is also available from Brigham Young University.

Conclusion

You will have to work at making the country/area studies portion of your training program as active and exciting as the other components, but the extra effort will be more than worth the trouble. After all, the information a good area studies component contains can spell the difference between the success or failure of the trainees as they move in-country. And if you have presented the material in a lively, engaging manner, you will also have stimulated and motivated them to continue to gather information while they are abroad.

References

Devine, Elizabeth, and Nancy L. Braganti. *Traveler's Guide to Asian Customs and Manners.* New York: St. Martin's Press, 1986.

Hoopes, David S., and Paul Ventura. *Intercultural Sourcebook: Cross-Cultural Training Methodologies.* LaGrange Park, IL: Intercultural Network, 1979.

Kohls, L. Robert, and V. Lynn Tyler. *A Select Guide to Area Studies Resources.* Provo, UT: Brigham Young University Press, 1988.

Thiagarajan, Sivasailam. "Twenty-five Ways to Improve Any Lecture." *Performance and Instruction Journal*, December (1985): 22–24.

Resources

Braganti, Nancy L., and Elizabeth Devine. *European Customs and Manners.* New York: Meadowbrook Press (Simon & Schuster), 1992.

Devine, Elizabeth, and Nancy L. Braganti. *Traveler's Guide to Middle Eastern and North African Customs and Manners.* New York: St. Martin's Press, 1991.

———. *Traveler's Guide to Latin American Customs and Manners.* New York: St. Martin's Press, 1988.

Simon, M. *Traveler's Reading Guide.* New York: Facts on File, 1994.

Culture-Specific Training: China

George W. Renwick

China, like many other countries, is a challenging environment for foreigners. The program that is described below and variations on it have been developed in response to the requests and real concerns of managers in European and North American organizations responsible for projects and personnel in the People's Republic. It is a predeparture program for employees and spouses who will be living in China for two years.

History and Development of the Program

Groundwork

Three sets of interests must be represented in the design of any program. The first steps in program planning articulate these interests. The findings from our investigation become the foundation for the whole program.

The organization. Clarify the purposes and goals for the program through interviews with people strategically placed in the organization. Take the organization's mission and requirements into consideration.

The host nationals. Estimate the attitudes, expectations, and abilities of the host nationals with whom the participants will interact.

The participants. Assess the participants' relevant education and life experience and strengths as well as weaknesses, spouses' strengths and weaknesses, motivation for going overseas (and participating in this program), what they are leaving behind, real feelings about the assignment, primary tasks and responsibilities in China, extent and kind of interaction with Chinese individuals and organizations, specific questions and concerns they bring to the program, knowledge of (and attitudes toward) China and its people and government, and preferred learning and contributing styles. Learn the one situation in which it is most important that they function confidently and effectively during their first three months in China (each of these becomes the basis for some of the critical incidents and role plays). Gather demographic data such as age, gender, family situation, length of assignment, and so forth.

The Strengths, Needs, and Tasks Assessment Questionnaire (see Appendix A) is the key to excellence in cross-cultural training. Most of the decisions, while the design is being created and as it is reexamined and modified during the program, must be based on comprehensive and accurate Participant Profiles and task descriptions. This is done through questionnaires, interviews with representative participants, and interviews with selected host country nationals and with people in the organization who know the participants and their new responsibilities well. It is also helpful to interview trainers who have designed and conducted well-received programs for the organization in the past.

For the purpose of this chapter, we will assume a group of fifteen people, all of them American. We have six couples (one African American couple and one Chinese American couple), two single men, and one single woman, all of whom bring very relevant (but different) life experiences to their foreign assignments. Some other findings from the assessment: most of the participants are definitely curious but uncertain and apprehensive about living for two years in Shenyang, Northeastern China (formerly known as Mukden, Manchuria). Most expect some benefit from the upcoming cross-cultural training program, but some resent the precious time it will take. A few are very skeptical. Most of them are practical people concerned about concrete situations. They definitely do not want what one called "another academic exercise." Another stated emphatically he did not want "any of that touchy-feely stuff."

Preparation: A Creative Process

Each of the next steps must take into account and do justice to the interests, the potential, and the constraints of the organization, the host nationals involved, and, especially, the participants who must carry out their tasks and responsibilities in new contexts overseas.

1. Formulate Objectives

Each objective should be meaningful and motivating for the diverse group of participants. Depending on the findings of the Strengths, Needs, and Tasks Assessment, the objectives should address one or more of the following: knowledge, attitudes, perceptions, expectations, attributions, skills, specific behaviors, and specific relationships. It is often best, when writing objectives, to specify *behaviors,* which can be observed (and perhaps evaluated) during the program itself, as well as related *competencies,* which can be practiced following the program in the real world. The behavior, for example, can be to describe clearly certain relevant subjects. Each subject can be listed; then the related competency will follow. The statement of objectives for our program might look like this:

Example

(Subject) When they have completed this program, participants will be able to describe clearly this significant subject.

> (Competency) *Later, when they are living in Shenyang, they will be more capable of functioning in this way.*

American Culture and Its Influence on Them

Discern how their own cultures equip and limit them. Explain their backgrounds to Chinese contacts in a concise and facilitative manner.

Foundations of Chinese Culture and Their Consequences for Chinese Today

Analyze accurately some of the reasons for the behavior of Chinese men and women. Interpret the significance of current events with a long-term perspective. Anticipate how the Chinese in Shenyang may perceive (and misperceive) the United States and the foreign guests from the United States.

Specific Barriers and Skills in Cross-Cultural Interaction

Communicate comfortably and effectively with a variety of Chinese in Shenyang. Learn a great deal from them. Gradually develop mutual respect with some of them and strong relationships with at least a few.

The Process of Transition

Take specific steps to deal constructively with culture fatigue and role shock. Find security and meaning as a minority.

Their Goals, Roles, and Resources as Members of the Participant Team

Be conscious of and committed to their common purposes. Respect their own differences and resolve their difficulties. Establish standards and norms for themselves as a group. Rely confidently on one another and enjoy their association throughout their time together in China.

Profiles of Thoroughly Adjusted Families in Shenyang

Carry out their responsibilities as partners and parents in mutually supportive and creative ways. Develop more depth and balance as individuals, more integrity and resilience as families. Contribute significantly to their communities, both in Shenyang and back home.

2. Create an Integrated Design

Before any methods are considered, it is important to make basic design decisions in a number of areas. The program design, once established, provides the framework, the parameters, the underlying pattern, and the character of the program. The design allows for the development of a distinctive rhythm and engaging momentum, and it accounts for much of the power of a program.

Given these participants with their particular tasks and responsibilities, and given these program objectives, we must decide which options within the following areas are most appropriate:

❖ **Duration** (One day, one week, perhaps one day this week and one day next week, then three consecutive days the following week, perhaps one evening each week for two months)

❖ **Dependence** (Degree of dependence on materials, trainers, participants, or equipment—computers, VCRs, and the like)

❖ **Setting** (Classroom, living room, training room, retreat facility, wilderness)

❖ **Climate/Atmosphere** (Cold, objective, competitive, combative, high pressure, cooperative, supportive, friendly, warm)

❖ **Personal disclosure (modeled and required)** (Virtually none, some, a great deal)

❖ **Pace** (Rapid at first then gradually slowing, or the reverse—slow at first then speeding up, steady, alternating—the hot and cold shower approach)

❖ **Proportion of conceptual and experiential** (90 percent conceptual, 10 percent strictly experiential, the reverse, half and half, perhaps alternating back and forth)

❖ **Focus** (Culture specific—China, culture comparative—U.S. and China, or culture interactive—Chinese and Americans together, in what order)

❖ **Content** (Specific subjects and their sequence)

❖ **Communication style** (High- or low-context; person-, problem-, or group-centered; one-way, two-way, or every which way)

❖ **Leadership (training) style** (Didactic, administrative, facilitative)

The options chosen in all of the above areas will work only if they are coupled with appropriate *program integrators*. These include the following:

❖ Continuity in key program staff: each is with the participants throughout the program and able to use a variety of integrators effectively.

❖ A solid cornerstone: the basic concept, image, situation, person, or common experience upon which the structure of the program is built and to which frequent reference is made.

❖ A compelling theme: the memorable phrase or quotation which represents the underlying strand woven through the whole program; this provides a consistent point of reference and a superordinate goal for the group.

❖ Coherent program principles and ground rules: the basic guidelines all staff members and participants live by and learn by during the program.

❖ Organic sequencing: If a program is to be highly effective, each part must be carefully orchestrated. Each concept, subject, method, experience, and additional staff member builds upon the previous ones and prepares the participants for subsequent sessions.

Integrating exercises serve the primary purpose of enabling the participants to relate their past experience to their current program experience and future in-country experience. Other exercises enable them to consolidate and integrate their learning during different parts of the program.

Participants, too, are part of the program—the central part. As rapport builds among them, and with the staff, they become increasingly integrated into a community of explorers. In a program where the design is fragmented, rapport among the participants cannot develop—unless, of course, they unite against the program or against the trainer. Much of the resistance we sometimes find in participants is their discomfort and understandable reaction to a program design that is not appropriate for them, is inherently contradictory, or is simply not in place at all. A lack of structure or design is an unnerving condition, especially for people who may be strangers to one another and are in the midst of a major transition. It can be especially distracting and disconcerting for participants if they are Asian.

There are four basic principles regarding the integrity of program design: (1) a fragmented design cannot yield integrated learning, (2) a fragmented design cannot yield an integrated group, (3) integrated learning cannot occur in a disintegrated group, and (4) learning which is not integrated is not retained and not used.

In planning our program for the fifteen participants going to Shenyang, the following design decisions have been made. The **duration** will be eight consecutive days with the afternoon of the fourth day off. The design will be more **trainer dependent** at the beginning, then become more **participant dependent** as training progresses. Some parts will be **materials dependent**; these will be set up and processed through individual reflection and discussion exercises.

The **settings** will be a small, quiet conference center and, of course, several noisy, crowded Chinese restaurants. The **climate and atmosphere** will be relaxed, accepting, candid, creative, and a combination of serious and humorous. As much **personal disclosure** will be encouraged as the participants are comfortable with and the trainers are capable of handling (which must be carefully assessed and monitored).

The **pace** will be fairly rapid at the beginning (American), moving to a slower pace (Chinese) toward the close. Therefore, participants will experience a change in their environment and will actually begin their adjustment during the program (which will be discussed). Much of the time (about 60 percent) will be devoted to **experience-based** activities (especially those involving the Chinese resource people) integrated with more **cognitive** subjects (altogether about 30 percent). The remainder of the program time will be devoted to pauses and restful or stimulating diversions. Opportunities for physical activity will be provided each day through practicing the graceful movements of Tai Ji Quan.

During early phases of the program the **focus** will be on specific cultures: first the American, then the Chinese. Then a systematic comparison of the two cultures will illustrate those particular differences that will be very much in evidence in the participants' lives once they get to China. This will provide a basis for the major **content** focus: analyzing and practicing interaction. The importance of interaction will be demonstrated and specific interactive skills practiced throughout the program.

The **communication style** will be continually interactive, beginning rather low context (American) during the early phases and moving toward higher context (Chinese). The **leadership and training styles** of the trainers will differ somewhat, but will usually be evocative and facilitative. The trainers will give some presentations. Rather than lecturing, however, they will involve the participants in a variety of engaging ways. One fundamental assumption of effective intercultural training designed for adults is that what we do in a program depends not on the schedule but on the thoughts, feelings, and readiness of the participants each moment. Program process respects and responds to internal, personal process. Program design and training style must therefore be flexible. This approach is expressed well in *The Tao of Leadership* (John Heider 1985, 33), a translation of the Chinese classic from the fifth century B.C., *The Tao Te Ching*:

> Remember that you are facilitating another person's process. It is not your process. Do not intrude. Do not control.
>
> If you do not trust a person's process, that person will not trust you.
>
> Facilitate what is happening rather than what you think ought to be happening.

With regard to the essential **program integrators**, there will be one male and one female trainer (because the participants include both men and women) who will be responsible for the design, conduct, and evaluation of the program. They will be with the participants throughout the eight days. The theme will be "Things Go Better with *Guan Xi*" (explained below). The cornerstone of the program will be a complex Chinese character, made up of simpler characters representing a person's ears, eyes, and heart. It means "to listen" and is pronounced "ting." Participants will have many opportunities to write, pronounce, and practice this during the program:

聽 　 ting (to listen)

Two principles of this program will be "Build on strength, make weakness irrelevant" (Drucker 1967) and "Respond to the person before the problem" (when with Chinese *and with family members*). Two ground rules will be (1) no smoking in program sessions and (2) no interruptions when another participant is speaking.

Integrating exercises will include structured reflection by each individual, then each couple, on other transitions and stressful situations they have faced in their lives, followed by discussion of insights and practical guidelines they can draw from this previous experience. Another integrating exercise is a collage of participants' impressions and images of China and Shenyang, begun early in the program as they introduce themselves and added to at several points over the eight days. Many integrating exercises are cumulative; that is, participants add to them throughout the program. As a part of the session on transition, participants will imagine themselves in the midst of everything in the collage (all those bicycles, the bitter cold, political uncertainty, and newfound friends) and then anticipate their reactions.

Cumulative recording of major points and specific implications is also effective, especially when these are reviewed periodically. At the close of each session, participants will write on a Strategy Sheet (provided at the front of their manuals) the specific steps they will take to prepare for their assignment, explore their new city, make the adjustments, support their family, and interact with the Chinese. These steps or strategies will be based on insights gained during that particular session. As participants review their strategies at the close of the program, the substance of each session will be recalled and the most important practical implications from the program will be reinforced. Priorities can then be established and constructive actions taken.

Conceptual integration will be enhanced through a cumulative diagram. Central concepts presented or generated early in the program will be visually represented in a simple diagram which will be expanded as other concepts are introduced. Clarifying connections can then be drawn (and more easily remembered and used). Concepts, if they are to be meaningful, must have context too. For example, the Chinese term for relationship is *guan xi*. If you apologize to someone for something you have done, that person would probably reply, *"Mei guan xi"* (Don't worry about it). Literally, the meaning is "It has no relationship." That which has no relationship, that which is not connected, does not matter. It has no value. This is true of actions and concepts. In China, it is especially true of people. An influential Chinese person has guan xi. Foreigners, if they want to get things done in China, must carefully cultivate guan xi. The participants add the concept of guan xi to their Strategy Sheets.

The organization of the program will also be illustrated with a diagram (see Appendix B). On the first morning the trainers will present and explain a flow chart, making clear to participants what the plan is, what their immediate future holds. This is especially important for American participants. The components and connectors will be explained, the underlying structure traced, the gestalt established. Progress through the plan can be marked as the work is completed (also important to Americans). Significant discoveries can be noted at the points where they occur.

Evaluation is one of the best occasions for integration and is a strong stimulus for it. All evaluation efforts, in fact, should contribute to participants' integration of their learning. An effective evaluation can actually train participants how to integrate and apply their learning and, of course, how to continuously evaluate their own learning. This program will provide such opportunities (as well as essential feedback to the staff) at the midpoint of the program, at the close, and then two months and five months after the participants arrive in China (a sample Final Evaluation questionnaire is provided in Appendix C).

Rapport will be developed among participants, and their efforts and resources will be integrated in a variety of ways. During each session their experience and distinctive strengths will be recognized and called upon. Their common concerns will be respected, shared, and addressed. Common goals and commitments will emerge and be confirmed. Some real problems will be solved—by them, together. As the inherent capability of their new community becomes clear, their confidence will grow, and their new context and their roles within it will take form. The result: each participant, in his or her own way (and in some new ways) will cultivate guan xi with one another during the program. We can watch this essential process, analyze it, experiment with it, discover how these individuals accomplish it, and discuss now very specifically how they can cultivate guan xi with Chinese acquaintances and coworkers in Shenyang. As we work out appropriate steps that each individual, each couple, and the whole group can take, these steps will be added to the Strategy Sheets.

Especially important in building rapport among the participants will be the rapport between the two cotrainers. The quality and resilience of their relationship, with their differing backgrounds and styles, will have a pervasive influence on all of the relationships throughout the program. When two trainers genuinely respect and trust one another, participants will more quickly develop respect for both of them, have more confidence in them, and learn more from them. As the cotrainers work in concert with each other, earn the respect of the participants, and develop rapport with them, participants will more quickly develop comfortable, respectful, cooperative relationships among themselves [see Fritz Heider (1958) and the balance theory in social psychology].

On the other hand, when the cotrainers dislike one another and are constantly at odds, participants will find it much more difficult to respect them, accept their leadership, or assimilate what they have to offer. Furthermore (and this is subtle but powerful), participants will find it difficult to join and learn from one another. Conflict and competition between cotrainers is contagious; dissension in the group will usually be the result. Integrated learning cannot occur in a disintegrated group. The program objectives cannot be met. The participants and their organization will not have been served.

The core staff should reflect, to the extent possible, the gender and cultural diversity of the participants. Cotrainers, therefore, are usually essential in cross-cultural training. Participants may learn more from how the diverse members of the staff communicate with one another than from anything else in the program. This may be especially true in predeparture programs. For this reason, an examination of staff relations will be an integral part of the final day in our program. We evaluate the participants' abilities to communicate; why shouldn't they evaluate (and thereby learn more from) ours?

3. Select and Prepare Appropriate Staff and Resource Persons

Members of the staff must be not only compatible with one another, they must also be compatible with the participants, credible to the organization, committed to achieving the objectives of the program, and capable of carrying out the design of the program. The lead trainers for our China program will be an American man and an American woman who have worked well together on other programs, both of whom are familiar with China and its challenges to American expatriates and their families living there.

In culture-specific training, the resource persons are critical. Ours will include an American couple and a single American woman who have returned recently from successful two-year assignments in Shenyang. Involved in several parts of the program and social activities will be an older Chinese man and a young Chinese woman, both of whom grew up in China and have lived most of their lives there. The woman went to school in Shenyang.

It is difficult to conduct responsible, effective culture-specific training without such qualified resource persons. The major benefit we offer participants in intercultural *training* (not education) is access to the most resourceful, perceptive people who have experienced what the trainees are about to go through as well as access to host nationals who are best able to serve as cultural informants and communication coaches. Not only do we provide access to such persons, we also enable participants to interact with them in constructive, illuminating ways, then analyze their interaction in order to understand, assimilate, and then plan to apply that learning once they are in the foreign country. More time is often spent on locating and selecting the most qualified resource persons than on any other part of culture-specific training. The lead trainer needs more professional skills as he or she prepares the resource persons and then structures, facilitates, and analyzes the interaction than during any other phase of the program.

Preparation of our resource persons will begin with a description of the participants (based on the Strengths, Needs, and Tasks Assessment) and an explanation of the objectives and basic design of the program. The social and structural context into which the participants are moving is important to resource persons, especially if they come from high-context cultures (like China). Describing this context is also important because an intercultural training program is profoundly foreign for many resource persons. Their comfortable entrance and integration will depend on clarifying exactly what their role will be. Most have never been a resource person before. Role ambiguity here (and for many Chinese in China and other peoples elsewhere) can lead to anxiety and paralysis.

Preparation will continue with the resource persons reflecting on their own cultural background, examining specific situations in which they have interacted with people of the other culture, clarifying and expressing (perhaps for the first time) cultural and communication insights, and rehearsing the sessions in which they will be involved during the program. One purpose of this process, of course, is to encourage the development of mutual respect, trust, and confidence between the trainers and the resource persons. To the extent that this actually develops, the resource persons will be more relaxed and effective during the sessions and, most importantly, the training team will be demonstrating the quality of communication and cooperation the participants should practice with Chinese men and women in Shenyang. Which brings us back, once again, to guan xi.

Interaction between the Chinese resource persons and the American cotrainers, *and between the Chinese and the participants*, will be the crux, the centerpiece, of the whole program. This will be the one dish in the Chinese banquet which is most carefully prepared, enthusiastically served, eagerly sampled, and vividly remembered.

We want to keep in mind some basic guidelines as we develop the staff and resource persons for our program. Search everywhere for the most suitable candidates. Build a program leadership team that is clear about the purposes of the program and about its own goals, roles, and responsibilities. Include the resource persons in comfortable (which usually means hosted and facilitated) social events, perhaps a dinner early in the program. Structure and facilitate especially carefully the sessions in which resource persons are involved. Remain quietly but definitely in charge of those sessions; the Chinese usually expect someone to be in charge. Do not expect the resource persons to be intercultural specialists (analyzing and comparing cultures in depth) or to come up with more effective ways they can contribute; this is up to the trainers. Do not expect the Chinese resource persons to represent all the people of China. They know they cannot. Instead, discover what each can best contribute to the participants and the program objectives. For example, most can tell the story of significant, relevant parts of their own lives. Some can do this in colorful, compelling, moving ways. Then leave it up to the participants, who have been listening, observing, and interacting, to discern (with some assistance from the staff) the underlying Chinese cultural themes and communication styles. Enable the participants to practice during the program what they will have to do every day they are in China. Give them real situations, real people. The best way to learn how to communicate with Chinese people is to communicate with Chinese people—in a safe, supportive environment and with the assistance of competent intercultural trainers.

4. Choose, Adapt, or Create Effective Methods and Exercises

In planning our program up to this point, we have (a) clarified the interests of the organization and the host nationals who will be involved in China; (b) identified the strengths, needs, and tasks of the participants; (c) formulated the program objectives; (d) made the basic design decisions; and (e) selected and begun to prepare the staff and resource persons. *Only now can we seriously consider the methods and exercises or activities.* Once the interests, objectives, program framework, and staff are in place, the most appropriate methods become clear. This systematic approach to program planning differs significantly from the tendency of some trainers to start with a favorite method, add a few more activities involving different methods, then put the assortment end to end and believe they have a program. This is something like lining up an engine from a motorcycle, seats from a sports car, tires from a tractor, a tailgate from a pickup, and air brakes from a moving van, and then think you have a comfortable, cost-effective car for your family.

Without an in-depth understanding of the purposes, participants, basic structure, and staff of the program, we have no basis upon which to decide which methods to use. Also, we have little incentive to create new, exactly appropriate methods or exercises and little direction in doing so. Creating new methods and activities and adapting existing ones are often required in effective culture-specific programs because our participants come from such different backgrounds, the working and living situations for which we are preparing them vary widely, and the resource persons who are available bring a challenging variety of strengths.

Some frequently neglected principles of effective training will be considered as various methods are weighed for our China program. Each method or activity should be exactly suited to, and engaging for, these particular participants. Each method and exercise should contribute directly to a specific program objective. Some of the methods and exercises should identify, affirm, and mobilize each participant's current strengths and resources. Most should include opportunities for participants to learn from their own experience and the experience of the other participants, since these experiences will be their primary—sometimes their only—source of learning during their two years on their own in China. An important part of experiential learning is to provide opportunities for participants to recall their life experience, reflect on it, understand it in a new light, then draw some valuable insights and helpful guidelines from it. Putting them through exercises, one after another, even if we take the time to process them, is not so much experiential learning as it is experiential teaching. Setting up one structured experience after another can be more trainer-centered than we usually admit. Instead, we must discover ways to *get out of the participants' way,* so they can learn more directly from their own, their spouses', and their fellow participants' experience. We can have more confidence in our participants than in our methods.

Each exercise should build upon previous ones and prepare participants for subsequent ones. Some exercises, carefully chosen or created, should serve the special function of integrating the other methods, exercises, and the whole program. (Among the integrators created for this program, in addition to the cumulative collage of participants' images of China, are the Chinese Profile and Participant Profile built during the program, the action plans recorded on the Strategy Sheet at regular intervals, the evaluation and follow-up evaluation, and the Chinese banquets that open and close the program.)

5. Gather Accurate Site Information on Shenyang

Fascinating historical information is available in a few books. Most participants, however, urgently want current information. This has been gathered by one of our trainers at the site. It has also been gathered through interviews with the resource persons and telephone conversations with others who have lived in Shenyang recently. The collected information covers all of the major areas about which expatriates must know as they get established in Shenyang. Included, of course, were the areas of particular concern expressed by the participants during the Strengths, Needs, and Tasks Assessment. This information will be condensed and included in the packet of background readings which the participants will receive before the program.

Especially effective are good quality slides and videotapes of the places where the participants will live, shop, work, go for medical care, send their children to school, and so forth. These will be shown and explained early in the program. Seeing exactly what their new home looks like, and getting some sense for what it feels (and smells) like, will be both reassuring and somewhat depressing for many of the participants. The effect is significant: their cultural adjustment will have begun while they are with us in the program. Nothing provides more opportunity for the trainers—or more responsibility.

6. Develop Engaging Audiovisual and Printed Materials

We do not have adequate audiovisual and printed materials to form the basis for a whole culture-specific program. It is doubtful whether this kind of intercultural training can ever be done effectively through a materials-dependent design. Our China program, therefore, will follow a design which is primarily trainer-dependent, especially during its early stages. The appropriate materials we do have (slides, videotapes, films, some instruments, and written exercises) will be used to supplement participant-trainer and participant-resource person interaction. Each one will be integrated with the various other methods, and these materials will themselves be sequenced to have a cumulative effect as the program progresses. Each of these materials, like the other methods, will serve specific program objectives.

One special kind of material developed especially for these participants will be a map of their new home city, Shenyang, with the places expatriates most often go clearly marked in both Chinese and English. This will be used early in the program as the participants learn to pronounce the name of each place in Mandarin, ask for directions, and give instructions to taxi drivers. It will also be used as the participants are taken on their slide and video tour of Shenyang.

Special video materials will include two taped tours of Shenyang. One will portray the city through the eyes of a foreigner who is curious, adventurous, determined to adjust well, learn a lot, and contribute as much as possible. The other, shorter videotape will portray the city through the eyes of an ethnocentric, negative foreigner looking for things to criticize and expecting to be dissatisfied. The two perspectives become a basis for discussing the effect of attitudes and expectations on perceptions, the effect of perception on behavior, and the effect of all of these upon the participants' adjustment and performance (and, ultimately, upon Chinese counterparts and friends). The two perspectives also reveal different aspects of Shenyang, a complex industrial city whose many aspects and four million inhabitants seem so intriguing and so isolating to the handful of foreigners living there. Many participants are likely to respond rather intensely to this, their new reality. The way the staff responds to them will influence the way they will respond to one another. Discussions of culture shock and role shock later in the program will connect with the participants' earlier feelings and allow for some personal clarification and resolution.

7. Send Introductory Letter and Overseas Assignment Inventory (OAI)

A few weeks before the program, the cotrainers send a letter to each participant, introducing themselves and explaining the purpose and content of the program. Brief introductions of the resource persons are also given. The reasons for including the OAI in the program are explained, and participants are encouraged to complete it soon. (For a description of the OAI, please see page 45.) Having read the letter, most participants will be more enthusiastic about attending this program.

8. Choose and Send Informative Background Readings

Participants are usually under a great deal of pressure during the weeks before the program and their departure. Preliminary readings, if they are to serve their purpose, must be immediately interesting and useful. The booklet of background readings for our program will include the following:
❖ Quotations on the importance of understanding Chinese culture and communicating effectively with the Chinese—and the commitment necessary to do so.
❖ A concise overview of the country and culture (along the lines of a Culturgram).
❖ A summary of the practical, current information about the site gathered through an examination of the site and interviews with Americans living there and others who have recently returned.
❖ Specific advice from expatriates in Shenyang for people about to move there. (If carefully gathered, this can be extremely useful and reassuring.)

❖ Excerpts from the diary of a Russian who lived in Shenyang in 1953, with colorful descriptions of the city and his reactions to it.

❖ Excerpts from two novels, one by Alice Tisdale Hobart (*Oil for the Lamps of China*, 1933); the other by John Hersey (*The Call*, 1985), stories of an American businessman and an American missionary in China with their families, struggling to come to terms with China (and with themselves), hoping, despairing, learning gradually to communicate and work with the Chinese, then coming home.

❖ Recent, brief interviews with a farmer, a student, a factory manager, and a government official in China in which they describe very candidly their memories and their lives today.

❖ A concise interactive study that describes Chinese and American perceptions and expectations as they get to know one another; explains specifically what each does that confuses, irritates, embarrasses, motivates, and earns the respect of the other; then provides guidelines on what Americans can do to communicate more comfortably and effectively with their Chinese contacts and counterparts.

❖ An annotated list of the most interesting books available in a variety of areas so the participants can begin to learn about China through the particular area they most enjoy. These include history, U.S.-China relations, the Chinese people, contemporary politics and economics, business, art, music, literature, expatriates in China, Chinese in the United States, and negotiation and communication between Americans and Chinese. All of the books listed will be available to the participants during their program.

With these readings will be a letter from the cotrainers. Included will be a brief instrument requesting the participants to indicate their perceptions of the Chinese people and the Chinese government. A similar instrument will be completed as a part of the evaluation at the close of the program, then another five months and one year after the participants have arrived in China. This will give the program staff and the participants' organization some evidence of changes in perceptions as a result of the program.

Structure and Content of the Program

Establishing Base Camp

The numbers in parentheses, below, refer to the session number within which that particular subject is discussed (see numbers 1–18, pages 297–309).

1. **Getting Acquainted.** (First afternoon and evening.) Introduction of staff, resource persons, and participants.

   a. Culture in microcosm. Preparation of participants to glimpse Chinese culture and communication patterns in a traditional Chinese banquet. Begin building the Chinese Profile (basic insights to be developed throughout the program). For example, some of the same cultural characteristics and communication patterns (along with new ones) that the trainees will be exposed to at the banquet will be discussed later during the sessions on area studies (7), cultural differences (8), communication (10), interaction practice/role plays (11), adjustment—Chinese experience (13), and creating a community—Chinese strategies (15).

b. Enjoyment of a traditional Chinese banquet, including appropriate opening toasts, with Chinese and American resource persons.

2. **Setting the Stage.** (Next morning.) Introduction of program schedule, intercultural learning assumptions, ground rules, recommended books, and the visual environment (maps, Chinese paintings, and calligraphy). Put the cornerstone in place: listening (ting).

3. **Confirming Program and Participant Objectives.** Identification of additional participant concerns. Establish theme for the whole program (which will be woven into each of the following sessions in a variety of ways, some of them surprising).

4. **Exploring and Affirming Participants' Own Culture(s) and Values.** Clarification of consequences of participants' cultures for them. Develop cultural self-awareness and cultural self-respect. Begin participant team building.

a. A brief values inventory.

b. Reflection by each participant on important values and attitudes learned in his or her family, schools, and organization. Discussion and consolidation. These values and attitudes will serve as the beginning of the construction by participants of the Participant Profile. Chinese values and attitudes will become part of the Chinese Profile. Both will be further expanded and refined later during the session on cultural differences (8).

c. Identification of the diversity within the participant group. Consider one of the basic points and purposes of the program: to the extent that participants recognize and respect the diversity in their own group and learn to communicate comfortably and effectively with one another, they will be equipping themselves to deal with the diversity they will find among the other expatriates in Shenyang and, of course, to deal with their hosts—the Chinese. Dealing with their own diversity will be reconsidered and practiced at several points in the program, especially during the later session on creating their own community in Shenyang (15).

5. **Opening Mandarin Windows.** Introduction to structures, tones, phrases, and characters ("window words") that reveal characteristics of Chinese culture and patterns of thinking, learning, and communicating. These will become a part of the Chinese Profile and will become integrators throughout the program.

a. An example of a window word: the character for "woman" is 女. The character for "son" or "child" is 子. When we put the two together we get another character 好, which is pronounced "hao" and means "good." In other words, whenever a Chinese person writes "good" (the weather is good; the food is good), he or she is writing "mother/child." Is the family important to the Chinese? Are parents? Children? Can they ever be separated?

Each Chinese cultural characteristic has implications for foreigners living in China. Some of the implications here will be considered later during the sessions on adjustment (13) and providing support for the participants' families in transition (14). Chinese insights on how to do this will be explained and, where appropriate, applied.

Each window word has a practical use. For example, if we put the word for "you," which is *ni,* together with the word for "good," we get *ni hao.* This means "Hello" or "How are you?" It is the standard greeting in many places in China. It will be the standard greeting for the participants and staff during the rest of the program.

b. Introduction during each session of the program of a few Chinese words, phrases, or brief dialogues. These will be relevant to the subject, revealing of cultural characteristics and communication patterns, and useful to the participants. They will be practiced regularly throughout the program.

Becoming Acquainted with the Terrain

6. **Living Each Day in Shenyang, Northeastern China.** Construction of a picture of participants' new reality. (We learned through the Strengths, Needs, and Tasks Assessment that none of the participants have been to China before.) The training staff will field participants' practical questions.

   a. Carefully sequenced slides and videotapes, following the special map, with periodic discussion of participant reactions. Relevant Mandarin will be introduced and practiced.

   b. Facilitated discussion with an American couple who recently returned from a difficult but rewarding assignment in Shenyang. Prior to the program they were alerted to the special situations and concerns of the participants (expressed in the Strengths, Needs, and Tasks Assessment), so they were able to do some special preparation.

   c. Additional concerns and specific questions. These will emerge during subsequent sessions, be faxed to the on-site contact (an American expatriate) in Shenyang, and then be responded to later as the participants consolidate their learning during the program (16).

7. **Exploring Participants' New Neighborhood, Discovering China.** Area studies. A practical approach. The results of our Strengths, Needs, and Tasks Assessment confirm that most of our fifteen participants would be most intrigued by, and get the most out of, a graphic, tangible, *personal* approach to area studies. For most of them, abstract theories, complex models, new terminology, and lots of numbers and names and dates and distant events would

present barriers to their understanding. Bear in mind that some of them have not been in a classroom for twenty-five years. Academic ways of reasoning and communicating are foreign to them. It will be more difficult for our participants to grasp and begin to adjust to the Chinese environment during the program if, at the same time, we are requiring them to adjust to an academic environment.

The key in working with these kinds of participants is to offer them people and places they can relate to—in fact must relate to if they are to survive in China. There is not time in this kind of intercultural training, nor at this point in these participants' lives, to provide what would merely be "nice" to know. We must concentrate on what they *need* to know, need to remember, and will be able to use.

Area studies: whose area should we study? The participants'. In presenting the area studies, we will recall several principles. Start where the participants are. Enable them to learn from where they live. Every aspect of China that is important for them to know is evident somewhere in their immediate surroundings in Shenyang. Then move out from their neighborhood to the city, the province (perhaps along an ancient trade route taken by nomads leaving Shenyang), and from there to the whole country. Once we have moved outward, it is important that we return to Shenyang and the immediate neighborhood. If it is a theme in history that is being traced, for example, we would describe how it is remembered by the Chinese next door, how it affects them, and how it affects foreign residents today.

Instead of a presenter "covering" an area of knowledge, participants begin discovering the area in which they must make a meaningful life for themselves. We might call this participant-centered area studies. What would it look like? Let's experiment with some possibilities:

a. *People of China*: Birth, family, education, occupation, marriage, child rearing, retirement, and death as expressed in the personal stories of Li Mei Yu and Go Ching Po, female and male resource persons. Listening and talking with them, trainees will participate briefly in five generations of Chinese lives, from his grandmother in China, whose feet were bound, to her daughter now in the United States studying physics. Some cultural characteristics and communication patterns are confirmed, additional ones are considered. Chinese values and attitudes will be noted here and in the following steps (continuing to build the Chinese Profile), then set beside the participants' values and attitudes during our session on cultural differences (8).

b. *History of China*. As represented by an ancient tomb in Shenyang and by previous events and guests—nationalists and communists—in the local landmark hotel.

c. *Chinese communism, socialism, and politics*. As illustrated in the bold banner and old monument in the park.

d. *Economy of China*. As demonstrated in the local bicycle factory.

e. *Basic Chinese attitudes.* As enacted by participants while learning some Tai Ji Quan and calligraphy, and reinforced while watching and discussing brief videos of accomplished Chinese doing both.

f. *Philosophies and religions of China.* As suggested in a lotus blossom.

g. *Chinese values underlying all of the above.* As reflected in a rice paddy.

During each of these sessions, participants will be introduced to a few relevant, revealing structures, words, or phrases in Mandarin. As an example, let's take the last topic. The Chinese character for rice paddy in fact looks like one: 田. If we put that with the character for labor, 力, we get 男. The meaning of this character is "man," the one who applies labor to the land. Do the Chinese identify closely with the land? Are they connected to their roots?

As always, we want to connect language with cultural insight. We also want the language to have immediate practical application. Recognizing this character when they see it on a door, the men in the program will now know which rest room to use.

8. **Recognizing Cultural Differences (and Similarities) that Can Make a Difference.**

a. Assignment of carefully chosen Chinese names. Trainees will learn to write and pronounce their Chinese names, then write them on their name tags. Chinese classical and folk music will now be playing each morning as the participants arrive and during the breaks for the rest of the program.

b. A review of Chinese values and attitudes discovered during area studies and other previous sessions (recorded in the Chinese Profile). Analyze a videotape in which Chinese actors manifest some of these values and attitudes in specific situations (fictional, role-played, or real). Add new insights to the Chinese Profile.

c. A review of the participants' own values and attitudes (the Participant Profile) constructed earlier in the program. Refine and add to these. Discuss situations during the program where some of these have been manifest, thereby deepening cultural self-awareness and team consciousness.

d. Comparison of the Chinese Profile and the Participant Profile. Decide on those differences and similarities which will probably affect the participants most directly as they live and deal with the Chinese in Shenyang.

e. Time for reflection on other situations in the experience of the participants where they have dealt with differences. When have they done this rather well? What exactly did they do? Why? With what results? When have some of the participants and trainers dealt rather well with differences in the group during the program? Consolidate the lessons learned. Consider new, especially appropriate strategies for dealing with the Chinese—and one another.

    f. Discussion of the advantages of the *similarities* in the Chinese Profile and the Participant Profile. Analyze the ways in which the program design has been built upon similarities among the participants and how their areas of similarity have been increasing during the program. Consider the implications for their creation of their own community in Shenyang (to be developed further during session 15) and for building relationships with the Chinese. Return once again to guan xi.

Everything is now ready, and the participants are prepared to explore that most central question: What happens when we bring participants and the local Chinese together in Shenyang and they try to communicate with one another?

9. Midprogram Evaluation and Break.

Face to Face: The Major Challenge

10. **Communicating with Confidence.** (Both the Chinese and the American resource persons participate in this session.)

    a. Choice of effective communication situation. The participants have been communicating with people all of their lives. One of the purposes of this program is to enable them to distill what they have already learned about communicating and apply this to their relations with Chinese. They begin by choosing one situation in which they communicated rather well with a person whose background was different from theirs. They recall the situation as vividly as they can, describe their communication styles and priorities, explain what happened and why, then draw some insights from this. (The African American and Chinese American participants may have especially helpful insights to contribute here.) Their styles and priorities are summarized and added to their values and attitudes in the Participant Profile. As they turn to a consideration of Chinese communication styles, they will keep these approaches and insights in mind to determine which might be most appropriate.

    b. Investigation of Chinese communication styles, priorities, and patterns (both verbal and nonverbal). Begin with the participants' own experience with the Chinese resource persons in the program so far. Then discuss the experience of other Westerners in China and the results of relevant research. Communication analysis skills will be further developed, and more cultural insights gained, through a few excerpts of dialogue from Chinese literature. Returning to the values and attitudes in the Chinese Profile, we will now add Chinese communication styles and patterns.

    c. Clarification of prevailing American communication styles, priorities, and interaction patterns (both verbal and nonverbal). This will be achieved through participants' own observations, studies from the intercultural field, and contrasting dialogues from American literature. Add to Participant Profile as appropriate.

d. Development of specific Communication Guidelines. Given what the participants now understand about Chinese and American interaction and about themselves when they communicate, what will probably work best when they want to communicate with Chinese in Shenyang?

11. **Interacting Effectively with the Chinese: Pitfalls, Possibilities, Practice and More Practice.** A review at this point of everything in the program that can be brought to bear on interaction. Communication strategies will be brought even more vividly to life.

a. Brief review of the Chinese Profile, the Participant Profile, and the Communication Guidelines generated so far.

b. Role plays of successful Chinese-American interaction. Who in the program can interact most effectively as Chinese? The Chinese resource persons. Who can interact most effectively as Americans with the Chinese? The Americans who recently returned from two years doing just that in Shenyang—our American resource persons. These Chinese and Americans, well prepared by the trainers for this moment, will therefore be our first role players. They will enact two situations which are comfortable for them and of real interest to the participants.

The situations will be chosen from those described by the participants (during the Strengths, Needs, and Tasks Assessment) as being the ones in which it is most important that they function most confidently and effectively during their first three months in China. We start with a simpler one, then move toward a very demanding one. During the analysis of each, everyone contributes: participants, Chinese resource persons, American resource persons, trainers, and, of course, the role players themselves.

c. Reconsideration of the Communication Guidelines. Refine and condense. (These, along with the Chinese Profile and the Participant Profile, will be typed up in a very clear format and given to participants during review session 16).

d. Closure. Wrap up this session with an explanation of the origin and implications of the Chinese character 信, which means "trust." Reaffirm the importance of listening in the development of trust.

Making a Meaningful Life as a Foreigner

12. **Fulfilling Special Responsibilities, Pursuing Special Opportunities in China.** Special concerns of the different groups among the participants that deserve attention during the program. The members of these groups often prefer to discuss these concerns with one another. Separate sessions, therefore, will be designed for the following:

a. *Employees.* This session will lay the groundwork for the second intercultural training program to follow this one. That program will concentrate on the professional insights and skills needed by the employees in Shenyang. Most of the time during this session, however, will be devoted to a compelling explanation of the needs and potential of those people who are essential to the project but are often overlooked: the spouses.

b. *Spouses.* Candid, personal discussion with the appropriate resource person.

c. *Single woman and single men.* Frank discussion with the appropriate resource person plus information and recommendations from other singles who have lived in China and were interviewed by the trainers prior to the program.

d. *African Americans and Chinese Americans.* Straightforward discussion about their special situations in China based on information and recommendations from African Americans and Chinese Americans who have lived in China and were interviewed prior to the program. Their names and telephone numbers are given to the participants for further conversations following the program.

13. **Adjusting Successfully, Contributing Significantly.** Careful consideration of the support requirements and resources available for families and singles in Shenyang.

a. Lessons from previous moves. Each participant chooses and reflects on the most difficult move he or she has made in life so far. Each step is discussed. Participants' feelings and findings (about themselves, their spouses, and the process of adjustment) are considered (sometimes privately). Their own cycles of adjustment are traced.

b. Impact of Chinese reality. The collage of salient realities of the Chinese environment is completed. Participants imagine themselves in the midst of these and sense more deeply their reactions to everything Chinese around them.

c. Experience and recommendations of American resource persons. Each recalls (and, to some extent, relives) his or her move to Shenyang. The fact that the spouses' pattern of adjustment is different becomes clear. Implications for each participant are considered.

d. Results of research on culture shock, role shock, and cycles of adjustment, including specific implications for participants—as individuals, partners, parents, and team members. This is done through a participative presentation during which a diagram is built representing the research results, the experience of the American resource persons, and the experience of participants during previous transitions. (The diagram will be reproduced and given to the participants during session 16.)

e. Experience and recommendations of Chinese resource persons. Each recalls (and, to some extent, relives) his or her move to the United States. Their expectations, perceptions, and reactions will reveal some underlying Chinese values and attitudes (which we will add to our Chinese Profile) as well as some basic characteristics of American culture (which will deepen still further the participants' cultural self-awareness). Also considered is the fact that, for centuries, Chinese people have experienced dislocations. What can Chinese philosophy and personal practice contribute to American families and individuals in transition?

f. Specific competencies necessary for satisfactory adjustment to Chinese culture and conditions in Shenyang. Staff and participants identify these competencies together. Many will already have been measured on the OAI. This is one point where the results of the OAI, which were studied by the trainers prior to the program, can be most useful. As participants mention each attribute that is especially important in adjusting to China (patience, for example), we can ask the participants who scored highest on that competency to reflect on what it is and how they developed it. They explain what having this competency can mean, then suggest to the other participants (and trainers) how we might develop it further. By doing this, we are following one of the original principles of the program: build on strength. And we are contributing further to building this diverse participant team.

Two essential competencies for the participants, who will live isolated lives in Shenyang, might be called "self-sourcing" and "family sourcing." These terms are chosen because the employees already know that the "local sourcing" of natural resources and manufactured materials will be critical to the success of this project in China. They also know this will be difficult and will require a lot of concentration and effort, as does drawing upon one's own strengths and those of the family and the participant team. What we were doing in discussing the results of the OAI was "team sourcing." One's self, family, and team are all one has for a long time in China.

Additional competencies are the knowledge, attitudes, and skills the participants already use in social and professional situations, and which they may want to concentrate on now as they prepare for challenges in China. One critical competency is the ability to listen (ting).

g. Case stories. Our participants in this program are not much interested in academic studies. They are, however, intrigued by colorful, relevant stories. The first is the story of the Taylor family, whose experience in China was difficult, meaningful, and successful. The second case story recounts the story of the Steele family, whose experience and response were so negative that they left China after eight months. The creative and destructive dynamics of these and other family systems are diagrammed and discussed. Each couple in the program considers the patterns and *potential* of their own family, anticipates the consequences in China, and plans accordingly. They do this together, in private, guided by an uncomplicated instrument created especially for this purpose.

14. **Planning Encouraging Entrance Strategies that Will Work for Each Participant and Family.**

a. Lessons from previous moves. Participants return to the most difficult moves they have made in their lives so far (chosen at the beginning of session 13). They recall as clearly as they can specific strategies they used that helped them, their spouses, and their children. They also clarify the things they did that did *not* help and those they now know they should have done. They discuss as many of these as they wish. Each participant then recalls specific actions others took (spouse, children, friends) that helped, actions which definitely did not help, and actions that would have been productive but no one took. These are discussed to whatever extent participants wish. Findings from recent research on stress management and health maintenance are introduced where relevant as participants raise the various issues.

b. Personal strategies. Participants plan and write down in a special section of their Strategy Sheet their own entrance strategies, specifying the specific steps they want to take during the first three months in Shenyang in order to ensure their own successful adjustment.

c. Couples' strategies. Guided by another special instrument, the couples (in private) consider their goals as a couple and the strengths and needs each partner brings to their first three months in Shenyang. They agree on what they can do, and will do, for one another, what they will do with one another to further strengthen their relationship, and what they will do together for their children.

d. Film. Participants and trainers discuss Going International film number three *(Beyond Culture Shock)* that is described beginning on page 95. Participants reconsider and refine their entrance strategies.

e. Coming home. Some of the participants have experienced returning to the same place after moving away. They explain what returning is like. Some of the background readings and the American resource persons described the unexpected difficulties of readjusting. The research on the reentry process is summarized. The participants' entrance strategies are reviewed, and the relevance of these strategies to reentry is demonstrated. The cultural insights, adaptation attitudes, and integrating skills developed during adjustment to the foreign environment are clarified. The value of these as the participants readjust to American culture and reintegrate into their home communities, families, and organizations is illustrated. Listening is now more important than ever.

This session comes at the close of one day of the program. The participants need some time to themselves at this point.

15. Creating (or Fragmenting) Your Foreign Community.

a. Critical incidents. These will simulate actual situations participants are likely to face within the foreign community in Shenyang. Constructive ways to deal with them will be discussed.

b. Consolidating the participant team. Living in Shenyang will give the participants an opportunity, probably the only such opportunity during their lives, to create the kind of group they most want to be a part of. While affirming their diversity, they now decide on the norms and standards for their group, what they stand for and what they stand against as a group, and what they will tolerate among their members and what they will not.

Participants then consider how they can continue building their team. They are given the graph from the OAI on which the averages of the whole group are plotted. This profile represents the strengths and possible weaknesses of the team. One trainer leads a discussion on how the team can take advantage of its strengths in China, the possible consequences of those attributes on which it scored the lowest, and what it can do as a team to develop those.

c. Contributing to the foreign community. The characteristics of small, isolated clusters of foreigners are illustrated: the rich diversity of nationalities (with the possibility of fascinating, lifelong friendships), together with the rumors, gossip, griping, and cliques (with tendencies toward conflict and demoralization). Participants then confirm the values and commitments they want to live by as a part of this community and the kind of influence they want to have on it.

d. Chinese strategies for building communities. Participants and trainers recall the opening dinner of the program. A Chinese banquet is, in important respects, a Chinese community. As they reflect on the banquet, participants will discover implications for the formation and sustenance of their own foreign community. The Chinese Profile of values, attitudes, and patterns of communication, which has been constructed during the program, is reviewed. Traditional Chinese insights into conflict, harmony, and interpersonal relations are more fully grasped, guan xi more deeply understood.

e. Specific strategies. Participants map out the steps they will take to continue building their team and to contribute to their new community as foreigners in Shenyang. They do this first individually, then in small groups, and finally as a whole team.

Connecting, Reviewing, Confirming

16. Consolidating Participants' Learning.

a. Conversation with an expatriate in Shenyang. Through an amplified speaker phone, the participants speak directly with a member of the foreign community in Shenyang. The participants' questions and concerns about living in Shenyang, seven thousand miles from home, which have not yet been addressed in the program, have been faxed to this person, the on-site contact. They will be dealt with now during this conversation. This person will also provide a summary of current developments in Shenyang and in the foreign community and will offer some further suggestions to the participants as they prepare to depart. This person will meet each participant at the airport in Shenyang.

b. *Participant Record.* The insights, guidelines, and plans generated by the participants during the program are bound in an attractive, convenient packet and presented to them. These are reviewed and discussed briefly. The *Record* contains

- ❖ a photograph of the participants and staff;
- ❖ participants' names (plus accompanying children's names) and addresses and phone numbers before they leave for China, and the name and phone number of the on-site contact;
- ❖ Participant Profile;
- ❖ Chinese Profile;
- ❖ Communication Guidelines;
- ❖ Entrance strategies (which were discussed); and
- ❖ humorous highlights of the program (put together by two participants with an especially good sense of humor).

c. Most significant learning from the program. Participants decide on this first individually, then as couples, and, finally, as a whole team.

d. The design of the program as a source of learning. Explain how the communication style and content have moved from low context (American) to high context (Chinese). Demonstrate how the growth of the participants and the evolution of their group has followed, in significant ways, classic Confucian and Taoist principles.

e. Return to the program theme ("Things Go Better with *Guan Xi*"). Discover where this concept represents the participants' most significant learning. Expand the theme so it represents much of their learning and planning. Suggest that in its expanded form this may become their theme and focus for their first two months in China.

f. Confirmation of the full meaning for the participants of the program's cornerstone: listening—to themselves, their spouses, their team members, other foreigners, and especially to the Chinese—more deeply and more accurately than they ever have before.

g. Closing. As the requirement to change, placed on the participants by the foreign environment, has become more acutely clear as the program has progressed, some participants, understandably, may have begun to resist and even resent such demands that they change. Some ask, with increasing urgency, "How much must I change?" A lot? A little? No one can answer that question. It's difficult to say. A more productive question is "*What* must I change?" Specific areas can be identified and addressed.

The best question, however, as participanats begin a major transition in their lives, is "What must I *not* change?" The trainers have been asking this question indirectly in a variety of ways, on behalf of the resource persons and the participants, throughout the program in order to affirm the participants' current strengths and to balance the inevitable pressures to change. Each of us has a core within us, that which makes us distinctly us, some basic values and ultimate commitments, the rock upon which we stand. To the extent that we are clear on our core and begin now to affirm it, and continue affirming and strengthening it throughout our transition, we are then free to change anything else—everything else if necessary. Those who do not have an established center in their lives can be thrown off by the slightest wind.

Each couple and each family has a center. The trainers now ask participants to think quietly about the center of their relationship as husband and wife, as a family. They are also asked to consider the essential qualities that make them distinctive as a couple, as a family; those fundamental values and commitments that the couple will hold to firmly and protect no matter what the challenges, no matter where the destination, be it Shenyang, Cairo, Buenos Aires, or back to Houston. Anywhere. If they are clear on this and continually confirm their primary relationships, these relationships will be secure and resilient, and they will be well prepared for the foreign environment.

This group of trainers has been developing a stable core, some central values, and its own ways of being and working together. The dinners they have enjoyed together during the week, the resource persons they have gotten to know, the situations they have discussed, and the things they have accomplished in the last eight days are all part of this process. At this point, participants are asked to reflect on what is distinctive about this group, different from other groups they have been a part of. What has become important to the group? What are some of the assets of the group at this point? The participants respond.

Then each of the trainers suggests special attributes of this group which they have discovered and have been indirectly affirming during the program. They also point out particular strengths of this group that the participants themselves probably could not see, strengths which will enable the whole group, and each of its members, to be resilient and creative during their two years in the People's Republic of China.

17. **Evaluation of Program.** A review and evaluation questionnaire, followed by discussion. The second reading is taken of participants' perceptions of the Chinese people and the Chinese government.

18. **Celebration and Farewell.** A Chinese banquet including appropriate closing toasts.

Follow-Up Programs, Evaluation, and Research

Much of the value of a culture-specific predeparture program will be lost and much of the participants' learning will be extinguished if it is not consistently reinforced, applied, and deepened. Building intercultural competence is a daily process, requiring attention, discipline, and discovery over many years.

1. *Professional Development Program (for Employees).*

The predeparture program outlined above has prepared individuals and couples for their initial entrance into China. It will enable them to go through their early phases of adjustment more confidently and successfully. Cultural adjustment, however, does not guarantee effective performance on the job. Consider the many Americans in their organizations in the United States who are extremely well adjusted to the culture (it is their own, after all) but who are not effective in working with others and cannot really carry out their professional responsibilities.

In culture-specific training, therefore, we must identify the professional intercultural skills required for our participants on their particular project. These may be in negotiation, communication with a local joint-venture partner, supervision, marketing and selling, training, or cooperation with a local counterpart. This requires a separate Professional Strengths, Needs, and Tasks Assessment.

Based on the results of this special assessment, the trainers have planned a three-day program on cross-cultural technology transfer for our China project. It will follow shortly after the predeparture program for couples and will build on relevant parts of it. The Participant Profile and the Chinese Profile will be reexamined and expanded to connect directly with the professional responsibilities of the employees. This program's objectives, design, content, staff, methods, and materials will be different from the couples' program and will address specifically the employees' competence for their cross-cultural jobs. Methods will include a specially designed simulation.

2. *Cross-Cultural Communication Workshops (for Employees and Chinese Counterparts).*

The best way for Chinese and Americans to learn how to work well together is for them to work well together (in a carefully structured, low-risk, enjoyable environment with experienced, culturally informed process facilitators).

One month after the employees arrive in China, they will meet away from the plant for two days with the Chinese with whom they work. Americans and Chinese will learn about one another *from* one another (their cultural backgrounds, life experiences, education, expectations of one another, and their attitudes toward work, efficiency, accountability, quality, safety, and other critical areas). They will discover *with* one another how to build a productive multicultural organization. This will be the first of an integrated series of workshops. One will be conducted every three months for the duration of the project.

3. *Assessment and Planning Sessions (for Participants Who Were in Predeparture Program Together).*

Two months after their arrival, the participants will reconvene for a day and a half during which they will evaluate their predeparture program; discuss how their entrance strategies are working; share the lessons they have learned so far about individual, couple, family, and team adjustment; exchange resources discovered so far in Shenyang; plan the next phase of their adjustment; and recommit themselves to creating a constructive expatriate community and to integrating, where they can, with the Chinese community. This will be the first of an integrated series of assessment and planning sessions, one to be held each three months for the duration of the project.

4. *Research on Perceptual Change.*

Toward the end of the second assessment and planning session (about five months into their assignment), the participants will record again their perceptions of Chinese people and the Chinese government. They will do so again at the one-year point. These data will be put with the data gathered before and at the close of the predeparture program, analyzed, then graphically displayed with implications explained for the participants themselves, for their organization, and for the design of subsequent predeparture and follow-up training programs. These data will be aggregated over the years, published, and presented periodically at summer institutes and international conferences.

Contexts in Which This Program Has Been Used Successfully

This basic format has been used in multinational corporations involved in China and (with different content and resource persons) in companies with operations in Taiwan, Korea, Malaysia, and Saudi Arabia. Since 1979 about five hundred personnel and spouses have participated.

This program has also been used with good results in condensed form for demonstration purposes. It has been condensed to two days as a part of a course, "Cross-Cultural Communication for International Managers," at the American Graduate School of International Management (Thunderbird). It has been condensed further for the workshop, "Cross-Cultural Training in International Corporations," at the Summer Institute on Intercultural Communication in Portland, Oregon. And it has been condensed to a half day in order to demonstrate integrated, experience-based training for managers considering cross-cultural training for their employees.

Problems to Be Avoided by Trainers

Assuming that this program equips employees to be much more effective in their jobs. It does not. This program concentrates on cultural adjustment, not professional performance. It does provide an excellent basis, however, for programs that should follow: organization-specific and job-specific intercultural training. Both kinds of training (for adjustment and for performance) are necessary for intercultural competence.

Underestimating the importance of language in communication. This program concentrates on the cultural dimensions of interaction, not language. Where written and spoken language is introduced, it is to assist in visual and auditory orientation and to provide insights into the culture. If the Strengths, Needs, and Tasks Assessment indicates that use of the language is important, systematic language training should be provided. If the language training builds upon this program and is integrated with it (returning, for example, to the same role plays and deepening cultural insights gained), the language training will be more effective. The integration will also make the intercultural training more effective by more firmly anchoring the participants' new insights and skills.

Overlooking single adults. This program is designed primarily for couples. Program staff must be careful to mobilize the unique resources of the single adults for the benefit of the whole group. They must also address the special concerns of these adults.

Overlooking the children. If children will be accompanying some of the participants, a separate children's program (or two separate programs if the age range is wide) should be designed and conducted by two trainers experienced in working with children in cultural transition. This should be integrated with the adults' program at appropriate points (for example, during some of the audiovisuals of the country, during some of the language learning and practice, and during some of the planning of family entrance strategies).

Overload. There is a lot in this program. It is usually manageable, conceptually and emotionally, for the participants. The stress that a program places on participants depends not so much on what is done but the *way* it is done, especially the way it is integrated. If there is continuity in staff, a supportive climate, and a design that flows easily from one phase to the next, the participants can usually concentrate, contribute, assimilate, and enjoy. The free afternoon midway through the program helps ensure that they can. Nevertheless, the staff must, as in any program, continually monitor energy levels and abilities to absorb and contribute, then make adjustments in the pace, sequence, and depth as appropriate.

Trying to do an eight-day program in three days. Often, this amount of time is not available. The program designers must then, as always, begin with the Strengths, Needs, and Tasks Assessment. The major priorities (of the organization, the host nationals, and the participants) must be determined. Then fewer objectives are established, a simpler design is created, fewer staff members are selected, and fewer methods and materials are chosen or developed. The result is another program, based on the same principles, which is exactly consistent with the strengths, needs, and tasks of the participants and with consideration to the time and financial and other constraints that are given. If a program is to be highly effective, in other words, it must be re-created each time it is requested.

References

Culturgram. Provo, UT: David M. Kennedy Center for International Studies, Brigham Young University.

Drucker, Peter. "Making Strength Productive." In *The Effective Executive,* 71–99. New York: Harper and Row, 1967.

Heider, Fritz. *The Psychology of Interpersonal Relations.* New York: Wiley, 1958. See also Susan T. Fiske and Shelley E. Taylor. *Social Cognition.* 2d ed., 472–75. New York: McGraw-Hill, 1991.

Heider, John. *The Tao of Leadership.* New York: Bantam, 1985.

Hersey, John. *The Call: An American Missionary in China.* New York: Alfred A. Knopf, 1985.

Hobart, Alice Tisdale. *Oil for the Lamps of China.* New York: P. F. Collier & Son, 1933.

Resources

Landis, Dan, ed. *International Journal of Intercultural Relations.* New York: Pergamon.

Landis, Dan, and Rabi S. Bhagat, eds. *Handbook of Intercultural Training.* 2d ed. Thousand Oaks, CA: Sage, 1996.

The primary resources for this program are Chinese men and women from the People's Republic of China now living in the United States, expatriates in Shenyang, returned expatriates (who have already learned some of what the participants want to learn), audiovisual materials (including selections from PBS programs on China), books, periodicals and newsletters from and about China, and the trainers' own experience.

The essential resources, however, are the only ones which the participants can continually draw upon during their two years in Shenyang: themselves. This is why the program concentrates on the participants' experience prior to and during the program, especially their experience with the Chinese resource persons and with Chinese culture and language as they begin to come to terms with it, and, of course, with one another. So the program closes as it began, with guan xi and the importance of concentrating our ears, minds, eyes, and hearts on 聽 .

Appendix A

Program Planning Questionnaire
(Strengths, Needs, and Tasks Assessment Questionnaire)

Cross-Cultural Program on Shenyang, China

Date

To each participant:

This program is for you. As the directors of this program, we want to be sure that each phase of the program is very interesting and useful for you.

In order to design a program that builds on your strengths and directly addresses your concerns, we would like to ask you for some information about yourself and your family. Therefore, we would appreciate your completing this questionnaire.

What you write here is confidential. Only the two of us will read your responses (and we will read them carefully). A summary of all participants' responses, without any names, will be discussed with our resource persons (who are Chinese or have had experience in China) as we plan with them how they can contribute the most to you and the other participants.

Please return the questionnaire with your responses WITHIN THE NEXT TWO DAYS. You may use the enclosed envelope or fax the questionnaire to us at the following number:

We look forward to meeting you and discussing a variety of important subjects with you.

Names of Trainers
Organization

1. Name: _____ Telephone (W) _____

2. Country of birth: _____ Telephone (H) _____

3. Age: _____

4. Gender: _____ male
   _____ female _____

5. Undergraduate college or university (if any): _____
   Major field of study: _____

6. Additional professional training (if any): _____

7. Current residence:

   _____
        city   state/province   country

8. Your first language: _____

   This program will be conducted in English. How much difficulty will you have understanding English and speaking in English?

   _____much _____some _____a little _____no difficulty

9. Have you lived in any country other than your own? _____ yes _____ no
   If yes, which countries and for how many years? e.g., <u>Spain</u> (5)

   _____ ( ), _____ ( ), _____ ( )

10. Have you been to Shenyang recently? _____ yes _____ no

    If yes, for how long? _____

    What are your impressions of

    a. the city? _____

    _____

    b. the people? _____

    _____

    c. the job site? _____

11. On what date will you probably move to China? _____

12. What are your concerns (if any) about leaving and being separated from family members and friends when you move to China?

    _____

    _____

13. Will you be taking children with you? _____ yes _____ no
    If yes, what are their names and ages? e.g., <u>Mary</u> (2.5)

    _____ ( ), _____ ( ), _____ ( )

    If you have any special concerns regarding your children in China, what are your concerns?

    _____

    _____

14. Do you know where you will be living in Shenyang? _____ yes _____no
    If yes, please describe: _____

    _____

15. How long do you plan to live in China? _____

16. What are your most important *personal goals* during the assignment?

    a. _____

    b. _____

17. What are your *goals for your family* during your time in China?

    a. _____

    b. _____

Spouse

18. Will you be leaving a job in order to go to China? _____yes _____no

19. During your first three months in China, what will your primary responsibilities be?

    a. _____

    b. _____

20. Please choose and describe one specific situation during your first three months in China in which it will be important that you function comfortably and very effectively:

    _____

    _____

21. What activities are you considering outside the home while you are living in China?

    _____

    _____

22. What outside activities are most enjoyable and fulfilling for you where you are living now?

    _____

    _____

    (Please go to question 29)

Employee

23. During your first three months in China, what will your primary responsibilities be?

    a. _____

    b. _____

24. To whom will you report in China? _____
                                                name/position

25. How many people will report directly to you? _____
    What are their nationalities and approximate ages? e.g., <u>Chinese</u> (58)

    _____ (   ), _____ (   ), _____(   )

    _____ (   ), _____ (   ), _____(   )

26. Please choose and describe one specific situation involving Chinese colleagues during your first three months in which it is important that you function comfortably and very effectively:

    _____

    _____

    _____

27. What activities are you considering outside your work and outside your home while you are living in China?

     _____

     _____

28. What outside activities are most enjoyable and fulfilling for you where you are living now?

     _____

     _____

Both Spouse and Employee

29. As you think about living in China for the full term of your assignment, what are your biggest concerns? (Please be as specific as possible.)

     a. _____

     b. _____

     c. _____

30. How much (if anything) have you done to prepare for this assignment?

     _____much _____some _____a little _____very little

     If you have done some preparation, what has that been?

     _____ read books: number of books _____ and (approximate) titles:

     _____

     _____ talked with individuals/couples who have been in China.

     _____ other initiatives (please describe): _____

     _____

31. Have you participated in a cross-cultural training program before?

     _____ yes _____ no

     If yes, what *specifically* was most valuable for you in that program?

     _____

     What *specifically* was least valuable for you?

     _____

32. Cross-cultural insights and skills can be developed through a variety of methods. From which method(s) do you learn the *most*?

     _____ lectures

     _____ presentations that involve participants

     _____ case studies

     _____ discussion with other participants

     _____ discussion with knowledgeable individuals brought in

     _____ experiential methods (simulations, role plays, etc.)

From which method(s) do you learn the *least?*

_____ lectures

_____ presentations that involve participants

_____ case studies

_____ discussion with other participants

_____ discussion with knowledgeable individuals brought in

_____ experiential methods (simulations, role plays, etc.)

33. What subjects could we cover and what could we do during this program that would be especially interesting and useful to you?

    a. _____

    b. _____

34. How much do you feel you need a cross-cultural training program to help you prepare for living and working in China?

    _____very much _____some _____a little _____not at all

35. In addition to what you have written on this questionnaire, what else would you like the program directors and staff to keep in mind as we plan and conduct this program for you?

    a. _____

    b. _____

36. Please make any other comments you would like.

    _____

    _____

    _____

    _____

We appreciate the time and thought you have put into completing this questionnaire and planning this program. We will do our best to design an enjoyable, valuable program for you.

Appendix B

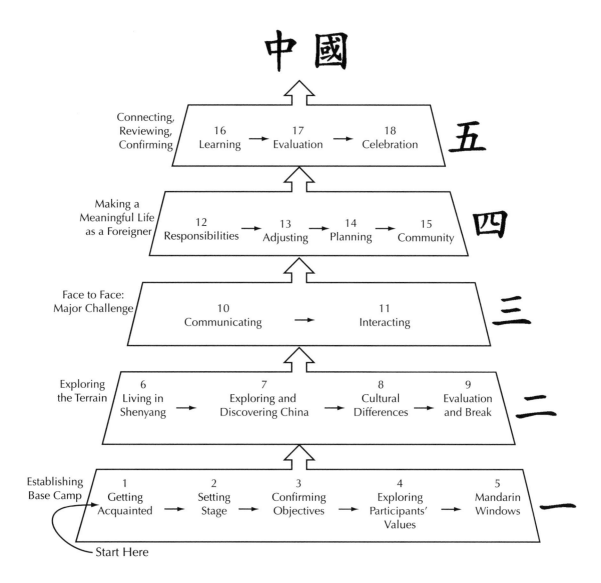

Program Itinerary

Appendix C

Final Evaluation

Cross-Cultural Program on Shenyang, China

[Program Dates]

1. What are the two *most valuable things* you have gotten out of this program?

   a. _____

   b. _____

2. Generally speaking, what do you feel the program has been for you? (Check as many as apply.)

_____ helpful	_____ fun
_____ stimulating	_____ frustrating
_____ confusing	_____ encouraging
_____ motivating	_____ discouraging
_____ boring	_____ challenging
_____ reassuring	_____ intimidating
_____ tiring	_____ other _____
_____ informative	

3. To what extent have the *program leaders* [names] responded to your particular interests and concerns? (Circle the appropriate number.)

   [not at all]   0   1   2   3   4   5   [exactly]

4. Please comment on the program leaders.

   [Name]: _____

   [Name]: _____

5. Several *resource persons* have been involved in the program [names]. Consider for a moment your sessions with them. How much have they, together, contributed to your learning?

   [not at all]   0   1   2   3   4   5   [a great deal]

6. Please comment on the resource persons (either individually or together).

   _____

   _____

   _____

7. During the first day of this program, we discussed the *program objectives* and the specific competencies you would develop. Some of these are given below. Please indicate the extent to which you have been able to develop each competency during the program. (Circle the appropriate number. Use the following scale.)

[not at all] 0 1 2 3 4 5 [a great deal]

a. Explain your own culture and background to Chinese contacts in a concise and facilitative manner.   0 1 2 3 4 5

b. Analyze accurately some of the reasons for the behavior and perceptions of Chinese men and women.   0 1 2 3 4 5

c. Communicate comfortably and effectively with a variety of Chinese in Shenyang and learn from them.   0 1 2 3 4 5

d. Take specific steps to deal constructively with culture fatigue and role shock.   0 1 2 3 4 5

e. Demonstrate commitment to the team going to Shenyang, respect members' differences, draw upon members' resources, and serve as a reliable team member yourself.   0 1 2 3 4 5

f. Carry out your responsibilities as a marriage partner and parent, or a friend to expatriate families, in supportive and creative ways.   0 1 2 3 4 5

g. Contribute significantly to your community, both in Shenyang and back home.   0 1 2 3 4 5

8. During your first three months in Shenyang, what two things do you think you will now do *differently* as a result of your participation in this program? Please be specific.

a. _____

b. _____

9. *Overall,* how valuable has this program been for you?

[not at all] 0 1 2 3 4 5 [a great deal]

10. What *changes* would you suggest to make this program more interesting and useful for other individuals in the company going to Shenyang?

a. _____

b. _____

11. Please make whatever other comments you would like.

_____

_____

_____

Adapting Intercultural Methods for Training across Cultures

Sheila Ramsey

Many intercultural trainers find themselves training people from a variety of cultures or training in cultures other than their own. Whomever we work with and wherever we work, we find that developing effectiveness in working across cultures requires an openness to change on a deeply personal level. This openness can create feelings of vulnerability. Additionally, an intercultural trainer is often cast in the role of a guide and counselor in transformations of major proportions. In order to create the "response-ability," trust, and credibility through which change can occur, a trainer must adapt to a variety of culturally specific training styles (Ramsey, Hofner, and Shimakawa 1988).

Adapting Training: The Issues

Several case studies will illustrate the importance of adapting intercultural methods to cultures other than one's own.

Incident: It is midsemester in an ESL class at an American university. A student of Czechoslovakian background who grew up in Argentina approaches the teacher.

"What qualifications do you have for teaching this class?"

"Why are you asking?" asks the teacher with a smile.

"Because you aren't teaching. You are just asking questions and writing what we say on the board."

The teacher continues the interaction by inquiring about the student's views on teaching and learning and by discussing some American approaches such as counselor-learning, adult education, and experiential learning.

Incident: An American professor is lecturing to a class of Japanese undergraduates. Ten minutes into the lecture, he pauses to ask,

"Any questions?"

Pause. Silence and more silence.

"Well, I guess no one is thinking very deeply about this topic."
He continues with his lecture.

Incident: A Japanese man and an American woman are cotraining in two programs. The first audience is made up of Japanese businessmen, and the topic is negotiating with Americans. The second program, immediately following, is for Americans doing business in Japan. At the close of the four-day sessions, the trainers commented about the programs.

American: "I knew it was me up there, but comparing the two programs, I really felt like a different person. Actually, even though I was more familiar with the style the Americans expected, the Japanese one was easier. I mean it was more evenly paced, we actually followed the plan, things were more ordered...I enjoy that American quick, spontaneous, answer questions on the spot, 'gotta keep them reined in' approach too, but it wears me out."

Japanese: "It wears me out too! And I get impatient when they don't listen until we finish and want to know an answer *right now* without looking deeper."

At the Heart of Our Work

These incidents illustrate a theme that lies at the heart of intercultural work: we cannot separate our product from the processes in which it is anchored. The preparation, design, implementation, and evaluation of our efforts will speak our intended meaning as loudly (and perhaps more loudly at times) than will the literal *content* of our programs. If we intend our programs to be of the highest quality and to speak to our audiences in ways they can receive most effectively, then our ability to adapt our methods to the cultural specificity of an audience is a matter of ethical concern.

We wish for our audiences to explore empathy and observation skills, increase their abilities to perceive the world from alternate perspectives, and learn to build relationships and accomplish tasks in these alternative realities. And yet, will we question our own favorite assumptions behind strategies we use to convey these themes? Will we conceive and deliver training by methods different from those we deem most effective, familiar, and comfortable? Can we actually *do* in the very act of design and delivery what it is that we are training about?

Another question arises: what kind of alternative perspectives do intercultural trainers need? One European colleague suggests the North American approach can be seen as a cultural preference resulting from specific value orientations.

> The systems perspective and the cultural framework model (value orientations, iceberg model of culture, etc.) seem to have been widely adopted in the training field as the way to conceptualize and teach intercultural communication "theory." It has affected the nature and sequencing of global training objectives which are now also almost standard: create awareness of difference (using an experiential exercise); describe difference and promote sensitivity to difference; and, finally, develop proficiency in dealing with difference. American assumptions as to trainer and trainee roles and motivations are built into the "standard" training ap-

proaches. A partial list of these assumptions flows directly from the "American" value orientations we use in training to develop self-awareness: people are curious, they naturally wish to grow and change in a supportive environment; they will readily self-disclose; they will take responsibility for their own learning, etc. So what we really have here is a cultural preference embedded in an approach, as the deductive French are quick to point out, especially when they refuse to play "naive games" in training contexts. An American trainer may diagnose this as "resistance to training," "fear of engaging affect." Yet who is to say the French are wrong? (Haeberle 1993)

In his discussion of trainer competencies, Michael Paige (1993) places the issue of cognitive and behavioral flexibility in an ethical framework.

What characterizes ethical pedagogy? For example, are there certain types of learning activities (such as experiential simulations) that would be inappropriate under certain circumstances?...an ethical trainer will seek to establish a climate of trust and will strive to fit the learning environment to the learning styles of the clients. (175, 177)

Today, thanks to personal experience and guidance from veterans in our field, intercultural trainers are at least conceptually aware of the importance of not designing a training program from a "common sense" perspective. We know that a "what fits for clients in my native culture" approach cannot be applied to different cultural arenas using the method of direct translation.

Dynamic Equivalence

When we have achieved a certain level of conceptual awareness, we begin to ask critical questions which point us in useful directions: Will Japanese participate in simulations? Shall I only lecture to the French? How much professional distance and formality do I need to keep as I work with mainland Chinese or Taiwanese? As we ask such questions, we are looking for perspectives that can move us toward a *dynamic equivalence* rather than a *direct translation* approach (to borrow from terms used in language translation).

In language translation theory, the ideal of dynamic equivalence involves modifying the original text to produce an effect on the reader similar to that experienced by the reader of the original. The translator's attention is focused on the intended effect rather than on the literal content of a message. Modifications are made with great care given to the thinking style, feelings, behaviors, and preferences of the reader in each language and culture (Nida 1964). The translator must move below surface structural concerns to access essential meaning and place this meaning within the appropriate context to create equivalence.

In application to intercultural training, a trainer willing to modify programs for use in a variety of cultural backgrounds might focus on the dynamic equivalence of *effect* rather than the direct translation of instructional *content*. But how is this accomplished? How can we go about creating the dynamic equivalent form of a training program for use with our German, Taiwanese, or Chilean clients?

In approaching this question, there are two important considerations. First, we must be sure that we are sufficiently prepared, doing our homework in learning the cultural specifics of the client relationship and participant expectations. Second, we must consider our own abilities as practitioners and remain mindful of the interactive nature of our work, paying particular attention to relationships established between ourselves and participants.

Adapting Methods for Training with Different Cultural Groups

As we encounter program participants with cultural identities different from our own, we are challenged to rethink and reshape our approaches at the most subtle levels of detail. Now we must do our own work within the contexts of the ambiguity and uncertainty we verbally encourage others to tolerate. The potential for increasing our own awareness and transforming our training style is clearly within our reach; the excitement as this potential becomes real is, for many in our field, highly motivating and valued.

Doing Our Homework

The task of preparation has several components. It is important to be very clear about the larger context of the work to be undertaken. Specifically, we need to

❖ know the client's reasons for inviting our assistance,

❖ arrive at clear agreement about the overall purpose of the training or consultation as well as about detailed programmatic objectives,

❖ know how our client has described us to the trainees with whom we will be working, and,

❖ understand our trainees' expectations regarding the work to be done.

We also need to gather as much information as possible about every culture represented among our participants. If the context is corporate, are the participants engineers or human services professionals? Do they have managerial or staff responsibilities? If the context is educational, what disciplines and degrees are represented? Do many of the participants have international experience?

While all of this information is important to a trainer preparing for any training program, it is particularly vital when working across cultures, for it is our baseline in deciding how to modify our familiar ways of working. These decisions can be made in the design stage, but sometimes they must be made in the very process of delivery, with little time to plan.

We should also gather information from colleagues who have conducted intercultural training in our culture of interest, and ideally from colleagues who are both native and nonnative to that culture. For instance, comparing how American and Chinese trainers work with Taiwanese trainees could provide additional illumination for our decisions. It could help us to locate the parameters regarding value orientation, learning styles, and expectations about trainer-trainee relationships within which we will work. Such information can also give us some sense of the latitude, or allowance for difference, present in the group. That is, how willing are they to participate in an intercultural learning event structured in ways that are untraditional and unfamiliar to them?

Illustration: An American Training in Taiwan and Mainland China

In China, a respect for authority, attention to saving face, and a didactic tradition of teaching are cultural parameters that will strongly influence the effectiveness of any training program. One American trainer learned that Chinese university students could come to enjoy and learn from experiential exercises (which at first shocked them) only after they developed trust in her.

She began her work with them by using more standard ways of delivering information and then slowly introduced experiential methods, careful to return again to a more didactic approach upon sensing signs of discomfort. She learned to accept the students' need to respect her and did not attempt to create a more informal learning atmosphere. It became clear that asking students in the beginning of a program to tell her what they wanted to learn was perceived to mean that she did not know how to teach and was asking for help. However, this question was received more as she had intended after some time had passed and her credibility more clearly established. She learned that pointing out mistakes in the group, for the sake of learning from mistakes, was never received positively. Criticism or negative feedback could be approached (if at all) only through individual or perhaps paired interactions (Liu 1995; McCoy 1995).

Illustration: Trainer Credibility in Japan

A study of the learning preferences of over two thousand Japanese management trainees (Ramsey, Hofner, and Shimakawa 1988) suggests how nonverbal dimensions of a program influence perceptions of trainer credibility. How is it that a non-Japanese trainer may be judged as competent from a Western perspective and yet not perceived in the same manner by the Japanese? What are the dimensions of such Japanese perceptions in a structured learning situation? To answer these questions, we explored several variables:

Program Structure
- ❖ beginnings and endings
- ❖ timing of activities
- ❖ agenda and objectives

Material
- ❖ presentation
- ❖ usage

Trainer Style
- ❖ demeanor
- ❖ delivery

We found that in corporate settings, Japanese trainees prefer clearly marked

beginnings and endings, an explanation of agenda, procedure, and time lines—
and trainers who adhere to all of the above. Materials are expected to be bound in
manual form and be notable for aesthetic and image-conveying qualities. All
material aspects of any program benefit from remembering the Japanese appreciation for attention to detail. Preparedness and thoroughness are the messages
that need to be communicated to trainees.

Regarding demeanor and delivery, there is greater comfort with a formal style
and little self-disclosure by the trainer about his or her personal experience. American trainers may prefer to establish their credibility by talking about their achievements and clients. The Japanese would prefer that trainers list their accomplish-
ments in the written material and be more discreet in referring to them while
conducting the training program.

Delivery style also distinguishes the credible non-Japanese trainers from less
credible counterparts.

> An important element of delivery style relates to the Japanese con-
> cept of *ma*, or short silences. A trainer sensitive to the Japanese
> expectation of *ma* will check others' intentions carefully before
> taking the floor or before filling in silence with relevant examples
> or humorous quips, and will encourage short "empty" time after
> questions or others' comments so that the points may be inte-
> grated by trainees. (Ramsey, Hofner, and Shimakawa 1988, 223)

Finally, for Japanese participants, a reluctance to participate in role plays or
simulations is usually related to their lack of preparation before the event and
having to jump into the experience somewhat spontaneously.

Identifying Our Assumptions

To uncover the assumptions behind our approaches to training, we must ask,
What are we taking as common sense? One of the most subtle and pervasive
blind spots for trainers and participants alike is in the realm of how we pay attention and how we learn. Habits and expectations in both of these areas grow out of
our personal and cultural histories. At times we can almost hear participants, and
perhaps ourselves, saying, "I'll accept all the new and unfamiliar content you
have to offer, but just serve it to me so that I really feel like I am learning something." If a program's required learning style causes sufficient confusion to prompt
questions such as, "Why are we here?" and "What are we supposed to be learning?" then the credibility of the leader might soon be in doubt.

As much as we may accept the premise that we must identify and examine the
assumptions upon which our training is based, it sometimes takes the actual experience of contrast and unfamiliarity to trigger a reaction. Such is the nature of
certainty and its loosening. We can become so enmeshed in our habitual ways of
training that we cannot even see these ways as habitual.

> Tradition is not only a way to see and act, but also a way to con-
> ceal. Tradition consists of all those behaviors that…have become
> obvious, regular and acceptable. Since they do not require reflec-
> tion to be generated, they are invisible unless they fail.… Only
> when some interaction dislodges us—such as suddenly being re-

located to a different cultural environment—and we reflect upon it, do we bring forth new constellations of relation that we explain by saying that we were not aware of them or that we took them for granted. (Maturana and Varela 1992, 242)

Impact of Our Assumptions. Mismatched assumptions about learning style can diminish the perceived credibility of the trainer. As we know, a partner to credibility is trust. If we expect trainees to move through confusion or hesitancy and be willing to learn in new ways, their trust in us is paramount.

I recall such a mismatch of assumptions that came close to completely undermining the credibility of the program leaders. My colleague, John Condon, and I were once training non-Japanese executives to work with the Japanese. Being new to business culture, we began with an experience more appropriate for college professors than for corporate presidents. After receiving the "Why are we here?" feedback, we spent until the early hours of the next morning redesigning the entire program.

> We were as blind as our clients in our out-of-awareness assumptions about how real learning should occur and how you create interest and establish rapport. We believed that one must first learn about self in order to be effective in another culture and that an interpersonal focus is the foundation for any effective interaction. All this was carried over from the academic experience and placed directly into a context which did not operate from these assumptions. (Ramsey 1996)

Similarly, Cornelius Grove reports a reaction to intercultural work by Africans from a variety of countries that further challenges us to examine habituated basic tenets of intercultural work. These professionals resisted the idea that people from different backgrounds should attempt to appreciate each other's differences or that flexibility is to be encouraged. In particular, Grove notes:

> Africans apparently dislike our suggestion that they should try to understand any social phenomenon without first making a judgment about it. For many of them, "to understand" is to be affected by the thing you are understanding. One must judge the thing first lest one be affected by it in a bad way. Perhaps this attitude arose out of the colonial experience.... Is it possible that this approach, caring and oh-so-gentle though it seems to us, is fundamentally ill-suited to certain peoples who already have had one horrendous experience with Westerners who also were preaching a gospel of understanding and acceptance? (Grove 1988)

Working with Our Assumptions. And yet, no matter how much culture-specific data we gather about a new cultural group of participants, we still may be surprised about what happens in the training room. If we are wedded to some small variation of delivery style or program design, it is more difficult to change our approach in the midst of a program. It is our familiarity with the assumptive base of our work that provides us with a certain ease and flexibility.

One American trainer who frequently works in Europe with expatriates from all over the world says that, in general, her work in Europe is more didactic than when she works in the United States. When she uses experiential activities, she always legitimizes them by making goals, learning outcomes, and applications quite clear. In debriefing, she is careful to connect the learning outcomes to research.

When working in the United States, she notes that emotions seem to have more prominence in the postactivity discussion. In the European context, she finds that discussion about feelings does not become as involved. She may pose a question about feelings, knowing it may provide reflection for participants, but without the expectation that it will be discussed. At times, she finds herself needing to address the question, Why does it matter what we feel?

She is also sensitive to alternative styles of creating credibility for herself. When working in the U.S. context, she finds a receptivity to self-disclosure and personal storytelling by the trainer, while in the European context she places more emphasis upon her credentials (Schaetti 1995).

Illustration: An American Trainer in Germany

The experience of another American trainer in Europe offers contrast. In this case, the trainer had asked for advice in preparation of the programs. All opinions pointed, once again, to the comfort with and expectation for a more logical, conceptual, and didactic approach. This was strongly emphasized, for the trainees were German government bureaucrats.

The trainer began with a lecture, but sensing less than full interest and involvement, moved rapidly into more practical aspects. The participants were very appreciative of a learning opportunity that enabled them to take action. Each day of the three-day program contained a simulation. In debriefing the simulations games *Ecotonos* and *Barnga*, the trainer noted that participants could easily make real-time applications and were in fact quite skilled in observing their own behavior. The participants even asked to repeat *Ecotonos* in order to use what they had learned the first time.

At the end of the program, the trainer asked the participants about her initial expectation regarding their preference for the conceptual, didactic approach. Their response, in laughter, affirmed the expectation and indicated that it was a stereotype which was not applicable in this case. Still, the trainer felt that it had been helpful to have talked to others who had worked in Europe and with Germans, specifically for the information received on how to build rapport and establish credibility. "People can learn a lot more and in more ways than they think they can. It is important to know how to show respect, to adjust behaviorally and also to trust what you feel" (Hofner Saphiere 1995). Her experience suggests that we must be so aware of our underlying assumptions that we are prepared even for the opposite of what is expected.

This example contains another important reminder. The American trainer had asked the German participants about a second specific behavior she had been told to expect, that is, Germans may take exception to and debate what is being presented. The participants indicated that yes, this is true, but only when they feel someone is being very adamant and making gross generalizations. They did not feel she was using such a style. The information she received as she prepared the program was not incorrect; it was simply not applicable as this particular training program evolved.

In order to effectively adapt our methods, we may make concerted efforts to learn from those who have gone before us about our intended audience and their expectations and preferences. However, may we be mindful of looking for generalizations that are comforting yet do not necessarily fit the context within which we will work. We suggest that our participants avoid contextually empty generalizations, and so must we.

Surely we must remember that intercultural training is an interactive experience; both participants and trainers will draw upon their cultural and personal repertoire of behaviors and act in particular ways. These ways of behaving are quite responsive to the experience of being and learning together. Accepting this involves us in the ongoing adventure of accessing our own creativity as we extend invitations for intercultural learning which our participants are eager to accept.

Conclusion

The dynamic equivalent approach to language translation rests on finding essential meaning and then placing such meaning within an appropriate context. Applying this to intercultural work requires us to anchor our work firmly in the explicit corporate or institutional culture of the client. We must also try to discover the audience's preferences and expectations about learning style. We must discover how to establish trainer credibility as well as how to build relationships and behave appropriately in a training setting.

All this information serves two purposes: (1) it helps us to identify assumptions inherent in our work, and (2) it can serve as a baseline from which we modify the design and implementation of our programs.

Remembering Ourselves

Plan as we will, as effective and responsible trainers we are engaged in a dance. When our preferred rhythm is the waltz, we may be called upon, at a moment's notice, to dance the reggae. It is our responsibility to hear the new beat and take the opportunity to change our steps. We must also consider with whom we are dancing. We hope we have as partners the client's purpose, the program objectives, and the needs and responses of the participants—rather than our own expectations and less-than-fully-conscious assumptions about how effective intercultural training should proceed.

To the extent that we dance only with our own preferences and comfort, we will be less inclined to notice when the rhythm calls for a shift. To the extent that we dance with our attention placed on inquiry and self-awareness, we are more available to try new steps.

References

Grove, Cornelius L. "To Search Again and Repeatedly." *Communique* 13, no. 4 (1988): 4.

Haeberle, Daniel. "Meta-Intercultural Communication (Intercultural Communication about Intercultural Communication)." Paper presented at SIETAR Europa's 3d Annual Symposium, Bad Nauheim, Germany, March 11–14, 1993.

Hofner Saphiere, Dianne. Personal communication, May 1995.

Liu, Lifong F. Personal communication, May 1995.

Maturana, Humberto R., and Francisco J. Varela. *The Tree of Knowledge: The Biological Roots of Human Understanding,* 242. Boston: Shambhala Press, 1992.

McCoy, Mary V. Personal communication, May 1995.

Nida, Eugene. *Towards a Science of Translation.* Holland: Brill and Leiden, 1964.

Paige, R. Michael. "Trainer Competencies for International and Intercultural Programs." In *Education for the Intercultural Experience,* edited by R. Michael Paige. Yarmouth, ME: Intercultural Press, 1993.

Ramsey, Sheila. "Creating a Context: Methodologies in Teaching and Training." In *Experiential Activities for Intercultural Learning*, vol. 1, edited by H. Ned Seelye. Yarmouth, ME: Intercultural Press, 1996.

Ramsey, Sheila, Dianne Hofner, and Yoichi Shimakawa. "The Binding of Culture: Nonverbal Dimensions of Credibility in Structured Learning Situations." In *Cross-Cultural Perspectives in Nonverbal Communication*, edited by Fernando Poyatos, 217–24. Lewiston, NY: Hogrefe, 1988.

Schaetti, Barbara. Personal communication, May 1995.

Adapting Cross-Cultural Training Methods for Different Age Groups

Lance Descourouez

There is an African proverb that goes, "Wherever something stands, something else will stand beside it." Nigerian novelist Chinua Achebe (1989) explains the proverb to mean there is no one way to anything and no absolute anything; that the world is, in effect, a world of duality. Achebe's words appeal to me because I believe they accurately depict reality. For example, children see the world differently from adults, and these worlds exist concomitantly—the children's world and the adults' world.

Conceptual Background

In the world of cross-cultural training, it is often assumed that what has worked for one group of people should work for another. One such example involves young people or children. (Throughout this chapter I use children to refer to all dependents, from young children to teenagers.) Much of the research that has led to the development of cross-cultural training has been drawn from the literature on international relocation, which has focused almost exclusively on adults, not children (see N. Adler 1991; P. Adler 1975; Church 1982; Garza-Guerrero 1974; Grove and Torbiörn 1986; Higginbotham 1979; Juffer 1986; Kohls 1996; Nagler 1977; Oberg 1960, 1972; Sargent 1970; Taft 1977; Weaver 1986).

The first step is to acknowledge what we are talking about. There are three conceptual parts to successfully adapting cross-cultural training for different ages. You need to know something about (1) the developmental process (stages of development, learning styles, and the like), (2) training (design, modification, and delivery), and (3) cross-cultural theory and knowledge.

The third part is beyond the scope of this chapter. All the books and articles mentioned above are a good place to find the substance and theory of intercultural training. In this chapter, I will focus on the other two parts: development and training.

Children and Adults Are Different

"Let's go to the ocean." Think about the differences that one could expect to see in the mind of a child or an adult on hearing this statement. Parents and adults are likely to think about sitting on the beach, taking in the whole scene with all its sounds, sights, and colors, or just basking in the warm sun and sand to experience a flood of memories. The memories might include romance—walking hand in hand through the surf with a loved one—or be philosophical, listening to the roaring waves and contemplating the small place we occupy in this majestic world. Their memories may also harken back to their childhood, when they played in this fairyland, creating untold worlds out of sand and surf.

Children, on the other hand, who are anticipating this event for perhaps the first time, have not built up a grand list of memories that simply hearing that the family is going to the ocean will trigger. They are caught up with the idea of experiencing the ocean through their senses: the strong salty taste of the water, the warmth of the sun on their backs, the grainy feel of the sand between fingers and toes, and the deafening roar of the crashing water, with its delicate trickle back from the shore and out to the ocean again.

In short, children seek to manipulate their world via the senses to experience the event; to touch it, taste it, smell it, listen to it, and most important of all, *to play with it.* In addition to their five senses, adults use a sixth sense to experience the event. The sixth sense may most appropriately be described as the wealth of experience adults bring to the event. This allows them an opportunity to react based on reflection. Herein lies the primary difference between children and adults: children have a concrete orientation; adults have an abstract orientation.

That means when we are teaching children about culture we cannot make the assumptions we would if we were teaching adults. Adults are willing to learn about different cultures, to understand the underlying nature of other people and places because "it will be good for me—I will learn more about myself and grow from the experience." Children, ages five through adolescence, want to know about the culture only insofar as it will help them assimilate: to make friends and *have fun.*

The Developmental Process

Ages 3–7: Preoperational Stage

Children between the ages of three and seven are at the stage of cognitive development commonly referred to as preoperational or symbolic functioning. They live in a world that is egocentric, concrete, and static. Using terms like "German" or "Japanese" has little meaning because such abstract inferences are currently outside of their realm of experience. Most importantly, children at this stage cannot yet understand another's point of view, although they can relate to another's emotional experience. They interpret events and information in terms of themselves. If I show a picture to a child of two other children laughing, I will likely be told about a time when he or she was laughing with another child.

One child about the age of six, who was on her way to Japan, asked me if it would hurt when her eyes changed shape. For a child at this stage *everything* is real. Although children within this age range cannot explain how one culture might appear to another, they can identify the emotional expressions of another culture and empathize in terms of their own experiences. Thus, historical approaches to cross-cultural training based on fact-finding geography or history lessons usually fall short of the intended goals. Cross-cultural training must be created and designed in a format that recognizes the developmental capabilities of the children being trained.

One way to teach children at this level is to allow them to experience geography in a personal and physical way. For example, I would instruct children at this stage of development that when they were living overseas, people would be asking them where they were from in the United States. To help them answer this question in a role-playing format, they would first *discover* that the United States was shaped like their hand and they could begin to point to the city or location they were from without having a map. Once this technique was illustrated, we could begin to use a map to discover what other countries looked like. One seven-year-old girl exclaimed, "Hey look, I'm moving to Korea and it looks like a rabbit!" Thereafter, she was always able to identify on any world map the country she was moving to and would be living in by the shape she assigned to it.

Ages 8–11: Concrete Operations Stage

Children between the ages of eight and eleven are at a stage when the formation of concrete mental operations is developed, and, therefore, simple abstract concepts can be used in training. Because the children no longer view the world strictly from their own unique vantage point, they can now solve problems which at an earlier time they could not complete. Still, their problem-solving efforts must be made and experienced in very concrete ways. They can begin planning for the future because they now begin to understand concepts such as "soon" and "later." This is a particularly good age to use role-playing methods. In addition, not only can simple maps be interpreted, but more importantly, the perspective of another viewer can be appreciated.

Ages 12–18: Formal Operations Stage

Not until the formation of conceptual thought (formal operations stage), from roughly the age of twelve through adolescence, can children begin to create new approaches in reasoning, not limited by "what is real" but to consider things that are hypothetically possible. Here, youngsters can construct a whole system of beliefs and engage in the world of ideas by reflecting on their own way of thinking and perceiving. Individuals at this stage can begin to contrast the value systems of different cultures, like that of Americans and Chinese.

During this period the teenager is capable of logical thought about what might occur rather than being restricted to actual events. This kind of thinking process enables the depth of understanding to truly synthesize cross-cultural differences and interactions. The only limitation is that not all individuals with the capacity for formal operational thought will use it consistently. Cross-cultural interactions can be overwhelming for someone who is just beginning to truly define himself or herself as a person. Adolescents often retreat somewhat in a move overseas to compensate for the level of emotional coping demanded of them.

Distinguishing One Stage from the Other

Age does not always tell the whole story. Generally speaking, development occurs at different paces. Whereas a young child may be slow to move from the preoperational to the concrete stages of development, an older child may reach the formal operations stage well ahead of other children of his or her same age (Dixon and Baltes 1986). One way to distinguish individuals at the concrete operations stage or the formal operations stage (to ensure that you are developing a training approach at the appropriate level) is to ask, "If I were visiting your country for the first time, please describe for me what to look out for—when is the situation dangerous?" Individuals at the formal operations stage are much more skilled at articulating such hypothetical settings than those at a concrete operations level. This type of question also allows one to begin to assess the level of cultural knowledge individuals may possess concerning their own culture.

In any case, children at a very early age learn to recognize differences in humans, and their interpretation of such differences will be based on the biases or prevailing attitudes of the adults and the environment around them. One such example came from an eight-year-old boy interviewed some six months after he had relocated from the United States to Belgium with his family. When I asked him about his impression of the country, his rather curt response was, "I think it is ridiculous that you have to give a waiter a tip even if the service is bad."

Children are not culture-free, which is a critical aspect to remember when developing cross-cultural training programs. In addition, children are less able to interpret and articulate their anxieties or concerns. All of these skills and abilities are being developed. While attending a cultural presentation on Japan to a group of fifth graders, I overheard one child comment to another, "I told you they were stupid, they eat with sticks!" Culture shock is a reality, be it for a child moving overseas or learning about cultural differences within his or her own classroom. As children encounter and experience unexpected responses in their social world, they are forced to deal with internal expectations that no longer apply. The developmental process is itself a type of culture shock. Children will not benefit from cross-cultural training until they are provided with both concrete experiences that create momentary perceptual imbalances and with realistic tools, designed at the appropriate developmental level to help them diagnose, understand, and cope with these differences.

Styles of Learning and Training

Just as it is important to attend to styles of learning when adapting cross-cultural training for people from different cultures, it is equally important to consider how children learn. Adults have long thought that children learn from them in a one-way manner. However, the research and the writings of Erika Landau (1976), of the Museum Haaretz in Tel-Aviv, have led to the following realization:

> The opinion that children live in a narcissistic world and seek instant gratification is not upheld when one looks at the questions posed by children. Children have much to teach us. One tends to look down on them, yet their thoughts are brighter and clearer than those of adults. Perhaps it is because they are not afraid to appear illogical or stupid, and their naive thoughts can awaken a yearning for the paradise adults have lost. (154–62)

Training based on the concept of experiential learning has existed for more than six decades. But children and adults use experience much differently. When adults attach their learning to prior experiences they will perform much better. This approach is what Malcolm Knowles (1984) calls "androgogy." According to Knowles, adults need a place where they validate their experience by using themselves as a measure of their own learning. Thus, an adult needs to learn *how to use experience.*

Older Adults

That need alone indicates why older adults require the same consideration as children and why cross-cultural training methods must be adapted at *all* age levels. Older adults may appear not to learn as quickly as younger adults or may be more resistant to it. In fact, a colleague who provides cross-cultural training for elderly diplomats describes them as being difficult to motivate and engage. In her opinion, older adults often believe they know everything already.

But current research tells a different story. In numerous studies done to assess levels of rigidity on the part of senior citizens, middle-aged adults, and younger adults, the senior citizens tended to be the least resistant group (Comfort 1976; Rosenfeld 1976). Again, the evidence on developmental patterns is clear: people move through life in an ever-increasing path from concrete to abstract—yes, you heard me right, even the elderly.

Learning a new language is one of the only areas where there is clear evidence that the younger you are, the easier it is. The best way I can explain this involves an extrapolation of the psychological term, *habituation*. Adults have simply become used to speaking a certain way. All of the physiological (vocal cords) and psychological aspects of acquiring and producing a specific language have become a habit. As any ingrained habit will make us look awkward and feel uncomfortable when trying a new way of doing something, so does beginning to speak another language (more so the older you are).

In any case, adapting training methods and developing cross-cultural training programs for older adults is not an issue of rigidity but of learning styles and developmental stages. Unless older adults are involved with a teaching and learning process that recognizes and uses their experience, they are more likely to resist training. Also, although physiological considerations are a reality, they are not a barrier. Those who want to learn a language will. Individual differences abound; yet aspects of the information available on how different age groups learn is still underutilized.

In my experience, most cross-cultural trainers tend to train others the way they themselves would like to be trained. This is why most of the approaches in cross-cultural training for younger children and older adults have been less than effective. This is also why (again based on my experience) older adults do a better job of training older adults. Older adults seem to understand intuitively the approaches that will be most effective to access and engage the knowledge and experience of someone or a group near their own age. Younger trainers can train older adults but only if they make the necessary adjustments.

Children

A child, on the other hand, needs to *experience how to learn*, an approach Knowles (1984) refers to as "pedagogy." *Pedagogy* literally means the "art and science of teaching children," since the word is derived from the Greek: *paid* meaning "child" and *agogus* meaning "leader of." The central difference between adults and children concerns aspects of intent. The goal of cross-cultural training for adults should be aimed at their developing the skill to use what they learn. Children need to develop learning skills (Malcolm 1994).

Children derive their self-identity largely from external definers such as their parents, brothers, sisters, and extended families, where they live, and what churches and schools they go to. As they mature, they increasingly define themselves in terms of the experiences they have had. For children, experience is something that happens to them; for adults their experience is who they are.

Children tend to be subject-centered in their orientation to learning (at least at school), whereas adults tend to be life-centered, task-centered, or problem-centered (Knowles). As children grow and develop, their need and capacity to be self-directing increases. They begin to use their experience in learning to identify their own readiness to learn and to organize their learning around life problems. This ability increases slowly and steadily from infancy to preadolescence, then increases rapidly during adolescence.

> The pendulum has swung from the "radiation theory" (just expose children and hope they learn) to the "carpentry theory" (just hammer knowledge into their heads). What has been missing is the understanding of how children learn. (Greenspan 1992)

Thus, cross-cultural training requires much more than cultural content and a series of training methods. Rather, an effective trainer must know how various age groups learn and then adapt his or her material to the participants at hand.

Training Starts with the Trainer

Although cross-cultural instructors for adults can be either educators or trainers or both, young people require coaches. The coach does not tell the athlete what to do but rather gives advice and counsel around the athlete's own natural approach to the sport he or she is playing. The coach focuses on recognizing and enhancing individual potential.

Coaching might not be a natural approach for many educators. For example, Lawrence C. Porter (1987) described the five phases of the learning cycle in his article "Game, Schmame! What Have I Learned?" as experiencing, data gathering, interpreting, generalizing, and applying. These phases will not mean much to most children. To transform it into coaching, I shortened the cycle to three parts (an idea my wife, Shawn, introduced me to). The experience and data collection phases become the "what" section, the interpretation and generalization phases become the "so what" section, and the application phase becomes the "now what" section. Children quickly grasp these aspects of learning, and the cycle makes sense to them.

Instructors of cross-cultural subjects need to develop what Greenspan calls "a child's core abilities to engage, focus, relate and communicate" if their goal is to provide the children with opportunities for cross-cultural understanding. All too often the approach used is one developed with adults. Thus, unknowingly the instructor is teaching above the child's or youth's developmental level and, worse yet, teaching in a one-way, top-down pedagogical manner rather than in the two-way communication style needed.

A Theoretical Foundation for Adapting Intercultural Training for Children

Much of my knowledge of cross-cultural training for children was developed during my seven years as a program manager at a cross-cultural training institute for corporate executives and their families being relocated abroad. During my time there I had the opportunity to work with approximately 5,000 families being relocated to over forty different countries. Shortly after I arrived, I was asked to develop a training program for the children, over which I would have primary responsibility for design, development, implementation, research, and evaluation. At the time I still knew very little about training design and facilitation, but I was provided with as many resources as I needed to create the best possible product.

It was important to me that everything I did be grounded in an appropriate theory to support whatever decisions I made concerning a particular approach, exercise, or activity in cross-cultural training. I discovered rather quickly that there was very little written about cross-cultural training, mobility adjustment, and identity development for children, so I was forced to develop not only an approach to training but a theoretical model upon which to ground my choices. Because there was so little available, much of what I developed was based on an intuitive sense about what would work the best. Although I have conducted several research studies to evaluate the effectiveness of the training and have worked to publish the specific approach, this is the first time I have attempted systematically to present the theory behind it.

Components of Cross-Cultural Training for Young People

Any cross-cultural training program for different age groups needs to include the following four components:
1. emotional exploration and development

2. cross-cultural interaction skill development

3. factual information

4. conceptual information

You will find a synopsis of these components illustrating key concepts for each age group in Appendix A. All four components are needed for a training program to be successful, but the amount of attention you give to each component is dependent upon the families being trained. Their particular needs determine whether you expand or contract the amount of time you spend in covering the material you have designed for each component.

1. *Emotional exploration and development.* The first component emphasizes understanding the young people being trained, taking into account all their knowledge (accurate and inaccurate), hopes, and concerns. I refer to this component as emotional exploration because it is an ongoing process that serves as a foundation for the other areas of the training. This component should start the training and be interwoven all the way through. Research indicates that children relate to differences at an emotive level first (Ramsey 1987).

Whether using structured role plays, culture-contrast sessions, simulation games, critical incidents, culture assimilators, or age-specific self-awareness inventories, you will also want to include unstructured elements. Unstructured elements in training children allow you to assess the developmental level of the child and ensure you are not going over the child's head. It is vital that the total child/individual be involved. As the exploration unfolds, constantly modify the training to ensure that skills for emotional adjustment and self-assessment are built upon and developed.

2. *Cross-cultural interaction skill development.* The cross-cultural interaction skill development component creates an opportunity to assess the child's readiness for cross-cultural interaction. A core aspect of this component involves helping the child through various culture-specific and culture-general activities to become a self-directed learner. A culture-specific activity is one that concentrates on the new country and culture. A culture-general activity is one that focuses on aspects of cross-cultural interactions that would take place in any transition to any culture or country. One of the things I have enjoyed the most is the large number of parents who have commented on how the training programs have helped their children excel in areas that go well beyond simply easing their adjustment and acculturation.

One example that comes to mind is a family that was having difficulty with their teenage son just prior to their move to Hong Kong. He was acting out, not communicating with his parents, and avoiding coming to terms with their move overseas. The parents sent a letter to me shortly after the training saying, "You did more than provide our son with short-term gains, you assisted him in aquiring long-term skills." The training had helped him not only adjust to Hong Kong but also take more responsibility in other aspects of his life, such as his social life and schoolwork.

3. *Factual information.* This component involves teaching the child factual, culture-specific information. I discovered that the culture-specific information the

child acquires is of less value than what the child learns about how to learn. Said another way, it is more important to look at what children do in response to this factual information than how much they retain about the country they are moving to. One of my favorite examples involves a delightful family with two young Vietnamese girls they had adopted when the girls were about one and two. The family was from Oklahoma and was moving to Saudi Arabia. The girls were seven and eight years old when I met them. They had just begun learning Arabic (as a part of the training) because it had been demonstrated to them that by learning some of the language they would more easily make friends with the local people. While on a tour at the Islamic Mosque in Washington, DC, we met a woman from the Middle East. I will never forget the look on the woman's face as these two Vietnamese-looking children cheerfully greeted the woman in Arabic, but with a distinct Oklahoma accent!

My point in this story is simple. If you ask an adult why they are going overseas they will often tell you, "to learn about another country and experience new things." Young people when asked the same question rarely answer that way. They are much more interested in making friends and establishing relationships. Culture-specific information is of use to them only if it helps them in this process. If the girls in this example had reacted in horror upon seeing a woman in an *abi,* or felt it was too strange, they would never have ended up learning about the country and culture. Knowing how to learn and ask questions about things that are different was of much more use to them than a grand list of memorized facts about Saudi Arabia. This brings us to the last component.

4. *Conceptual information.* Closely associated with the factual information component is the conceptual component. Where factual information provides the "what," the conceptual component offers the "why." Asking why takes you below the surface. For example, it is not just that Belgian chocolate tastes better than American chocolate or that the Japanese bow when greeting and Germans shake hands, but there is an underlying reason for the differences they will notice in their new country. Simply knowing what is different will not be enough. Therefore, a cultural analysis tool such as the learning cycle was introduced so that the child or youth could begin to understand the "why" behind the "what."

In the case of the difference between Belgian chocolate and American chocolate, an eight-year-old boy was able to use the learning cycle and construct his own understanding about the difference. He made the connection that when his mother and father took more time preparing a meal, it tasted better—thus, might it not be the case that the Belgian people took longer to prepare their chocolate than did the Americans? This was not a one-time event. Given the tools and the appropriate design, children can and do make extraordinary strides toward cross-cultural insight, understanding, and behavior.

In the conceptual component, just as with the others, the total child is emphasized because his or her values and beliefs are at issue concerning the things often viewed as weird or different. The ways in which children can develop self-directed learning skills will determine their ability to locate and interpret the reasons behind a host of strange thoughts, attitudes, and behaviors.

Training as an Art Form

Another aspect of this work I want to note is that cross-cultural training design and practice is an art form, because it is best achieved through the intuitive abilities, creativity, and communication skills that exist within the trainer. Specific techniques or tools are best understood and used by trainers who have developed their intuitive capabilities.

Let me provide you with an example. The best cross-cultural trainers for children are those who are able to capture what the child is really trying to express. This particular tool does not originate in a tool bag. Rather it is a trainer's ability to make himself or herself totally available to the participants and to be fully aware of what is taking place at any given moment. Children respond to the behaviors the trainer models. It is not what the trainer says, but how the trainer acts in a cross-cultural setting that children respond to and truly learn from. There is an intuitive quality about that skill that can only be developed over time and with experience, but one that begins with an understanding of its existence and importance in training.

Points to Consider

When I am called upon to provide training for families, I often use a checklist of issues children face during their adjustment to living in another culture (see Appendix B). Some of the items on this list suggest points to consider when you are adapting cross-cultural training for children. You must select training methods and design training programs to

- ❖ recognize and use the whole person, especially identifying the child's level of cognitive, social, and even physical development;
- ❖ assist the children in letting go of the things that inhibit their learning;
- ❖ help the children do their own personal diagnosis and help them to be responsible for their own investigation and development of cross-cultural knowledge and skills;
- ❖ create a design that is fluid and can be changed to accommodate what the children truly need in order to grow; and
- ❖ always be aware of your own cultural values, which you are consciously and unconsciously communicating to the participant.

And finally, remember that children, far more than adults, will respond to the behavior you are modeling in terms of cross-cultural interactions.

Conclusion

Because intercultural understanding is ultimately self-development,
in the end the intercultural challenge is a personal challenge.

—Anon.

Although there are numerous methods for teaching someone cross-cultural information and knowledge, the goal is really one of learning how to act as a trainer, which includes having a grounding in training theory and practice. In working with children, the key elements are to bring enthusiasm to the training situation, to remain open and humble, and to always make an effort to leave arrogance outside the door. Build an approach that allows you to keep on learning.

References

Achebe, Chinua. In *Bill Moyers: A World of Ideas*, edited by B. S. Flowers. New York: Doubleday, 1989.

Adler, Nancy T. *International Dimensions of Organizational Behavior.* 2d. ed. Boston: PWS-Kent Publishing, 1991.

Adler, Peter S. "The Transitional Experience: An Alternative View of Culture Shock." *Journal of Humanistic Psychology* 15, no. 4 (1975): 13–23.

Blohm, Judith. *Where in the World Are You Going?* Yarmouth, ME: Intercultural Press, 1996.

Church, Austin T. "Sojourner Adjustment." *Psychological Bulletin* 91, no. 3 (1982).

Comfort, Alexander. *A Good Age.* New York: Crown, 1976.

Dixon, Robert, and P. Baltes. "Intelligence: A Life-Span Developmental Perspective." In *Handbook of Intelligence: Theories, Measurements and Applications,* edited by Benjamin Wolman. New York: Wiley, 1986.

Garza-Guerrero, A. C. "Culture Shock: Its Mourning and the Vicissitudes of Identity." *Journal of American Psychoanalytic Association* 22, no. 2 (1974): 408–29.

Greenspan, Stanley I. "How Children Learn: Why the New Education Initiative Is a Step in the Wrong Direction." *Washington Post,* 21 April 1992.

Grove, Cornelius L., and Ingmar Torbiörn. "A New Conceptualization of Intercultural Adjustment and the Goals of Training." In *Cross-cultural Orientation, New Conceptualizations and Applications*, edited by R. Michael Paige, 71–109. Lanham, MD: University Press of America, 1986.

Higginbotham, Howard N. "Cultural Issues in Providing Psychological Services for Foreign Students in the United States." *International Journal of Intercultural Relations* 3, (1979): 49–85.

Juffer, Kristin A. "The First Step in Cross-Cultural Orientation: Defining the Problem." In *Cross-cultural Orientation, New Conceptualizations and Applications*, edited by R. Michael Paige, 175–92. Lanham, MD: University Press of America, 1986.

Knowles, Malcolm. *The Adult Learner: A Neglected Species.* Houston: Gulf, 1984.

Kohls, L. Robert. *Survival Kit for Overseas Living.* 3d. ed. Yarmouth, ME: Intercultural Press, 1996.

Landau, Erika. "The Questions Children Ask." *Futures,* April 1976.

Malcolm, Henry W. "The Secret to Effective Training Designs: Laboratories for Adult Learning." Paper presented in a graduate course, Training Design and Facilitation, at The American University/National Training Labs, Washington, DC, May 1994.

Nagler, Scott F. "Ego and Vicissitudes of Culture Change: Proposed Theory of Culture Shock." Ph.D. diss., Smith College, 1977, Dissertation Abstracts International, 48, 70.

Oberg, Kalvero. "Culture Shock: Adjustment to New Cultural Environments." *Practical Anthropology* 7 (1960): 177–82.

———. "Culture Shock and the Problem of Adjustment to New Cultural Environments." In *Readings in Intercultural Communication,* edited by David S. Hoopes. Pittsburgh: Intercultural Communications Network, Regional Council for International Education, 1972.

Porter, Lawrence C. "Game, Schmame! What Have I Learned?" In *Training Theory and Practice*, edited by Brendon W. Reddy and Clenard C. Henderson Jr. Alexandria, VA: NTL Institute for Applied Behavioral Science and University Associates, 1987.

Ramsey, Patricia G. *Teaching and Learning in a Diverse World: Multicultural Education for Young Children.* New York: Teachers College Press, 1987.

Rosenfeld, Albert. *Prolongevity*. New York: Alfred A. Knopf, 1976.

Sargent, Clyde B. "Psychological Aspects of Environmental Adjustment." Manuscript, The American University, Washington, DC, 1970.

Taft, Robert. "Coping with Unfamiliar Cultures." In *Studies in Cross-Cultural Psychology,* vol. 1, edited by N. Warren. New York: Academic Press, 1977.

Weaver, Gary R. "Understanding and Coping with Cross-Cultural Adjustment Stress." In *Cross-cultural Orientation, New Conceptualizations and Applications,* edited by R. Michael Paige, 71–109. Lanham, MD: University Press of America, 1986.

Appendix A

Four Components of Cross-Cultural Training for Children

The following four components need to be considered when designing and delivering cross-cultural training for children:

1. Emotional Exploration and Development

Age 0–6	Emotional adjustment dependent on parent
Age 7–11	Wide range of emotional maturity
Age 12–14	Inconsistent emotional maturity, but often the best age to relocate
Age 15–18	Emotionally mature with strong peer group focus

2. Cross-Cultural Interaction Skill Development (How)

Age 0–6	Asking questions of parents
Age 7–11	Asking questions and making friends
Age 12–14	Becoming a self-directed learner/making new culture friends
Age 15–18	Being a self-directed learner, responsible for your own adjustment

3. Factual Information: Culture-Specific (What)

Age 0–6	Concrete thought patterns
Age 7–11	Moving from concrete to abstract thought
Age 12–14	Abstract thought in place
Age 15–18	Abstract more important than concrete

4. Conceptual Information and Abilities (Why)

Age 0–6	Can understand very simple concepts, explanations
Age 7–11	Enjoy figuring out *why*; use the modified learning cycle
Age 12–14	Teach tools for understanding and dealing with differences; use the learning cycle
Age 15–18	Same as above; can understand more complex and subtle concepts

Appendix B

Issues of Cross-Cultural Adjustment for Children: A Parent's Guide

a. Be prepared for periods of little movement within developmental patterns and/or for levels of regression, which can be brought about by the disruption of the relocation.

b. Recognize that children enjoy novelty but do not like change.

c. Be patient; time is required to reestablish social links and sense of self in the new culture.

d. Create opportunities to share and express feelings.

e. Be especially aware of your own attitudes and behaviors.

f. Reaffirm acceptable and unacceptable behaviors—identify clear distinctions regarding rules and chores.

g. Assist your children in achieving a nonjudgmental view of behavior in their own culture and the other culture(s). Example: weird versus different.

h. Avoid feeling guilty about taking children overseas.

i. Assist your children in assuming responsibility for their own feelings and adjustment.

j. Establish links; for example: (a) burying something at your old home to find later, (b) identifying something special that will go with them anywhere, (c) decorating their new room.

k. Reinforce new friendships.

Intercultural Training: The Future

Sandra M. Fowler and Sheila Ramsey

Edward T. Hall, when asked how he pictures the future of intercultural training, said he sees "a stream of water flowing" (personal communication, 1994). This age-old metaphor is a good place to begin when imagining the future of intercultural training. While we cannot see far enough ahead to know exactly how and where the stream flows, certainly what lies ahead must resemble what is already part of our experience of the stream. Indeed Mel Schnapper claims, "There's no more future than there has been—the books and materials and courses and programs are out there" (personal communication, 1995). We find ourselves in a time of paradox and creativity. Certainly what is currently "out there" is providing a firm and credible foundation, but it must be reshaped to meet the demands of the contexts and situations within which we will be working in the future. Does this imply we already know the future? Perhaps not, for the future is for imagining.

In preparation for this chapter, we read literature in and out of our field and interviewed several interculturalists whose ideas are sprinkled throughout. We hope their comments and our own serve as a springboard for your imagination. We invite you to join us in imagining the field of intercultural relations, roles and functions, competencies, and contexts in which we might work in the future. What intrapersonal realities, paradoxes, group and systemic realities face us in the future? And finally we examine the purpose of our work and the need to sustain a dialogue that will ensure that we will be the best we can be.

Intercultural Relations: A Field or a Focus?

When the founders of SIETAR International met in Estes Park amid the aspens and vistas of the Rocky Mountains in 1966, they envisioned a discipline of intercultural relations and cross-cultural communication with culture as its central focus. They felt that what they were doing with the U.S. Peace Corps and in their university classes would develop into a field, supported by research and practiced by the people they were currently training—people who would have the overseas experiences that would change their lives and make them empathic and sophisticated trainers of those who would follow. Now, several decades later it is fair to ask if the founders were on the right track. Is there such a thing as an intercultural field? And what does the answer mean for the future?

It would seem that their vision has to some extent come to pass; in other words, it is and is not a field. An intercultural field exists in the minds of many people—at least those who practice in this field, if not the general public. However, as yet the intercultural field does not have the rigor and boundaries characteristic of most established academic disciplines. By and large, it does not have an academic home—its academic base is spread among many different departments. When it exists at all, it is most likely housed in the speech/communication department in large universities, but relevant courses can be found in psychology, anthropology, sociology, education, economics, and foreign language. For many people who were prepared to do something else, intercultural understanding is a focus, not a field.

Many of the old-timers in intercultural training majored in something else when they were in college, so intercultural relations and cross-cultural communication might be considered a focus for them, but increasingly the new professionals are products of intercultural relations graduate programs. We can imagine a future in which many more universities and colleges offer degrees in intercultural relations. That suggests the continued development of an intercultural *field*, not a focus.

The issues of the new millennium will increasingly require people educated in intercultural relations to respond to the demands of global civilization. Speaking in Philadelphia on the Fourth of July, 1994, in a "declaration of interdependence," as reported in *Newsweek* (Woodward 1994), Czech president Vaclav Havel commented that the end of the century is an age of transition and that Western culture has entered a postmodern phase where "everything is possible and almost nothing is certain." Havel "wants a shared global vision that enables diverse peoples, multicultural societies and competing religions to transcend their particularities" (66). According to Havel a single, interconnected civilization is emerging underneath which, like shifting geological plates, is the countervailing assertion of local cultures which cling to the ancient tribal values. As reported in the same article, sociologist Robert Bellah of the University of California, Berkeley, declared that it is amazing that the president of anything—especially of a small country—would think of such things. To those of us who have made the understanding between cultures central to our lives, this is not so amazing. Unwittingly, President Havel makes a strong case supporting the need for educated interculturalists who can help people make sense of their world.

Intercultural Trainers and Training: The 21st Century

At the end of the twentieth century, we already see people being trained in new ways. In the future, these young professionals will bring new technologies to intercultural training, for example, using the World Wide Web with ease and confidence. This electronic communication forum is guaranteed to shape changes in intercultural training. Trainers of the future are likely to incorporate interactive computer methods, teleconferencing, virtual reality, artificial intelligence, and hologram technology into their training in ways we can only imagine.

Cyberspace is regarded as the next frontier (O'Hara-Devereaux and Johansen 1994). The dawning of the cyberspace era extends our imagination. Cyberspace is communication as space, and not just a version of current communication technology. This is a subtle but profound shift from communication as a link between two locations to communication as a destination in its own right. Cyberspace is where meetings will take place, decisions will be made, deals will be struck—among people of many different cultures, with their kaleidoscope of worldviews. How can we help multicultural teams who never meet to work together? How does one develop trust under these circumstances? How are deadlines conveyed to team members when words like *time* and *completed* mean something quite different in each of their cultures? The intercultural trainers of the future will be pioneers who help prepare their trainees for sojourns in unbounded cyberspace just as trainers of today help trainees learn to cross real-world cultural and geographic borders.

In addition to developing cyberspace skills, Edward T. Hall (1994) suggests that cross-cultural trainers must learn a lot more about perception, about human beings as psychological and physiological beings. The whole neurological/perceptual system is influenced by culture, and we need to become more sophisticated in our understanding of this interaction. At this point in time, almost all of our training deals with learned or explicit culture, but we must begin to learn how to prepare people for acquired culture—the implied, tacit, not-expressed part of culture. Preparing people to operate in internal and external environments in which there are different ways of identifying strengths and talents represents a radical change. Two examples are provided by Hall: Native Americans can carry much more in their minds than Anglo Americans can. Eskimos have a sense of directionality not possessed by outsiders to that ethnic group. Hall reminds us that holding on to the world we are given to the extent that we cannot see another world may prevent us from realizing there are many such strengths yet to discover.

New Roles and Functions for Intercultural Training

Traditionally, we have focused on preparing people for international transitions in educational, religious, governmental, or corporate contexts. Nancy Adler (1994), in her keynote address at the annual SIETAR International Congress in Ottawa, said she feels that our role as interculturalists is to transcend this traditional focus. If we continue on the same path, our current success can lead to future demise. According to Adler, we must move away from training international managers and preparing people for expatriate transfers. We need to develop transnational leadership models and train to those models. Her higher purpose is to create a better world by sending better global citizens out into it. These global citizens will be able to keep their balance when they are overwhelmed by cultural conflicts because we will help them operate from strength, flexibility, and "proprioception." She describes *proprioception* as "learning to attend to internal messages, vision, and values to regain balance and stability." Intercultural trainers need the skills to do this; we need to strengthen who we are in order to contribute to the world. She sees us facing a highly challenging next twenty years.

New roles and functions for intercultural training have been emerging in the recent past and will only continue to take on critical importance. For example, our work can be informed by those who are directly involved in such areas as crisis negotiation, health services, and dispute resolution. In illustrating this by citing specific work, we do not mean to imply that others are not seriously involved in doing important work in these and other areas. For reasons of economy we cannot give reference to all, even if we knew everything that is happening. Realizing that our knowledge is limited reminds us of the opportunity offered by cyberspace. As people become accustomed to sharing their work electronically, the Internet could be a great help for future articles chronicling the work of interculturalists as well as supporting us all in being resources for each other as we step toward challenges demanding that we work in new ways. A few examples of people who are working on the challenging frontiers help us look to the future.

Working with law enforcement officers, Mitchell Hammer is applying a communication-based model to study cultural aspects of crisis negotiation (Rogan, Hammer, and van Zandt 1997). Hammer (1996) says that the major cultural considerations are language, paralinguistics, verbal style, and nonverbal behavior. He describes a situation in which a group of Vietnamese young men took about forty people hostage in a California store. The Vietnamese language pattern is high-pitched, staccato, repetitive. These characteristics describe an emotionally charged communication pattern to most Americans. The negotiators became convinced that the situation was escalating out of control because they interpreted what they heard from their own cultural perspective—with a disastrous outcome.

Deena Levine and her associates have also directed their attention toward building awareness and skills in the context of multicultural law enforcement. Focusing on improving relationships within police agencies and communities, they work with the culturally influenced interactions of citizens, victims, suspects, and coworkers (Shuster, Levine, Harris, and Wong 1995).

In another example, the work of Michelle LeBaron and Craig Darling addresses public policy dispute resolution in Canada and the United States. They recognize that culture, broadly defined, operates strongly in negotiations and public policy decision-making processes. For example, at least three cultures exist in a specific negotiation regarding decisions about natural resources: the culture of the government and its ministries; the culture of the professional groups involved such as biologists, engineers, and lawyers; and the culture(s) of those directly affected by the decisions—perhaps ethnicity and/or urban-rural differences. In this work it is critical that constituents who previously have not had a voice now be heard. Acknowledging and honoring cultural perspectives is crucial to reaching wise solutions in areas of concern that can be heavily laden with issues of power and privilege, with emotion, and with adversarial position (LeBaron 1992; LeBaron and Darling 1997).

Another application is provided by John Berry of Queens University, who has set out to answer the question, How can we apply cross-cultural knowledge to the area of health? He believes that health concepts and definitions, health norms and values, and health practices and professional health roles are heavily influenced by culture. Berry (1996) states that the ways people conceptualize health and the specific health needs of culturally diverse populations need to be studied so that culturally appropriate services can be developed. Training needs to include the special needs of cultural minorities, immigrants, and refugees. Our work will take on more and more importance for health providers in managed care, hospitals, community health centers, and clinics.

Carlos Cortes alerts us to the critical importance of working at the intersection between the media and intercultural issues. He tells us that the media are educational curricula, therefore we must question the responsibilities of those who are creating our entertainment and our education. He suggests the following dimensions of media study: content analysis regarding the messages found in visual and auditory images; control analysis regarding the decisions that are made in designing programs, advertisements, and their specific messages; and impact analysis focused upon what people are learning through this influential channel of communication. He encourages interculturalists to work with those who create programming to become involved in training people to become media-literate and, from a constructivist perspective, use media in training that tap into the images that people bring into the training situation (personal communication, 1996).

Our stream is broadening; new roles, functions, and contexts widen Hall's metaphor for intercultural training. Law enforcement, health care, dispute resolution, and the media are only four examples of contexts that will need many more intercultural specialists in the future who understand both the industry or profession and the intercultural issues. Imagination and a very current awareness of our global condition are the only limits to identifying contexts in which we can work in new and creative ways.

Our Work: What Now?

While it is certainly interesting to consider the future of intercultural training, it is more than merely interesting, for is it not the case that we are already futurists, defined as those who study and envision what might be? From our infancy, marked in 1959 by the publication of Edward Hall's *The Silent Language*, we have been sending a consistent message to our colleagues and clients in education, in the corporate sector, in government, and in international development.

We have been saying, Wake up and pay attention. Please! Context is relative and relevant; multiple perspectives and behavioral differences exist and are a source of creativity; entering another's assumptive world as well as empathically living and working there is a challenging, growth-producing, and useful practical experience. Learning how to learn may be the most important key to effectiveness. And, we have consistently added, the need for such perspectives and for the skills of people who see themselves as global citizens and who can be *living bridges* is only going to grow. This is not just about a nice and interesting way of being in the world but rather a necessity, because international relationships, networks, and alliances are the future. Over the years our voice has grown stronger and our messages are more self-evidently true.

Some of the original concerns that brought our work into being seem even more relevant in light of current-day interpersonal, political, and economic realities. In describing our work as "holy work," Robert Kohls speaks to some of these original concerns in suggesting that, as we all retain our ethnic uniqueness and our common connection, we must be sure that the work we do does not promote separateness. "Overcoming gross ignorance and separateness is our goal" (Kohls 1995).

It seems thus appropriate that as futurists we look closely at ourselves; to what extent have our perspectives, our methods, and our approaches kept pace with the experiences and needs of the people who are now living in this world of networks and alliances that we predicted? How are we serving the original concerns from which we grew?

After several decades of doing this work, we have become quite skilled in facilitating the awareness of habitual, culturally influenced behavior and in teaching a variety of conceptual schema for the analysis of such behavior. However, the opinions of experienced practitioners and academicians alike suggest that we are encrusted in our own habits and familiar ways, that we need to rise from our comfortable rocking chairs, shake ourselves, look around, and seriously ask, "What is needed now?"

Speaking to American trainers, Renwick and Clarke (1996) said, "We need to be more creative. There have been few new methods developed in the last twenty years. The field is caught in old assumptions and paradigms, which often no longer meet the needs of trainees and corporations" (2). Shall we critically judge ourselves for this standstill, for being caught in the old and familiar? Perhaps not, for we can only understand and teach about the assumptions and mechanisms that have led us here. Our colleagues in the field of biology have said,

> By existing, we generate cognitive 'blind spots' that can be cleared only through generating new blind spots in another domain. We do not see what we do not see, and what we do not see does not exist. Only when some interaction dislodges us, as being suddenly relocated to a different cultural environment, and we reflect upon it, do we bring forth new constellations of relation that we explain by saying that we were not aware of them or that we took them for granted." (Maturana and Varela 1992, 242)

Holding on to the very heart of our work and thanking our clients and program participants for their questions and feedback, let us begin to gently dislodge ourselves so we can prepare for the future.

To mark the twentieth anniversary, in 1996, of the Summer Institute for Intercultural Communication (known as SIIC and begun on the Stanford University campus, but now located in Portland, Oregon), the conveners called upon a panel to address the question, What now? Much of what was said is directly relevant to the future of training.

Lee Kneflecamp asked, "How may we find ways to live our lives finally realizing that we do so in the context of others?" This was followed by a possible answer: "In a commitment to work on diversity, people must choose to stay in dialogue in some authentic common space." In assessing research, Stella Ting-Toomey echoed a similar theme as she requested that we adopt approaches less focused on individuals as isolates but rather on individuals in co-orientation with each other. How do people influence each other's responsiveness and awareness? Regarding the change process, what are the turning points that move people into different stages in the development process? She stressed that the role of feeling or affect in the change process needs to become more central.

Taking a different look at research and training development, Harry Triandis (personal communication 1996) suggested that, while our work in the 1960s began with a cognitive emphasis (which is the way we were trained), the intervening years brought the integration of the experiential approach and the inclusion of the emotional needs of sojourners. However, he sees a current fragmentation of concepts and opposing methods that have brought us to a standstill. He feels that research might push us out of the quagmire. He encourages us to continue asking questions about the criterion problem. How is the length of training related to producing different kinds of effects? How do we measure intercultural effectiveness? If we cannot measure it, we cannot train for it. Triandis reminds us that we need to be clear about the effectiveness of our training for changing behavior, changing the situation, and changing economic outcomes in terms relevant to both sojourner and host. Are the enduring questions answerable? Will the answers force changes in the way we train? In our opinion, the answer must be yes.

Paradoxes: Present and Future

Intrapersonal Realities

How may our work expand inwardly to focus on personal strengths when our goal is to train people to participate outwardly in intercultural interactions? How do we deal simultaneously with paradoxical intrapersonal and interpersonal realities?

The answer may lie in reframing our work as a transformation process. We envision intercultural work of the future focusing much more on the intrapersonal transformation process because it is evident to all of us that living and working effectively with culturally distinct others and in culturally different systems is an experience that challenges us on very fundamental levels. The resulting upheaval provides an opportunity for reorganizing and renewing our worldview, creating a subtle change in the habits of the heart and mind. How we manage our state of being—the affective component of the experience—is directly related to our effectiveness (Ramsey 1994).

Peter Adler was one of the first to draw our attention to the learning/growth outcomes of cultural transition (Adler in Luce and Smith 1987). Mansell suggests that in effective intercultural experiences, there is much more going on than acquisition of skills and knowledge; rather there is a "consciousness which transforms an individual's perceptions of the world and imparts a sense of unity between self and surroundings" (Mansell 1994).

Edward Taylor makes a clear connection between the shifts in perspective that can occur during intercultural experiences and his studies of transformational learning in the area of adult education. "A possible explanation of the process of becoming interculturally competent lies in the concept of perspective transformation. When we change significant meaning structures (meaning perspectives), we change the way we view and act toward our world" (Taylor 1994, 154). In his research, cultural disequilibrium is seen as the catalyst of such a learning process. Such learning can move an individual "toward a more inclusive, differentiated, permeable (open to other points of view), and integrated worldview" (Kim 1994).

In the long run, participants make personal choices about how they will integrate and be affected by intercultural interactions; they decide whether or not to become a cultural go-between, a living bridge. Although there is a developmental impact available to partakers of intercultural experiences, we know that some people resist the opportunity for personal change. Transformational learning may not be for everyone.

We can be of great service to our trainees to the degree that we can and are willing to explore this potential on an individual basis. Certainly we lead people through intercultural simulations with the intention that they partake—in a safe place—of the processes that set the stage for personal reflection and change. However, perhaps because of the number of others involved in simulations, because of time constraints, or perhaps due to our own hesitancies, we do not often venture into the intrapersonal domain. In this domain, we would explore how participants relate to change in their lives.

In our future work we need to ask, What strengths do participants draw upon and what lessons have they learned? Have they ever been in situations where previous knowledge and experience was not particularly useful? How do they learn and make sense when nothing makes sense? Can they allow nothing to make sense and discover what emerges? What frees them to perceive in new ways and to live beyond judgment and fear? Could they construct a personal *theory of change* to which they could refer and research during their times of entry and reentry? What encourages them to remain in dialogue in frustrating and challenging situations? How do they return to balance following highly emotional states?

We are suggesting that it is not enough to tell participants, "You cannot go home again," "Notice how your cultural glasses led you to that interpretation," or "Try not to avoid culture shock—and good luck." We who have left home and live more comfortably in some home of our own creation can—and indeed have a responsibility to—encourage and support deeper exploration of the potential for transformation. Speaking to the pivotal decision to address the intrapersonal world, Kim suggests,

> Intercultural communication competence is explained not as communication in dealing with a specific culture but as the cognitive, affective and operational adaptability of an individual's internal system…. In reality, there are those who have achieved impressive intercultural adaptability as well as those who seriously lack this internal capacity. In the end, the critical difference between these two groups may well be the willingness (or lack of willingness) to go through the challenges and to creatively restructure oneself as situations demand. (259, 271)

Another basic belief found within our work is that difference is a resource for creativity and a critical element from which understanding grows. Creating and calling attention to interactions that potentiate this learning as well as exploring the possibility for personal development can perhaps best be approached not through engaging in skill-building role plays or lectures about value orientations but through less linear methods. These methods permeate the traditions of many cultures and are nontraditional only in light of the familiar training methods in the formalized intercultural arena. Such nonlinear methods include metaphor, myth and archetypes, reflective journaling, dialogue/appreciative inquiry, and personal narrative (Ramsey 1996; Ramsey and LeBaron; Ramsey and Sorrels 1997; Seelye and Wasilewski 1996; Watanabe 1997).

More Paradoxes

According to Stephen Rhinesmith (1994), the world of the future will demand that we manage paradox—working on many things simultaneously even when they go in opposite directions. We must become experts at working with people and situations that exhibit inexplicable or contradictory aspects. Meshing *our* values and behavioral styles with *foreign* values and styles is a form of managing paradox which uniquely helps build the expertise we need to work with managers whose daily lives are filled with paradox.

The contradictory nature of our work is embedded in understanding, accepting, and responding to the perspective of another culture while carrying our own perspective within us. We have been working within this paradox for so long that we see it as simply a reality that we enjoy and part of what draws us to this work.

Our clients often ask us to forecast outcomes, which implies a structured, predictable training program, run by the book. At the same time, we must also be prepared for the unexpected, be willing to change original program objectives in response to unforeseen events, and be able to continually turn resistance or mistakes into learning events. In this way we certainly give our participants the most relevant and personal guidance (Ptak, Cooper, and Brislin 1995). Most important, we are modeling an approach that is at the essence of the competence we teach about. As the groups that we work with become more culturally diverse, this way of working will be a necessity for the successful intercultural trainer of the future.

Moving Forward: Group and Systemic Realities

An additional dilemma confronts intercultural trainers of today. In the previously mentioned What now? panel discussion, George Renwick examined our work in relationship to the corporate context. He emphasized the necessity of customizing our work to meet the individual and function-specific needs of clients. At the same time, his experience suggests that when clients want to train large numbers of people, there is more likelihood of a request for standardized training programs. He feels that while the need for predeparture work will continue, there are additional requirements for people with intercultural expertise to assist in the design of new corporate cultures, management development programs, and organizational systems. He echoed a common theme of the panel members, saying that we must move from a focus on the individual to a focus on organizations and whole systems. From our training perspective, however, we believe the future will hold a solution to the challenge of working simultaneously with individuals, groups, and systems—and that solution may lie in cyberspace.

There are exciting and challenging opportunities before us in global and domestic corporations, educational systems, and public and governmental services. Despite the advent of cyberspace, where people do not physically meet, groups of people having diverse cultural identities are coming together to solve problems, move through conflicts, make decisions, and take actions. How can such groups focus their interests, priorities, and abilities? How can such groups be together and work together in ways that support and engender a commitment to create together? There is exacting and rewarding work to be done. Are we ready to step right into the middle and wear whatever hat is called for, whether it be that of resource, adviser, leader, coach, facilitator, or mediator?

Wearing such hats suggests that we understand working from a systems perspective as well as understanding the larger systems within which work groups or communities of interest are placed. From a systems perspective, we focus upon relationships and interactions rather than only upon internal processes or the efficiency of an individual as a single unit. We know that to survive and thrive an individual depends upon transactions with the environment. Intercultural work certainly has incorporated from its inception the critical notion of context; continuing to value the systems approach leads us further into considering the interplay between individual and group boundaries as well as the permeability of these boundaries. In exploring the dynamics of self-regulation we can assist clients in understanding the bases of their choices regarding how they integrate themselves into workplaces and neighborhoods that are markedly unfamiliar. We are also led into working with the critical relationship between goals, purpose, and the outcome of interactions.

The future will force us to deal with larger systems. We must examine and become more knowledgeable about national and functional culture, reward and recognition policies and practices, conflict resolution, problem-solving and decision-making strategies, structural designs of organizations, and relationships with the larger community and customers (in the sense of all who are served and affected by the actions of the group). In the past, we have not been particularly adept at recognizing that all systems live within particular power relationships and have political overtones, the dynamics and effects of which in the future will be even more crucial to the effectiveness of our work.

There is a growing tendency for corporate clients, in particular, to request that intercultural consultants be able not only to assist them with culturally specific information, but that this information be placed within very specific organizational contexts. This suggests some melding of intercultural expertise and organizational development. As an illustration of the specificity of the work we may be asked to do, we might be asked to assist in creating performance appraisal systems and management development plans appropriate for an international mix of research scientists in the Singapore-based center of a company's U.S.-Japanese joint-venture consumer-products division.

Systems are not only to be understood, as they form the setting for how group members are able to interact, but they are also to be examined and potentially redesigned to encourage the commitment to engage and the potential to create. It is challenging to be creative across cultures, and we must educate our clients regarding the implications of policy, structure, and decision making on the creative process. As Renwick suggested, our role becomes that of introducing cultural insight to complex organizational processes.

Sustaining the Dialogue

Synergy is often considered a highly desirable outcome when people with diverse experiences work together. If this is the case, we need to examine the purpose of any work we have set before ourselves, because in reality, our training goals are rarely that lofty. There are common training objectives with which we are all familiar: "to identify and practice key skills for effectively interacting with German scholars," "to identify competencies and strategies for making successful intercultural transitions," or "to learn to interpret unfamiliar behavior accurately according to the intention of the other-culture actor." Such objectives have proven themselves over time to be foundational ones. However, future work calls for us to connect to the larger perspective already noted.

> What of connection to a larger purpose?… When managers, doctors, or teachers working as a multicultural team learn skills that can help them communicate more effectively, we must also inquire about and help them articulate how their new abilities can now support them in serving the greater purposes which have brought them together. Examples of such purpose might include creating products that exceed customer expectations while valuing the unique talents of all employees, educating patients in ways to maintain the highest level of health, or valuing the diversity of all people in the creation of intercultural partnerships. As leaders, we must be able to identify, articulate and hold the objectives...of the entire program...in alignment with the answers to "so what?" As participants become consciously involved in the creation of this thread of connection, the learning has relevance, it makes sense and, more important, becomes motivating and inspiring. (Ramsey 1996, 20–21)

Our purpose can become one of being with groups in whatever ways are appropriate to promote synergistic processes and outcomes in which parts truly do optimize each other and in which a whole-system intelligence develops, guiding decision into action. This asks that we go beyond delivering culturally specific information and examining perception or attribution processes.

What Next?

What lies beyond this familiar way of working? To begin, let us intentionally continue to develop our own cultural fluencies, our own capacities and knowledge. From this place of continual learning, let us invite our clients to experience the alignment and commitment that grow from finding common ground and shared purpose; let us acknowledge and build capacities—not only knowledge and skills— for honoring and engaging with diversity and ambiguity; and let us engender the appreciation of and desire for ongoing learning. There is a fundamental assumption underlying these suggestions. This assumption relates to how we, who consider ourselves intercultural trainers, need to reconceptualize our relationship to the arenas of work that are newly presenting themselves every day. Continuing to think of ourselves as trainers, with all the familiar approaches to *doing training*, is a limiting and potentially self-defeating frame. Perhaps it will help if we call ourselves *consultants* or *resources*. The label we use is our choice, but it needs to anchor us in a more expansive and responsive perspective. Structuring our work to serve the largest challenge, it is possible to create environments and connections within which people feel interested and motivated to become permeable to others, to be affected by others, to sustain the challenging and rich dialogues that, most important, we must ourselves believe in.

We began by likening the future of intercultural training to a stream along which we are all traveling together. As we wonder about what lies beyond the bends and turns ahead, we need to use the natural flow of the current to carry us. The most dangerous risk is that of becoming stuck, caught in a whirlpool, or snagged on the branch of a submerged log. Flexibility and creativity are the traits we need to develop in order to navigate rapidly evolving change.

References

Adler, Nancy. Keynote address presented at the annual congress of SIETAR International, Ottawa, Canada, 1994.

Adler, Peter. "Culture Shock and the Cross-Cultural Learning Experience." In *Toward Internationalism*, edited by Louise Fiber Luce and Elise C. Smith, 24–35. Cambridge: Newbury Press, 1987.

Berry, John. Session presented at the annual meeting of the International Association of Applied Psychology, Montreal, Canada, 1996.

Cortes, Carlos. Personal communication, July 1996.

Hall, Edward T. Personal communication, June 1994.

———. *The Silent Language.* 1959. Reprint, New York: Anchor/Doubleday, 1981.

Hammer, Mitchell R. *Crisis Negotiation across Cultures.* Lecture at the Smithsonian Institution, Washington, DC, March 1996.

Kim, Young Y. "Communication and Cross-Cultural Adaptation: An Integrative Theory." In *Intercultural Competence: A Transformative Learning Process. Adult Education Quarterly* 44, no. 3 (Spring 1994): 154–74.

Kohls, L. Robert. *Paradigms for the New World Order.* Presentation at the Summer Institute for Intercultural Communication, Portland, OR, July 1995.

LeBaron, Michelle. *Conflict and Culture: A Literature Review and Bibliography.* Victoria, BC: University of Victoria Institute for Dispute Resolution, 1992.

LeBaron, Michelle, and Craig Darling. *Leadership and Environmental Conflict Resolution.* Victoria, BC: Accord Canada, 1997.

Mansell, M. "Transcultural Experience and Expressive Response." In *Intercultural Competence: A Transformative Learning Process. Adult Education Quarterly* 44, no. 3 (Spring 1994): 154–74.

Maturana, Humberto R., and Francisco Varela. *The Tree of Knowledge: The Biological Roots of Human Understanding.* Boston: Shambhala Press, 1992.

O'Hara-Devereaux, Mary, and Robert Johansen. *Globalwork: Bridging Distance, Culture, and Time.* San Francisco: Jossey-Bass, 1994.

Ptak, Cynthia, Joanne Cooper, and Richard W. Brislin. "Cross-Cultural Training Programs: Advice and Insights from Experienced Trainers." *International Journal of Intercultural Relations* 19, no. 3 (1995).

Ramsey, Sheila. *Creativity: The Heart of Intercultural Competence.* Manuscript in preparation.

———. "Creating A Context: Methodologies in Intercultural Teaching and Training." In *Experiential Activities for Intercultural Learning,* vol. 1, edited by H. Ned Seelye, 7–24. Yarmouth, ME: Intercultural Press, 1996.

———. "Riding the Waves of Culture: Intercultural Communication at the End of the 20th Century." *Intercultural Communication Studies* no. 7. Intercultural Communication Institute, Kanda University of International Studies, Japan, 1994.

Ramsey, Sheila, and Michelle LeBaron. *The Place of Metaphor in Intercultural Relations.* Manuscript in preparation.

Ramsey, Sheila, and Kathryn Sorrels. "Creative Methods for Intercultural Training." Workshop presented at the Summer Institute for Intercultural Communication, Portland, OR, July, 1997.

Renwick, George W., and Clifford Clarke. "Intercultural Training: Where Are We and Where Are We Going?" *Insider's Line,* Intercultural Press, author newsletter, June 1996.

Rhinesmith, Stephen, H. "Managing Change in the 1990s." Presentation at the annual congress of SIETAR International, Ottawa, Canada, June 1994.

Rogan, Randall G., Mitchell R. Hammer, and Clinton van Zandt, eds. *Dynamic Processes of Crisis Negotiation.* Westport, CT: Praeger, 1997.

Schnapper, Mel. Personal communication, December 1996.

Seelye, H. Ned, and Jacqueline H. Wasilewski. *Between Cultures: Developing Self-Identity in a World of Diversity.* Lincolnwood, IL: NTC, 1996.

Shuster, Captain Robert, Deena R. Levine, Philip Harris, and Herbert Wong. *Multicultural Law Enforcement: Strategies for Peacekeeping in a Diverse Society.* New York: Prentice Hall, 1995.

Taylor, Edward E., ed. *Intercultural Competence: A Transformative Learning Process. Adult Education Quarterly* 44, no. 3 (Spring 1994): 154.

Triandis, Harry C. Personal communication, August 1996.

———. *Culture and Social Behavior.* New York: McGraw-Hill, 1994.

Watanabe, Gordon. "Exploring Edges: Using Metaphor to Develop Intercultural Competence." Manuscript, 1997.

Woodward, Kenneth, with Bruce Shenitz. "More Than Ourselves." *Newsweek,* 18 July 1994, 66.

About the Authors

Michael Gottlieb Berney currently works for the Federal Judicial Center in Washington, DC, where he designs and delivers management development programs (including various types of field studies) for federal court personnel. He owes his understanding of cross-cultural training to the International Society for Intercultural Education, Training and Research and to two wonderful years spent at Meridian International Center (then the Washington International Center of Meridian House), working with Bob Kohls, Carole Watt, and a very special team of program staff and faculty.

Chris Brown is the president of Global Associates, Ltd. (GAL), in Cary, North Carolina. He learned about cross-cultural communication out of necessity while living overseas for eight years and traveling to more than sixty-five countries. He now specializes in the Latin American and Middle Eastern regions, using his knowledge of languages and cultures. Chris has presented and consulted extensively on the development and benefits of multicultural teams, while still finding time to be the father of a cross-cultural family.

Pierre Casse is a professor of leadership/organizational behavior and the associate dean for International Affairs at the University of Aix-en-Provence (France). He is also a visiting professor at the Kellogg Graduate School of Management in Chicago and the Templeton College of Oxford. He has just completed a new book (in cooperation with Paul Claudel) on philosophy and business. He lives in Geneva, Switzerland.

Robert Cyr specializes in designing training programs and strategies for effective management, customer service, and international business communication. He previously managed training at Underwriters Laboratories. He is a lecturer at Northwestern and Loyola Universities and has been published extensively in business periodicals.

Lance Descourouez, trained as a cultural psychologist, has worked extensively with families in transition. He is the former director of intercultural training and organization development for Geonexus Communications, where he provided cross-cultural training, consulting, and organization development for public and private sector organizations in the United States and overseas. He currently resides in northern California, with his lifelong bride, Shawn, young son, Andrew John, and their dog, Dar.

Mitchell R. Hammer is an associate professor in the School of International Ser-vice at The American University in Washington, DC, where he specializes in intercultural communication and conflict negotiation. He has published widely, with over fifty articles in various academic and professional books and journals. Federal agencies and corporations consult him on intercultural communication, crisis negotiation, and conflict resolution issues. Dr. Hammer frequently provides expert analysis for the media, including NBC News, CNN, and NHK television in Japan, Voice of America, *USA Today,* and the *Washington Post.*

Cay Hartley was director of training services at Youth For Understanding for eight years and has had extensive experience in training design and delivery. Ms. Hartley is cofounder of Counseling & Training Resources, Inc., and maintains a general psychotherapy practice with specialties in cross-cultural adjustment and issues of loss and bereavement.

Robert Hayles is an effectiveness/diversity consultant based in Arden Hills, Min-nesota. He was formerly (until 1995) vice president, human resources and diver-sity, for The Pillsbury Company and recently (1996) served as chair of the board of directors of the American Society for Training and Development. He is also coauthor of the book titled *The Diversity Directive: Why Some Initiatives Fail and What to Do About It.*

Robbins S. Hopkins is president of Hopkins & Hopkins, Inc., a consulting firm specializing in organizational development for international, educational, and business organizations. She helps clients develop self-managing teams and uses participant-centered conference strategies to enable groups to utilize their own leadership for strategic planning and problem solving. She also offers a public series of experiential workshops to enable participants to rediscover ways to con-nect with the Divine to bring greater peace and satisfaction to their lives.

Colleen Kelley has been a human relations consultant in La Jolla, California, since 1973. She has traveled extensively and lived abroad for three years. She holds degrees in modern languages, French language and literature, educational psychology, human resource development, human communication systems, and professional psychology. Besides cross-cultural training and team building, she does training and consulting in a variety of other areas.

Kasey Knight is vice president of Global Associates, Ltd. (GAL), and has been a consultant, designer, and facilitator of communication programs for the past fif-teen years. She has lived, worked, and traveled extensively overseas. In her role as mother of a cross-cultural family, she finds her knowledge and skills in the communication area to be critical in dealing with her two Costa Rican teenagers.

L. Robert Kohls, a cultural historian by profession, had the rare opportunity of entering the training field in the mid-1960s, just as its new technology and its new methodologies were being invented (as an unexpected spin-off of program-ming data into computers). Out of that exciting experience, he left the university classroom to become one of our best-known cross-cultural trainers. He is the author of *Survival Kit for Overseas Living* and a book which he coauthored with John M. Knight, *Developing Intercultural Awareness.* He was the second winner of SIETAR's *Primus Inter Pares* award.

Alfred J. Kraemer (now retired), was raised in Vienna and Paris and was for many years senior staff scientist at the Human Resources Research Office (HumRRO) in Alexandria, VA. In 1987 he chaired the SIETAR Commission on Intercultural Training, Research and Development, which included Paul Kimmel, Jackie Wasilewski, and the late Ned Seelye.

Terri Lapinsky, formerly director of language services at Youth For Understanding, has been working in the field of intercultural education for twenty-five years as a teacher, trainer, materials developer, and consultant. Currently, she is on contract as education specialist with the Peace Corps Office of Training and Program Support.

Nessa Loewenthal, consultant and trainer to a variety of corporations and public service and educational institutions, designs and implements programs in change management; culture, communication, and effectiveness; value-based decision-making programs; and international effectiveness. As a faculty member of the Summer Institute for Intercultural Communication (Portland, OR), she trains trainers to develop and present programs in international relocation and in the development of international effectiveness. She has written several books and articles on international living and management of cultural difference. A graduate of Stanford University, Loewenthal received SIETAR International's Senior Interculturalist award and serves as the organization's Ethics Chair.

Norma M. McCaig is the founder and former president of Global Nomads International, a nonprofit organization in association with the United Nations serving those who lived abroad before adulthood because of a parent's career. A cross-cultural consultant, trainer, and writer specializing in global nomad issues, transcultural transitions, and cross-cultural awareness, she spent sixteen childhood years abroad in Asia. Publications include several booklets in the series USA in Brief and *The Participant Guidebook,* a cross-cultural orientation manual. All were produced during her seventeen-year tenure with what is now Meridian International Center in Washington, DC. For over twenty years she has presented workshops and sessions for both SIETAR and NAFSA: Association of International Educators.

Louis M. Meucci is currently at Showa Boston Institute for Language and Culture. In 1988 he received a Fulbright grant for international education administrators and studied in Japan and Korea. Before Showa, Meucci was assistant director of programs at the University of California Berkeley International House. Earlier, Meucci was assistant director for student development in the International Students and Scholars Office at Boston University. He has been cochair of the International Careers Consortium of New England and also served as a Peace Corps volunteer in the Kingdom of Tonga in the South Pacific.

Judith Meyers is a licensed clinical psychologist who lives in San Diego. Dr. Meyers began her clinical practice in California in 1978. Her interest has always been clinical assessment, and she has applied this skill to the fields of child psychology, sexual abuse, forensic psychology, and cross-cultural issues. She has also applied the Rorschach test to the assessment of cross-cultural adaptation.

Noriko Ogami, a native of Kyoto, Japan, obtained her master's degree in broadcasting and film from Boston University's College of Communication. She has worked for Hakuhodo (public relations/advertising) in Tokyo, producing television commercials, and for TELL Systems, International, Inc., as a cross-cultural consultant and production manager in the development of laser videodiscs for language and cultural training. She joined Clarke Consulting Group in September 1987 as an intercultural specialist and works with Japanese and American corporate clients.

Jun Ohtake was graduated from a Japanese international university in Tokyo, where he wrote a thesis on the concept of a culture hero. Since entering his working life, he has been employed by a major Japanese company for which he conducts training, first in Hokkaido and now in Hong Kong.

Paul B. Pedersen is a professor in the Department of Human Studies, School of Education, University of Alabama. He has worked in Indonesia, Malaysia, and Taiwan for six years and has taught at the University of Minnesota, University of Hawaii, and Syracuse University. He has authored or edited thirty books and 160 articles or chapters.

Margaret D. Pusch (Peggy) is associate director of the Intercultural Communication Institute, a cross-cultural trainer, and a writer and editor. Throughout her career, she has been involved in international educational exchange and is a past president of NAFSA: Association of International Educators. She authored the chapter "Cross Cultural Training" in the NAFSA publication *Learning Across Cultures* edited by Gary Althen. Peggy cofounded the Intercultural Press, Inc., and was its president for nearly fifteen years.

Sheila Ramsey is founder and principal of the Crestone Institute, Washington, DC, the purpose of which is to design human communication processes promoting creativity, innovation, and human development. She has focused on intercultural relations for over twenty years and is known internationally for her work in coaching leaders to develop more creative organizations and for her consultation in strategic planning, visioning, and Japan-U.S. relations.

George W. Renwick is president of Renwick and Associates, a consulting and training firm founded in 1975. He began working with the Chinese in 1963 when he joined the faculty of the Chinese University of Hong Kong and has been going to China once or twice every year since 1982 to work with U.S. corporations, often on technology transfer projects. He was director of the State-of-the-Art Study of Intercultural Education, Training and Research, during which he analyzed thirty thousand intercultural courses, training programs, and research projects which have been conducted in ninety countries. He was the fourth winner of SIETAR's *Primus Inter Pares* award.

Fanchon J. Silberstein is an intercultural trainer who has lived and worked in South and Southeast Asia and Latin America. She designs and provides predeparture, reentry, and training of trainers programs and workshops using art as a vehicle for intercultural training. She serves as a member of the board of directors for the National Multicultural Institute and is a docent for the Smithsonian Institution's Hirshhorn Museum and Sculpture Garden.

Dorothy A. Sisk specializes in the field of creative behavior, leadership development, and multicultural training. She currently directs the Center for Creativity, Innovation and Leadership at Lamar University, Beaumont, Texas. Some of her clients include Xerox, Turner Broadcasting Company, Procter & Gamble, American Cyanamid, AT&T and Bell Laboratory, Warner Davis Park Lambert, and American Marine Products.

Edward C. Stewart is a cultural psychologist who has spent many years teaching and doing research in Japan, Germany, and Scotland as well as in many other countries where he has lived and worked. He writes and conducts training based on the paradigm of cultural differences called the "cultural trilogy." Since 1994 he has concentrated on cultural memories of war, conducting research on the meaning of pain and the role of emotion in cultural identity.

Craig Storti is the author of *The Art of Crossing Cultures, The Art of Coming Home, Cross-Cultural Dialogues, Figuring Foreigners Out* (all published by Intercultural Press), and *Incident at Bitter Creek*. He is the director of Craig Storti and Associates, an intercultural communication training and consulting company.

Nan M. Sussman is assistant professor of psychology at the College of Staten Island, City University of New York, specializing in cross-cultural social psychology. Her research focuses on cultural transitions, in particular cultural repatriation, the psychological process of returning home following an overseas sojourn. She is the recipient of the Outstanding Junior Interculturalist award by SIETAR and a senior Fulbright research grant to Japan.

Michael F. Tucker is president of Tucker International, LLC, and author of the Overseas Assignment Inventory, having directed its research and development. He is a leading international human resource consultant, with some thirty years' experience in the field. He and Loretta Sunter-Tucker founded Moran, Stahl & Boyer Int'l. in 1982, developing it into a leading firm providing a broad range of international human resource management services to major multinational corporations in over ninety countries. He and Loretta organized Tucker International, LLC, in 1994, providing services directly to a select group of multinational corporations.

V. Lynn Tyler, recently retired from Brigham Young University, is enjoying a busy life writing books such as *Illustrating Discoveries on a World Campus*, a history of intercultural and related research representing work done over his career. He was the original editor of the Culturgrams and a charter member of SIETAR International. He served SIETAR on the governing council and the executive committee for six years and was one of the first winners of the Senior Interculturalist award.

Albert R. Wight is a specialist in institutional and organizational development and training. He has developed and conducted cross-cultural training for the Peace Corps, VISTA, Teacher Corps, Job Corps, New Careers, New Start (Canada), teachers on or near Indian reservations, and employees and families of international companies. He conducted training in entrepreneurship and small business management under contract with the government of Malaysia and for over ten years worked with the World Bank or the Harvard Institute for International Development in Pakistan and Russia.